Martin Collie

Contentious Pr...
the law and

"Let's talk of g...
Make dust our ...
Write sorrow on ... ...arth.
Let's choose execu... ...alk of wills"
(William Shakespea... , Richard II, Act 3, Sc. 2, 1. 145).

FENNERS CHAMBERS
3 Madingley Road
Cambridge CB3 0EE
Tel: 01223 368761

AUSTRALIA
Law Book Co.
Sydney

CANADA and USA
Carswell
Toronto

HONG KONG
Sweet & Maxwell Asia

NEW ZEALAND
Brookers
Auckland

SINGAPORE and MALAYSIA
Sweet & Maxwell Asia
Singapore and Kuala Lumpur

Contentious Probate Claims: the law and procedure

First edition

Andrew Francis
MA Oxon
11 New Square

Hedley Marten
MA Cantab, A Bencher of Lincoln's Inn
11 New Square

SWEET & MAXWELL

Published in 2003 by
Sweet & Maxwell Ltd, 100 Avenue Road,
Swiss Cottage, London NW3 3PF
http://www.sweetandmaxwell.co.uk

Typeset by J.P. Price, Chilcompton, Somerset
Printed in Great Britain by
TJ International Ltd, Padstow, Cornwall

No natural forests were destroyed to make this product;
only farmed timber was used and replanted.

A CIP catalogue record for this book is available from the
British Library

ISBN 0 421 849 401

All rights reserved. UK statutory material in this publication is
acknowledged as Crown copyright.

No part of this publication may be reproduced or transmitted in
any form or by any means, or stored in any retrieval system of
any nature without prior written permission, except for permitted
fair dealing under the Copyright, Designs and Patents Act 1988,
or in accordance with the terms of a licence issued by the
Copyright Licensing Agency in respect of photocopying and/or
reprographic reproduction. Applications for permission for other
use of copyright material including permission to reproduce
extracts in other published works shall be made to the publisher.
Full acknowledgement of author, publisher and source must be
given.

©
Sweet & Maxwell
2004

Foreword

Contentious probate claims originated in the Ecclesiastical Courts and came to the Chancery Division in 1971 via the Probate Court and the Probate, Divorce and Admiralty Division. Their air of mystery is enhanced by the description of substances which, as recorded in Megarry's *Second Miscellany at Law*, have been admitted to probate. The following pages may not tell the reader how to obtain a grant of probate in solemn form of a will inscribed on an egg-shell, a step-ladder, or a nurse's petticoat, but they do give practical guidance what to do in contentious probate proceedings of a more normal sort.

Part I deals with the substantive law, including associated topics such as mutual wills, secret and constructive trusts, proprietary estoppel and rectification. Part II deals with practice and procedure. It directs the practitioner to the requirements of the Civil Procedure Rules in general and Part 57 and its associated practice direction in particular. In both parts the reader will appreciate the directness of the author's approach and the absence of footnotes.

For many years practitioners have felt the need for a text-book devoted to the topic of Contentious Probate Claims alone. They will, I am sure, be well pleased with the way it has been met by this work.

The Rt Hon Sir Andrew Morritt
The Vice-Chancellor
July 31, 2003

Preface

Contention over wills is perennial.

At the present time, there is a greater wealth among a larger number of persons in this country than earlier generations and many people are living longer than their ancestors. So expectations held by those who consider themselves entitled to inherit this wealth on the death of parents and other relations, are all the more heightened. The dashing of such expectations leads the disappointed party to seek the assistance of the Court in setting aside the last expression of wishes of the deceased. So the contentious probate claim is born.

We have tried in a modest amount of space to explain what a contentious probate claim is all about, and how it may be started, carried on, and finished. We are very conscious of the cost of litigation and we stress how these claims can be prevented, if not settled early in their lives, and we show the extent of the risks in terms of costs for all parties. This is high stake litigation if embarked upon without sound advice and financial security.

In the present century it is curious that probate claims should still present themselves to the world (even the legal world) in the antique garments worn in previous ages. They also seem to possess an aura based on the descriptions in the novels of Charles Dickens written over 150 years ago. These conceptions reveal a gloomy picture depicting a disastrous miasma of confusion, delay and costs, with pettifogging rules and traps for the unwary. Such conceptions are wrong and based on ignorance. This book strips them away, leaving a modern picture, on a canvas of practical size, in bold, clear colours.

To an outsider we must confess that the impression of the law in this field being in a state of senescence is not assisted by the fact that the Act of Parliament governing the formal validity of wills dates from 1837 (albeit amended in 1982) and that the leading case of testamentary capacity dates from 1870. Even the most "recent" decision in the House of Lords on want of knowledge and approval was handed down nearly 45 years ago. With these factors in mind the book leads the reader as gently as possible into the law of how the validity of wills may be challenged, but with extensive reference to recent decisions. (By "recent" we mean within the last 10-15 years). This shows how modern judicial minds work. From there we take the reader into the rules of procedure and the Family and Chancery Divisions of the High Court which apply in probate claims. Whilst such rules are not uncomplicated, they are at least modern and designed for the twenty-first century litigant to a broad degree. We have also looked in outline at some of the other claims which may be made against an estate, such as how a will may be rectified to correct an error. These claims often run in tandem with probate claims.

We have had great assistance from Professor Malcolm Hodkinson who has written a chapter on the medical aspects of testamentary capacity, thus assisting the lawyer in his understanding of that topic, which often lies at the heart of the challenge to a will.

We gratefully acknowledge the assistance given by the following people to the individual authors:

Andrew Francis: Keith Biggs, the District Probate Registrar at the Winchester District Probate Registry, who has shed light on the inner workings of the Registries and the practice after Orders of the Court have been obtained.

Hedley Marten: John Pennycuick (the younger) whose lucidity of thought triggered many of his (the author's) own lucid intervals; Hedley's son Alexander Marten, who threatened to write first, and did; and above all Arabella von Friesen, who without a second's hesitation provided him with a paradise in which to work. Without these three the first part of the book (the law) would be missing.

Jointly we thank: The Vice-Chancellor of the Chancery Division of the High Court, The Right Hon. Sir Andrew Morritt, for agreeing to write the Foreword at the end of a busy Term.

Our publishers (in particular Steven Warriner, Annie Kemsley and Susan Sidebotham) who have kept us to time and coped with the odd moment of crisis when our professional commitments threatened to engulf the task of writing.

Notwithstanding such invaluable contributions to our labours all our errors are our own.

We have endeavoured to state the law as at September 1, 2003.

Andrew Francis
Hedley Marten
11 New Square
Lincoln's Inn
September 2003.

Contents

Foreword	v
Preface	vii
Table of Cases	xiii
Table of Statutes	xxi
Table of Statutory Instruments	xxv

PART I

1 Challenging the Will — 1–001

2 Interest Claims — 2–001
- Introduction — 2–001
- Personation — 2–004
- Parentage — 2–005

3 Lack of Testamentary Intention — 3–001
- Introduction — 3–001
- Evidence of testamentary intention — 3–004
- Burden of proof of testamentary intention — 3–008
- Incorporation of documents — 3–009
- Conditional Wills — 3–015

4 Lack of Due Execution
- Introduction — 4–001
- Section 9(a) — 4–002
- Section 9(b) — 4–006
- Section 9(c) — 4–007
- Section 9(d) — 4–011
- The presumption of due execution — 4–015
- Privileged wills — 4–017
- Foreign wills — 4–023

5 Lack of Testamentary Capacity
- Introduction — 5–001
- Testamentary capacity: the *Banks v Goodfellow* test — 5–003
- Delusions — 5–010
- Burden of proof — 5–014
- The rule in *Parker v Felgate* — 5–020
- Conclusion — 5–021
- Assessing testamentary capacity — 5–022

CONTENTS

6 Lack of Knowledge and Approval
Introduction — 6–001
The rule in *Barry v Butlin* — 6–007
Burden of Proof — 6–010

7 Undue Influence
Introduction — 7–001
Undue influence in equity — 7–002
Undue influence in probate — 7–009
Burden of proof — 7–012

8 Fraud and Forgery
Introduction — 8–001
Fraud — 8–002
Forgery — 8–008

9 Revocation
Introduction — 9–001
Modes of revocation — 9–003
Revocation by operation of law — 9–004
Burden of proof — 9–032

10 Related Non-probate Claims
Introduction — 10–001
Mutual wills — 10–003
Proprietary estoppel — 10–010
Constructive trusts — 10–023
Secret trusts — 10–028
Rectification — 10–041

PART II PROCEDURE

11 The Rules as to Starting Claims
Caveats, citations and subpoenas — 11–002
Problem areas and special cases — 11–041
Costs in non-contentious probate business — 11–043
Bringing a probate claim — 11–045
General conclusions — 11–140

12 Dealing with Claims Once Started: Pre-trial
The court's power to manage claims — 12–002
Preparation for the CMC hearing — 12–004
Mediation and Alternative Dispute Resolution ('ADR') — 12–045

13 The Final Hearing
General observations	13–001
The final hearing	13–002
The order of speeches	13–003
Evidence	13–007
Opening and closing speeches	13–015

14 Discontinuance and Compromise
Where the parties agree to discontinue the claim, or where a party applies for such discontinuance	14–002
Where there is a general compromise of the claim, parties may have a choice	14–009
Without prejudice offers	14–019
Without prejudice save as to costs, or "Calderbank" letters	14–020
Open offers	14–022
Offers to mediate	14–023
Taxation and the effect of orders made by consent in probate claims varying the disposition of the deceased's estate	14–024

15 Orders which the Court Can Make
The effect of an Order for proof in solemn form	15–002
Orders for a grant in common form	15–005
Revocation orders	15–008
Declarations against the validity of an alleged will	15–010
Carrying out the Order	15–011

16 Costs
The general rule	16–001
Exceptions to the general rule	16–005
Some "special rules"	16–010
Taking indemnities	16–015
Assessment of costs	16–016
The position of the "neutral" personal representative	16–018
Wasted costs orders, etc.	16–022
Costs-only proceedings and claims which have been settled save as to the costs	16–023

17 Enforcement of Orders and Terms of Settlement
Enforcement of Orders	17–001
Enforcement of Tomlin Orders: applying to lift the stay	17–004
Problems post-grant	17–005

18 Funding Probate Claims
Private funding	18–001
Legal Service Commission funding	18–003
Funding from insurance policies	18–005
Conditional fee agreements	18–006

19 Appeals
The route of appeals	19–001
The relevant rules which apply to appeals	19–005
Deciding whether to appeal or not	19–006
The time limit for filing a notice of appeal	19–008
How can permission to appeal be obtained and when will it be given?	19–011
The principles on which an Appellate Court will act	19–019
Appeals to the House of Lords from the Court of Appeal	19–029

20 Claims to rectify Wills
Introduction	20–001
Time limits	20–004
Procedure in s.20 claims generally	20–012
Other procedural features of rectification claims	20–019
The effect of an order for rectification under s.20, or under the inherent jurisdiction	20–021
Recording the Order of the Court	20–025
Costs in rectification claims	20–028

Appendix 1 Forms and Precedents	A–001
Appendix 2 Statutes and Rules of Court and other procedural material	B–001
Appendix 3 Mental and medical conditions relevant to testamentary capacity	C–001
Index	443

Table of Cases

Adams (Dec'd), Re [1990] Ch. 601; [1990] 2 W.L.R. 924; [1990] 2 All
 E.R. 97, Ch D 9–019
Adams v Schofield, unreported, (1981) 20–006
Ali Reza-Delta Transport Co. Ltd v United Arab Shipping Co. (No. 2).
 See Ali Reza-Delta Transport Co. Ltd v United Arab Shipping Co.
 (Costs)
Ali Reza-Delta Transport Co. Ltd v United Arab Shipping Co. SAG
 (Costs) [2003] EWCA Civ 811; *The Times*, July 4, 2003; *Independent*,
 June 20, 2003, CA 14–015
Allan v Morrison [1900] A.C. 604, PC (NZ) 9–022
Allcard v Skinner (1887) L.R. 36 Ch D 145, CA 7–005
Allen v Maddock (1858) 11 Moo. P.C. 427 3–013
Allen v McPherson (1847) 1 H.L.C. 191 8–004
Alsop Wilkinson v Neary [1996] 1 W.L.R. 1220; [1995] 1 All E.R. 431,
 Ch D 16–019, 20–030
Anston, Re (1929) 73 Sol. Jo. 6–006
Assicurazioni Generali SpA v Arab Insurance Group (BSC) [2002]
 EWCA Civ 1642; [2003] 1 W.L.R. 577, CA 19–019, 19–023, 19–024

Bank of Montreal v Stuart [1911] A.C. 120, PC (Can) 7–007
Banks v Goodfellow (1869–70) L.R. 5 Q.B. 549, QB 5–002, 5–003, 5–005,
 5–010, 5–021
Barclays Bank Plc v O'Brien [1994] 1 A.C. 180 HL; affirming [1993]
 Q.B. 109; [1992] 3 W.L.R. 593; [1992] 4 All E.R. 983; [1993] 1 F.L.R.
 124; [1993] 1 F.C.R. 97; (1993) 66 P. & C.R. 135; (1992) 11 Tr. L.R.
 153; [1992] C.C.L.R. 37; [1993] Fam. Law 62; (1992) 89(27) L.S.G.
 34; (1992) 142 N.L.J. 1040; (1992) 136 S.J.L.B. 175; [1992] N.P.C. 74;
 The Times, June 3, 1992; *Independent*, June 17, 1992; *Financial Times*,
 June 10, 1992, CA 7–007
Barder v Caluori; sub nom. Barder v Barder [1988] A.C. 20; [1987] 2
 W.L.R. 1350, HL 11–127, 17–002
Barry v Butlin (1838) 2 Moo. P.C. 480 .... 6–007, 6–008, 6–010, 6–011, 6–012
Basham (Dec'd), Re [1986] 1 W.L.R. 1498; [1987] 1 All E.R. 405,
 Ch D 10–012, 10–013
Bateman, Re (1970) 1 W.L.R. 1463 10–039
Bell, Re [2002] EWHC 1080 20–019
Berger (Dec'd), Re; sub nom. Englander v Berger [1990] Ch. 118;
 [1989] 2 W.L.R. 147, CA 3–002
Birch v Birch [1902] P. 130, CA; reversing [1902] P. 62, PDAD 8–006,
 15–004
Birks v Birks (1865) 4 Sw. & Tr. 23 9–015
Birmingham v Renfrew (1937) C.L.R. 666 10–008
Blackwell v Blackwell; sub nom. Blackwell, Re [1929] A.C. 318; 67
 A.L.R. 336, HL 10–039
Boughton v Knight; Marston v Knight (1872–75) L.R. 3 P. & D. 64, Ct
 of Probate 5–011
Boyce v Rossborough (1857) 6 H.L.C. 2 .... 5–021, 7–012, 8–004
Brawley v Marczynski (No. 2); sub nom. Brawley v Marczynski [2002]
 EWCA Civ 1453; [2003] 1 W.L.R. 813, CA 16–017, 16–023

TABLE OF CASES

Brawley v Marczynski. *See* Brawley v Marczynski (No. 2)
Brown v Deacy [2002] W.T.L.R. 781, Ch D 5–019
Buckenham v Dickinson [2000] W.T.L.R. 1083, QBD   6–015, 11–137, 16–007
Bullivant v Attorney General of Victoria; sub nom. R. v Bullivant [1901]
    A.C. 196, HL; affirming [1900] 2 Q.B. 163, CA 12–014

Cadell v Wilcocks [1898] P. 21, PDAD 9–014
Campbell v Griffin [2001] EWCA Civ 990; [2001] W.T.L.R. 981, CA .. 10–022
Carapeto v Good. *See* Good (Dec'd) (Costs), Re
Chana v Chana [2001] W.T.L.R. 205, Ch D 5–018, 9–022
Chapman, Re; sub nom. (National Trust v RNIB) 12–040
Cheese v Lovejoy (No. 2); sub nom. Harris (Dec'd), Re (1876–77) L.R.
    2 P.D. 251 [1876 H. 16.], CA 9–017, 9–019
Chichester, Re [1946] Ch. 289 4–018
Chittock v Stevens; sub nom. Chittock (Dec'd), Re [2000] W.T.L.R. 643;
    (2000) 97(16) L.S.G. 42, Ch D 10–045, 20–005
Clancy v Clancy, *The Times*, September 9, 2003 5–020
Cleaver (Dec'd), Re; sub nom. Cleaver v Insley [1981] 1 W.L.R. 939;
    [1981] 2 All E.R. 1018, Ch D 10–005, 10–028
Cole, Re [1962] 106 Sol. 837 16–011
Coleman, Re (1971) 1 Ch. 1 9–009
Cooke v Henry [1932] I.R. 574 4–010
Cooper, Re; sub nom. Le Neve-Foster v National Provincial Bank;
    Cooper (Dec'd), Re [1939] Ch. 811, CA; affirming [1939] Ch. 580,
    Ch D 10–038
Corbett v Newey [1998] Ch. 57; [1996] 3 W.L.R. 729, CA 3–016, 11–075
Couser v Couser [1996] 1 W.L.R. 1301; [1996] 3 All E.R. 256, Ch D ... 4–013
Crabb v Arun DC [1976] Ch. 179; [1975] 3 W.L.R. 847, CA 10–016
Craig (Dec'd), Re; sub nom. Meneces v Middleton; Craig, Re [1971]
    Ch. 95; [1970] 2 W.L.R. 1219; [1970] 2 All E.R. 390, Ch D 7–005
Craig v Lamoureux [1920] A.C. 349, PC (Can) 7–012

D'Abo v Paget. *See* D'Abo v Paget (No. 2)
D'Abo v Paget (No. 2); sub nom. D'Abo v Paget [2000] W.T.L.R. 863;
    (2000) 97(38) L.S.G. 43, Ch d 16–020, 20–030
Daintree v Butcher. *See* Daintree v Fasulo
Daintree v Fasulo; sub nom. Daintree v Butcher (1888) L.R. 13 P.D.
    102, CA; affirming (1888) L.R. 13 P.D. 67, PDAD 4–009
Dale (Dec'd), Re; sub nom. Estate of Monica Dale (Dec'd), Re; Proctor
    v Dale [1994] Ch. 31; [1993] 3 W.L.R. 652, Ch D 10–005, 10–007
Daniel v Abiola [2003] EWHC Civ 1562 .... 11–042, 11–125, 12–032, 15–006,
                                                                15–007
Davies (Dec'd), Re; sub nom. Russell v Delaney [1951] 1 All E.R. 920,
    Assizes (Gloucester) 9–029
Den v Vancleve 2 Southamp. 660 5–006
Dunnett v Railtrack plc (2002) 2 All E.R. 850 12–046
Denning, In the Estate of; sub nom. Denning, Re; Harnett v Elliott
    [1958] 1 W.L.R. 462; [1958] 2 All E.R. 1, PDAD 4–016
Dennis (Dec'd), Re; sub nom. Dennis v Lloyds Bank Plc [1981] 2 All
    E.R. 140; 124 S.J. 885, Ch D 20–005
D'Eye v Avery [2001] W.T.L.R. 227, QBD 6–025
Dickson (Dec'd), Re [2002] W.T.L.R. 1395; (1984) 81 L.S.G. 3012,
    CA 9–022
Diplock, Re [1948] 465 Chapter 11–127
Douglas-Menzies v Umphelby [1908] A.C. 224, PC (Aus) 3–001
Dufour v Pereira (1769) 1 Dick. 419 10–004

TABLE OF CASES

Edgar v Edgar [1980] 1 W.L.R. 1410; [1980] 3 All E.R. 887, CA 11–127, 17–002
Emerson, Re (1992) 9 L.R.Ir. 443 4–004
English, Re (1864) 3 Se. & Tr. 586 3–005
Escritt v Escritt (1982) 3 F.L.R. 280 10–045
Excelsior Commercial & Industrial Holdings Ltd v Salisbury Hamer Aspden & Johnson (Costs); sub nom. Excelsior Commercial & Industrial Holdings Ltd v Salisbury Hammer Aspden & Johnson [2002] EWCA Civ 879; [2002] C.P. Rep. 67, CA 14–015

Ferguson-Davie v Ferguson-Davie (1890) L.R. 15 P.D. 109, PDAD 3–004
Finnemore (Dec'd), Re [1991] 1 W.L.R. 793; [1992] 1 All E.R. 800, Ch D 9–030, A–023
Fitzhugh Gates v Sherman. *See* Sherman v Perkins
Flynn (Dec'd), Re; sub nom. Flynn v Flynn [1982] 1 W.L.R. 310; [1982] 1 All E.R. 882, Ch D 5–020, 11–121, 14–008
Fuld (Dec'd) (No. 2 A), In the Estate of; sub nom. Hartley v Fuld (Privilege: Witness of the Court) [1965] P. 405; [1965] 3 W.L.R. 162, PDAD 11–033, 12–015, 12–016, 13–001, 13–012
Fuld (Dec'd) (No. 3), In the Estate of; sub nom. Hartley v Fuld (Conflict of Laws) [1968] P. 675; [1966] 2 W.L.R. 717, PDAD 6–012, 13–001, 13–006
Fuller v Strum [2001] EWCA Civ 1879; [2002] 1 W.L.R. 1097, CA 6–002, 6–006, 6–007, 6–013, 8–005, 13–001, 13–005, 19–024, 20–003
Fulton v Andrew; Fulton v Wilson (1874–75) L.R. 7 H.L. 448, HL 6–027, 8–005

G v G (Minors: Custody Appeal) [1985] 1 W.L.R. 647; [1985] 2 All E.R. 225, HL 19–023
G (A Minor) (Child Abuse: Standard of Proof), Re [1987] 1 W.L.R. 1461; [1988] 1 F.L.R. 314, Fam Div 2–006
Gardner v Gardner (1877) 2 App.Cas. 723 2–007
Gibson, Re [1949] P. 434; [1949] 2 All E.R. 90, PDAD 4–008
Gillett v Holt [2001] Ch. 210; [2000] 3 W.L.R. 815, CA 10–014, 10–016
Gissing v Gissing [1971] A.C. 886; [1970] 3 W.L.R. 255, HL 10–023
Godman v Godman [1920] P. 261, CA; affirming [1919] P. 229, PDAD 3–007
Good (Dec'd), Re; sub nom. Carapeto v Good; Brennan v Good [2002] EWHC 640; [2002] W.T.L.R. 801, Ch D .. 16–005, 16–007, 16–012, 19–012
Good (Dec'd) (Costs), Re; sub nom. Carapeto v Good; Brennan v Good [2002] EWHC 640; [2002] W.T.L.R. 1305, Ch D 6–026, 7–012
Good (Dec'd) (Permission to Appeal), Re [2002] EWCA Civ 944; [2002] W.T.L.R. 1311, CA 19–012, 19–017
Goodchild v Goodchild; sub nom. Goodchild (Dec'd), Re [1997] 1 W.L.R. 1216; [1997] 3 All E.R. 63, CA 10–006, 10–009
Graham v Murphy [1997] 1 F.L.R. 860; [1997] 2 F.C.R. 441, Ch D ... 14–022
Grant v Edwards [1986] Ch. 638; [1986] 3 W.L.R. 114, CA 10–023
Grattan, Re. *See* Grattan v McNaughton
Grattan v McNaughton; sub nom. Grattan, In the Estate of; Grattan, Re [2001] W.T.L.R. 1305, Ch D .. 20–006, 20–013, 20–019, 20–028, 20–033
Gray v Perpetual Trustee Co. Ltd; sub nom. Grey v Perpetual Trustee Co. Ltd [1928] A.C. 391; 60 A.L.R. 613, PC (Aus) 10–006
Grey v Perpetual Trustee Co. Ltd. *See* Gray v Perpetual Trustee Co. Ltd
Guardian Trust and Co. v Public Trustee of New Zealand [1942] A.C. 115, PC (NZ) 15–007

H (Children), Re. *See* H (Children) (Paternity: Blood Tests), Re
H (Minors), Re. *See* H (Minors) (Sexual Abuse: Standard of Proof), Re
H (Children) (Paternity: Blood Tests), Re; sub nom. H (Children), Re
  [2002] EWCA Civ 383; [2002] 1 F.L.R. 1145; [2002] 2 F.C.R. 469 ... 2–009
H (Minors) (Sexual Abuse: Standard of Proof), Re; sub nom. H
  (Minors) (Child Abuse: Threshold Conditions), Re; H and R (Child
  Sexual Abuse: Standard of Proof), Re; H (Minors), Re [1996] A.C.
  563; [1996] 2 W.L.R. 8, HL 6–013
Hall v Warren (1804) 9 Ves. 605 5–014
Hamilton v Al-Fayed (No. 2) (2003) 2 W.L.R. 128 16–022
Hammond v Osborn [2002] EWCA Civ 885; [2002] W.T.L.R. 1125,
  CA 7–002, 7–008
Hanoksley's Settlements, Re [1934] Ch. 384 9–015
Harris v Knight (1890) L.R. 15 P.D. 170, CA 4–015
Hart v Dabbs; sub nom. Dabbs (Lawrence Stanley) (Dec'd), Re [2001]
  W.T.L.R. 527, Ch D 6–003
Harwood v Baker 13 E.R. 117; (1840) 3 Moo. P.C. 282, PC (UK) 5–008
Heys (Dec'd), Re; Walker v Gaskill; sub nom. Heys, In the Estate of
  [1914] P. 192, PDAD 10–003
Hollins v Russell; Tichband v Hurdman; Dunn v Ward; Pratt v Bull;
  Worth v McKenna; Sharratt v London Central Bus Co. Ltd [2003]
  EWCA Civ 718; (2003) 153 N.L.J. 920, CA 18–008
Holmes v McMullan; sub nom. Ratcliffe (Dec'd), Re [1999] S.T.C. 262;
  [1999] B.T.C. 8017, Ch D 20–021
Hornal v Neuberger Products [1957] 1 Q.B. 247; [1956] 3 W.L.R. 1034,
  CA 8–008
Horsefall v Haywards; sub nom. Horsfall v Haywards [1999] 1 F.L.R.
  1182; [1999] Lloyd's Rep. P.N. 332, CA 20–006
Howard, Re (1869) L.R. 1 P. & D. 636 9–014
Huck v Robson [2002] EWCA Civ 398; [2003] 1 W.L.R. 1340, cA 14–015,
                                                                 14–017

Isaac v Kenny, unreported, February 16, 2000 16–003

Jenkins v Gaisford and Thring (1863) 3 Sw. & Tr. 93 4–004
Jennings v Rice [2002] EWCA Civ 159; [2003] 1 F.C.R. 501; [2002]
  W.T.L.R. 367, CA 10–017
Jolly v Jay [2002] EWCA Civ 277; *The Times*, April 3, 2002; Independent, March 15, 2002, CA 19–018
Jones (Dec'd), Re [1981] Fam. 7; [1981] 2 W.L.R. 106 4–020
Jones (Dec'd), Re; sub nom. Evans v Harries [1976] Ch. 200; [1976] 2
  W.L.R. 457, CA 9–026, 9–027, 9–028, 9–032, A–023
Jones v Harding (1887) 58 L.T. 60 9–020

Kasperbauer v Griffith [2000] W.T.L.R. 333, CA 10–033, 10–037
Keen, Re; sub nom. Evershed v Griffiths [1937] Ch. 236, CA 10–038
Kennell v Abbott (1799) 4 Ves. Jr. 802 2–004
Kenward v Adams; *The Times*, November 29, 1975 5–021
Kieran, Re [1933] I.R. 222 4–004
Killick v Pountney; sub nom. Killick (Dec'd), Re [2000] W.T.L.R. 41;
  The Times, April 30, 1999, Ch D 7–012
King v Bonnar (1998) LTL, CA 16–012
King's Proctor v Daines (1830) 3 Hagg.Ecc. 218 3–005
Kingsley, Re 1981 11–038

Ladd v Marshall [1954] 1 W.L.R. 1489; [1954] 3 All E.R. 745, CA 19–021

TABLE OF CASES

Langston, Re; sub nom. Langston, In the Estate of [1953] P. 100; [1953] W.L.R. 581, PDAD 9–009
Langton, In the Estate of; sub nom. Langton, Re; Langton v Lloyds Bank [1964] P. 163; [1964] 2 W.L.R. 585, CA 15–003
Larke v Nugus; sub nom. Moss, In the Estate of [2000] W.T.L.R. 1033; (1979) 123 S.J. 337, CA .. 11–130, 11–131, 11–132, 11–133, 11–134, 11–135, 11–136, 11–137, 11–138, 11–139, 11–140, 12–005, 12–015, 12–016, 12–036, 16–009
Lawrence's Will Trusts, Re; sub nom. Public Trustee v Lawrence [1972] Ch. 418; [1971] 3 W.L.R. 188, Ch D 9–014
Lewis, Re (1858) 1 Sw. & Tr. 31 9–022
Lloyds Bank Plc v Rosset [1991] 1 A.C. 107; [1990] 2 W.L.R. 867, HL 10–024, 10–027
Lord Walpole v Lord Orford. *See* Walpole v Orford

McCormick v Grogan (1869–70) L.R. 4 H.L. 82, HL (UK-Irl); affirming (1866) 1 Ir. Eq. 313 10–032
McNulty v McNulty [2002] EWHC 123; [2002] W.T.L.R. 737, Ch D .. 20–005 20–005
Magson (dec'd), Re [2003] 11–015, 11–024, 11–042
Marsland, Re; sub nom. Lloyds Bank Ltd v Marsland [1939] Ch. 820, CA; affirming Ch D 10–009
Midland Bank Plc v Cooke [1995] 4 All E.R. 562; [1997] 6 Bank. L.R. 147, CA 10–026
Morris, Re; sub nom. Lloyds Bank v Peake [1971] P. 62; [1970] 2 W.L.R. 865, PDAD 6–004, 20–001

National Trust v RNIB, sub nom. Re Chapman unreported 24 January, 1999 12–040
Newell v Weeks (1814) 2 Phil. Ecc. 224 15–003
Newland (Dec'd), Re; sub nom. Newland, In the Estate of; Newland, In the goods of [1952] P. 71; [1952] 1 All E.R. 841 4–021

Ottaway v Norman [1972] Ch. 698; [1972] 2 W.L.R. 50, Ch D 10–040

Parfitt v Lawless (1869–72) L.R. 2 P. & D. 462; (1872) 36 J.P. 722, Ct of Probate 7–009
Parker v Felgate (1883) L.R. 8 P.D. 171, PDAD 5–018, 5–020, 6–005
Parsons, Re [2002] W.T.L.R. 237   4–004, 4–008, 4–015, 5–014, 5–019, 12–023, 13–001, 16–007
Patten v Poulton (1858) 1 Sw. & Tr. 55 9–022
Piercy, Re (1845) 1 Rob. 278 4–008
Pilot v Gainfort [1931] P. 103, PDAD 9–009
Plimmer v Wellington Corp.; sub nom. Plimmer v Mayor, Councillors, and Citizens of the City of Wellington (1883–84) L.R. 9 App. Cas. 699, PC (NZ) 10–016
Posner, In the Estate of; sub nom. Posner v Miller [1953] P. 277; [1953] 2 W.L.R. 1149, PDAD 2–004
Powlett Peerage Case, The [1903] A.C. 395 2–006
Prodmore v Whatton (1864) 3 Sw. & Tr. 449 9–022

R. v Ewing [1983] Q.B. 1039; [1983] 3 W.L.R. 1, CA (Crim Div) 8–008
Ramsden v Dyson; Ramsden v Thornton (1866) L.R. 1 H.L. 129, HL   10–011
Rapley (Dec'd), Re; sub nom. Rapley v Rapley [1983] 1 W.L.R. 1069; [1983] 3 All E.R. 248, Ch D 4–021
Ratcliffe (Dec'd), Re. *See* Holmes v McMullan

Ratcliffe v Barnes (1862) 2 Sw. & Tr. 486 15–003
Reynette-James (Dec'd), Re; sub nom. Wightman v Reynette-James
 [1976] 1 W.L.R. 161; [1975] 3 All E.R. 1037, Ch D 20–001
Richards v Allan [2001] W.T.L.R. 1031, Ch D 5–015, 6–014
Richards v Allan W.T.L.R. 12–021
Right v Price (1779) 1 Doug. K.B. 241 4–008
Royal Bank of Scotland Plc v Etridge (No. 2); Barclays Bank Plc v
 Coleman; Barclays Bank Plc v Harris; Midland Bank Plc v Wallace;
 National Westminster Bank Plc v Gill; UCB Home Loans Corp. Ltd
 v Moore; Bank of Scotland v Bennett; Kenyon-Brown v Desmond
 Banks & Co. (Undue Influence) (No. 2) [2001] UKHL 44 HL;
 affirming in part [1998] 4 All E.R. 705; [1998] 2 F.L.R. 843; [1998] 3
 F.C.R. 675; (1999) 31 H.L.R. 575; [1998] Fam. Law 665; (1998)
 95(32) L.S.G. 31; (2001) 151 N.L.J. 1538; (1998) 148 N.L.J. 1390;
 [1998] N.P.C. 130; (1998) 76 P. & C.R. D39; *The Times*, August 17,
 1998, CA 7–002, 7–008
Royal Brunei Airlines Sdn Bhd v Tan; sub nom. Royal Brunei Airlines
 Sdn Bhd v Philip Tan Kok Ming [1995] 2 A.C. 378; [1995] 3 W.L.R.
 64, PC (Bru) 8–003

Sallis v Jones [1936] P. 43, PDAD 9–008
Salmon (Dec'd), Re; sub nom. Coard v National Westminster Bank Ltd
 [1981] Ch. 167; [1980] 3 W.L.R. 748, Ch D 10–045, 20–005
Sebag-Montefiore, Re; sub nom. Sebag-Montefiore v Alliance
 Assurance Co. Ltd [1944] Ch. 331, CA 3–014
Segelman (Dec'd), Re [1996] Ch. 171; [1996] 2 W.L.R. 173, Ch D ... 10–042,
 10–043, 20–019
Shephard v Wheeler [2000] W.T.L.R. 1175; *The Times*, February 15,
 2000, Ch D 15–007, 15–009
Sherman v Perkins; sub nom. Woolnough (Dec'd), Re; Perkins v
 Borden; Fitzhugh Gates v Borden Sherman [2003] EWCA Civ 886,
 CA; reversing [2002] W.T.L.R. 603, Ch D   11–122, 15–007, 16–019, 16–022
Simpson v Foxon [1907] P. 54, PDAD 9–010
Smart, Re [1902] P.238 3–014
Smee v Smee (1879) 5 P.D. 84 .... 5–010, 5–012
Snowden (Dec'd), Re [1979] Ch. 528; [1979] 2 W.L.R. 654, Ch D 10–031
Snowden (Dec'd), Re [1979] Ch. 528; [1979] 2 W.L.R. 654, Ch D 10–040
Societe Internationale de Telecommunications Aeronautiques SC v
 Wyatt Co. (UK) Ltd (Costs) [2002] EWHC 2401; (2003) 147 S.J.L.B.
 27, Ch D 12–046
Sohal v Sohal (Application for Permission to Appeal) [2002] EWCA Civ
 1297, CA 15–004, 19–021, 19–026
Sotheran v Dening (1881–82) L.R. 20 Ch D 99, CA 9–014
Southenden, Re (1925) P. 177 9–029
Spiers v English [1907] P. 122, PDAD 16–005, 16–007
Spratt, Re [1897] P.28 3–014
Stephens v Taprell (1840) 2 Cust. 458 9–019
Stevens v Vancleve 4 Washington 267 5–007
Stone v Hoskins [1905] P. 194, PDAD 10–009
Stott (Dec'd), Re; sub nom. Klouda v Lloyds Bank Plc, [1980] 1 W.L.R.
 246; [1980] 1 All E.R. 259, Ch D 11–073
Sugden v Lord St Leonards (1875–76) L.R. 1 P.D. 154; [1874–80] All
 E.R. Rep. 21, CA 11–038

Taylors Fashions Ltd v Liverpool Victoria Trustees Co. Ltd [1982] Q.B.
 133 10–011
Tchilingirian v Ouzounian [2003] EWHC 1220; [2003] W.T.L.R. 709,
 Ch D 5–019

TABLE OF CASES

Three Rivers DC v Bank of England. *See* Three Rivers DC v Bank of England (Disclosure) (No. 3)
Three Rivers DC v Bank of England (Disclosure) (No. 3) ; sub nom. Three Rivers DC v Governor of the Bank of England (No. 5); Three Rivers DC v Bank of England [2003] EWCA Civ 474; (2003) 100(23) L.S.G. 37, CA 12–014
Tibbs v Dick [1998] 2 F.L.R. 1118; [1999] 2 F.C.R. 322, CA 11–127
Tufton v Sperni [1952] 2 T.L.R. 516; [1952] W.N. 439, CA 7–006
Tweedale, Re (1874) L.R. 3 P. & D. 204 4–022

Vernon, Re (1916) 33 T.L.R. 11 4–022

W v K (Proof of Paternity) (1987) 151 J.P. 589; [1988] 1 F.L.R. 86 2–009
Wagstaff v Colls [2003] EWCA Civ 469; (2003) 147 S.J.L.B. 419, CA   17–004
Walker v Geo H Medlicott & Son; sub nom. Walker v Medlicott [1999] 1 W.L.R. 727; [1999] 1 All E.R. 685, CA 10–044, 20–006, 20–019
Walker v Medlicott. *See* Walker v Geo H Medlicott & Son
Wallgrave v Tebbs (1855) 2 K. & J. 313 10–039
Walpole v Orford (1797) 3 Ves. Jr. 402 10–031
Weatherhill v Pearce [1995] 1 W.L.R. 592; [1995] 2 All E.R. 492, Ch D 4–010
Welch v Philips (1836) 1 Moo P.C. 299 9–022
White (Dec'd), Re; sub nom. Barker v Gribble [1991] Ch. 1; [1990] 3 W.L.R. 187, Ch D 4–006
Williams (Dec'd), Re; sub nom. Wiles v Madgin [1985] 1 W.L.R. 905; [1985] 1 All E.R. 964, Ch D 20–001
Williams v Johns [1988] 2 F.L.R. 475; [1988] Fam. Law 257, DC 12–034
Willmott v Barber (1881) L.R. 17 Ch D 772, CA; affirming in part (1880) L.R. 15 Ch D 96, Ch D 10–011
Wingham, Re; sub nom. Andrews v Wingham [1949] P. 187; [1948] 2 All E.R. 908, CA 4–019
Wingrove v Wingrove (1885) 11 P.D. 81 7–011
Wintle v Nye (No. 2); sub nom. Wells, In the Estate of [1959] 1 W.L.R. 284; [1959] 1 All E.R. 552, HL 6–008, 6–011, 6–013, 8–005, 13–001, 13–006, 19–029
Wood v Smith [1993] Ch. 90; [1992] 3 W.L.R. 583, CA 4–006, 19–025
Worby v Rosser [1999] Lloyd's Rep. P.N. 972; [2000] P.N.L.R. 140, CA 11–048
Wordingham v Royal Exchange Trust Co. Ltd [1992] Ch. 412; [1992] 2 W.L.R. 496, Ch D 10–043
Wright v Sanderson (1884) 9 P.D. 149 4–015
Wynn (Dec'd), Re [1984] 1 W.L.R. 237; [1983] 3 All E.R. 310, Ch D .. 4–023

Young (Dec'd), Re; sub nom. Young v Young [1951] Ch. 344; [1950] 2 All E.R. 1245, Ch D 10–029
Young v Holloway [1895] P. 87, PDAD 15–003

Zamet v Hyman [1961] 1 W.L.R. 1442; [1961] 3 All E.R. 933, CA 7–002

Table of Statutes

1837 Wills Act (c.26) 4–021, 11–066, 13–004, A–023
    s.1 .... **B–001**
    s.3 .... **B–002**
    s.7 .... **B–003**
    s.9 .... 2–004, 3–011, 3–013, 3–016, 4–001, 4–007, 4–016, 4–017, 4–021, 4–023, 5–020, 9–012, 9–016, 9–023, 11–033, 11–037, 11–048, 11–050, 11–140, 12–023, 13–012, 14–009, 15–010, 16–007, A–023, A–024, **B–004**, C–0177
      (a) 4–002
      (b) 4–006
      (c) .. 4–007, 4–010, 4–011
      (d) 4–011, 4–013
    s.10 .... **B–005**
    s.11 ... 4–018, 4–020, 4–021, **B–006**
    s.13 .... **B–007**
    s.14 .... **B–008**
    s.15 ... 9–030, 9–031, **B–009**
    s.16 .... **B–010**
    s.17 .... **B–011**
    s.18 .. 9–007, 9–009, 15–010, A–023, **B–012**
      (1) 9–005
    s.18A 9–010, **B–013**
      (1) 9–010
      (2) 9–010
      (3) 9–010
    s.19 .... **B–014**
    s.20 .. A–023, A–024, 9–012, 9–016, 9–017, 9–019, 9–031, 11–038, 11–055, 13–012, 15–010, 20–001, **B–015**
    s.21 ... 9–023, 9–024, **B–016**
    s.22 .. 3–014, 11–104, **B–017**
    s.23 .... **B–018**
    s.24 .... **B–019**
    s.25 .... **B–020**
    s.26 .... **B–021**
    s.27 .... **B–022**
    s.28 .... **B–023**
    s.29 .... **B–024**

1837 Wills Act—*cont.*
    s.30 .... **B–025**
    s.31 .... **B–026**
    s.33 .... **B–027**
    s.34 .... **B–028**
    s.35 .... **B–029**

1918 Wills (Soldiers and Sailors) Act (c.58)—
    s.1 .... **B–030**
    s.2 .... **B–031**
    s.3 .... 4–018, **B–032**
    s.4 .... **B–033**
    s.5 .... **B–034**

1925 Law of Property Act (c.20)—
    s.177 .... 9–007, 9–009
    s.204 ...... 11–124, 12–031, 15–007, **B–035**

Administration of Estates Act (c.23)—
    Pt II **B–036**
    Pt III **B–037**
    s.27 .... 11–124, 12–031, 15–007, **B–036**
    s.37 .... 11–124, 12–031, 15–007, **B–037**

1963 Wills Act (c.44) A–021, A–023, A–024
    s.1 .... 4–023, **B–064**
    s.2 .... 4–023, **B–065**
    s.3 .... 4–023, **B–066**
    s.4 .... **B–067**
    s.6 .... **B–068**
    s.7 .... **B–069**

1969 Family Law Reform Act (c.46)—
    s.20 2–009

Administration of Justice Act (c.58)—
    s.12 19–029

1974 Solicitors Act (c.47)—
    s.50 17–003
    s.71 .... 11–048, 16–011, 16–015, 16–021

TABLE OF STATUTES

1975	Inheritance (Provision for Family and Dependants) Act (c.63) 1–007, 9–010, 11–003, 11–098, 11–102, 11–125, 11–127, 12–032, 12–033, 12–034, 12–035, 14–020, 17–002, 18–004, 19–022, 20–004, 20–005, 20–006, 20–007, 20–010, 20–011, 20–013, 20–017, 20–018, 20–022, 20–024, 20–028, A–028, B–139, D–001, D–003, D–006
	s.1(2) 11–127
	s.2 14–025
	s.3 .... D–003, D–005
	s.4 10–045
	s.19 .... 11–127, 14–025
	(3) 11–125
	s.20(1) 20–024
1980	Limitation Act (c.58) 11–126
1981	Supreme Court Act (c.54) 1–003, **B–161**
	Pt V .... **B–038—B–061**
	s.22(1) 11–126
	(2) 11–126
	s.25 11–060
	s.33 .... **B–161**
	s.34 .... **B–161**
	s.49(2) 17–004
	s.51 .... 16–009, **B–161**
	(3) 16–022
	s.105 .... **B–038**
	s.106 .... **B–039**
	s.107 .... **B–040**
	s.108 .... **B–041**
	s.109 .... **B–042**
	s.110 .... **B–043**
	s.111 .... **B–044**
	s.112 .... **B–045**
	s.113 .... **B–046**
	s.114 .... **B–047**
	s.115 .... **B–048**
	s.116 ...... 11–013, 11–043, 17–003, 20–031, **B–049**
	s.117 ...... A–026, 11–004, 11–016, 11–042, 11–078, 11–081, 12–028, 12–031, 14–006, 16–013, 19–006, 19–018, **B–050**
	(3) 11–042
	s.118 .... **B–051**
1981	Supreme Court Act—*cont.*
	s.119 .... **B–052**
	s.121 .... 11–027, **B–053**
	s.122 ...... 11–029, 11–030, 11–131, 11–033, 11–035, 11–036, 11–037, 11–040, 11–043, 12–005, 12–016, 13–001, 13–012, **B–054**
	s.123 ...... 11–029, 11–031, 11–033, 11–036, 11–038, 11–040, 11–043, 11–078, 12–012, A–006, **B–055**
	s.128 .... 11–060, **B–056**
	Sch.1, para.1(g) 20–012
1982	Administration of Justice Act (c.53) 9–005, 9–010, **B–163**
	Pt IV **B–062, B–063**
	s.17 4–001
	s.18(2) 9–005
	(3) 9–005
	(4) 9–005
	s.20 .. 6–027, 9–006, 10–041, 10–042, 10–043, 10–044, 10–045, 20–001, 20–003, 20–004, 20–005, 20–006, 20–007, 20–008, 20–009, 20–010, 20–012, 20–017, 20–018, 20–019, 20–021, 20–022, 20–023, 20–030, 20–033, 20–034, 20–036, 20–040, **B–057**
	(1) 10–042, 20–026
	(a) .. 10–043, 20–029
	(b) 20–029
	(2) 10–045, 20–004
	(3) 20–024
	(4) 20–004
	s.21 ... 3–011, 9–006, 9–015, 20–002, **B–058**
1983	Mental Health Act (c.20) 5–021, 11–065, A–011
1984	County Courts Act (c.28) **B–161**
	s.23(a) 20–012
	(d) 20–012
	(g) 20–012
	s.25 12–033
	s.32 .... 11–059, 20–012
	s.52 .... **B–161**
	s.53 .... **B–161**
1984	Inheritance Tax Act (c.51)—
	s.142 14–025

TABLE OF STATUTES

1985	Administration of Justice Act (c.61)—		1990	Courts and Legal Services Act—*cont.*
	Pt IV ...... **B–064—B–067**			Sch.18, para.43 ..... **B–161**
	s.20 .... A–027, A–028			para.44 ..... **B–161**
	(1)(a) A–028		1992	Taxation of Chargeable Gains Act (c.12) 14–025
	(b) A–028		1995	Law Reform (Succession) Act (c.41) ... 9–010
	(2) A–028			
	s.47 .... 11–065, **B–059**			Disability Discrimination Act (c.50)—
	s.48 .... 20–002, **B–063**			s.1 18–004
	s.49 .... 14–006, 14–009, 14–011, 14–012, A–026, **B–061**, B–139		1996	Trusts of Land and Appointment of Trustees Act (c.47)—
	s.50 .... 15–007, 17–002, 20–031, **B–062**			s.14 18–004
1986	Family Law Act (c.55) 9–010		1998	Human Rights Act (c.42) 11–066, 19–012
	Pt II 9–010			
	s.53 9–010			Data Protection Act (c.29)—
1989	Children Act (c.41) **B–162**			s.35(1) 12–016
1990	Access to Health Records Act (c.23) 12–017, 12–019		1999	Access to Justice Act (c.22) **B–162**
	s.1 12–017			Pt I **B–068**
	s.3(1)(f) 12–017			s.4(2) 18–004
	(4) 12–018			s.6(8) 18–004
	Human Fertilisation and Embryology Act (c.37) 2–010			s.10(7) 18–004
				s.11 16–014, 18–004, **B–063**
	s.28 2–010			s.27 .... **B–130**
	Courts and Legal Services Act (c.41) ... **B–130, B–161**			(1) **B–130**
				s.29 18–005
	s.4(1) **B–161**			Sch.2, para.1(d) 18–004
	s.58 .... 18–006, **B–130**		2002	Land Registration Act (c.9) 11–126
	s.58A 18–006			
				s.35 12–029

Table of Statutory Instruments

1965 Rules of the Supreme Court (SI 1965/1776—
Ord.45 17–003
    r.7(4) A–007
Ord.52 17–003
Ord.76, r.9(3) 11–073
Ord.99 .... B–139
1987 Non-Contentious Probate Rules (SI 1987/2024) ...... 1–003, 11–015, 11–066—A–026, **B–163**
r.1 .... **B–070**
r.2 .... **B–071**
r.3 .... **B–072**
r.4 .... **B–073**
r.5 .... **B–074**
r.6 .... **B–075**
r.7 .... **B–076**
r.8 .... **B–077**
r.9 .... **B–078**
r.10 .... **B–079**
r.11 .... **B–080**
r.12 .... **B–081**
rr.12–16 5–014
r.13 .... **B–082**
r.14 .... **B–083**
r.15 .... **B–084**
r.16 .... **B–085**
r.17 .... **B–086**
r.18 .... **B–087**
r.19 .... **B–088**
r.20 .... **B–089**
r.21 .... **B–090**
r.22 .... **B–091**
r.23 .... **B–092**
r.24 .... **B–093**
r.25 .... **B–094**
r.26 .... **B–095**
r.27 .... **B–096**
r.28 .... **B–097**
r.41 .... 15–007, 15–009
    (2) 15–009
r.42 .... A–001
r.43 .... 11–003, 20–010
    (1) A–002
r.44 11–002, 20–010, **B–099**
    (1) 11–042, 11–081

r.44(2) A–003
    (3) 11–004, 11–015, 11–017
    (5) A–004
    (6) 11–013
    (7) 11–013
    (10) A–005
    (11) 11–010, 11–018
    (12) 11–018
    (13) 11–015, 11–042
r.45 ... 11–, 11–015, 11–081, **B–100**
    (1) 15–003
    (3) 11–017, 14–005
r.46 .... **B–101**
    (2) 11–021
    (3) 11–021
    (5) 11–021
    (6) 11–021, A–005
rr.46–49 11–019
r.47 .... 17–003, **B–102**
    (1) 11–020
    (2) 11–021
    (3) 11–020
    (5) 11–021
    (b) 11–021
    (7) 11–021
r.48 11–020, 11–022, **B–103**
    (2)(a) 11–023
    (b) 11–024
r.49 .... 11–002, **B–104**
r.50 .... **B–105**
    (1) 11–030
    (2) 11–031
r.51 .... **B–106**
r.52 .... 11–042, **B–107**
r.53 .... **B–108**
r.54 .... **B–109**
r.55 .... 20–003, 20–012, 20–027, 20–034, **20–035**, 20–036, 20–037, 20–038, 20–039, 20–040, 20–014, A–028, **B–110**, B–136
    (1) 20–036
    (3) 20–036
    (4) 20–040
r.57 .... **B–111**
r.58 .... **B–112**
r.59 .... **B–113**

TABLE OF STATUTORY INSTRUMENTS

r.60 11–044, 20–037, **B–114**
   (9) 11–045
r.61 . . . . 11–030, 20–036,
                A–028, **B–115**
   (1) 11–025, 20–036
r.62 . . . . **B–116**
r.62A **B–117**
r.63 . . . . 11–043, 20–037,
               20–038, **B–118**
r.64 . . . . **B–119**
r.65 . . . . **B–120**
r.66 . . . . 20–036, **B–121**
r.67 . . . . **B–122**
r.68 . . . . **B–123**
1991 High Court and County Courts Jurisdiction Order (SI 1991/724) 11–059, 20–012
(SI 1991/1876) **B–134**
1998 Non–Contentious Probate (Amendment) Rules (SI 1998/1903) **B–134**
Civil Procedure (Modification of Enactments) Order (SI 1998/2940) **B–132**
Civil Procedure Rules (SI 1998/3132) . . 1–003, 11–074, 12–002, 13–020, 14–008, 20–005, 20–010, A–024, **B–138,** D–002, D–006
r.1.1 . . . . 11–131, 20–005
r.1.1(2)(a) B–138
r.2.2(2) 20–034
r.2.8 19–009
Pt 2 PD B, para.5.1(a) . . . . .
              14–007, 20–012
Pt 3 11–102
r.3.1 12–025
r.3.4 . . . . . . 11–117, 11–119, 11–121, 12.025
Pt 6 . . . . 11–086, 11–089
rr.6.1–6.5 11–086
r.6.3 PD 11–092
r.6.7 11–105
r.6.8 11–086
r.6.17ff 11–087
r.6.22 11–092
r.6.23 11–095
Pt 6 PD 11–087, 11–095
Pt 7 . . . . . . 11–062, 11–068, 12–001, 12–032, 20–013, 20–014, 20–036, 20–039, A–022, A–028

r.7.1(2)(b) 11–085
r.7.4(1) 11–068, 11–097
r.7.5 11–088
r.7.5(2) 11–068, 11–097
r.7.6 11–088
r.7.10 11–115
   (1) 11–115
   (2) 11–115
   (3) 11–115
   (4) 11–115
   (5) 11–115
Pt 7 PD A–022
Pt 8 . . . . . . 12–032, 12–033, 16–023, 20–002, 20–013, **B–139**
Pt 9 . . . . 11–094, A–024
r.10.1(3) 11–089
Pt 12 11–115
PD B, para.5.1(a) . . . . . .
              14–011
Pt 15 . . . . A–024
r.15.4 11–109
   (1)(b) 11–094
r.15.9 11–111
r.15.18 11–105
Pt 15 PD A–024
      para.3.3 . . 11–106
Pt 16 . . . . . . 11–075, A–024, A–025
r.16.5 . . . . A–024
   (2) **B–140**
r.16.7 . . . . A–025
   (1) 11–103
   (2) 11–103
Pt 16 PD . . 11–075, A–024, **B–140**
Pt 17 . . . . . 11–076, 11–104, 11–111
Pt 18 11–120
Pt 19 . . . . . . 11–056, 12–004
r.19.3 15–002
r.19.6 11–065
r.19.7 . . . . . 11–065, 14–009, 14–010, 14–011, 15–002, 15–003
   (6) 14–011
   (7) 14–011
r.19.8A 11–065, 12–004, 14–011, 15–002, 15–003, B–137, B–139
   (6) 14–011
Pt 20 . . . . . 11–096, 11–106, 11–112, 11–113, 11–114, 12–046, A–024, A–025, D–003
r.20.3 11–109
r.20.4(2) 11–069
r.20.5 . . . . . . 11–112, 11–113

TABLE OF STATUTORY INSTRUMENTS

Pt 20 PD A–024
    para.3 ... 11–109
    para.6.1 ....
        11–106A–024
    para.6.2 .. A–025
    para.7.1 .. 11–112
    para.7.2 .. 11–113
Pt 21 ..... 11–065, 12–004,
    12–012, 14–025, 17–002,
    20–023, A–026
r.21.10 ..... 14–018, B–130
Pt 22 .... A–022, A–024
Pt 22 PD A–022
Pt 23 ..... 11–097, 12–007,
    12–012
Pt 23 PD, para.6 ... 12–009
    para.7 ... 12–009
Pt 24 ..... 11–118, 11–124,
    12–031, 14–002, 17–004,
    A–024, **B–139**
r.24.2 11–118
r.24.3(2) 11–118
Pt 25 ...... 11–117, 12–027
r.25.12 12–027
r.25.13 ..... 12–027, 19–018
r.25.15 19–018
r.26.3 ...... 11–105, 12–002
    (6) 11–105
    (6A) 11–105
r.26.8 20–015
Pt 26 PD 12–002
Pt 29 ..... 12–002, 12–003,
    12–038, A–016, A–017
r.29.2(b) 12–002
r.29.3(2) 12–007
r.29.5 12–009
r.29.6 12–002
r.29.7 12–038
r.29.14 12–008
r.29.16 12–038
Pt 29 PD 12–003
    para.2.6(7) .....
        12–009
    para.3.8 .. 12–007
    para.4 ... 12–008
    para.4.6 .. 12–008
    para.4.7(2) .....
        12–008
    para.4.10(4) .....
        12–004
    para.5 ... 12–004
    para.5.2 .. 12–007
    para.5.2(3) .....
        12–007
    para.5.3 .. 12–005
    para.5.5(1) .....
        12–004
    para.5.5(2) .....
        12–004

Pt 29 PD, para.5.7(1) .....
        12–007
    para.5.8 .. 12–007
    para.6 ... 12–009
    para.7 ... 12–025
    para.7.4 .. 12–025
    para.8.1(5) .....
        12–002
    para.8.3 .. 12–002
para.14.10(5) 12–004
para.14.10(6) 12–004
Pt 31 ..... 12–004, 12–010,
    12–013, 12–014
r.31.3 12–010
r.31.6 12–010
r.31.7 12–010
r.31.10 12–011
r.31.12 12–010
r.31.15 12–010
r.31.15(c) 12–010
r.31.16 .... 12–010, 12–012,
    12–027
    (3) 12–012
r.31.17 ..... 12–010, 12–012
r.31.17(3) 12–012
r.31.23 12–010
Pt 31 PD 12–010
    para.1 ... 12–010
    para.2 ... 12–010
    para.3 ... 12–011
    para.4 ... 12–011
    para.5 ... 12–010
    para.7 ... 12–010
    para.8 ... 12–010
Pt 32 ...... 12–004, 12–022
r.32.1 13–020
Pt 32 PD 12–022
Pt 33 12–005
r.33.3(b) 12–005
Pt 34 ...... 11–040, 13–013
r.34.5 ...... 12–039, 13–013
r.34.7 12–039
r.35.7 12–004
r.35.12 12–004
Pt 36 ..... 12–039, 13–019,
    14–013, 14–014, 14–015,
    14–016, 14–017, 14–018,
    14–020, 14–021, 14–023,
    16–017, 19–028, 20–032
r.36.1 .... **B–130**
r.36.2 .... **B–130**
    (4) 14–017
r.36.3 .... **B–130**
    (b) 14–016
r.36.4 .... **B–130**
r.36.5 .... **B–130**

TABLE OF STATUTORY INSTRUMENTS

r.36.6 .... **B–130**
r.36.8 .... **B–130**
r.36.9 ...... 14–016, **B–130**
r.36.10 ..... 14–017, **B–130**
r.36.11 .... **B–130**
   (1) 14–018
   (2) 14–018
r.36.12 .... **B–130**
r.36.13 ..... 14–018, **B–130**
r.36.14 ..... 14–018, **B–130**
r.36.15 ..... 14–016, **B–130**
   (4) 14.018
r.36.16 .... **B–130**
r.36.17 .... **B–130**
r.36.18 .... **B–130**
r.36.19 .... **B–130**
   (2) 14–016
r.36.20 .... 14–015, 14–018, **B–130**
r.36.21 .... 14–015, 14–018, 16–017, **B–130**
   (2) 14–015
r.36.22 .... **B–130**
r.36.23 .... **B–130**
Pt 38 ...... 14–002, 20–023
r.38.6 14–002
r.38.12 13–002
   (1) 14–002
r.39.3 15–002
   (3) 15–002
Pt 39 PD, para.3 ... 12–039, **B–140**
Pt 43 .... 11–044, **B–131**
r.43.1 .... **B–131**
r.43.2 .... **B–131**
r.43.3 .... **B–131**
r.43.4 .... **B–131**
Pt 43 PD, para.6 ... 12–007
Pt 44 ..... 11–044, 14–017, 20–037
r.44.1 .... **B–132**
r.44.2 .... **B–132**
r.44.3 ..... 11–136, 11–136, 16–001, 16–009, 16–019, 20–028, **B–132**
   (2) 11–076
   (3)(b) 16–010, 19–027
   (4)(c) 14–017, 14–021
   (5) ... 11–136, 12–046
r.44.3A **B–132**
r.44.3B **B–132**
r.44.4 .... **B–132**
r.44.4(3) 16–017
r.44.5 .... **B–132**
r.44.6 .... **B–132**
r.44.7 ...... 13–019, **B–132**
r.44.8 .... **B–132**

r.44.9 .... **B–132**
r.44.10 .... **B–132**
r.44.11 .... **B–132**
r.44.12 .... **B–132**
r.44.12A ... 13–019, 14–003, 16–023, **B–132**
r.44.13 .... **B–132**
r.44.14 ..... 16–017, **B–132**
r.44.15 ..... 18–005, **B–132**
r.44.16 .... **B–132**
r.44.17 .... **B–132**
Pt 44 PD ... 18–005, 18–008
   para.13 .. 13–019
   para.13.6 13–019
   para.22 ... A–026
   para.23 ... A–026
Pt 44 PD 2, s.8, para.8.2 11–076
Pt 44 PD, para.22 .. 18–004
   para.23 .. 18–004
Pts 44–48 16–016
Pt 45 .... **B–130**
Pt 46 .... **B–130**
Pt 47 .... 11–044, **B–130**
r.47.2 13–019
r.47.6 .... A–026
Pt 47 PD, para.29 .. 13–019
Pt 48 ..... 11–044, 16–011, 18–002, **B–130**
r.48.1 .... **B–133**
r.48.2 ...... 16–022, **B–133**
r.48.3 .... **B–133**
r.48.4 .... A–026, **B–133**
r.48.5 ...... 14.018, A–026, **B–133**
r.48.6 .... **B–133**
r.48.7 ..... 11–076, 11–135, 16–022
r.48.16 16–022
Pt 48 PD, para.51 ... A–026
Pt 52 ...... 19–003, 19–005
r.52.1 .... **B–134**
r.52.2 .... **B–134**
r.52.3 ...... 19–003, **B–134**
   (2) 19–003
   (4) 19–017
   (6) ... 19–012, 19–014
r.52.4 19–009, A–027, **B162**
r.52.5 ..... 19–008, 19–010, 19–015, 19–018, **B–134**
r.52.6 .... **B–134**
r.52.7 ...... 19–006, **B–134**
r.52.8 .... **B–134**
r.52.9 .... **B–134**
r.52.10 .... **B–134**
r.52.11 ..... 19–019, **B–134**
r.52.11(2) 19–021
   (3)(a) 19–020

TABLE OF STATUTORY INSTRUMENTS   xxix

r.52.11(3)(b) 19–020
r.52.12 ..... 19–028, **B–134**
Pt 52 PD ... 19–005, 19–008
  para.2A.1 ......
    19–001, 19–004
  para.2A.2 ......
    19–001, 19–004
  para.2A.3 ......
    19–002
  para.2A.4 ......
    19–002
  para.4.4 .. 19–004
  para.4.5 19–004,
    19–013
  para.4.6 .. 19–003
  para.4.7 .. 19–003
  para.4.15 19–016
  para.4.16 19–016
  para.5.6 .. 19–011
  para.5.10 19–011
  para.5.11 19–011
  para.5.12 19–011
  para.5.15 19–011
  para.5.16 19–011
  para.6 ... 19–018
Pt 57 ...... 1–004, 11–027,
  11–037, 11–038, 11–039,
  11–046, 11–096, 11–105,
  11–106, 11–118, 20–003,
  A–020, A–022, A–024,
  A–025, **B–137**, **B–139**
r.57.1 ..... 12–032, 15–010,
  19–001, 20–003, A–006
  (2) ... 11–046, 15–002,
    20–003
    (a) 1–002, 11–060,
      11–098
      (i) 15–001
      (ii) 15–008
      (iii) 15–010
    (b) 11–084
    (c) 11–077
r.57.2 ..... 11–060, 20–003,
    20–012, **B–135**
  (2) 20–012
  (4) ... 11–105, 12–001,
    12–002
r.57.3 .... **B–135**
  (b) ... 11–062, 11–068
r.57.4 .... **B–135**
  (1) ... 11–089, 11–090
  (2) 11–092
  (3) ... 11–087, 11–092
  (4) 11–094
r.57.5 ..... 11–049, 11–077,
  11–081, 11–090, 11–093,
    14–011, **B–135**
  (2)(b) 11–092

r.57.5(3) 11–077
  (4)(b) 11–092
  (5) ... 11–090, 11–091
r.57.6 .... **B–135**
  (1) ... 11–049, 11–124,
    14–011
  (2) ... 11–079, 15–006
  (3) 11–092
r.57.7 ..... 11–069, 11–073,
  11–097, 11–107, 11–110,
  11–120, 11–130, 12–004,
  A–021, A–023, A–024,
    B–135
  (1) 11–069
  (2) 11–069, A–024
  (3) ... 11–069, 11–071,
    11–072, 11–074, 11–096,
    A–023
  (4) ... 11–069, 11–071,
    11–072, 11–074, 11–096,
    A–023
  (c) 8–007
  (5) ... 11–097, 11–119,
    13–006, 16–008, A–024
r.57.8 ..... **11–096**, 11–097,
    B–135
r.57.8(2) 11–097
r.57.9 ..... 11–098, 11–101,
    B–135
  (4) 11–099
  (a) 11–100
  (b) 11–100
  (5) 11–099
r.57.10 ..... 11–118, A–026,
    B–135
r.57.11 .... 14–002, 14–004,
  14–005, 14–008, 15–005,
  A–026, **B–135**, B–137
  (1) ... A–028, B–139
r.57.12 .... **B–136**
  (2) .. 20–016, 20–030,
    A–028
r.57.15 11–064
r.57.16 12–032
  (1) 20–013
  (3) A–028
r.57.17 11–067
Pt 57 PD .. 11–046, 11–067,
  A–011, A–012, A–020,
    B–137, B–139
  para.1.1 .. **B–137**
  para.1.2 .. **B–137**
  para.2 ... 11–063,
    15–003, 20–003, 20–012
  para.2.1 .. A–022,
    B–137
  para.2.2 .. **B–137**

Pt 57 PD, para.2.3   11–080,
        B–137
     para.2.4   11–081,
        B–137
     para.3 ... 11–064,
        11–077, 11–078
     para.3.1 .. **B–137**
     para.3.2   11–081,
        B–137
     para.3.2(2) .....
        11–082
     para.3.3   11–083,
        11–091, **B–137**
     para.4 ... 11–056,
        11–065, **B–137**
     para.4(1)   11–065
     para.5.1   11–118,
        A–024, **B–137**
     para.5.2 .. A–024,
        B–137
     para.6.1 .. **B–137**
     para.6.1(1) .....
        14–009, B–137, B–139
     para.6.1(2) .....
        14–011
     para.6.1(3) .....
        14–011, B–137, B–139
Pt 57 PD, para.6.2   11–084,
        14–011, **B–137**
     para.7 ...   11–040
     para.7.1 .. **B–137**
     para.7.2 .. **B–137**
     para.7.3 .. **B–137**
     para.7.4 .. **B–137**
     para.8 ...   11–042,
        12–028
     para.8.1 .. **B–137**
     para.8.2 .. **B–137**
     para.8.3 .. **B–137**
     para.8.4 .. **B–137**
     para.8.5 .. **B–137**
     para.9 .... **B–138**
     para.10 ..   20–026
     para.10.1 ....
        20–017, **B–138**
     para.10.2 ....
        20–017, **B–138**
     para.11 ... **B–138**
     para.11.1   20–025
     para.15 ... **B–137**
Pt 57, Annex   11–081
Pt 64 .....   11–122, 16–020,
        20–024, 20–030
Pt 64 PD   16–020
Pt 74   17–002
Sch.1 ....   A–007

1999 Non–Contentious Probate Fees Order
        (SI 1999/688)—
     art.1 .... **B–124**
     art.2 .... **B–125**
     art.3 .... **B–126**
     art.5 .... **B–127**
     Sch.1, para.1 .... **B–128**
        para.11   11–021
        para.4   11–004,
           11–017, 11–021
        para.10   11–045
     Supreme Court Fees
        Order   (SI
        1999/687)   11–045,
           11–061
     Non–Contentious Probate Fees Order
        (SI 1999/688) ... **B–125**
     art.1 .... **B–125**
     art.2 .... **B–126**
     art.3 .... **B–127**
     art.5 .... **B–128**—
     Sch., para.1 .... **B–129**
     Non–Contentious Probate (Amendment) Rules (SI
        1999/1015) **B–134**
2000 Conditional Fee Agreements Regulations (SI
        2000/692)   18–006
     Access to Justice Act
        1999 (Commencement No.3, Transitional Provisions
        and Savings)
        Order (SI
        2000/774) **B–130**
     Access to Justice Act
        1999 (Transitional
        Provisions) Order
        (SI 2000/900) ... **B–130**
     Access to Justice Act
        1999 (Destination
        of Appeals)
        Order (SI
        2000/1071)—
     art.14(b)   19–001
2003 (SI 2003/185)   11–044
     Destination of Appeals
        Order (SI
        2003/490)—
     art.1(2)(c)   19–002
     art.2   19–001
     (SI 2003/1240)   18–006

Part I

The law

Chapter 1

Challenging the Will

The death of a person may give rise to many possible claims. 1–001
The primary object of this book is to cover the law and procedure in relation to contentious probate claims. Statute has long made a broad distinction between contentious and non-contentious probate, and procedurally that distinction is preserved under the CPR. In procedural terms the boundary between the two is marked by the moment of issue of the claim form. It remains both an appropriate and a convenient boundary.

A contentious probate claim means a claim for: 1–002

"(i) the grant of probate of the will, or letters of administration of the estate, of a deceased person;
(ii) the revocation of such a grant; or
(iii) a decree pronouncing for or against the validity of an alleged will;

not being a claim which is non-contentious (or common form) probate business." (CPR r.57.1(2)(a)).

Non-contentious probate, with which this book is not primarily concerned, is defined by statute as: 1–003

"the business of obtaining probate and administration where there is no contention as to the right thereto, including the passing of probates and administrations through the High Court in contentious cases where the contest has been terminated, and all business of a non-contentious nature in matters of testacy and intestacy not being proceedings in any action, and also the business of lodging caveats against the grant of probate or administration." (Supreme Court Act 1981, s.128)

Non-contentious probate remains, despite the introduction of the CPR, governed by the Non-Contentious Probate Rules 1987, for the good reason that the CPR are concerned with contentious probate claims, whereas the Non-Contentious Probate Rules are not.

1–004 Probate claims within the definition in CPR r.57 (above) fall into three general categories:

(1) interest claims (see below, para. 2–001);

(2) claims for a decree pronouncing for or against an alleged will (see below, paras 3–001 to 9–001); and.

(3) claims for the revocation of a grant already made.

1–005 Claims under (2) and (3) above will involve a common range of grounds upon which a will may be challenged. These grounds are the primary subject of this book, and in summary are as follows:

(1) lack of testamentary intention (see below, para. 3–001);

(2) lack of due execution (see below, para. 4–001);

(3) lack of testamentary capacity (see below, para. 5–001);

(4) lack of knowledge and approval (see below, para. 6–001);

(5) undue influence (see below, para. 7–001);

(6) fraud and forgery (see below, para. 8–001); and

(7) revocation (see below, para. 9–001 below);

In practice, most probate claims are for a decree pronouncing for, or against an alleged will.

1–006 In order to put probate claims in a broader context, however, it is also appropriate to have regard to some of the more frequent claims, other than probate claims proper, which may arise on the death of a person. Such claims may often provide a remedy where for one reason or another a probate claim proper is unavailable. They may in an appropriate case be available in addition to a probate claim. The non-probate claims we deal with in this book are as follows:

(1) mutual wills (see below, para. 10–003);

(2) proprietary estoppel (see below, para. 10–010);

(3) constructive trusts (see below, para. 10–023);

(4) secret trusts (see below, para. 10–028); and

(5) rectification (see below, para. 10–041).

We do not in this book cover either the subject of claims against **1–007** the net estate of a deceased person under the Inheritance (Provision for Family and Dependants) Act 1975, or the subject of professional negligence in the preparation of wills. Both subjects have their own textbooks, to which the reader should refer.

Chapter 2

Interest Claims

Introduction

The essential issue raised by any interest claim is whether a particular individual is or is not a person entitled to any interest in a deceased person's estate, whether under the will of the deceased person or (as is more usual) under the statutory trusts arising on the death of that person. 2–001

The issue may arise between individuals claiming under a particular will, or under an intestacy, where one or more persons claim that a particular person is not entitled to share under that particular will, or under that intestacy. But it may equally arise when there are competing wills, or when a party challenges a will and claims on a resulting intestacy. 2–002

The factual issues raised by an interest claim will typically be one of the following: 2–003

(1) Is X the person he claims to be, or is this person impersonating X (personation)?

(2) Is X the issue of the deceased (parentage)?

Personation

The issue whether X is the person he claims to be involves proof of identity, and will invariably arise as a result of somebody fraudulently attempting to impersonate X and claim X's inheritance (whether under a will or an intestacy). But an interest claim may also arise from the application of the rule that where a legacy is given to X under a particular description which X has falsely assumed, and which alone can be supposed to be the testator's motive for giving the legacy, X cannot claim the legacy (*Kennell v Abbott* (1799) 4 Ves. 802). The converse of this is that 2–004 a mere misdescription of a legatee will not defeat the legacy. For example, if a testator leaves a legacy to "my wife Rose", where she was not his lawful wife and he did not know that she was not his lawful wife, Rose's interest claim would succeed. Only if she had fraudulently assumed the character as his lawful wife would her interest claim fail (*Posner v Miller* [1953] P. 277).

Parentage

2–005 The issue of parentage arises most commonly in the context of intestacy, where X comes along claiming to be an illegitimate child of the intestate entitled to share under the statutory trusts arising on the intestacy. But it can equally arise where a person presumed to be legitimate and thus to be entitled under the will or intestacy of a supposed parent is challenged as not being the natural issue of the deceased at all.

The common law presumption of legitimacy
2–006 The common law rebuttably presumes that a child born to a married woman during the subsistence of her marriage is also the child of her husband (*Re G (A Minor)* (1988) 1 F.L.R. 314). This presumption of legitimacy applies even if the child must have been conceived before the marriage (*The Powlett Peerage Case* [1903] A.C. 395), or where the child is born within the possible period of gestation after the husband's death, or a final decree of divorce. In every case the husband and wife must have had the opportunity of access to each other during the period in which the child could have been conceived and born in the course of nature, and the husband must not be proved to be impotent.

2–007 The presumption does not apply where the spouses are living apart under a decree of judicial separation, but it has been held to apply in other circumstances notwithstanding, for example, the fact that the parties were living apart under a separation deed or agreement. The presumption exists even where, from the date of the child's birth, it is clear that the child must have been conceived out of wedlock (as where it is born the day after the marriage), for the act of marriage is a recognition by the husband of the child as his own. The presumption, though not so strong as it would be if the child were conceived after the marriage, is not defeated merely by proving that someone else had intercourse with the woman (*Gardner v Gardner* (1877) 2 App. Cas. 723).

The presumption is not affected where the mother, living apart from her husband, is maintained by him under an order of a magistrates' court which contains no provision that the parties be no longer bound to cohabit with one another. Where the parties are living apart by agreement, whether by deed, writing under hand, oral agreement or agreement implied by conduct, the presumption is that the child is legitimate. The presumption is reversed, however, if the parties are separated under an order of the court, such as a decree of judicial separation, which ends the duty of the spouses to live together.

Rebutting the presumption of legitimacy
The presumption may in any civil proceedings be rebutted by evidence which shows that it is more probable than not that the child is illegitimate, but it is not necessary to prove that fact beyond reasonable doubt in order to rebut the presumption. But the standard of proof may depend on the gravity of the particular issue to be resolved, and since parentage is a serious matter, the standard of proof required to rebut the presumption which is implicit in the presumption of legitimacy is somewhat higher than the mere balance of probabilities.

2–008

Evidence rebutting any of these common law presumptions increasingly involves scientific evidence. An example of the degree to which scientific testing may define who, on the balance of the evidence, is the father, is *W v K (proof of paternity)* (1988) 1 F.L.R. 86, where the evidence showed that a man with whom a married woman had sexual intercourse was 97.4 per cent more likely to be the father, on the evidence of blood tests, than her husband, with whom she had also been having intercourse. But other cases show that the evidence may not be so conclusive; and there is always the interest of the child to be considered in deciding whether tests should be ordered. Now that DNA tests can be used under the amended Family Law Reform Act 1969, s.20, the uncertainty of blood tests is much reduced, if not eliminated, for practical purposes. Various laboratories provide facilities for testing and producing DNA test reports. The procedures no longer require the production of blood samples; mouth swabs are equally effective. As all the world knows, an individual inherits half his genes from his mother and half from his father. Scientific samples obtained from the mother and the alleged father would allow a decisive DNA test to be undertaken. However, there are cases where a DNA test report may not be decisive. For example, if it is alleged that a child born during the marriage of the deceased was not the natural child of the deceased, but of the mother and another man (so that the child would not be entitled to take under the intestacy of the deceased), DNA samples taken from a blood relation of the deceased may produce an indecisive result. These developments in science are nonetheless now preferred by the courts as a more reliable means of establishing

2–009

paternity than the application of the common law presumptions (*Re H (Children)*) (2002) 2 F.C.R. 469).

2–010 Meanwhile, science is constantly developing, and the law of parentage is in consequence also developing. In particular, the development of human-assisted reproduction and surrogacy means that natural parturition (the act of giving birth by the mother) is no longer the sole criterion for motherhood. For example, the Human Fertilisation and Embryology Act 1990 defines who is the mother of a child by reference to the placing in the woman who has carried the child of an embryo (which has implanted) or of sperm or eggs. In the case of a married woman, the father of the child is the other party to the marriage at the time of the placing of the embryo or the sperm or the eggs, or the insemination of the woman. There are special provisions which apply to sperm donors, so as to exclude the donor's parentage in favour of the father who is the party to the marriage with the woman who carries the child conceived by such sperm: s.28.

Now by the Human Fertilisation and Embryology (Deceased Fathers) Act 2003 a dead father of children born posthumously as a result of IVF treatment conceived by the widow after the death using the dead father's sperm is recognised as the father of such children.

Chapter 3

Lack of Testamentary Intention

Introduction

The function in English law of a probate court is to ascertain **3–001** and determine what testamentary paper or papers is or are to be regarded as constituting the last will of the testator, and who is entitled to be constituted his legal personal representative. However many testamentary documents a testator may leave, it is the aggregate or the net result that constitutes his will, or, in other words, the expression of his testamentary wishes. In this sense it is inaccurate to speak of a person leaving two wills; he does leave, and can leave, only one will (*Douglas-Menzies v Umphelby* [1908] A.C. 224).

English law does not require a document which is intended to **3–002** have testamentary effect to assume any particular form or to be couched in language technically appropriate to its testamentary character. It is sufficient that the instrument, however irregular in form or artificial in expression, discloses the intention of the maker regarding the posthumous destination of his property. It is from the document so admitted to probate together with any other relevant testamentary instruments that an English court will ascertain the testator's testamentary intentions and determine their effect and validity (*Re Berger* [1990] 1 Ch. 118).

The underlying principle is that a document will only operate **3–003** as a will if it was intended by its maker to operate as a will. Without such testamentary intention it will not operate as a will and hence will not be admitted to probate as a will. Hence a document put forward by one party as a will may be challenged by another on the ground that the document was not intended by its maker to operate as a will. This in turn frequently leads to two other related issues: incorporation of documents (see below, para. 3–009) and conditional wills (see below, para. 3–015).

Evidence of testamentary intention

3–004 Normally, an intention that a document should operate as a will is expressed in the form of the document itself, the clearest possible expression of such intention being words such as "this is the last will and testament of me William Shakespeare". But the form of the document may not be so clear and may leave genuine doubt as to whether the document was indeed intended to operate as a will. At the other extreme, the document itself, although testamentary in appearance, may be expressed not to be a will, in which case the lack of testamentary intention is clear. For example, a testator left a will and then executed in accordance with the requirements of s.9 of the Wills Act 1837 a further document which a party mentioned in it attempted to propound as a codicil. The document, although testamentary in appearance, was headed "This is not meant as a legal Will, but as a Guide". Probate was refused because the document contained what amounted to a positive assertion by the person who had executed it that it was not intended to operate as a will (*Ferguson-Davie v Ferguson-Davie* (1890) 15 P.D. 109).

3–005 Between these two extremes are documents which are silent as to the maker's testamentary intention. In such cases extrinsic evidence is admissible as to the maker's intention (*King's Proctor v Daines* (1830) 3 Hagg. Ecc. 218). Even a simple document saying "I, X, give Y full authority to draw the amount of money contained in my bank book" but duly executed was admitted to probate on evidence that the maker's intention in writing the document was to make Y all right so that the money could be drawn if anything happened to X, such evidence being regarded by the court as sufficient to establish X's testamentary intention (*Re English* (1864) 3 Sw. & Tr. 586).

3–006 There is a further class of document containing an expression of the writer's wishes as to the disposition of his property at his death which may be admitted as a will even though it contains ambiguous expressions, provided that the court is satisfied by parol evidence and by the document itself that it really was a fixed and final expression of the testator's wishes, and not a mere deliberative and temporary document compiled for consideration and not for stating final intention. Whatever the form of the instrument, whatever its appearance, whatever its construction, in whatever terms it may have been expressed, or on whatever material it may have been written, the court has only one question to ask: was it the intention of the testator that that document should operate as his will? However informal or imperfect it may be, if satisfied that the deceased did intend it to operate as his will, the court is bound to give effect to it.

CONTENTIOUS PROBATE

This class of document is to be distinguished from the class of document which is imperfect or unfinished, when the writer obviously contemplated doing something more. To admit this latter class of document to probate, two conditions are required: 3–007

(1) that the deceased had a fixed and final intention to make the disposition of his property expressed in the document; and

(2) that he never abandoned that intention, and was only prevented by death from proceeding to the completion of his will (*Godman v Godman* [1920] P. 261).

Burden of proof of testamentary intention

Where the document itself is not clearly testamentary, the burden of proof of the maker's testamentary intention is on the party propounding the document as a will. But if it is apparently testamentary, the burden of proof that it was not intended to have testamentary effect is on the party challenging it. 3–008

Incorporation of documents

An issue may arise as to which of a number of documents left by the testator after his death should be admitted to probate. Here again the essential issue is the testator's intention. Where the testator's testamentary intention is established in relation to one document, the question can arise as to whether certain related but not duly executed documents should be included. This requires consideration of the rule relating to incorporation of documents. 3–009

The rule permits incorporation only if certain factual circumstances are established by the evidence. These in summary are: 3–010

(1) that the document sought to be incorporated was already in existence at the time of the duly executed testamentary document (whether will or codicil) in which it is sought to be incorporated;

(2) that the duly executed document must refer to the document sought to be incorporated as one already in existence; and

(3) that it must be referred to so expressly as to identify it (and not some other possible document) as the document in question.

14 LACK OF TESTAMENTARY INTENTION

3–011 Given that the effect of the rule is to include in the probate documents which themselves have not been duly executed in accordance with s.9 of the Wills Act 1837, it is not surprising that the onus on those seeking incorporation of such documents is a heavy one. The evidence required is evidence to establish the necessary factual conditions for the application of the rule. Consequently, evidence of what the testator wished or intended is not, subject to one exception, relevant. That exception is where the terms of the will are such as to be ambiguous in the light of the surrounding circumstances, as (for example) where there is ambiguity as to which of one or more persons or things the testator was referring. It would seem that here, as elsewhere, extrinsic evidence including evidence of the testator's intention may now be admitted to assist in the interpretation of the will (Administration of Justice Act 1982, s.21).

3–012 The limits of the rule are strict. Thus a document which is not dispositive will not be admitted. A statement in a will referring to an intended or future document will not permit incorporation. Words in the will too general to refer to any particular existing document will be insufficient to effect incorporation. However, the principle "that is certain which can be rendered certain" may allow a document referred to in a will to be identified with sufficient certainty so as to be incorporated. There is no reason, for example, why a general reference in X's will to the piece of paper he left in the garden shed on Y's birthday could not be identified by appropriate evidence and incorporated in X's will, much though some might wish it not to be incorporated.

3–013 The rule can successfully be invoked even to save a will which is itself invalid as not having been duly executed in accordance with s.9 of the Wills Act 1837. This can happen where the testator has subsequently duly executed a codicil to his supposedly valid will. Where the will is clearly referred to in the subsequent codicil as the testator's will, and is clearly referred to as already in existence, then the rule of incorporation will apply and allow the invalidly executed will to be included by incorporation in the duly executed codicil and admitted to probate as incorporated in it (*Allen v Maddock* (1858) 11 Moo. P.C. 427). This might be seen as driving a coach and horses through s.9, and it is likely that the court would require the facts to be very clear before applying the rule. The same result could be reached as between two codicils, the first not duly executed, where the second refers to the first as an existing codicil. But here again the reference would have to be nothing less than clear.

3–014 The most surprising application of the rule perhaps is in its interface with the doctrine of revival, whereby no will or codicil or any part of them which has been revoked can be revived (*i.e.* revalidated) other than by re-execution, or by a duly executed codicil, showing an intention to revive the will or codicil in question (Wills Act 1837, s.22). Naturally, all the same considerations as to due execution apply to the re-execution of the will or the execution of the subsequent codicil. The expression of the intention to revive is essential, and must be clear and unequivocal. It will not easily be inferred (*Re Sebag-Montefiore* [1944] Ch. 331). The doctrine of revival, where it applies to revival of a will by a subsequent codicil, has effect as if the revived will was re-executed at the same time as the subsequent codicil. The rule of incorporation of documents may then have the surprising (but logical) effect of letting in documents which did not exist at the time of original execution of the will before its subsequent revocation, provided such documents were in existence at the time of the deemed re-execution of the will under the doctrine of revival. But all the requirements for incorporation, albeit applied as at the later date (*i.e.* the date of the deemed re-execution) must be satisfied. The document sought to be incorporated by this back-door route must accordingly be referred to in the will as already in existence, which of course in actuality it was not, at the date of original execution. If the will refers to the document as a future document (as was at the time of original execution the case), the rule will not apply so as to allow incorporation (*Re Smart* [1902] P. 238).

Conditional Wills

A will may be intended by its maker to become operative only 3–015 on some condition being satisfied. In that event its operation is conditional on the satisfaction of the condition. As has been seen, the court is in every case concerned to establish what was the intention of the testator and to give effect to it. The testator's intention that his will should be conditional on some event is as much part of his testamentary intention as any other part of such intention.

The testator's intention that the will should only operate on 3–016 satisfaction of some condition, or on the happening of some future event, may only be established by the intrinsic terms of the will itself. Extrinsic evidence to establish the testator's intention that the will was to be conditional in its operation is not admissible (*Corbett v Newey* [1998] Ch. 57). Thus where a testator executes a will but refrains from dating it in the mistaken belief that this will postpone the operation of the will until the date is inserted (in other words intending the operation of the will to be conditional on a future event), not only is the condition ineffective but so also is the entire will. It is true that the dispositions under any will will remain inchoate until death, but they operate immediately as ambulatory provisions varying in range or subject-matter according as to how the assets in the ownership of the testator during his lifetime may change in nature, value or extent. Since a will operates from the moment of execution, it necessarily follows that to possess the necessary testamentary intention the testator must intend that this dispositive (though revocable and ambulatory) regime will be called into play immediately and not postponed to, or made dependent upon, some future event or condition. That is why, surprising though the distinction may at first sight be to a laymen, it is possible to have a will which is on its face conditional, and yet impossible to have a will which though unconditional on its face purports, through some direction imposed externally by the testator at the time of its execution, to be made conditional in its operation (*ibid.* at 65 *per* Waite L.J.). Furthermore, to admit extrinsic evidence of the testator's intention that the will was to be conditional when on its face it was unconditional would be tantamount to writing into the will an additional provision which failed to satisfy the requirements for due execution stipulated by s.9 of the Wills Act 1837 (*ibid.* at 67).

3–017 An issue may nonetheless arise over the interpretation of the terms of the particular will claimed to be conditional. Here the cases make a basic distinction between words which merely express a reason for the making of the will, and words which have the effect of imposing a condition. Two criteria are regarded by the court as useful in establishing the distinction: first, whether the nature of the disposition made appears to be related to the time or circumstances of the condition or contingency; secondly, where the condition or contingency is connected with a period of danger for the testator, whether it is coincident with that period. If it is, it may be concluded that the danger was regarded by the testator merely as a reason or occasion to make the will; if it is not, the court may conclude that the reasons for the reference to a particular period was to make the operation of the will conditional by reference to that contingency (*Re Spratt* [1897] P. 28).

Chapter 4

Lack of Due Execution

Introduction

For deaths on or after January 1, 1983, a will to be duly **4–001** executed must, unless it is a privileged will (see below, para. 4–017), comply with the requirements of s.9 of the Wills Act 1837 as amended by s.17 of the Administration of Justice Act 1982. Under these provisions no will is valid unless:

"(a) it is in writing, and signed by the testator, or by some other person in his presence and by his direction; and
(b) it appears that the testator intended by his signature to give effect to the will; and
(c) the signature is made or acknowledged by the testator in the presence of two or more witnesses present at the same time; and
(d) each witness either—

 (i) attests and signs the will; or
 (ii) acknowledges his signature,

in the presence of the testator (but not necessarily in the presence of any other witness) but no form of attestation shall be necessary."

Each limb of these statutory requirements will now be considered in turn.

Section 9(a)

A will must be in writing. Any form of writing (handwritten, **4–002** typed, or printed by any form of technology) will suffice, as long as it is on some substance (normally paper) which will bear a signature and can be produced to a probate registry. This

18   LACK OF DUE EXECUTION

requirement would appear to allow almost anything, except perhaps wills written on the sand, which could not easily be produced to a probate registry.

4–003 What amounts to a signature is ultimately an evidential question as to the testator's intention. The essential purpose of a signature is to authenticate a document as a document emanating from the person who signs it.

4–004 Thus an indecipherable scrawl has on the evidence been held to constitute the signature of the testator (*Re Kieran* [1933] I.R. 222), as has the testator's personal stamp (*Jenkins v Gaisford* (1863) 3 Sw. & Tr. 93), his initialled seal (*Re Emerson* (1992) 9 L.R. Ir. 443), and even just his thumb print (*Re Parsons* [2002] W.T.L.R. 237).

4–005 A will may be validly signed by some other person than the will-maker, at the will-making location, where for instance the testator is blind or paralysed. In such cases there is obviously a practical need for signature by an agent. In any other circumstances there would have to be very clear evidence that the signing was indeed done at the testator's direction.

Section 9(b)

4–006 The former requirement that a testator's signature must be at the foot or end of the will has gone. For deaths on or after January 1, 1983, statute is no longer concerned with the position of the signature but simply with the testator's intention. Clearly the position of the signature still has some relevance as evidence of intention. So also has the proved stage at which the signature was made. A signature made by the testator in the following circumstances will satisfy s.9(b). First, the testator takes a blank piece of paper and signs it at the bottom. Secondly, as part of the same continuing process, he writes above his signature "This is my last will and testament. I leave everything to my wife." Thirdly, he gets his signature attested by two witnesses. In such a case it does not matter that he wrote his signature on the document before the dispositive wording of the will, because it is all one operation (*Re White* [1991] Ch. 1). Thus a will will be valid where a testator uses a standard will form and fills it out in his own handwriting, heading it "my Will by X", but does not sign it at the bottom after writing out the dispositive provisions, provided that there is affirmative evidence to establish that the testator had indeed intended his initial signature to give effect to the provisions which then followed (*Wood v Smith* [1993] Ch. 90). The object of the new s.9(b) was to simplify the requirements for the execution and witnessing of wills, and the complementary requirements of s.9(a) and (b) of a signature

CONTENTIOUS PROBATE 19

and a proved intention that the signature should give effect to the will demand a practical approach (*ibid.* at 111 *per* Scott L.J.). Nonetheless, whether what happened consisted of one operation or not could still arise as an issue.

Section 9(c)

A will remains unique among all legal documents in requiring to be witnessed by not one but two witnesses, in the manner prescribed. This is in recognition of the exceptional need for authenticity, given that the will-maker is thereby disposing of his entire worldly goods, probably in old age, and probably in the context of conflicting claims and expectations. It is most commonly for failure to satisfy the requirements of this particular subsection of s.9 that wills are successfully attacked on the ground of lack of due execution. 4–007

The essential requirement is that both witnesses should be present at the same time when the testator signs or acknowledges his signature. The testator may rightly believe that he needs two witnesses to his will. But many wills with two witnesses have been successfully challenged because it was established by the evidence that the witnesses were not simultaneously present at the signing or acknowledgement. Whether a person is in the presence of another person may itself constitute an issue of fact. In *Re Parsons* [2002] W.T.L.R. 237 one of the two attesting witnesses claimed not to have been in the room when the will was signed; but the court rejected that evidence. A testator is not present in the required sense if he is physically present when his will is witnessed but unconscious (*Right v Price* (1779) 1 Doug. 241). Nor can a blind witness be present in the required sense (*Re Gibson* [1949] P. 434). It matters not that the testator himself is blind, although in such a case it must be established that he could have seen the witnesses had he not been blind (*Re Piercy* (1845) 1 Rob. 278). 4–008

In the case of acknowledgement by the testator, what has to be acknowledged is not that the document is the testator's will, but only that the signature thereon is the testator's signature (*Daintree v Butcher* (1888) 13 P.D. 102). That the witnesses may believe that the document is something altogether different is accordingly immaterial. 4–009

Section 9(c) does not stipulate what amounts to sufficient acknowledgement by a testator of his signature already on the document; nor is any express declaration required by the subsection to indicate whether the testator signed in the presence of two witnesses present at the same time or merely acknowledged his signature already on the document to them. 4–010

No particular form of expression is required, for example by using the actual word "acknowledge"; nor indeed need the testator speak a single word, provided that the testator's signature is physically visible to him and the two witnesses, and he can see and acquiesce in the witnesses signing the will as his witnesses (*Cooke v Henry* [1932] I.R. 574). The modern approach is for the court to give effect to clear testamentary wishes if it is possible and proper to do so, and as the law leans against intestacy the court will not be astute to undermine a will unless there is clear evidence of non-compliance with the rules to be observed in its making (*Weatherhill v Pearce* [1995] 1 W.L.R. 592). It is accordingly a sufficient acknowledgement for the purpose of s.9(c) for a testator to sign a will beforehand and then just proffer it as a document for the witnesses to sign that all concerned know is a will (*ibid.* at 598).

Section 9(d)

4–011 It is not, however, necessary for both witnesses to be together at the same time when they come to sign or acknowledge their own signature. In practice, if the witnesses are together at the same time when the testator signs or acknowledges his signature, as they have to be to satisfy s.9(c), they will normally themselves sign on that same occasion, and thereby more than satisfy s.9(d).

4–012 The law as to what constitutes a witness's signature is the same as that for the signature of the testator himself (see above, para. 4–003), as is the law as to what constitutes an acknowledgement. The same evidential issue can arise as to the nature of the intention which accompanied the witness's signature or acknowledgement. That intention must be to act (whether by signature or acknowledgement) in the capacity as witness, as opposed to any other capacity.

4–013 A will will be validly executed even where, at the time at which the testator and the two witnesses are together, both the testator and one of the witnesses have already signed, provided that the witness who has already signed acknowledges that fact on that occasion. Where, on such facts, the witness who had already signed protested on that occasion that what was happening was not due attestation, her very protests recognising and acknowledging that something had happened and that she had already indeed signed the document as a witness amounted to sufficient acknowledgement to satisfy s.9(d) (*Couser v Couser* [1996] 1 W.L.R. 1301).

4–014 In summary, the possibilities which the section raises are various. The will can validly be signed by the testator in the absence of the witnesses but then shown by the testator to the two witnesses with the testator acknowledging the testator's signature in their presence. That acknowledgement by the testator must be in the presence of them both at the same time. However, it would in fact be a perfectly valid execution if both witnesses then left and each severally or separately returned on a subsequent occasion then to attest and sign the will in the presence of the testator; alternatively, it would be sufficient that they had already signed the will and that they came back subsequently and acknowledged their signature to the will (*ibid.* at 1304).

The presumption of due execution

The application of this presumption may itself put an end to a dispute about due execution. It is a particular application of a more general presumption which applies in other areas of the law too, that everything is to be presumed to have been done properly: *omnia praesumuntur rite esse acta* to those who only speak Latin. In essence it is a presumption of evidence. It is the expression of an inference which may reasonably be drawn when an intention to do some formal act is established, where the evidence is consistent with that intention having been carried into effect in a proper way, and where there is no positive evidence either way (*Harris v Knight* (1890) 15 P.D. 179). The courts have been and continue to be robust in their application of the presumption. In one case the presumption was not rebutted even in the face of evidence from the two attesting witnesses that the testator did not sign in their presence, on the ground that they were confused and forgetful in the witness box (*Wright v Sanderson* (1884) 9 P.D. 149). In *Re Parsons* [2002] W.T.L.R. 237 the court disbelieved a witness who claimed not to have been in the room when the will was signed. In cases where lack of due execution would result in an intestacy, the presumption will be reinforced by the public policy principle whereby the law leans against an intestacy.

4–015

Some forms of attestation will attract the application of the presumption more strongly than others, bearing in mind always the proviso to s.9 that no particular form of attestation is necessary. Accordingly, where a will has what might be called a regular attestation clause, which carries the inference that the testator knew the statutory attestation requirements, the presumption will be compelling, on the footing that persons who signed their names to such a clause must have known and meant what they were doing. Where the will has what might be called an informal attestation clause, which carries the inference that the testator did not know the statutory attestation requirements,

4–016

the presumption may be less compelling, but may nonetheless be applied in the absence of evidence to the contrary. Thus a holograph will, which was the only testamentary document found after the deceased's death, consisted of a small single sheet of writing paper. On one side appeared the date and the words "I give all I possess to my cousins Mary Jane and John Harnett . . .", followed by the signature of the deceased. On the other side and upside down, two names were written in different hands, "Edith Freeman" and "Dorothy Edwards" one below the other. There was no attestation clause and no indication as to why Edith Freeman's and Dorothy Edwards's names were on the back of the document. It was held that, applying the maxim *omnia praesumuntur rite esse acta*, probate would be granted since the only practical reason why the names of Edith Freeman and Dorothy Edwards were on the back of the document must have been that their names were there for the purpose of attesting the will (*Re Denning* [1958] 2 All E.R. 1).

Privileged wills

4–017 A privileged will is exempt from the requirements of s.9 of the Wills Act 1837. Hence, where a will does not comply with those requirements, the issue can arise as to whether it falls within the exemption accorded to privileged wills.

The exemption

4–018 Section 11 of the Wills Act 1837 provides that any soldier being in actual military service, or any mariner or seaman being at sea, may dispose of his personal estate as he might have done before the making of that Act. The position before the Act was that no formalities were required (it might have been simpler if s.11 had said just that). Personal estate includes property over which the testator has a general or special power of appointment (*Re Chichester* [1946] Ch. 289). The exemption accorded to personal estate now extends to realty as well (Wills (Soldiers and Sailors) Act 1918, s.3). That Act also extended the exemption to all persons (whether man or woman) serving in the Army, the Royal Navy, the Royal Marines or the Royal Air Force, provided always that they are "in actual military service".

4–019 The issue may accordingly arise as to whether an individual is a member of the above armed forces, and whether he is in actual military service. The statute has been interpreted (*Re Wingham* [1949] P. 187) as meaning that any soldier, sailor or airman is entitled to the privilege if he is actually serving with

CONTENTIOUS PROBATE 23

the armed forces in connection with military operations which are or have been taking place or are believed to be imminent. It does not include officers on half-pay or men on the reserve, or the territorials, when not called up for service. They are not actually serving. Nor does it include members of the forces serving in this country, or on routine garrison duty overseas, in time of peace, when military operations are not imminent. They are actually serving, but are not in actual "military" service, because no military operations are afoot. It does, however, include all men and women serving or called up for service. It includes not only those actively engaged with the enemy but also all those who are training to fight him. It also includes those members of the forces who, under stress of war, both work at their jobs and man the defences, such as the Home Guard. It includes not only the fighting men but also those who serve in the forces, *e.g.* doctors, nurses, chaplains, and so forth. It includes them all, whether they are in the field or in barracks, in billets or sleeping at home. It includes them although they may be captured by the enemy or interned by neutrals. It includes them not only in time of war but also when war is imminent. After hostilities are ended, it may still include them, as, for instance, when they garrison the countries which they occupy, or when they are engaged in military operations overseas.

Although a person claiming the exemption has to prove it, it **4–020** seems that in a doubtful case the court will give him or her the benefit of the doubt (*Re Jones* [1981] Fam. 7). In that case the deceased, while serving as a soldier in Northern Ireland, had been sent out on a military patrol with an officer and a warrant officer. An unknown assailant shot him and, before he died, he made an oral testamentary declaration to the two soldiers with him, leaving his possessions to the applicant whom he was to have married the following week. She applied to have the declaration admitted to probate as a privileged will under s.11 of the Wills Act 1837. The court held that it was the nature of the duties a soldier was called upon to perform which determined whether he was on actual military service; that, provided the service was both active and military, it could be either within the United Kingdom or abroad against a force that need not be organised along conventional military lines; and, therefore, that when the soldier was called upon to go out on patrol at a time when there was clandestinely organised insurrection, he was on actual military service and his oral declaration would be admitted to probate.

Similar issues may arise as to whether or not a mariner or **4–021** seaman was "at sea" so as to attract the exemption. The term is interpreted expansively (*Re Newland* [1952] P. 71). In that case an apprentice in the merchant navy while on leave in wartime, executed a testamentary document shortly before rejoining his ship, which sailed a day or so later. The document was executed in compliance with the formalities of the Wills Act 1837, but as he was then a minor the question arose on his death whether he was at the material time a "seaman being at sea" within the meaning of s.11 of the statute. The court held that since the document was executed in contemplation of a fresh voyage, and the deceased was under orders to rejoin his ship before a certain date, he was "a seaman at sea" when he made his will. But the exemption will not extend so far as to include leave at a time when the deceased is under no orders to join any ship (*Re Rapley* [1983] 1 W.L.R. 1069). In that case the deceased, who was then an apprentice seaman aged about 19, went on leave to his family home in Sussex having been discharged from the *SS City of Ely* and not yet having received any orders to join another ship. On October 22, 1980, he signed a document which he intended to be his will, but which was unattested, and which was therefore invalid under s.9 of the Wills Act 1837, unless he could be regarded as a "mariner or seaman being at sea", within the terms of s.11, at the date when he signed the document. On November 29, he received an order to join the *SS City of Melbourne*. He died subsequently when the ship in which he was then serving foundered in a typhoon in the Pacific Ocean. By the terms of the document the deceased had purported to leave all that he should die possessed of to the plaintiff, his mother. She obtained letters of administration to his estate on January 9, 1981, but subsequently sought to propound the document as a seaman's will. The defendant was the deceased's father who was the only other person interested in any estate in respect of which the deceased died intestate. The court held that a seaman on leave who was liable at any time to be instructed to join a particular ship but who had not received such instructions and was not part of the complement of any particular ship was not "at sea" within the meaning of s.11 of the Wills Act 1837; and that, accordingly, since the deceased had not received orders to join another ship when he signed the document on October 22, 1980, he was not a "seaman being at sea" and the plaintiff was not entitled to the relief sought.

4–022 Provided always that the necessary testamentary intention is present (see Chapter 3), a privileged will does not have to be in any particular form. It may even be merely verbal. If in writing, it does not need to be witnessed or even signed. It may be in a letter, or part of a letter, or more than one letter (*Re Vernon* (1916) 33 T.L.R. 11). Alterations or interdelineations on a privileged will are presumed also to be subject to this privilege (*Re Tweedale* (1874) LR 3 P. & D. 204).

Foreign wills

By foreign wills is here meant wills, other than privileged wills, not subject to the provisions of s.9 of the Wills Act 1837. An English court will treat a foreign will as properly executed if its execution conforms to the internal law in force either:

4–023

(1) in the territory where it was executed (see *Re Wynn* [1984] 1 W.L.R. 237); or

(2) in the territory where, either at the time of its execution or at the time of the testator's death, the testator had his habitual residence, or was domiciled; or

(3) in a state of which, either at the time of its execution or at the time of the testator's death, the testator was a national. (See Wills Act 1963, s.1.)

In addition, an English court will treat as properly executed:

(4) a will executed on board a vessel or aircraft of any description, if the execution of the will conformed to the internal law in force in the territory with which, having regard to its registration (if any) and other relevant circumstances, the vessel or aircraft may be taken to have been most closely connected;

(5) a will so far as it disposes of immovable property, if its execution conformed to the internal law in force in the territory where the property was situated;

(6) a will so far as it revokes a will which under the Act would be treated as properly executed or revokes a provision which under the Act would be treated as comprised in a properly executed will, if the execution of the later will conformed to any law by reference to which the revoked will or provision would be so treated; and

(7) a will so far as it exercises a power of appointment, if the execution of the will conformed to the law governing the essential validity of the power. (See Wills Act 1963, s.2.)

Furthermore, an English court will disregard a foreign law in so far as such law treats as other than a formal requirement any law whereby special formalities are to be observed by testators answering a particular description, or witnesses to the execution of a will are to possess certain qualifications. (See Wills Act 1963, s.3.)

4–024 Foreign wills are not otherwise dealt with in this book. For the issues of conflict of laws which may arise in relation to a foreign will, see Dicey and Morris, *Conflict of Laws* (13th ed.), Vol. 1, Ch. 27.

Chapter 5

Lack of Testamentary Capacity

Introduction

This issue has in recent years become a very definite growth area in probate litigation, and is set to become even more so. This is because lengthening life expectancy has resulted in dementia, "the scourge of old age", becoming over the population as a whole an increasingly widespread disease. The Alzheimer's Disease Society estimates that there are over 670,000 people in the United Kingdom suffering from dementia and that approximately 70 per cent of them have Alzheimer's disease, and that 1 in 5 of those over 80 years old have dementia. According to the Office for National Statistics, the number of people in the United Kingdom aged 65 and over rose by nearly half between 1961 and 2003 to 9.3 million, and will reach 12 million in the year 2021, while the number of people aged 85 and over has risen from nearly 350,000 in 1961 to nearly 1.1 million in 2003. In the absence of dramatic advances in medical science, the number of people with dementia is liable to increase proportionately.

The case law on testamentary capacity remains firmly rooted in the nineteenth century. It is striking to recall that in 1870, the year in which the ruling case of *Banks v Goodfellow* ((1870) L.R. 5 Q.B. 549) was decided, Gladstone had only recently formed his first ministry, and Stanley had yet to meet up with Dr Livingstone in what was then regarded as darkest Africa. More particularly, medical science had a long way to go before Dr Alois Alzheimer identified in 1907 the mental disease which bears his name. Unquestionably, a knowledge of the manifold forms of mental illness currently known to medical science is extremely relevant; and that will necessarily present a constantly changing picture. (See the medical overview by Professor Hodkinson in Appendix III). Assessment of testamentary capacity necessarily involves a medico-legal assessment. But when all

5–001

5–002

the medical evidence has been considered, and the nature and extent of the mental disease in question has been assessed, the issue for the court remains the same: Is the nature and extent of the mental disease such as to remove testamentary capacity as that concept is understood by the law? To that concept we now turn.

Testamentary capacity: the *Banks v Goodfellow* test

5–003 In *Banks v Goodfellow* Cockburn C.J. famously said:

> "It is essential that a testator shall understand the nature of his act and its effects; shall understand the extent of the property of which he is disposing; shall be able to comprehend and appreciate the claims to which he ought to give effect, and, with a view to the latter object, that no disorder of the mind shall poison his affections, pervert his sense of right, or prevent the exercise of his natural faculties, that no insane delusion shall influence his will in disposing of his property and bring about a disposal of it which, if his mind had been sound, would not have been made." (*ibid.* at 565)

This passage in effect deals in two separate parts with two separate matters:

(1) what the testator must be capable of understanding; and

(2) the relevance or otherwise of any disorder of the mind or insane delusion to which the testator may be subject.

5–004 What the testator must be capable of understanding is:

(a) the nature of his act and its effect;

(b) the extent of the property of which he is disposing; and

(c) the claims to which he ought to give effect.

These three constituents of (1) above are so lucidly expressed that they do not require elaboration. Equally lucid is the expression of (2): that neither a disorder of the mind nor an insane delusion are relevant unless they are active in bringing about a disposal which the testator would otherwise not have made.

5–005 The peculiar force and staying power of *Banks v Goodfellow* can only be fully understood by a consideration of the whole of the 20-page judgment of Cockburn C.J. It has many notable aspects. In the first place, Cockburn C.J. was giving the judgment of a quite exceptionally distinguished court which included (apart from himself) Blackburn J., Mellor J. and Hannen J. In the second place, the issues before the court did not in fact require it to formulate a new definition of testamentary capacity, so that a bright law student (and even a not so bright one) would be entitled to point out that the whole of the first part of Cockburn C.J.'s dictum was merely *obiter dictum*. That is because the court was required to assume, as a result of a jury verdict at trial which there was ample evidence to support, that although the testator laboured under a certain insane delusion, these delusions had no influence on him in the disposal of his property and irrespective of these delusions the state of his mental faculties was such as to render him capable of making a will (*ibid.* at 555). The actual issue requiring the decision of the court was whether partial unsoundness of mind, not affecting the testator's general faculties, and not operating on his mind in regard to the particular testamentary dispositions made by him, was sufficient to deprive him of the power of disposing of his property (*ibid.* at 556).

It is hardly surprising to a modern mind that Cockburn C.J. **5–006** held that partial unsoundness of mind (the "disorder of the mind and insane delusions" referred to in the second part of his dictum) not affecting the testator's general faculties did not deprive the testator of testamentary capacity. In reaching that decision, however, he wholeheartedly approved certain earlier authorities which add useful substance and very illuminating colour to his own pithy dictum. First was *Den v Vancleve* (2 Southamp 660), where it was said that:

> "by the terms 'a sound and disposing mind and memory' it is not meant that a testator must possess these qualities of the mind in the highest degree; otherwise, very few could make testaments at all; neither must he possess them in as great a degree as he may have formerly done; for even this would disable most men in the decline of life; the mind may have been in some degree debilitated, the memory may have become in some degree enfeebled; and yet there may be enough left clearly to discern and discreetly to judge, of all those things, and all those circumstances, which enter into the nature of a rational, fair, and just testament. But if they have so far failed as that these cannot be discerned and judged of, then he cannot be said to be of sound and disposing mind and memory."

Thereafter Cockburn C.J. cited *Stevens v Vancleve* (4 Wash- **5–007** ington 267), where it was said that:

"the testator must, in the language of the law, be possessed of sound and disposing mind and memory. He must have memory; a man in whom the faculty is totally extinguished cannot be said to possess understanding to any degree whatever, or for any purpose. But his memory may be very imperfect; it may be greatly impaired by age or disease; he may not be able at all times to recollect the names, the persons, or the families of those with whom he had been intimately acquainted; may at times ask idle questions, and repeat those which had before been asked and answered, and yet his understanding may be sufficiently sound for many of the ordinary transactions of life. He may not have sufficient strength of memory and vigour of intellect to make and to digest all the parts of a contract, and yet he may still be competent to direct the distribution of his property by will. This is a subject which he may possibly have often thought of, and there is probably no person who has not arranged such a disposition in his mind before he committed it to writing. The question is not so much what was the degree of memory possessed by the testator, as this: Had he a disposing memory? Was he capable of recollecting the property he was about to bequeath; the manner of distributing it; and the objects of his bounty? To sum up the whole in the most simple and intelligible form, were his mind and memory sufficiently sound to enable him to know and to understand the business in which he was engaged at the time he executed his will?"

5–008 Finally, Cockburn C.J. cited the trenchant judgment of Erskine J. in *Harwood v Baker* (1840) (3) Moo. P.C. 282), where he said that:

"in order to constitute a sound disposing mind, a testator must not only be able to understand that he is by his will giving the whole of his property to one object of his regard, but he must also have capacity to comprehend the extent of his property, and the nature of the claims of others, whom by his will he is excluding from all participation in that property; and that the protection of the law is in no cases more needed than it is in those where the mind has been too much enfeebled to comprehend more objects than one; and more especially, when that one object may be so forced upon the attention of the invalid as to shut out all others that might require consideration. And, therefore, the question was not whether Mr Baker knew, when he executed this will, that he was giving all his property to his wife, and excluding all his other relations from any share in it, but whether he was at that time capable of recollecting who those relations were, of understanding their respective claims upon his regard and bounty, and of deliberately forming an intelligent purpose of excluding them from any share of his property. If he had not the capacity required, the propriety of the disposition made by the will is a matter of no importance. If he had it, the injustice of the exclusion would not affect the validity of the disposition, though the justice or injustice of the disposition might cast down some light upon the question as to his capacity."

From all that, Cockburn C.J. concluded that it was to be 5–009 inferred that the standard of capacity in cases of impaired mental power was the capacity on the part of the testator to comprehend the extent of the property to be disposed of, and the nature of the claims of those he was excluding. He concluded with the rhetorical question: Why should not this standard also be applicable to mental unsoundness produced by mental disease? He could hardly more eloquently have acknowledged his debt to these earlier authorities.

Delusions

The delusions from which the testator in *Banks v Goodfellow* 5–010 suffered, which it was conceded did not affect his testamentary capacity, was that a man called Featherstone Alexander who had died many years before nonetheless pursued and molested him; he also believed that he was pursued and molested by devils or evil spirits whom he claimed to be able to see. In *Smee v Smee* ((1879) 5 P.D. 84), by contrast, the testator suffered from the insane delusion that he was the son of George IV, who, when Prince Regent, had (as we all know) built Brighton Pavilion. Under two successive wills the testator left his estate to his widow for life and then to the Corporation of Brighton, to found a free public library for the people of Brighton. The jury held that this insane delusion affected the testator's mind when he was considering how he should dispose of his property; and the court accordingly pronounced against both wills.

However, cases arise which raise the issue whether the 5–011 testator was or was not suffering from a delusion, which in turn requires some definition of delusion. Hannen J.'s definition in *Boughton v Knight* ((1873) L.R. 3 P. & D. 64) remains serviceable, and is formulated as a jury question: "Can I understand how any man in possession of his senses could have believed such and such a thing?" This must of course be judged in the context of the testator's own religious and cultural background, and in the general context of the time at which the question is asked.

5–012 A further issue, which is essentially an evidential issue, is whether or not the delusion affected the testamentary disposition in question. In *Smee v Smee* (above) the court adopted a graphic analogy with the physical world: there might be a little crack in some geological stratum of no importance in itself, and nothing more than a chink through which water filters into the earth; but it might be shown that this flaw had a direct influence upon the volume, or colour, or chemical qualities of a stream that issued from the earth many miles away. So with the mind. Upon the surface all may be perfectly clear, and a man may be able to transact ordinary business or follow his professional calling, and yet there may be some idea through which in the recesses of his mind an influence is produced on his conduct in other matters.

5–013 The question then is whether the crack in the testator's mind affected his testamentary disposition. Whatever the modern medical diagnosis, it is the causal connection between the delusion and the disposition with which the court itself is concerned.

Burden of proof

5–014 The basic principle is that for a will to be valid the testator's mind must go with his testamentary act, and one element of this basic principle is that the court will not admit to probate any testamentary document unless satisfied, on the balance of probabilities, that the testator's mind did indeed go with his testamentary act. However, although the standard of proof is that of the balance of probabilities, that itself carries with it a degree of flexibility (*Re Parsons* [2002] W.T.L.R. 237). It is not surprising that in the absence of the main witness (the testator), the court relies on various rebuttable presumptions in the process of reaching its decision. For instance, where probate in common form is sought, and there is no dispute, the court will presume, subject to its own power to make its own inquiries (Non-Contentious Probate Rules 1987, rr.12–16), that the testator possessed testamentary capacity. Where the validity of the will is in dispute, the burden of proof of the testator's testamentary capacity rests on those who seek to propound it; put another way, there is an initial rebuttable presumption that the testator did not have testamentary capacity. That presumption will be more difficult to rebut where it is conceded that the testator had previously suffered from mental disease, or where the will itself shows signs of irrationality. Where delusions exist, the burden of proof that they did not affect the testamentary dispositions is on those who seek to propound the will; in other words, there is a rebuttable presumption that they did. Sometimes it is conceded that the testator was suffering from a mental illness which generally rendered him not of testamentary capacity, but that he executed his will during a lucid interval. There the burden of proof that such a lucid interval occurred is on those who seek to propound the will: it is up to them to rebut the presumption that the testator remained testamentarily incapable throughout (*Hall v Warren* (1804) 9 Ves. 605).

In reaching its conclusion on the evidence, the court will be concerned both with the general factual context of the making of the challenged will as well as with the immediate factual details of the execution. A good modern example is *Richards v Allan* [2001] W.T.L.R. 1031. There the testatrix ("Olive") died on July 31, 1995. On May 13, 1994, aged 84, she signed a will which appointed the defendant, Miss Allan, to be her sole executor and beneficiary. Olive had met Miss Allan in 1974 and worked for her in her antique shop for six afternoons a week, from 1977 until 1988. A friendship developed between them. After Olive retired, Miss Allan visited her from time to time and assisted her with some daily tasks which she needed help with as her health began to fail. Among other things, Olive suffered from non-insulin dependent diabetes. From time to time Olive made the odd reference to the house passing to Miss Allan. By the spring of 1994 Olive was seriously ill. She was admitted to hospital on April 8 with various problems, including uncontrolled diabetes and dehydration, having been increasingly confused for a few days before admission, although she knew her name, age, whereabouts, the year and the identity of the monarch. She was discharged on April 26, 1994. Her mental state had improved but she required help. 5–015

A few weeks before the will was executed, Miss Allan asked Olive if she wanted to make a will. Olive said she would and agreed that Miss Allan ought to speak to Mr Tickner, Miss Allan's brother-in-law, who was a solicitor. In addition, they discussed the possibility that Olive might require residential care, and Olive wanted Miss Allan to be able to arrange for payment of fees and to deal with her finances if that were to happen. Miss Allan asked Mr Tickner to draw up a will for Olive, leaving everything to her (Miss Allan). She also asked him to draw up an enduring power of attorney. He drew up the short will which contained errors, including an error in the address of Miss Allan, and an enduring power of attorney. All this took place between the date Olive came out of hospital (April 26) and May 13. Within two weeks there were further difficulties. She had numerous falls and a domiciliary visit was requested from Dr Ali, a G.P. specialising in geriatric medicine, stating that Olive was experiencing "a little confusion". 5–016

5–017 On May 13, the day the disputed will was signed, Dr Ali visited Olive some time in the morning, probably about 10am. He found her confused, diagnosing her as possibly having suffered a recent stroke. He decided that she should go to hospital for further tests. She was diabetic, she had a recent history of poor control and she was taking a number of drugs, some of which were capable of affecting her mental state relating to capacity. The home help found Olive very confused — she could hardly talk and did not recognise her. Miss Allan made two visits to Olive on May 13. The first was one of her regular visits, probably at the end of the morning, although she had it in mind to get the will executed later that day. Olive complained to her about Dr Ali's examination. Miss Allan said that on the previous occasion, when she had left the will with Olive, she had explained that two witnesses were required; that she had asked Dennis Ballard (who was already known to Olive) and Brenda Chown (who was not) to fulfil that role; and that she planned to have the execution done on the Friday afternoon because that was a time at which she knew that Olive's sister Rose would be out shopping because she feared disputes. Mr Ballard and Ms Chown went to Olive's house. She was in bed but apparently well. She appeared to read the will, but no one checked that she understood what was on the paper before her and its effect and significance. Olive signed the will and the power of attorney. There was between 5 and 15 minutes of conversation, and the witnesses left. Olive did not appear confused. Later, Mrs Johnson, a neighbour, went to see Olive at about 4pm for a cup of tea. She found Olive lying down, but Olive could not recognise her. She could hardly talk. Olive was admitted to hospital the next day. The admission record described her as "alert and orientated" but two days later it was noted that she remained "confused at times". The will was contested by those entitled on an intestacy — her surviving sister and the estate of another sister who survived Olive but had since died. The court approached the evidence of Olive's testamentary capacity on the day of execution by dividing the events of the day into three phases. First there was the phase witnessed by Dr Ali and the home help, which demonstrated a serious degree of disability. Then there was the phase seen by the witnesses to the will, which, on its face, seemed to indicate no real mental impairment at all. Finally, there was the phase witnessed by Mrs Johnson, which again showed a significant degree of mental impairment. The crucial time was the middle phase. Did the testatrix have capacity at that point? If it stood by itself with nothing immediately before or afterwards which cast doubt on capacity, then capacity at that point would be proved. However, that was not the case. Since capacity was not established at points of time immediately on either side of the occasion, was it possible that the testatrix could have recovered capacity during this period and then lost it again? Medical expert evidence indicated that the testatrix was subject to intermittent attacks of confusion, indicating toxic confusional states which could vary over a short period of time, so that it would be possible for a person to have seriously diminished capacity at 10am, proper capacity at 1pm, and then to lapse into lack of capacity again by 4pm. In that scenario, the events at 1pm would amount to a lucid interval, but the experts differed as to the likelihood of that having happened here. The court held that, on balance, the burden of establishing capacity was not discharged.

Testamentary incapacity may be merely temporary, as where 5–018 the testator is drunk or on drugs at the time he executes his will. In *Chana v Chana* [2001] W.T.L.R. 205 the will was challenged on the ground that the testator was drunk at the time he signed it, but the court held on the evidence that to invalidate the will, drunkenness must have such an effect on the testator that he does not know the nature and quality of the act which he is carrying out, and furthermore that the measure of testamentary capacity need not be as complete at the time of execution as it had been at the time of giving instructions (see the rule in *Parker v Felgate* (1883) 8 P.D. 171, para. 5–020).

More commonly, however, the testamentary incapacity is the 5–019 end state of a long period of mental decline, where the court will consider the whole history. For a recent case where a challenge based on testamentary incapacity failed on the facts, see *Re Parsons* [2002] W.T.L.R. 237. Such a challenge succeeded, however, in *Brown v Deacy* [2002] W.T.L.R. 782 and *Tchilingirian v Ouzouhian* [2003] W.T.L.R. 709.

The rule in *Parker v Felgate*

This important rule of evidence (in this authority reported at 5–020 (1883) 8 P.D. 171) is that if the testator, when of undoubted testamentary capacity, has given instructions for a will and it is prepared in accordance with those instructions, only a very slight degree of mental capacity is required at the time of actual execution. In this case the testatrix had given her Solicitor full instructions for her will by August 10; he then went on his summer holiday; on August 26 she fell ill and was thereafter basically comatose, although she remained capable of being roused. On August 29 the engrossed will was proffered for execution, although the testatrix was so physically weak that it had in any event to be signed by a friend of hers on her behalf (as allowed by s.9 of the Wills Act 1837). She opened her eyes. A doctor rustled the will in front of her face, thus rousing her.

He then said, "This is your will. Do you wish this lady to sign it?" She replied, "Yes". The doctor deposed that as far as he could judge, she understood what she was doing. This case established that:

(1) it is not necessary that a testator when the will is executed remembers and understands the instructions he had previously given while of testamentary capacity;

(2) it is not necessary that a testator when the will is executed could have understood each clause if it had been put to him; and

(3) all that is necessary when the will is executed is that the testator is capable of understanding, and does understand, that he is engaged in executing the will for which he had previously given instructions.

It is clear, however, that the onus of proving the matters in (3) above is squarely on the person seeking to uphold the will (*Re Flynn* [1982] 1 W.L.R. 310 at 320). This may be difficult to achieve where the testator is virtually in a coma. The rule was applied in *Clancy v Clancy* (*The Times,* September 9, 2003).

Conclusion

5–021 Most contested probate cases now involve a combination of lay evidence and professional medical evidence. The professional medical evidence is likely to involve not just that of the testator's own G.P. or of nurses in hospitals where he may have been confined. It will normally extend to the professional opinions of psychogeriatricians who have never met the patient and who reach their usually conflicting opinions on the basis of their analysis of G.P. medical records, hospital medical records and any mental tests that the testator may have undergone. This in our view perhaps leaves behind, for modern purposes, the "golden but tactless" routine suggested by Templeman J. in *Kenward v Adams* (*The Times,* November 29, 1975) of having a testator's G.P. present when he executes his will. Furthermore the various categories of mental illness defined in the Mental Health Act 1983 do not sit comfortably with the *Banks v Goodfellow* test for testamentary capacity. Finally, although there are a whole range of mental tests routinely used on patients, much depends on the analysis of the results of such tests. In almost every case the question will be one of degree. As Lord Cranworth said in *Boyce v Rossborough* ((1857) 6 H.L. C. 2 at 45), there is no possibility of mistaking midnight for noon; but at what precise moment twilight becomes darkness is hard to determine.

Assessing Testamentary Capacity: when should a doctor be asked to express a view on whether the patient has testamentary capacity?

The short answer is when the solicitor, or other person prepar- 5–022
ing the Will has doubt about the patient's capacity. As a matter of professional duty, solicitors (if not others) must observe the "golden if tactless" rule, that where the client is old or has been seriously ill, that client should be examined by a medical practitioner who should record his examination and his findings. The issue of capacity will usually arise when the client asks the solicitor to draw the Will. This is often referred to as the time when *the instructions* for the Will are given. In some cases the time when instructions are given and the time when the will is executed may be separated by only a short distance. This is often the case when the solicitor attends the client as a patient in hospital as a matter of urgency. In other cases there may be a distance of more time; even weeks. Often the solicitor takes instructions, and in order to be sure arranges for the doctor to assess capacity when the will is executed. Because of a rule in the law that the test of capacity is to be made either at the time of execution, or at the earlier time when instructions were given if the will is executed in conformity with those instructions, the doctor may, therefore, be concerned to assess capacity at the earlier stage when instructions are given, if not at the later stage of execution. In practice, and to avoid any doubt, he may be asked to confirm his assessment at the later stage too. But the will may be valid even if he cannot confirm capacity at that later stage, because capacity was present when the instructions were given.

What is clear as a matter of legal ethics is that the application of the "golden if tactless" rule is one exception to the rule that a solicitor is under a duty to keep his client's affairs confidential.

By the same token, the doctor's duty of confidentiality is threatened if he is asked to express a view on the capacity of his patient. Here the medical ethics are potentially less clear.

Because the task of assessing capacity and conveying the result of the test to third parties is not therapeutic (where patient consent to disclosure in the context of care and treatment to other health professionals may be implicit), the consent of the patient to disclosure cannot be assumed. This means that the doctor must explain his role and the purpose of the assessment at the outset. If the patient refuses assessment, or disclosure, the doctor has to be guided, at least initially, by what he considers to be the patient's best interests. It is in the patient's best interest to make a valid will which records the wishes which he has conveyed to his solicitor, or which he is about to convey. The doctor will invariably be party to discussions with not only the patient but also relatives, carers, and the solicitor who is in doubt. If it is plain that the patient lacks capacity to give consent, that rather answers the question whether the patient has testamentary capacity. If there is a firm refusal to consent to an assessment, that is the end of the matter, and the doctor should record that refusal and any reasons given. It is not thought that in a case where assessment of testamentary capacity was refused by a patient capable of such refusal, such an assessment should still be made, and if disclosure only is refused, it is thought unlikely that a doctor would be justified in making such disclosure without consent.

How should the doctor deal with the request?

5–023 He should first consider whether he is the appropriate person to carry out the task. If he is not the patient's GP, is there any reason why the GP cannot be asked. Often there is urgency, or some other reason why the referral has to be to the first choice — as opposed to a more "obvious" choice. Ultimately the doctor asked should be certain that he can make the assessment competently. That requires an ability to administer not only a general test of capacity (see the "baseline" referred to above) but also the ability to administer an assessment of testamentary capacity. Do not be afraid to say no — or refer the solicitor to someone else.

Secondly the doctor must consider and deal with the question of patient consent outlined above.

If the patient says yes, the doctor must then carry out a medical assessment of the patient, by reference to records and notes and to his own diagnosis. He may take the views of others into account (*e.g.* a clinical psychologist's reports) but must take care when gaining information from those with an interest in the outcome: *e.g.* well meaning, but very interested relatives. The rule is to diagnose the patient first.

The doctor must then take the time to be briefed by the solicitor about the patient, his estate, his family, the claims of others. Until this is done he cannot begin to assess the patient's testamentary capacity.

In any given case the doctor will have to determine whether the patient's medical, or mental condition is permanent or transient. In some cases the doctor may be able to express a view that capacity may be restored on a degree of probability, and advise awaiting that outcome. (This occurs in some instances where the (young) victims of car, or rail accidents have lost capacity through mental trauma, or actual injury, but stand a fair prospect of future recovery). In some cases there is the "lucid interval", and if instructions are given for a Will, or it is signed during such an interval, the Will should be valid.

Never be afraid to ask the solicitor for guidance on what is the test of testamentary capacity, and for further details of the patient and his estate and family.

Remember that the patient should be able to comprehend and appreciate the nature of the task, etc. unaided. Of course there will have to be an explanation of the nature and effect of the will — but in the end it is the capacity of the patient which is in issue, not the persuasive powers of the solicitor, or the relatives, or even the doctor.

Never feel pressured into giving an opinion which will please one side or the other.

If you (the doctor) are not only asked to assess capacity to make the Will, but also to act as a witness consider (a) whether your employer allows or prohibits this (b) whether your insurer allows or prohibits this and (c) whether you have done your job properly in assessing the patient's capacity to make that will.

Note that as a matter of formal validity an English or Welsh Will must have two witnesses to the testator's signature, and in simple terms, all three of you must all be there together at the "signing".

Confirm your assessment in writing. Always do so in specific terms, stating in particular:

(1) The circumstances of the request for an assessment and recording the patient's consent to it. (The latter will, no doubt, be recorded elsewhere).

(2) The diagnosis — and where you obtained this — apart from your own observations.

(3) The application of the test of what is testamentary capacity dealing with each limb of the test and the answers which allowed you to conclude that there was, or was not, capacity. Note, as is mentioned below, that this is a report which may be used in Court.

(4) Any other facts of specific relevance.

Do not delay doing it — however rushed you may be.

Finally, and this is a MUST, buy the latest edition of "Assessment of Mental Capacity — Guidance for Doctors and Lawyers", published jointly by the Law Society and the BMA, currently 1995 edition, ISBN 0 7279 0913 4.

What are the consequences of a doctor's response to the request?

5–024 By accepting the request to make an assessment of testamentary capacity, the doctor is placing himself in the position of an expert witness. This means that the doctor can not only be responsible for matters of fact, but also for matters of opinion.

It is beyond the scope of this section to deal with the issues which doctors face when they are in the position of expert witnesses. However, in the context of will making and the assessment of testamentary capacity, the doctor who has made such an assessment may well be asked to support that assessment at a later date, after the death of the patient, if there is a challenge to the validity of the Will.

Because the Court is concerned to examine the validity or otherwise of a document, *viz*, the Will under attack, the Court will be astute to discern weaknesses in the case of the parties supporting, or attacking, the Will. If the doctor's Report is crucial to the case of either party, it is obvious that the doctor will also be a crucial witness. He will be at the mercy of tough cross-examination. It is not a happy sight to see a doctor unprepared for this.

This is why the doctor who undertakes the task of assessing testamentary capacity MUST understand what tests to administer, and MUST produce the clear and concise Report along the lines recommended above. It is fatal for a doctor to assess a patient as capable without the "task specific" questions having been administered, and further to produce a report which shows a failure to appreciate the task which he (apparently) undertook.

In cases where the doctor has also acted as one of the witnesses to the Will, the presence of his signature as an attesting witness carries the strong implication that the testator had capacity, and if he did not, the doctor's professional reputation may well be at stake.

In cases where the doctor has assessed the patient and has concluded that there is a lack of capacity, that evidence may be crucial for a number of reasons, and which may not be directed towards a will made "in spite" of that assessment. The evidence may clearly point forwards so that a later will may be invalid unless it could be shown that the lack of capacity was transient. The evidence may even point backwards so as to suggest that the patient's mental state was such that capacity could be said to be in doubt before the date of the critical assessment. In some cases this has been done where there has been a diagnosis of Alzheimer's disease, where the onset can be traced back prior to the assessment and where other factual and medical evidence suggests a lack of testamentary capacity even at the date of an earlier Will.

Finally, doctors should be aware in the medico-legal context of the jurisdiction which is exercised by the Court of Protection to make "Statutory Wills" on behalf of persons who by reason of mental disorder are incapable of managing their property or affairs, and are incapable of making a will for themselves. In cases where the doctor is unable to certify that testamentary capacity is present, the use of this jurisdiction is to be recommended.

Chapter 6

Lack of Knowledge and Approval

Introduction

The basic principle, as we have already seen in Chapter 5, is that **6–001** for a will to be valid, the testator's mind must go with his testamentary act. A further element of this basic principle is that the court must be satisfied that the testator knows and approves the contents of the testamentary document he executes.

Where this is not in issue, the court presumes that, provided **6–002** the testator possessed testamentary capacity and the will was duly executed, he also knew and approved its contents. Where, however, the testator's knowledge and approval are put in issue by those seeking to challenge the will, the court must be satisfied on the evidence put before it that the testator did indeed know and approve its contents. It is appropriate to emphasise at the outset that, despite a degree of confusion generated by earlier cases, there exists no separate requirement of proving *"the righteousness of the transaction" (Fuller v Strum* [2002] 1 W.L.R. 1097, at 1107C *per* Peter Gibson L.J., 1119B *per* Chadwick L.J. and 1123 *per* Longmore L.J.).

In the nature of things there may be an infinite variety of **6–003** factual circumstances which may throw into doubt whether or not the testator knew and approved his will. So-called suspicious circumstances (as to which, see below, para. 6–007) are but one. In all cases alike the court having heard the witnesses must decide whether it is satisfied from the evidence that the testator knew and approved his will. It may quite properly satisfy itself merely by inference from all the evidence. For instance in *Hart v Dabbs* ([2001] W.T.L.R. 527) the propounder of the will made by a wealthy 74-year-old man was a person who was alleged to have killed the deceased unlawfully. The propounder was an executor under the will, was named as a specific legatee and the sole residuary legatee, had played an active part in the preparation of the will, and had organised the process of the signing of the will by the deceased and the witnesses. There was no professional assistance or involvement of any kind in the will-making process, no evidence that the deceased prepared the will himself or gave instructions for its preparation, and no evidence that the deceased read the will or had it read to him before or after it had been made or that he retained a copy or, apart from what can be inferred from evidence that he told one legatee of what he intended to do by his will (and that was partly inaccurate), that he knew about its terms. The propounder did not give evidence. Nevertheless, Lloyd J. was satisfied that the will should be admitted to probate. This was because knowledge and approval could be inferred in all the circumstances. Lloyd J. heard evidence from the attesting witnesses that the will and certain other documents executed at the same time were duly executed, that there was reference during the signing ceremony to the fact that the purpose of the attendance of the witnesses was to witness the deceased's signature of his will, and that the deceased covered up some of the documents. Lloyd J. commented that that evidence showed that the deceased was not being deceived as to the nature of the document he was signing and that he had at least had the opportunity of seeing the documents before they were covered up. He also noted that the provisions of the will were neither complex nor difficult to grasp. He said: *"So long as he read the document he would have had no difficulty in taking in its provisions, even if someone else had prepared it"*. He said that apart from the gift of residue to the propounder, there was not much in the will to provoke suspicion in itself as being different from what one might expect the deceased to do. He found that the evidence showed the deceased to have been alert and not likely to allow himself to be persuaded to do what he did not want to do. On that evidence the will was admitted to probate.

6–004 Many other factual circumstances will by themselves give rise to sufficient doubt as to the testator's knowledge and approval of his will as to require the court to be satisfied about it. Even the reading over of the will to the testator may not be conclusive if the testator is deaf or hard of hearing, or if it is read over at too great a speed for him to follow. Indeed, there is no rule of evidence that a testator must have known and approved the contents of the document even if he read it over (*Re Morris* [1971] P. 62), since every case turns on its own particular facts. Clearly, if a testator is blind the will must be read over slowly and clearly for the court to be satisfied that he knew and approved its contents. Where a testator is mute or paralysed, appropriate means of communicating the contents of the will must be proved, as also must the testator's understanding and response to those means of communication.

However, there is no rule that the instructions for the will **6–005**
have to have come from the testator himself. Where they have
done, the court will find it easier to be satisfied that he knew
and approved of the subsequent document, provided it embodied those instructions and had no material additions or subtractions. Indeed, where a testator, in a state approaching
insensibility, executes a will drawn up in accordance with
previous instructions, though he may not remember them and
could not understand the will even if read to him clause by
clause, yet, if he is capable of understanding and does understand that he is engaged in executing the will for which he has
given instructions, he has been held to know and approve of its
contents (*Parker v Felgate* (1883) 8 P.D. 171). (see further at
5–020 above). Where the instructions have not come from the
testator the court will be less easily satisfied that he knew and
approved the contents of the document he executes.

It is in principle possible that the testator may have known **6–006**
and approved part of the contents of the document but not the
remainder (*Re Anston* (1929) 73 S.J. 545). But this is unlikely.
As Peter Gibson L.J. observed in *Fuller v Strum* [2002] 1 W.L.R.
1097, where a will has been duly executed by a deceased of
testamentary capacity who knew that he was making a will and is
shown to have known and approved of a specific part of the will,
the court must consider how real is the possibility that the
deceased did not know and approve of the remainder of the will;
and that requires a careful examination of all the circumstances,
including the directions and dispositions of the will.

The rule in *Barry v Butlin*

We now turn to the line of cases which have been concerned **6–007**
with so-called suspicious circumstances in the preparation of the
testator's will. Before considering them, two preliminary points
of clarification need emphatically to be made:

(1) The suspicion with which the court is concerned is not
the so-called suspicious behaviour of individuals involved
in the preparation of the will, suspicious as that
behaviour may indeed be. The suspicion with which
alone the court is concerned is its own suspicion that the
testator may not have known and approved the will he
executed (*Fuller v Strum* [2002] 1 W.L.R. 1097, at 1123
per Longmore L.J.).

(2) As we have emphasised at the outset, there exists no
separate rule or requirement that those propounding the
will should prove *"the righteousness of the transaction"*.

That concept, redolent of nineteenth-century morality, is nothing more than a grandiloquent way of saying that the court must be satisfied that the testator indeed knew and approved of the will. It is not a separate concept (*ibid.* at 1123 *per* Longmore L.J.).

6–008 The starting point is *Barry v Butlin* ((1838) 2 Moo. P.C. 480), where the testator left his estranged son out of his will and gave his entire estate to an acquaintance (Mr Butlin) after large pecuniary legacies to his brother and to his lawyer who drew up the will. The son challenged the validity of the will on the ground that it had been procured by the fraud and conspiracy of the three individuals who benefited. That challenge failed on the evidence, but the court then proceeded to state two rules of law which both sides had in any event conceded to be applicable to the case: the first being that the onus of proof lay in every case on the party propounding the will, who had to satisfy the conscience of the court that the instrument propounded represented the last will of a free and capable testator; the second being that if someone writes or prepares a will under which he takes a benefit, that circumstance ought generally to excite the suspicion of the court and calls upon it to be "vigilant and jealous" (a phrase used again over a century later in *Wintle v Nye* [1959] 1 W.L.R. 284) in examining the evidence in support of the instrument, in favour of which it should not pronounce unless the suspicion is removed and the court is satisfied that the instrument propounded does indeed express the true will of the testator. That suspicion is that the instrument did not express his true will — in other words, that he did not know and approve its contents.

Burden of Proof

6–010 The rule in *Barry v Butlin* is no more than a rule of evidence. As the onus of proof is always on those seeking to propound the will, it is not correct to say that the rule is a rule that shifts the onus of proof. It is a rule which requires in certain circumstances further affirmative evidence than is normally required before the court can be satisfied that the instrument did indeed express the true will of the testator. As Parke B. said in *Barry v Butlin* (at 484), the strict meaning of the term *onus probandi* is that if no evidence is given by the party on whom the burden is cast, the issue must be found against him. In all cases the onus is imposed on the party propounding a will:

> "It is in general discharged by proof of capacity, and the fact of execution, from which the knowledge of, and assent to the

contents of the instrument are assumed, and it cannot be that the simple fact of the party who prepared the will being himself a legatee, is in every case, and under all circumstances, to create a contrary presumption, and to call upon the court to pronounce against the will, unless additional evidence is produced to prove the knowledge of its contents by the deceased."

Parke B. then tested the rule by taking a factual example. A man of acknowledged competence and habits of business, worth £100,000, leaves the bulk of his property to his family, and a legacy of £50 to his confidential attorney, who prepared the will: would this fact throw the burden of proof of actual cognisance by the testator, of the contents of the will, on the party propounding it, so that if such proof were not supplied, the will would be pronounced against? The answer is obvious: it would not:

"All that can truly be said is, that if a person, whether attorney or not, prepares a will with a legacy to himself, it is, at most, a suspicious circumstance, of more or less weight, according to the facts of each particular case; in some of no weight at all, as in the case suggested, varying according to circumstances; for instance the quantum of the legacy, and the proportion it bears to the property disposed of, and numerous other contingencies: but in no case amounting to more than a circumstance of suspicion, demanding the vigilant care and circumspection of the court in investigating the case, and calling upon it not to grant probate without full and entire satisfaction that the instrument did express the real intentions of the deceased."

Nor can it be necessary, that in all such cases, even if the testator's capacity is doubtful, the precise species of evidence of the deceased's knowledge of the will is to be in the shape of instructions for or a reading over of the instrument. They form, no doubt, the most satisfactory, but they are not the only satisfactory description of proof by which cognisance of the contents of the will may be brought home to the deceased. The court would naturally look for such evidence; in some cases it might be impossible to establish a will without it, but it has no right in every case to require it.

In *Wintle v Nye* [1959] 1 W.L.R. 284, where the rule in *Barry v Butlin* was applied, an elderly woman, unversed in business, signed a will and subsequently a codicil prepared by her solicitor, who was not an intimate friend. The solicitor was named as sole executor and, after provision had been made for **6–011** various legacies and gifts, he was to take the residue, which amounted to the bulk of her large estate. The will was complex; she was not independently advised and no copies of the documents were given to her. The validity of the will and codicil was challenged on the ground that she did not know or approve of their contents, but no allegation of fraud was made in the pleadings. There was no evidence except that of the solicitor as to the instructions given by the testatrix.

6–012 Viscount Simonds there reiterated that it is not the law that in no circumstances can a solicitor or other person who has prepared a will for a testator take a benefit under it.

"But that fact creates a suspicion that must be removed by the person propounding the will. In all cases the court must be vigilant and jealous. The degree of suspicion will vary with the circumstances of the case. It may be slight and easily dispelled. It may, on the other hand, be so grave that it can hardly be removed." (*ibid.* at 291).

In *Re Estate of Fuld (No. 3)* [1968] P. 675 at 697, Scarman J. accepted the purely evidential nature of the rule in *Barry v Butlin*. In his opinion the whole point of the rule was evidential; it was concerned with the approach required of the court to the evidence submitted for its consideration. In the ordinary case, proof of testamentary capacity and due execution sufficed to establish knowledge and approval; but in certain circumstances the court must require further affirmative evidence.

6–013 The standard of proof nonetheless remains the civil standard of proof, that is to say, the court must be satisfied, on the balance of probability, that the contents of the will do truly represent the testator's intentions (*Fuller v Strum* [2002] 1 W.L.R. 1097 at 1120 *per* Chadwick J.). There is built in to this balance of probability standard a generous degree of flexibility in respect of the seriousness of the allegations in question, so that even in civil proceedings a court should be more sure before finding serious allegations proved than when deciding less serious or trivial matters (*Re H (minors)* [1996] A.C. 563 at 586). Thus the circumstances of a particular case may raise in the mind of the court a suspicion that the testator did not know and approve the contents of the will that he has executed which is indeed so grave that, as Viscount Simonds said in *Wintle v Nye*, it can hardly be removed.

6–014 Although lack of knowledge and approval is a ground for challenging a will separate from the ground of lack of testamentary capacity, it is now clear that evidence relevant to establishing lack of testamentary capacity may be equally relevant to establishing lack of knowledge and approval. This was the case in *Richards v Allan* [2001] W.T.L.R. 1031, the facts of which are set out at para. 5–015 above. On those facts the court held that the state of the testatrix's mental capacity was a relevant and admissible fact contributing to her lack of knowledge and approval of the document she signed.

Buckenham v Dickinson [2000] W.T.L.R. 1083 is a recent case **6–015** where, although a claim of testamentary incapacity failed, a claim of lack of knowledge and approval succeeded. In that case the testator was born on May 3, 1896 and died on October 1, 1989. He was married twice, first of all to Betty, with whom he had two children — John (the claimant) and George. The family home was at 6 Albany Road, Maltby. When the testator retired in 1960, he and Betty moved to 2 Ivanhoe Way ("the bungalow"), where he lived until his death, and 6 Albany Road was let out to tenants. Betty died in 1966.

In January 1973, the testator married Edith, who had a **6–016** daughter of her own from a previous marriage. The claimant and his second wife, Ann, had one child. George had two children by his first wife. The testator made a will in 1973, when he married Edith, under which she was to have a roof over her head and a small income, and subject to that, the sons got the residue less some small legacies.

In 1975 he made a further will. It was drawn up by George, **6–017** who was a chartered accountant. The will appointed the two sons as executors, and gave directions for Edith to use and occupy the bungalow, together with its contents. He directed that payments would be made for her for the rest of her life from the net rents of 6 Albany Road, together with such cash as might be in his possession at the date of his death, and any money in building society accounts and the like. Various items such as a gold signet ring and watches were to be divided between the grandsons, and the residue was to pass to the two sons.

By January 1986, both Edith and the testator were very frail, **6–018** and the testator was assessed by a doctor for the purposes of obtaining an attendance allowance. The doctor found him to be very deaf and partially blind, and said that he would become muddled due to a hardening of the arteries.

On October 21, 1988, George died. The testator had to be **6–019** told again and again what had happened, and how. On October 26, the testator executed a codicil prepared by the claimant, giving the whole of the residue to the claimant, although the claimant did not believe this would have any effect, as he did not think the testator had capacity and did it merely to pacify him. A witness to the codicil said that she tried to get some response from the testator, but that it was impossible.

Following George's death, Albany Road had to be dealt with. **6–020** It was empty and in a poor state. The claimant thought he had got the old people's agreement for him to deal with the sale, deposit the proceeds in an account in his name and, as interest rates were then high, pay them an income, but they believed he intended to pocket the lot, and Edith instructed agents and solicitors to sell the property. The claimant and his wife got to know of the sale, and this caused a major breakdown of family relationships. As a result of the sale, Mr Dickinson of Hinchcliffe and Dickinson, an experienced solicitor and the first defendant, came to see the testator and Edith. When he went for a signature on the contract of sale, on May 15, 1989, he got instructions for the will through Edith. He simply asked the testator to confirm them. The third to seventh defendants, that is his grandchildren and her grandchildren, were to get £2,000 each. Those instructions were changed on June 2, and the legacies increased to £5,000 each.

6–021 On June 6, Mr Dickinson and his two secretaries attended on the execution of the will, which one of the secretaries read out loud. The testator was periodically asked if he agreed, but made no comment other than somewhat inarticulate affirmatives. On October 1, the testator died suddenly. As soon as the claimant found out what was in the will, there was a challenge. On November 8, Mr Dickinson set out very briefly, in a letter, his account of the will-making, but he took no steps to record the detail. Probate was granted on December 4, 1989. The writ was issued three years later on February 4, 1992. The will was attacked for lack of capacity, and also for want of knowledge and approval.

6–022 On those facts the court revoked the probate, and held that further affirmative evidence of knowledge and approval is required where the testator is deaf and dumb or blind, and to establish the will of a testator wholly blind or so nearly as to be incapable of discerning writing, such as this testator, it must be shown to the satisfaction of the court that the will was read over in the presence of witnesses or that he was otherwise acquainted with its contents (*ibid.* at 1090E–1091B).

6–023 Although the testator's infirmities had increasingly cut him off and made it difficult to communicate with him, if it had been possible to communicate with him properly there was no evidence that he would have lacked the elements of a sound disposing mind. However, knowledge and approval was a different and much more complex matter. There was nothing whatever to indicate any positive input from the testator to Mr Dickinson. All he did was to reply in the apparent affirmative to questions, and sign when his hand was put in the right place. The change in testamentary disposition was complex, and the testator needed to know what he was being asked to do, if it did not come from him, and to agree with it. If the instruction came from him, the solicitor and he needed to be in clear communication with one another. There are irreducible minima in establishing this, which include the use of non-leading questions. The solicitor must be sure that he is getting something in the way of a reasoned answer from his client and not merely an apparent approval of somebody else's proposition. On the balance of probability, the evidence suggested strongly that Mr Dickinson did not get the instructions that he honestly believed he did have, and that the reading through of the will was only an idle ceremony.

The court emphasised finally that when a will that a solicitor makes is challenged, he ought to immediately give a short and accurate statement of the circumstances in which it was made (*ibid.* at 1099B–D). In the letter he wrote, Mr Dickinson got some of the way there, but not far enough. Furthermore, the making of a will by an old and infirm testator ought to be witnessed and approved by a medical practitioner who satisfies himself as to the capacity and understanding of the testator. **6–024**

In *d'Eye v Avery* [2001] W.T.L.R. 227 the court held that although the testator just had, on the balance of probabilities, a sufficient grasp of affairs and receptive comprehension to be capable of making a will, the will was invalid on the ground that there was insufficient evidence of his knowledge and approval. The handicaps of the testator, who had suffered a stroke, required a laborious reading and a skilled communication of the will's contents to him. That did not occur. There was no need to consider where the burden of proof lay because the whole execution of the will was suspicious. The fact that its existence was kept from those who were responsible for the testator until after his death only fed the suspicion, which was so strong as to go beyond the civil burden of proof and compel the conclusion that, on the balance of probabilities, the testator had not fully understood the disposal which he was making by his will. He lacked knowledge and approval. The state of mind of the testator, both generally in relation to his testamentary capacity and specifically in relation to his knowledge and approval of the will, was crucial; and the distinction between the words *"generally"* and *"specifically"* encapsulated the distinction to be drawn between the two concepts of, on the one hand, testamentary capacity (a general ability to do something) and, on the other, *"knowledge and approval"* (an awareness and appreciation of a specific instrument). **6–025**

By contrast, in *Carapeto v Good* [2002] EWHC 640, Ch, a challenge to the will on the ground of lack of knowledge and approval failed. It was accepted that the circumstances gave rise to a suspicion that the testatrix did not know and approve the contents of her will and that the burden of proof that she did was accordingly cast on those seeking to propound it. After an exhaustive investigation into all the circumstances, the court held that they had, on the balance of probabilities, succeeded in discharging that burden. **6–026**

6–027 Finally, it must be emphasised that the circumstances which may result in a testator's lack of knowledge and approval of the contents of his will are infinitely variable. They may range from fraud (see *Fulton v Andrew* (1875) 7 H.L. 448) to the most innocent mistake. Most mistakes will now be rectifiable under s.20 of the Administration of Justice Act 1982 (see below, para. 10–041), but those that are not rectified or rectifiable under s.20 may support a lack of knowledge and approval claim. Every case will turn on its own unique facts.

Chapter 7

Undue Influence

Introduction

In principle a Court will pronounce against the validity of a will **7–001** if it was the result of undue influence. But as a ground for attacking a will, it will not often be needed, because the ground of lack of knowledge and approval will in almost all cases be easier to establish evidentially. Moreover, undue influence in probate is not the same as undue influence in equity: it is a narrower concept. This distinction is so important that we will first deal with undue influence in equity in order to identify clearly where the two concepts overlap and where they do not.

Undue influence in equity

In equity, cases of undue influence are now classified in three **7–002** categories. Class 1 consists of cases of actual (or express) undue influence. In these cases it is necessary for the complainant to prove affirmatively that he entered into the impugned transaction not of his own free will but as a result of actual undue influence exerted against him. Class 2 consists of cases of presumed undue influence. In these cases it is sufficient for the complainant to establish the existence of a relationship of trust and confidence between him and the wrongdoer of such a nature that it is fair to presume that the wrongdoer abused the relationship in procuring him to enter into the impugned transaction. Once such a relationship has been established, the burden shifts to the wrongdoer to prove that the complainant entered into the impugned transaction with his full and free informed thought (*Zamet v Hyman* [1961] 1 W.L.R. 1442 at 1444 *per* Lord Evershed M.R.; *Royal Bank of Scotland v Etridge* [1998] 4 All E.R. 705 at 711). For a recent case in which the presumption was not rebutted, see the court of Appeal decision in *Hammond v Osborn* [2002] W.T.L.R. 1125.

7–003 The necessary relationship can be established in either of two ways. Class 2A consists of certain well-known relationships which are by presumption of law irrebuttably treated as relationships of trust and confidence. Class 2B consists of other cases where the complainant establishes by affirmative evidence that he was accustomed to repose trust and confidence in the wrongdoer.

7–004 The expressions *"actual undue influence"* and *"presumed undue influence"* might be taken to indicate that the difference between them lies merely in the means by which the exercise of undue influence is proved. But this is not the case. Presumed undue influence is concerned with the abuse of a relationship of trust and confidence. Since the vice of the transaction lies in the abuse of a position of trust, the transaction must result in some unfair advantage to the person in whom trust is reposed (or to another at his request) at the expense of the person who relies upon him; for even a dealing between a fiduciary and his principal will be upheld if it is affirmatively shown to be fair to the principal.

7–005 The equitable doctrine of undue influence, however, is not confined to cases of abuse of trust and confidence; it is also concerned to protect the vulnerable from exploitation. It is brought into play whenever one party has acted unconscionably in exploiting the power to direct the conduct of another which is derived from the relationship between them. This need not be a relationship of trust and confidence; it may be a relationship of ascendancy and dependence. In such cases, actual undue influence has been said to involve some unfair and improper conduct, some coercion from outside, some overreaching, some form of cheating, and generally, though not always, some personal advantage obtained by a donee placed in some close and confidential relation to the donor (*Allcard v Skinner* (1887) 36 Ch.D. 145; [1886–90] All E.R. 90; see also *Re Craig dec'd* [1970] 2 All E.R. 390; [1971] Ch. 95, which involved a housekeeper and an elderly employer who had become dependent upon her).

7–006 This is often described in terms of the domination by the wrongdoer of the mind and will of the complainant so that the mind of the latter becomes a mere channel through which the wishes of the former flow (*Tufton v Sperni* (1952) 2 T.L.R. 516, at 532 *per* Morris L.J.).

7–007 Importunity and pressure, if carried to the point at which the complainant can no longer exercise a will of his own, amounts to undue influence, but pressure is neither always necessary nor always sufficient. In one case the wife succeeded in establishing that she was the victim of actual undue influence even though no pressure was exerted on her by her husband because none was needed:

"She had no will of her own. Nor had she any means of forming an independent judgment even if she had desired to do so." (*Bank of Montreal v Stuart* [1911] A.C. 120)

Today, perhaps, this would more readily be classified as a Class 2B case. It may be contrasted with the circumstances in which Mrs O'Brien signed the charge in *Barclays Bank plc v O'Brien* [1992] 3 All E.R. 983, at 1001; [1993] Q.B. 109. At 141–142, Scott L.J. said:

"Mr O'Brien was, Mrs O'Brien said, extremely insistent that she should sign. He made an emotional scene on the day she signed and told her that, if she did not sign, the company would be bankrupt and her son John would lose his home. These were heavy family pressures but not particularly unusual nor sufficient, in my opinion, to overset and bear down the will of Mrs O'Brien. She signed because she was persuaded that it was the right thing to do, not because her husband's pressure deprived her consent of reality."

Legitimate commercial pressure brought by a creditor, however strong, coupled with proper feelings of family loyalty and a laudable desire to help a husband or son in financial difficulty may be difficult to resist. They may be sufficient to induce a reluctant wife or mother to agree to charge her home by way of collateral security, particularly if they are accompanied by family pressure or emotional scenes. But they are not enough to justify the setting aside of the transaction unless they go beyond what is permissible and lead the complainant to execute the charge not because, however reluctantly, he is persuaded that it is the right thing to do, but because the wrongdoer's importunity has left him with no will of his own (*Royal Bank of Scotland v Etridge (No. 2)* [1998] 4 All E.R. 705; see also the recent restatement of the principle by Nourse L.J. in *Hammond v Osborn* [2002] W.T.L.R. 1125. **7–008**

Undue influence in probate

The concept of undue influence in probate is narrower because it is in all cases confined to actual undue influence. Undue influence will never be presumed (*Parfitt v Lawless* (1872) L.R. 2 P. & D. 462). Accordingly, in a probate claim challenging a will on the ground of undue influence, actual undue influence must be alleged and proved. Class 2A and 2B presumed undue influence in equity has no place in probate. The only issue which can arise in probate litigation is whether the actual influence **7–009** alleged amounts to undue influence as that concept is understood in probate.

7-010 To make a valid will, a person must be a free agent. Persuasion, appeals to the affections or ties of kindred, to a sentiment of gratitude for past services, or pity for future destitution, or the like, are all legitimate, and may be fairly pressed on a testator. On the other hand, pressure of whatever character, whether acting on the fears or the hopes, if so exerted as to overpower the volition without convincing the judgment, is a species of restraint under which no valid will can be made. Importunity or threats, which the testator has not the courage to resist, or moral command asserted and yielded to for the sake of peace and quiet, or of escaping from distress of mind or social discomfort, if carried to a degree in which the free play of the testator's judgment, discretion or wishes, is overborne, will constitute undue influence, though no force is either used or threatened. In summary, a testator may be led but not driven, and his will must be the offspring of his own violition, and not the record of some one else's (*Hall v Hall* (1868) L.R. 1 P. & D. 481).

7-011 The essential element, accordingly, is coercion. Without coercion the influence does not, for the purpose of probate claims, amount to undue influence. The coercion may of course be of different kinds: it may be of the grossest form, such as actual confinement or violence; or a person in the last days or hours of life may have become so weak and feeble that a very little pressure will be sufficient to bring about the desired result, and it may even be that the mere talking to him at that stage of illness and pressing something upon him may so tire the brain that the sick person may be induced, for quietness' sake, to do anything. This would equally be coercion, though it would not involve actual violence. The test in every case is whether the testator would say, after all is said and done, *"This is not my wish, but I must do it"* (*Wingrove v Wingrove* (1885) 11 P.D. 81).

Burden of proof

7-012 Where actual undue influence is alleged, the burden of proof is on the party alleging it. In all cases it must be proved affirmatively since, as already stated, undue influence will never be presumed. In practice, this presents an evidential hurdle which is very hard to surmount. In particular, it is not enough to show that the proved facts were consistent with undue influence having been applied: it must be shown that the proved facts were inconsistent with any other hypothesis (*Boyce v Rossborough* (1857) 6 HLC 2 at 51; *Craig v Lamoureux* [1920]

A.C. 349). *Carapeto v Good* [2000] EWHC 640, Ch, is a recent example of failure to surmount this hurdle. However, a claim based on actual undue influence succeeded in *Killick v Pountney* [2000] W.T.L.R. 41, but this was aided by the fact that the defendants put in no defence to the allegations made. The facts were that the testator, Norman Killick ("T"), died on October 26, 1994 aged 87. He had never married. The plaintiff, Geoffrey Killick, was his nephew and he and his family were T's only living relatives. Since the early 1940s, T had lodged with the second defendant, Nellie Pountney, and her husband, and this was his home, to which he was greatly attached. The first defendant ("the defendant") was the Pountney's son born in 1947. On July 30, 1993, T entered hospital for an emergency operation. He was readmitted in September 1993. He was enfeebled both physically and mentally. On October 6, he told the plaintiff and his wife that the defendant had *"banned him"* from seeing them, threatening that he, T, would not be allowed to return to his lodgings with the defendant's parents unless he complied. T was very upset, and the plaintiff and his wife complied with his wishes until, at Christmas, Nellie Pountney indicated that they could visit T again. On October 22, 1993, T's solicitors were contacted by Nellie Pountney and arrangements were made for them to visit T in hospital and take instructions for a new will. There was no question regarding T's competence and the will was prepared. On November 4, 1993, the solicitors attended T to have the will executed but T refused, saying that he was reluctant to sign the will without further discussions with the defendant, even though it was explained to him that the will was in accordance with his instructions, that it had nothing to do with the defendant and that the solicitors' costs would increase if they made extra visits. The solicitors returned on November 5 when the defendant was present, and after the defendant had left the room T executed his will.

Contrary to earlier wills which had named as executor the plaintiff or his father, when alive, the will named the defendant as executor, with his mother in default. The will made gifts of £20,000 each to the defendant and his father and mother. This was unexpected, since T had been most distressed by the defendant's behaviour. The defendant owed T more than £9,000, had let down Mr Belton, a friend and ex-business associate of T, leaving him with a debt of £1,500, and had borrowed £1,500 from his father, which T clearly considered he would not repay. He had also said words to T to the effect that he had *"got one over on you now"* or *"taken you for a ride"*. T had discussed these matters with the plaintiff and with Mr Belton.

7–013

7–014   T died on October 26, 1994. The day after he died the defendant swore his oath as executor with a view to obtaining probate and the plaintiff lodged a caveat. Very little was done for over a year and the plaintiff commenced proceedings for a declaration that the will was invalid because its execution was obtained by the undue influence of the defendant. The defendant and the second defendant served no defence, nor did they reply to the affidavits served by the plaintiff. Neither of the defendants was present at the trial, which the Master had directed should be tried on affidavit evidence alone in the absence of any defences. The court held that the defendant had exercised undue influence over T, and that if there is evidence showing the exertion of improper influence in relation to the execution of a will, it will be easier, where the testator is enfeebled in body or in mind, and all the more so if he is enfeebled in both body and mind, to find that such influence was in all the circumstances undue and that it was by means of the exercise of such influence that the execution of the will was obtained.

Chapter 8

Fraud and Forgery

Introduction

This chapter considers two separate, but often linked, methods **8–001** of challenging the validity of a will.

Fraud

Fraud invalidates a will for exactly the same reason as all other **8–002** substantive grounds for challenging the validity of a will, namely that the mind of the testator did not go with the document he signed. The essence of fraud in probate is, as in all other areas of the law, dishonesty. As a ground for challenging a will, it is accordingly entirely distinct from undue influence, the essence of which in probate is, as we have seen in Chapter 7, coercion.

In general, acting dishonestly simply means not acting as an honest person would in the circumstances. This is an objective standard. At first sight this may seem surprising. Honesty has a connotation of subjectivity, as distinct from the objectivity of negligence. Honesty, indeed, does have a strong subjective element in that it is a description of a type of conduct assessed in the light of what a person actually knew at the time, as distinct from what a reasonable person would have known or appreciated. Furthermore, honesty and its counterpart dishonesty are mostly concerned with advertent conduct, not inadvertent conduct. Carelessness is not dishonesty. Thus, for the most part, dishonesty is to be equated with conscious impropriety. However, these subjective characteristics of honesty do not mean that individuals are free to set their own standards of honesty in particular circumstances. The standard of what constitutes honest conduct is not subjective. Honesty is not an optional scale, with higher or lower values according to the moral standards of each individual. If a person knowingly appropriates another's property, he will not escape a finding of dishonesty simply because he sees nothing wrong in such behaviour.

8–003 In most situations there is little difficulty in identifying how an honest person would behave. Honest people do not knowingly take others' property. Unless there is a very good and compelling reason, an honest person does not, for instance, participate in a transaction if he knows it involves a misapplication of trust assets to the detriment of the beneficiaries. Nor does an honest person in such a case deliberately close his eyes and ears, or deliberately not ask questions, lest he learn something he would rather not know, and then proceed regardless (*Royal Brunei Airlines v Tan* [1995] 2 A.C. 378).

8–004 Fraud in probate most commonly involves some dishonest misrepresentation made to the testator by those seeking to benefit under his will. For example, a will would be invalid on the grounds of fraud if it were established that the testator made it in favour of X rather than Y as a result of a dishonest misrepresentation by X about Y which prejudiced the testator's mind against Y (*Boyce v Rossborough* (1857) 6 H.L.C. 3 at 53). Similarly, a dishonest misrepresentation by X about Y which resulted in a testator revoking a codicil in favour of Y, leaving his will in favour of X free of the codicil in favour of Y, would on the grounds of fraud invalidate the revocation (*Allen v McPherson* (1847) H.L.C. 1, 191).

8–005 Fraud may also be involved in the preparation and drawing up of a will. If fraud is involved, or even a sufficient suspicion of fraud, then the court will refuse to pronounce for the validity of a will. A typical case is where persons who are strangers to the testator, who have no claim on his bounty, have themselves prepared for their own benefit a will disposing in their own favour of a large portion of the property of the testator. In that case the court in its capacity as both judge and jury may well conclude that there was a failure on the part of those who propounded the will of a duty to bring home to the mind of the testator the true effect of his testamentary act, and that such failure amounted to fraud on their part (*Fulton v Andrew* (1875) L.R. 7 H.L. 448 at 463 *per* Lord Cairns). What is at issue is the honesty of the persons involved. The court is concerned, as always, with whether the testator's mind went with his act. This concern is expressed as a rule, which is a rule of evidence. It is that a person who is instrumental in the framing of a will, and who obtains a bounty by that will, is placed in a different position from other ordinary legatees who are not called upon to substantiate the truth and honesty of the transaction as regards their legacies. It is enough in their case that the will was read over to the testator and that he was of sound mind and memory, and capable of comprehending it. But there is a further onus upon those who take for their own benefit, after having been instrumental in preparing or obtaining a will. They have thrown on them what used to be called the *"onus of showing the righteousness of the transaction"* (*ibid.* at 471–472 *per* Lord Hatherley), a phrase now disapproved (*Fuller v Strum* [2002] 1 W.L.R. 1097 at 1107C *per* Peter Gibson L.J., at 1119B *per* Chadwick L.J. and at 1123 *per* Longmore L.J.) but which means the same as the onus of removing the suspicion that the testator did not know and approve the will he made (*ibid.* at 1123 *per* Longmore L.J.). In summary, the suspicion of fraud is sufficient to invalidate a will, but in practice it is introduced more conveniently as one available ground (among many other possible grounds) for attacking a will on the ground of lack of knowledge and approval (*Wintle v Nye* [1959] 1 W.L.R. 284).

Fraud may also result in the setting aside of an order pronouncing for a will in solemn form. The evidence required of such fraud will have to be as convincing as the evidence of fraud required to set aside any other judgment or order of a court. The setting aside on the ground of fraud of an order pronouncing for a will in solemn form may adversely affect other beneficiaries under such a will who are wholly innocent of any fraud, but the court nonetheless has the power to do this (*Birch v Birch* [1902] P. 130). However, if only a particular bequest in the will has been procured by fraud, the court also has the power to pronounce for the will but excluding that bequest. **8–006**

An allegation of fraud, involving as it does an accusation of dishonesty, is a serious matter. Consequently, any party who wishes to contend that the execution of a will was obtained by fraud must set out the contention specifically and give particulars of the facts and matters relied on (CPR r.57.7(4)(c)). **8–007**

Forgery

Forgery, although usually treated as a separate ground for challenging the validity of a will, is merely one form of fraud among others — and to it all the same considerations apply as apply to fraud. The forging of a will will usually involve the typing or printing of the dispositive parts and then the forging of the signatures of the testator and the witnesses. The evidence of forgery will usually consist of the evidence of a handwriting expert alone, since direct evidence of the act of forgery is very unusual, although obviously possible, for instance where one of the conspirators confesses. So serious an allegation as forgery requires a high standard of proof. (*Hornal v Neuberger Products* [1957] 1 Q.B. 247; *R. v Ewing* [1983] Q.B. 1039). **8–008**

Chapter 9

Revocation

Introduction

9–001 A will is ambulatory until the death of the testator. It is accordingly inherently revocable. Indeed, it remains revocable even if it is expressed to be irrevocable. As a result of the revocable nature of a will, however, certain related actions may arise:

(1) An action for breach of a contract not to revoke a will. The court will not grant specific performance of such a contract because that would be inconsistent with the revocable nature of the will, but it may award damages for the breach of contract, provided that a legally enforceable contract exists according to the normal law of contract.

(2) An action based on equitable estoppel where a person promises to make a will, or not to revoke an existing one.

(3) An action to enforce an agreement to make mutual wills (see below, para. 10–003).

9–002 The issue as to whether a will has been revoked will normally be raised by persons entitled under an earlier will of the testator, or under the resulting intestacy if there be no valid unrevoked will.

Modes of revocation

9–003 The various modes by which a will may be revoked fall into three basic categories:

(1) revocation by operation of law (see below, para. 9–004);

(2) revocation by instrument in writing (see below, para. 9–011); and

(3) revocation by physical act of the testator (see below, para. 9–017);

Revocation by operation of law

9–004 This section deals with the circumstances in which and the extent to which a will may be automatically revoked by:

(1) marriage; or
(2) dissolution or annulment of marriage.

Marriage

9–005 In the case of wills made on or after January 1, 1983, which will now be the case in respect of the majority of wills, a will is, subject to the three cases mentioned below, revoked by the testator's marriage (Wills Act 1837, s.18(1) as substituted by Administration of Justices Act 1982). The three cases are the following:

(1) A disposition in a will exercising a power of appointment (whether given under a settlement or under someone's will) takes effect despite the testator's subsequent marriage, except where the property so appointed would in default of such appointment pass to the testator's own personal representatives (s.18(2)).

(2) Where it appears from a will that at the time it was made the testator was expecting to be married to a particular person and that he intended that the will should not be revoked by the marriage, the will will not be revoked by his marriage to that person (s.18(3)).

(3) Where it appears from a will that at the time it was made the testator was expecting to be married to a particular person and that he intended that a particular disposition in the will should not be revoked by his marriage to that person,

 (a) that disposition will take effect notwithstanding the marriage; and
 (b) any other disposition in the will will take effect also, unless it appears from the will that the testator

intended the disposition to be revoked by his marriage (s.18(4)).

9–006 These provisions removed various areas of uncertainty under the pre-1983 law (as to which, see below, para. 9–007). Under these provisions, the will itself has to express the relevant expectation. Only if the expressions used in the will give rise to ambiguity can extraneous evidence be admitted for the purpose of construing the expressions used (Administration of Justice Act 1982, s.21). The provision only bites if the testator subsequently marries the particular person in question; it has no application if the stated expectation is not realised. Subsequent marriage to another person therefore has no relevance. It is to be observed here that a solicitor drawing up a will for a client has a duty to advise him of the revocatory provisions of s.20 (*Hall v Meyrick* [1957] 2 Q.B. 455). A common pitfall is where a testator has a new will drawn up on the occasion of his marriage to reflect his new obligations, but which is not expressed to be made in contemplation of that marriage. If such a will is executed after the wedding service, all will be well; but if out of excess of efficiency the testator executes it before the service, it will automatically be revoked as he says "I will" to his new wife.

9–007 It remains necessary to deal with the pre-1983 position. Section 18 of the Wills Act 1837 provided that every will made by a man or woman shall be revoked by his or her marriage (except a will made in exercise of a power of appointment, when the real or personal estate thereby appointed would not in default of such appointment pass to his or her heir, customary heir, executor, administrator, or the person entitled as his or her next of kin, under the Statute of Distributions). But this was eased by s.177 of the Law of Property Act 1925, which provided that a will expressed to be made in contemplation of a marriage shall, notwithstanding anything in s.18 of the Wills Act 1837 or any other statutory provision or rule of law to the contrary, not be revoked by the solemnisation of the marriage contemplated.

9–008 The presence of the "a" in "a marriage" gave rise to much uncertainty and much litigation. The cases may be classified under three headings. First, there are the "general contemplation" cases. In these, the will merely expressed a contemplation of marriage in general, so that the will could not be said to have been made "in contemplation of a marriage" within the section. "Marriage" and "a marriage" are two different concepts, and this is emphasised by the concluding words of the section, "the solemnisation of the marriage contemplated". Thus in *Sallis v Jones* [1936] P. 43, the last sentence of the will stated that "this will is made in contemplation of marriage", and it was held that this did not satisfy the section.

9–009 Secondly, there are the "wife" cases, where in the will the testator describes as his "wife" someone who was not in fact married to him. In the earliest of these cases, *Pilot v Gainfort* [1931] P. 103, a gift to X, "my wife", was held to satisfy the section. The testator's wife had disappeared three years before he began to live with X, six years before he made his will, and seven years before he married X. Lord Merrivale held (at 104) that the testator had made his will at a time when that marriage was obviously within the contemplation of the testator, if he could validly contract it. He said that the section prescribed that the solemnisation of his marriage should not revoke his will made in contemplation of that marriage, and that the will was in contemplation of the subsequent marriage and practically expressed that contemplation.

Thirdly, there are the "my fiancée" cases. In *Re Langston* [1953] P. 100, the testator gave his entire estate "unto my fiancée Maida Edith Beck" and appointed her sole executrix. It was held that the proper test under s.177 was "Did the testator express the fact that he was contemplating marriage to a particular person?" and held that it was satisfied. The last fiancée case, before the Law Commission decided it was time to redefine the law, was *Re Coleman* (1971) 1 Ch. 1. In that case the testator, by his will dated September 10, 1971, appointed, by clause 1, the plaintiff and the third defendant as executors and trustees. By clause 2, he gave and bequeathed some gifts "unto my fiancée", naming the first defendant. By clause 3, he gave, devised and bequeathed "unto my said fiancée", naming the first defendant, his freehold house absolutely. The testator then disposed of the residue. On November 18, 1971, he married the first defendant and died on November 8, 1972. The plaintiff, as one of the executors, issued a writ seeking the will to be pronounced in solemn form, contending that the will, by describing the first defendant as his fiancée, was expressed to be made in contemplation of the testator's marriage with the first defendant and so, by virtue of s.177 of the Law of Property Act 1925, was saved from being revoked on his marriage by s.18 of the Wills Act 1837. The first defendant tendered evidence of the testator's intention when making the will and counterclaimed, asking the court to pronounce against the will on the ground that the testator's marriage to her, subsequent to making the will, revoked the will, so that he died intestate. Megarry J. held that the operation of s.177 was a matter of construction on which extrinsic evidence of intention or purpose was inadmissible; that a testamentary gift to a named person described in the will as being the testator's fiancée would normally express a sufficient contemplation of marriage to that person, but for the section to apply, the will had to contain an expression which sufficiently showed that the will, as a whole, was made in contemplation of the particular marriage in fact celebrated; that expressions in the will which merely showed that parts of the will were made in contemplation of the marriage celebrated would not suffice, unless those parts amounted, at least, to substantially the whole of the beneficial dispositions made by the will; and that the will in that case was not expressed to be made in contemplation of the marriage within the meaning of s.177, so that it was revoked by the testator's marriage, and, accordingly, there should be a pronouncement in solemn form against the will.

Divorce or annulment of marriage

Before 1983 divorce or annulment of marriage did not revoke a will. The Administration of Justice Act 1982 inserted a new section 18A into the Wills Act 1837, s.18A(1) of which provided that where, after a testator has made a will, a decree of a court dissolves or annuls his marriage or declares it void, the will is to take effect as if any appointment of the former spouse as an executor or as the executor and trustee of the will were omitted, and any demise or bequest to the former spouse is to lapse, except in so far as a contrary intention appears in the will itself. Section 18A(2) preserves the former spouse's right to apply for reasonable financial provision out of the testator's net estate after his death under the Inheritance (Provision for Family and Dependants) Act 1975, although a properly drawn order on divorce will involve the former spouse giving up that right. Section 18A(3) provided for the acceleration of interests in remainder where a former spouse had a life interest which lapsed under s.18A(1). This was the position for deaths between January 1, 1983 and April 4, 1988, when s.18A(1) was slightly amended by the Family Law Act 1986, s.53 to limit decrees of a court to decrees of a court of civil jurisdiction in England and Wales, and to limit divorce or annulment to divorce or annulment entitled to recognition in England and Wales by virtue of that 1986 Act. Since January 1, 1996 the position has been reformulated, although not fundamentally changed, by the Law Reform (Succession) Act 1995, as a result of which, for deaths from January 1, 1996 onwards, s.18A of the Wills Act 1837 is now in the following form:

9–010

"18A. Effect of dissolution or annulment of marriage on wills

(1) Where, after a testator has made a will, a decree of a court of civil jurisdiction in England and Wales dissolves or annuls his marriage or his marriage is dissolved or annulled and the divorce or annulment is

entitled to recognition in England and Wales by virtue of Part II of the Family Law Act 1986—

(a) provisions of the will appointing executors or trustees or conferring a power of appointment, if they appoint or confer the power on the former spouse, shall take effect as if the former spouse had died on the date on which the marriage is dissolved or annulled, and

(b) any property which, or an interest in which, is devised or bequeathed to the former spouse shall pass as if the former spouse had died on that date, except in so far as a contrary intention appears by the will.

(2) Subsection (1)(b) above is without prejudice to any right of the former spouse to apply for financial provision under the Inheritance (Provision for Family and Dependants) Act 1975."

Revocation by instrument in writing

9–011 Revocation by this means will be a voluntary act, and the essence of this voluntary act of revocation lies in the intention of the testator to revoke. If that intention is absent, there will be no revocation. Normally, however, but not always, the necessary intention to revoke will be evident from the instrument itself.

9–012 Revocation by this means may take either of two forms, both provided for by s.20 of the Wills Act 1837:

(1) revocation by another later will or codicil duly executed in accordance with s.9; or

(2) revocation by some writing declaring an intention to revoke and executed in accordance with s.9.

Revocation by another later will or codicil duly executed

9–013 The issue frequently arises as to whether a later will or codicil has or has not had the effect of revoking an earlier will or codicil. In every case, as cannot too often be emphasised, it is a question of ascertaining the intention of the testator, whether that is ascertained expressly or only by inference. The potentially infinite variety of different facts naturally fall into two categories:

(1) where there is an express revocation clause; and

(2) where there is no revocation clause.

CONTENTIOUS PROBATE

Revocation where there is an express revocation clause
Here it is a matter of construing the words of the clause to **9–014**
ascertain the extent of the intended revocation (since a testator
may intend to revoke part or parts only of a previous will or
codicil). A revocation clause clearly expressed to revoke all and
any previous wills, codicils or other testamentary documents
leaves no doubt that all are intended to be revoked (*Sotheram v
Dening* (1881) 20 Ch.D. 99). This has the effect of deleting them
all as if they had never been made in the first place. But if the
revocation clause is expressed in less than comprehensive terms,
issues as to the intended extent of the revocation can arise. Even
describing the will as the last and only will will not necessarily
operate to revoke all previous testamentary dispositions (*Simpson v Foxon* [1907] P. 54), although the court may conclude on
reading the will as a whole that such was the testator's intention.
A revocation clause revoking bequests and dispositions in a
previous will will leave the appointment of executors under that
previous will unrevoked (*Re Howard* (1869) L.R. 1 P. & D. 636).
In general, the court will not treat an earlier testamentary
disposition as revoked unless the full extent of the testator's
revocatory intention is clear. Thus, where a particular disposition in a will was revoked by a codicil which not only revoked
the disposition but went on to direct that the will was in all
respects to be construed as if the gift had not been made, the
court held that this additional direction merely reiterated the
particular revocation but left the rest of the will unrevoked (*Re
Lawrence's Will Trusts* [1972] Ch. 418). In general, where a
previous will has included the exercise of a power of appointment, revocation of that will will revoke the exercise of the
power of appointment included in it (*Cadell v Willcocks* [1898]
P. 21).

Revocation where there is no revocation clause
Here there is naturally more scope for uncertainty. Since there **9–015**
is no law which says that a later will automatically revokes an
earlier will, there is nothing to prevent several testamentary
documents of successive date being admitted to probate
together. Here also the court has to find out the testator's
intention. This it may do from both intrinsic and extrinsic
evidence. The intrinsic evidence will be derived from the terms
of the documents themselves, which the court will endeavour to
construe as a whole. There is no particular formula of words
(other than express words of revocation, with which we are not
here concerned) which serve as a universal test of revocatory
intention (*Birks v Birks* (1865) 4 Sw. & Tr. 23). Obviously, if the
dispositions in the later will are wholly inconsistent with those in
the earlier will, the court will conclude that the testator intended

to revoke the whole of the earlier will (*Re Hanoksley's Settlements* [1934] Ch. 384). If the dispositions are only partly inconsistent, the court may conclude that the testator intended to revoke only those parts of the earlier will as are inconsistent with the later will, and the remainder of the earlier will will be admitted to probate along with the later will. Where the intrinsic evidence is insufficient to ascertain the testator's revocatory intention, the court has always been able to revert to extrinsic evidence to construe the document. Until 1982 it could only do this by admitting such evidence, excluding evidence of the testator's intention, as was necessary to put itself in the testator's own armchair at the time he was making the will. Since 1982 extrinsic evidence, including evidence of the testator's intention, has been admissible in construing the document and ascertaining that intention (Administration of Justice Act 1982, s.21). By allowing in evidence of instructions given by the testator to his solicitor, or conversations he had with family or friends, this has made it easier to ascertain a testator's revocatory intentions when the later will is silent or ambiguous on the point.

Revocation by some writing declaring an intention to revoke

9–016 Normally, of course, revocation is part of a subsequent will or codicil, but stand-alone revocation in writing is also provided for by s.20. As stated by the section, for such a document to be valid it must pass the same test for due execution under s.9 as wills and codicils themselves.

Revocation by physical act of the testator

9–017 Section 20 of the Wills Act 1837 provides that no will or codicil, or any part thereof, shall be revoked otherwise than by the burning, tearing or otherwise destroying the same by the testator, or by some person in his presence and by his direction, with the intention of revoking the same. Revocation by this means accordingly requires proof of two things:

(1) a sufficient physical act of destruction; and
(2) the intention of the testator thereby to revoke the will or codicil in question.

Proof of one without the other is not enough (*Cheese v Lovejoy* (1877) 2 P.D. 251).

A sufficient act of destruction

9–018 What will amount to a sufficient act of destruction cannot be stated objectively, since it will vary from case to case depending on the particular circumstances of each case, and depending above all on the evidence available in the particular case about the testator's intention (as to which, see below, para. 9–021). This important general point explains the apparently differing decisions of the court in the numerous reported cases on this topic.

9–019 It is not necessary for the document to be destroyed completely. In the case of burning, the document does not have to be reduced to cinders. A very slight burning will be sufficient destruction if the evidence of the testator's revocatory intention is very strong. However, if the actual burning is very slight, that might suggest that the testator had merely attempted destruction without achieving it. An attempted or uncompleted destruction does not suffice; nor does merely screwing up the will and throwing it in the wastepaper basket, even with the words "This is revoked" written on the back of the will (*Cheese v Lovejoy* (1877) 2 P.D. 251). In the case of tearing, the document need not be completely torn in half, but it must be torn sufficiently to amount to physical destruction consistent with the testator's knowing intention of revocation. Merely crossing out the whole document may be consistent with the testator's known intention of revocation, but it does not amount to "otherwise destroying" within s.20 (*Stephens v Taprell* (1840) 2 Cust. 458). The physical destruction, whether by burning, tearing or otherwise, must, to be sufficient, in every case be such as to destroy its essential nature. Thus destruction of the testator's signature and nothing else will be sufficient. This can be effected by cutting it out, by burning that part of the document, or by obliterating it such that that part of the document is no longer apparent to experts, using magnifying glasses if necessary to decipher it, albeit without physically interfering with the document. This last circumstance amounts to "otherwise destroying" within s.20 (*Re Adams* [1990] 2 All E.R. 97).

9–020 If a will has been executed in duplicate, the question may arise whether destruction of one part amounts to destruction of the whole. There is a rebuttable presumption that destruction of one part amounts to destruction of the whole (*Jones v Harding* (1887) 58 L.T. 60), but such presumption may be rebutted by evidence of the testator's intention.

The intention of the testator to revoke
9–021 Destruction of a will or codicil may not necessarily be the result of the testator's intention to revoke it. It may be the result of some accident; it may be the result of a mistake on the testator's part; or it may have been destroyed when the testator was drunk. In such cases the testator's intention to revoke is lacking, and there is accordingly no effective revocation.

REVOCATION

9–022   The general rule is that the burden of proof of revocation lies on the party seeking to establish such revocation. Since the testator's own evidence as to his revocatory intention or otherwise is normally lacking, the court resorts as usual in such situations to certain presumptions about the testator's intention, which may be rebutted by actual evidence to the contrary.

(1) The court presumes that, where a will is known to have been in the possession of the testator before his death, but cannot be found following his death, the testator destroyed it with the intention of revoking it. The presumption has no application where the testator has passed the will to a third party for safekeeping (*Chana v Chana* [2001] W.T.L.R. 206). This presumption is a matter of common sense, since it is reasonable to suppose that a document of such importance would be carefully looked after by a person of ordinary caution and would not be lost or stolen (*Welch v Phillips* (1836) 1 Moo. P.C. 299). Naturally, this presumption only applies if a thorough search has been made of all the places the testator was likely to have kept the document. If such a search has been carried out by someone who had an interest in establishing revocation, the court may be somewhat cautious before applying the presumption, and in an appropriate case will decline to do so *(Prodmore v Whatton* (1864) 3 Sw. & Tr. 449). But there is a rebuttable presumption against fraudulent destruction by an interested party (*Allan v Morrison* [1900] A.C. 604).

A case where the presumption of destruction by the testator was rebutted was *Re Dickson* [2002] W.T.L.R. 1395. In that case the deceased ("D") married for the first time in 1941 and had two children, the first and second defendants. He made a will in 1946, by which he left his estate to his first wife, but left her to live with the plaintiff, with whom he lived until the date of his death, and they had four children, the third, fourth, fifth and sixth defendants. In 1967, D bought a property, Placewood Farm, and on June 18, 1969, after they had moved there, D made a second will revoking the first, leaving the farm to the plaintiff and ordering his residue to be divided into three equal parts, leaving one part to his wife and two-thirds to the plaintiff. Following a crisis in his relationship with the plaintiff, he divorced his first wife, marrying the plaintiff in November 1977. Financial arrangements were reached with his first wife and D thereafter executed the will (the subject-matter in the proceedings) in which he left the whole of his estate to the plaintiff, appointing her his executrix. The will was prepared by a solicitor, duly executed and witnessed, and the original handed to him, the solicitor keeping a copy. That was the last time the will was seen. D was a meticulous man who kept neat files, but one of the children's birth certificates had gone astray, and there were at least two occasions of domestic upheaval when the document could have gone astray — once in 1980, when D moved his office, and the other when the parties, having sold the farm, had moved into rented accommodation, which they occupied up to D's death. D had periodic contact with a solicitor up until his death and, up to a couple of months before his death, was declaring that he had made a will leaving everything to his wife, although it was clear that their relationship was a stormy one and that, following the move from the farm, they had few, if any, interests in common, a fact set out in a memorandum prepared by D shortly before his death when trying to decide what to do and where to live in the face of the considerable expenses occasioned by the plaintiff's hobby of horse breeding. D died on December 29, 1981.

On those facts the Court of Appeal held that there was nothing in the evidence before the learned judge which countervailed against the clear evidence on the primary facts which he found, of a clear inference of a continuing intention to benefit the plaintiff. The presumption which undoubtedly did arise in a case where a will was traced to the testator's possession but could not be found at his death — the presumption of destruction *animo revocandi* — was on these facts accordingly rebutted.

The Court observed that declarations by a testator, and certainly declarations coupled with, and consistent with, conduct, were of weight in proof of intention. It held that in the absence of evidence pointing to a different state of mind on the part of the testator in the weeks elapsing between the second declaration and his death, it was a matter of common sense that the declarations made in circumstances such that they were made without any reason for suspicion as to their genuineness, and certainly without any pressure, had great weight as pointing to the fact that the will, made so many years before, was still regarded by the testator as being in force.

(2) The court presumes that, where a will is known to have been in the possession of the testator before his death, and is found sufficiently destroyed after his death, the testator destroyed it with the intention of revoking it. Thus, even where a testator made his will a mere week

before his death, but it was discovered after his death under the bolster of his deathbed with the part containing his and the witnesses signatures torn off and missing, the court applied the presumption of an intention to revoke (*Re Lewis* (1858) 1 Sw. & Tr. 31). However, the presumption may be rebutted by appropriate evidence (*Patten v Poulton* (1858) 1 Sw. & Tr. 55).

Partial revocation by obliteration, interlineation or alteration

9–023 Section 21 of the Wills Act 1837 provides that no obliteration, interlineation, or other alteration made in any will after the execution thereof shall be valid or have any effect, except so far as the words or effect of the will before such alteration shall not be apparent, unless such alteration is executed in accordance with s.9. However, the will, with such alteration as part thereof, is deemed to be duly executed if the signature of the testator and the subscription of the witnesses is made in the margin or on some other part of the will opposite or near to such alteration, or at the foot or end of or opposite to a memorandum referring to such alteration, and written at the end or some other part of the will.

9–024 Where as sometimes happens there are unattested alterations to a will, there is a presumption that they were made after the execution of the will and are accordingly invalid as not satisfying s.21. But such presumption is rebuttable by actual evidence that they were made before execution, and are accordingly valid; this may well be inferred by examining the document, possibly with the help of a handwriting expert.

Conditional revocation

9–025 Conditional revocation (traditionally called dependent relative revocation) is revocation coupled with the intention that the operation of such revocation should be conditional on the happening of some future event or some assumed fact being true. As always, it is a question of establishing the testator's true intention. Here, it has to be established (1) that the testator possessed the necessary revocatory intention (see above, para. 9–021), and (2) that he intended such revocation to be conditional, not absolute.

9–026 Establishing requirement (2) involves asking the following questions:

(1) Was the revocation absolute or qualified?

If qualified:

(2) What was the nature of the qualification?

(3) Has such qualification been performed or satisfied?

If the condition or contingency which qualified the revocation has not been satisfied or has not occurred, the revocation remains ineffective; if and where it has been satisfied or has occurred, the revocation becomes unconditional and effective (*Re Jones* [1976] Ch. 200).

Perhaps the most common factual case is where an existing valid will or codicil is destroyed in anticipation of making a new will. In this situation the evidence of the testator's exact intention is all important. The fact that at the time of the mutilation or destruction the testator intended or contemplated making a new will is not conclusive of the question as to whether his intention to revoke was dependent upon his subsequently making a new will. A testator who has made a will in favour of A may become disenchanted with A and decide not to benefit him. He may well at the same time decide that in these circumstances he will benefit B instead of A. It does not by any means follow that his intention to disinherit A will be dependent on his benefiting B, or making a will under which B could take. The test is, if the testator were told that for some reason B could or would not benefit under his new will, would he say, "In that case, I want my gift to A to stand", or would he say, "Well, even so, I do not wish A to benefit"? In the former case, his intention to revoke at the time of the destruction or mutilation of his will could properly be regarded as dependent on the execution of a new will, but not in the latter. It is consequently necessary to look closely at the circumstances surrounding the mutilation or destruction of the will to discover whether any intention that the testator then had of revoking the will was absolute or qualified, and if qualified, in what way it was qualified (*ibid.* at 206 *per* Buckley L.J.). **9–027**

It must be emphasised that every case turns on its own particular facts, which may fall on one side of the line or on the other. There may, for example, be the case where the testator or testatrix says to himself or herself that, however certain may then be his or her intention of making a new will and however certain or uncertain he or she may be of the likely content of that new will when made, he or she is determined to ensure forthwith that the old will shall no longer have any effect at all, and to that end he or she mutilates or otherwise destroys that old will with that specific intent. Such a revocation should in most cases at least be regarded by the courts as absolute and not as conditional upon the subsequent execution of a new will. A **9–028** mere present intention to make a new will at some future date is not enough in such a case to prevent such an act of revocation being absolute (*ibid.* at 214 *per* Roskill L.J.).

9–029 The doctrine of conditional revocation applies equally where the revocation is conditional on some assumed fact being true. This will usually involve some mistaken belief on the part of the testator. For example, where a testator destroys a previous will in the mistaken belief that he has already executed a valid new will, and in fact it is invalid for lack of due execution, the previous will is not revoked, its revocation by destruction being conditional on such mistaken belief (*Re Davies* [1951] 1 All E.R. 920). The mistaken belief may consist of a mistake of law, for instance a mistake of law by the testator that by revoking his will his widow would take his entire estate on his intestacy (*Re Southenden* [1925] P. 177).

9–030 The doctrine may even result in a general revocation clause in a later will being held to be conditional in respect of some provisions of an earlier will but not others. This was the case in *Re Finnemore* [1991] 1 W.L.R. 793. There the testator made three successive wills, on April 12, 1984, November 4, 1986 and November 26, 1986, each of which contained a clause revoking all previous wills. Each will contained a devise of the testator's house and its contents to the first defendant and directed three-quarters of the residuary estate to be held on trust for the first defendant. The later two wills were witnessed by the first defendant's husband, with the result that by reason of s.15 of the Wills Act 1837, the gifts therein to the first defendant were defeated. The first of the three wills gave the fourth quarter of the residuary estate to the second defendant and her husband, but under the terms of the second will the fourth quarter was given to two named charities. Under the last will a third charity was to share equally in the remaining fourth share of the testator's residuary estate.

9–031 On an originating summons issued by the sole executor and trustee under the last will to determine whether, the gifts to the first defendant in the later wills having failed, the assets comprised therein were held in trust for the first defendant under the earlier will or for those entitled on a partial intestacy, it was held that, although the gifts to the first defendant contained in the last of the three wills were rendered null and void by operation of s.15 of the Wills Act 1837, the court was not thereby precluded from looking at the words of gift in order to ascertain the testator's true intention when he executed that will; that determination of the question whether the last will, which was formally capable of revoking all previous wills pursuant to s.20 of the Act of 1837, actually did so depended on the intention of the testator, ascertained by construing the will without the need for extrinsic evidence; that the revocation clause had to be construed in its context and in the light of all the surrounding circumstances, which included the previous wills of November 4, 1986 and of April 12, 1984; that, on the evidence, the testator had had a settled intention since April 1984 that the first defendant should receive the house and its contents and three-quarters of the residuary estate and nothing in his last will suggested any alteration in that intention; that, accordingly, the testator could not have intended to revoke the earlier gifts to the first defendant; that, furthermore, since the testator had clearly laboured under the mistake that his last will would validly dispose of his property to the first defendant, the revocation of his two earlier wills was conditional on his last will being effective for that purpose; but that, since it was clear that the testator did intend to revoke the gifts relating to the fourth quarter of his residuary estate, contained in the first and second wills, and to substitute the gift to the three named charities contained in the last will, it was necessary to treat the revocation clauses in the last two wills as having a distributive effect, so as to confirm the gifts to the first defendant in the first will and to replace the dispositions as to the fourth quarter of the residue with a gift to all three named charities.

Burden of proof

It might be expected that there would be a heavy onus of proof on those attempting to establish that a revocation was conditional rather than absolute. However, no particular burden lies on those alleging that the revocation was merely conditional: it remains a question of what is the proper inference to be drawn in the light of all the evidence as a whole (*Re Jones* [1976] Ch. 200, at 218 *per* Goff L.J.).

9–032

Chapter 10

Related Non-probate Claims

Introduction

This section deals with various claims which are liable to arise on the death of a person but which do not constitute probate claims proper. As has already been seen, probate claims proper consist either of interest claims (see section 2 above) claims for a decree pronouncing for or against an alleged will (see above, paras 3–001 to 9–001), and claims for the revocation of a grant already made (to which the same considerations apply). **10–001**

The non-probate claims with which this section deals are the following: **10–002**

(1) mutual wills (see below, para. 10–003);

(2) proprietary estoppel (see below, para. 10–010);

(3) constructive trusts (see below, para. 10–023);

(4) secret trusts (see below, para. 10–028); and

(5) rectification (see below, para. 10–041.)

Mutual wills

As has already been seen (above, Chapter 9), a will is by its very nature revocable (*Re Heys* [1914] P. 142). Thus the court would never order specific performance of an agreement to make a will in some agreed form, still less grant an injunction preventing a testator from revoking an existing will and making a fresh one. The doctrine of mutual wills operates despite the revocable nature of wills, and despite the revocation of a particular will which the testator had agreed not to revoke. **10–003**

The basic doctrine of mutual wills is long settled (*Dufour v Pereira* (1769) 1 Dick. 419; see also (as more fully reported) Hargrave, *Juridical Arguments and Collections,* Vol. 2, p.311). It **10–004** is to the effect that where two individuals (typically husband and wife, but it can be any two individuals) have agreed to the disposal of their property after their respective deaths and have executed mutual wills in pursuance of that agreement, on the death of the first the property of the survivor (the subject-matter of the agreement) is held on an implied trust for the beneficiary named in the will of the survivor. The survivor may thereafter alter his will, because a will is inherently revocable; but if he does, his personal representatives will take the property subject to the trust.

10–005 For the doctrine to apply, there must be a contract in law. What it is necessary to establish in evidence is an agreement to make and not revoke mutual wills. The terms of such agreement must be definite (*Re Cleaver* (1981) 1 W.L.R. 939 at 944), since without a definite agreement there is nothing sufficiently certain to which the court can give effect. On the assumption that the first testator and the second testator agree to make and not to revoke the mutual wills in question, the performance of that promise by the execution of the will by the first testator is sufficient consideration by itself. But, in addition, to determine whether a promise can constitute consideration, it is necessary to consider whether its performance would have been so regarded. Thus, it is to be assumed that the first testator did not revoke the mutual will notwithstanding his legal right to do so. This too is sufficient detriment to the first testator to constitute consideration. Equally, what is necessary to obtain a decree of specific performance of a contract in favour of a third party is not a relevant question when considering the doctrine (*Re Dale* [1994] Ch. 31, at 38).

10–006 The onus of proving the existence of such an agreement is on the party invoking the doctrine of mutual wills. In principle, it may be established either from the express terms of the wills themselves or by extrinsic evidence of the necessary agreement. Proof of the existence of some loose understanding between the parties, or of a sense of moral obligation felt by one or both of them, will not suffice to trigger the operation of the doctrine (*Re Goodchild* [1997] 1 W.L.R. 1216). The execution of "mirror wills" is not, by itself, evidence that they were intended to be mutual wills (*Grey v Perpetual Trustee Co Ltd* [1928] A.C. 391). In *Re Goodchild* for instance, the testator and his first wife decided to make simultaneous wills in favour of their only son, the plaintiff. They were advised by a solicitor on the drafting of their testamentary wishes and both executed wills in identical terms, leaving their respective estates to each other absolutely in the event of surviving the deceased spouse for 28 days, but otherwise on trust for the first plaintiff. There was evidence that their intention was that after their deaths the first plaintiff would inherit the estate. After the death of his first wife the testator married the defendant and three months later made a new will leaving his entire estate to her. Six weeks later the testator died. The plaintiff brought an action seeking a declaration that after the death of his first wife the testator held her estate on trust for the plaintiff and that after the testator's death the defendant held his estate similarly. The court held that the evidence of the parties' intentions fell short of establishing a clear agreement, and that accordingly the doctrine of mutual wills did not apply.

It might be thought from the expression "mutual wills" that **10–007** the doctrine only applies where there are mutual benefits. It is now clear that it is not so limited (*Re Dale* (above, at 38). It can equally be invoked by a third-party beneficiary. The reason for this is that the underlying principle is to prevent fraud on the first testator to die. It is no less a fraud on the first testator if the agreement was that each testator should leave his or her property to particular beneficiaries, for example their children, rather than to each other. It should be assumed that they had good reason for doing so and in any event that is what the parties bargained for. In each case there is a binding contract. In each case it has been performed by the first testator on the faith of the promise of the second testator, and in each case the second testator would have deceived the first testator to the detriment of the first testator if he, the second testator, were permitted to go back on his agreement. There is thus no reason why the doctrine should be confined to cases where the second testator benefits when the aim of the principle is to prevent the first testator from being defrauded. A fraud on the first testator will include cases where the second testator benefits, but the principle is not confined to such cases, since the doctrine is in furtherance of equity's original jurisdiction to intervene in cases of fraud (*ibid.* at 48).

The enforceability of the mutual agreement depends not on **10–008** the continued existence of the former will as such, but on a species of trust which is held binding in equity, notwithstanding the revocation of the will. It is an unusual form of trust, since it does not prevent the surviving testator using the assets during his lifetime. It is a kind of floating trust which finally attaches to such property as the second testator leaves upon his death. It is by the special doctrine of equity that such a floating obligation, suspended during the lifetime of the survivor, can descend upon his assets at his death and crystallise into a trust. Gifts and settlements *inter vivos,* if calculated to defeat the intention of the agreement, could not be made by the survivor, and his right of disposition *inter vivos* is therefore not unqualified. But, substantially, the purpose of the arrangement will often be to allow full enjoyment for the survivor's own benefit and advantage upon condition that at his death the residue shall pass as arranged (*Birmingham v Renfrew* (1937) 57 C.L.R. 666 at 689).

10–009 Two final points on the operation of the doctrine need to be noted. First, it seems that either side can withdraw from the agreement with impunity during the lifetime of the other. This is apparently because if the first testator alters his will and then dies, the survivor is not prejudiced, since on receiving notice of the alteration, whether during the lifetime of the first testator or following his death, he is then free to alter his own will (*Stone v Hoskins* [1905] P. 194). Secondly, although the remarriage of the survivor to a mutual wills agreement would by operation of law revoke his own mutual will (*Re Marsland* [1939] Ch. 820), the floating charge which came into existence on the death of the first testator will not be affected by such subsequent remarriage. The floating charge will crystallise on his death regardless of his remarriage and regardless of any further wills he may make subsequently (*Re Goodchild* above).

Proprietary estoppel

10–010 A claim to property based on the principle of proprietary estoppel may arise in the course of administration of an estate, either as a claim against the estate or as a claim made by the personal representatives of the deceased against a third party. As a claim by a third party against the estate, its effect, if successful, will be to diminish the size of the net estate. As a claim by the personal representatives of the estate against a third party, its effect, if successful, will be to increase the size of the net estate.

10–011 Both in its origin and in its present application, the principle of proprietary estoppel is based on the equitable test of unconscionability. In its origin it involved the broad basic proposition that a person is not to be deprived of his legal rights unless he has acted in such a way as would make it fraudulent for him to set up those rights (*Ramsden v Dyson* (1866) L.R. H.L. 12). The requisites necessary to constitute fraud of that description followed a rather rigid five-fold formula (see Fry J. in *Willmott v Barber* (1880) 15 Ch.D. 96 at 105–106). But in *Taylors Fashions Ltd v Liverpool Victoria Trustees Co Ltd* [1982] Q.B. 133, Oliver J. made it clear that in the light of more recent cases, the so-called *Ramsden v Dyson* principle requires a very much broader approach, which is directed rather at ascertaining whether, in particular individual circumstances, it would be unconscionable for a party to be permitted to deny that which, knowingly or unknowingly, he has allowed or encouraged another to assume to his detriment, than to inquiring whether the circumstances can be fitted within the confines of some preconceived formula serving as a universal yardstick for every form of unconscionable behaviour.

In its modern form the principle of proprietary estoppel may **10–012**
be stated as follows: Where one person, A, has acted to his
detriment on the faith of a belief, which was known to and
encouraged by another person, B, that he either has or is going
to be given a right in or over B's property, B cannot insist on his
strict legal rights if to do so would be inconsistent with A's
belief.But where the belief is that A is going to be given a right
in the future, it is properly to be regarded as giving rise to a
species of constructive trust, which is the concept employed by a
court of equity to prevent a person from relying on his legal
rights where it would be unconscionable for him to do so (*Re
Basham* [1986] 1 W.L.R. 1498 at 1503).

In *Re Basham* (above), which has subsequently received the **10–013**
endorsement of the Court of Appeal in more recent cases (see
below), the plaintiff's mother married the deceased in 1936
when the plaintiff was 15. She lived with them until her marriage
in 1941. She continued to help them to run their business, was
never paid, but understood that she would inherit the deceased's
property when he died. In 1947 the plaintiff's husband was
considering moving to a job with a tied cottage, but the
deceased was opposed to that, saying that he was willing to help
them get another suitable house. Shortly afterwards the
deceased purchased a tenanted cottage with money provided
largely by the plaintiff's mother. She died in 1976 and the
deceased moved into the cottage, which had become vacant.
There was then a boundary dispute between the deceased and
his neighbour, and the plaintiff took advice from her own
solicitors, the deceased having told her that it was for her
benefit because the house was hers. The plaintiff and her family
lived near the deceased, and although the plaintiff's husband did
not get on well with the deceased, he provided food for him,
kept the garden in order and helped the plaintiff with work
about the house. The plaintiff bought carpets for it, which she
laid herself, and regularly prepared meals for the deceased. She
was told by the deceased that she would lose nothing by doing
those acts for him. A few days before his death the deceased
indicated that he wanted to make a will leaving money to the
plaintiff's son and that she was to have his house. The
remainder of his estate consisted of cash, money on deposit in
the national savings bank, and furniture and other chattels. The
deceased died intestate and the plaintiff claimed a declaration
against two of his nieces who were administrators *de bonis non*
of his estate that she was absolutely and beneficially entitled to
the house and to the deceased's furniture and other property.
On the plaintiff's claim the court held that the principle of
proprietary estoppel was not limited to acts done in reliance on
a belief relating to an existing right, but extended to acts done in
reliance on a belief that future rights would be granted; that a

proprietary estoppel could be raised in relation to the grant of rights over residuary estate; and that, accordingly, since the plaintiff had established that she had acted to her detriment in reliance on her belief, encouraged by the deceased, that she would ultimately benefit by receiving the deceased's property on his death, she was absolutely and beneficially entitled to the deceased's residuary estate, including the house.

10–014 The present application of the principle of proprietary estoppel recognises that all the elements of the principle are permeated by the fundamental principle that equity is concerned to prevent unconscionable conduct (*Gillett v Holt* [2001] Ch. 210). It recognises that although the element of detriment is an essential ingredient of proprietary estoppel, the requirement is to be approached as part of a broad inquiry as to whether repudiation of an assurance is unconscionable in all the circumstances; that where assurances given are intended to be relied on, and are in fact relied on, it is not necessary to look for an irrevocable promise, since it is the other party's detrimental reliance on the promise which makes it irrevocable; and that, when ascertaining whether promises and assurances repeated over a period of many years as to future rights over property are sufficient to found a successful claim for equitable relief, it is necessary to stand back and look at the claim in the round (*ibid.*).

10–015 In that case, the plaintiff spent his working life as a farm manager for and as a friend of the first defendant, a landowner of substantial means, who made repeated promises and assurances over many years, usually on special family occasions, that the plaintiff would succeed to his farming business, including the farmhouse in which the plaintiff and his family had lived for over 25 years. After 1992 relations between the plaintiff and the first defendant deteriorated rapidly. In 1995 the plaintiff was dismissed and the first defendant made lifetime dispositions to the second defendant, in whose favour he also altered his will, making no provision for the plaintiff. The plaintiff sought equitable relief based on proprietary estoppel. The Court of Appeal held that the conduct of the first defendant had given rise to an estoppel. The question then was how to satisfy the equity.

10–016 The aim of satisfying the equity is to look at the circumstances in each case to decide in what way the equity can be satisfied (*Plimmer v Wellington Corporation* (1883–84) L.R. 9 App.Cas. 699 at 714). The court approaches this task in a cautious way, in order to achieve the minimum equity to do justice to the claimant (*Crabb v Arun DC* [1976] Ch. 179 at 198). The range of possible relief is wide. The matter is one for the exercise of the discretion of the court. In *Gillett v Holt,* (above) for example, the court decided that the minimum equity to do justice to the plaintiff was for the defendant to convey to him the freehold of the farmhouse plus £100,000, which represented a sufficient sum of money to compensate him for his exclusion from the rest of the farming business.

In exercising its discretion in satisfying (or valuing) the equity, **10–017** the court will seek to achieve proportionality between the expectation of the claimant and the actual detriment suffered by him (*Jennings v Rice* [2002] W.T.L.R. 369). In that case Mrs Royle ("the deceased") died intestate in August 1997 at the age of 93 as a childless widow. Her estate was valued at approximately £1.3 million net, the value of her house and furniture being about £435,000. The claimant was self-employed and began to work for the deceased in 1970 as a part-time gardener for a wage of 30p per hour. Over the following years, he gradually took on more work on behalf of the deceased, including taking her shopping, running errands and doing minor maintenance work. The deceased ceased paying him in the late 1980s, but gave him £2,000 towards the purchase of his home, although she was otherwise very frugal with her money. At about this time, the deceased said to the claimant that he did not need to worry about not being paid, since he would be "all right" and she would "see to it". She also said to him "this will all be yours one day", or words to that effect.

During the 1990s, the deceased became more dependent on **10–018** the claimant, especially after a burglary in 1993. At her request, he spent almost every night on a sofa in a sitting room in her house from 1994 until her death. He also helped her to dress, attended to her personal hygiene, ran errands for her, ensured that she had food and drink, and continued to work in her garden. His wife also came to help for the last few months of the deceased's life, despite the claimant's time away from home putting a strain on his marriage. After the deceased's death, the claimant continued to live at her house.

At first instance, it was held that the claimant had believed **10–019** that he would receive all or part of the deceased's estate on her death, and that he had proved his claim under the doctrine of proprietary estoppel. The estate was ordered to pay the claimant £200,000, the assessed value of the "equity in the present case". In deciding upon this sum, the judge had taken into account the relevant circumstances (*ibid.* at 372H–373C).

The claimant appealed against the award, contending that he **10–020** was entitled to the deceased's entire estate, or alternatively to a sum representing the value of the house and furniture. The basis for his contention was that he had expected to be left the entire estate and that equity should be satisfied by making good this expectation. Alternatively, he claimed that the minimum he had expected was the house and furniture and that was therefore the minimum he should be awarded.

10–021 The respondents submitted that the claimant's expectation represented the maximum award that could be made, but that the award should be proportionate to the expectation and detriment suffered. In dismissing the appeal, the Court of Appeal stated that the issue was how to give effect to the estoppel which had arisen (*ibid.* at 376A–B). According to the judge's findings of fact, there could not have been an expectation by the claimant that he would receive the deceased's entire estate, since when she said "this will all be yours one day", she was referring to the house and furniture. Furthermore, the claimant did not know that the deceased owned anything other than the house and furniture. Therefore, any award on the basis of the claimant's expectation could not exceed £435,000.

10–022 See also *Campbell & Griffin* [2001] W.T.L.R. 981, where the Court of Appeal awarded the claimant a fixed sum only, charged on the property claimed.

Constructive trusts

10–023 When the assets of the deceased are being gathered in by his personal representatives, an issue may arise as to whether the deceased, despite being the sole legal owner of an asset, nonetheless held it on a constructive trust for someone else, or partly for himself and partly for someone else. The most typical case is the former matrimonial home. This may often have been bought in the sole name of the deceased, but following his death his widow may claim that he nonetheless held it on a constructive trust partly for himself and partly for her. In that case the part held for her belongs to her beneficially, and never forms part of the deceased's estate at all. Similar issues can arise between the deceased and other third parties, such as a co-habitee or partner. It must be emphasised that in the context of constructive trusts, the law makes no distinction between parties who have been spouses and parties who have not. English law does not yet recognise the concept of "family assets" (*Gissing v Gissing* [1971] A.C. 886; *Grant v Edwards* [1986] Ch. 638).

10–024 Under the present law the first and fundamental question which must always be resolved is whether, independently of any inference to be drawn from the conduct of the parties in the course of sharing the house as their home and managing their joint affairs, there has at any time prior to acquisition, or exceptionally at some later date, been any agreement, arrangement or understanding reached between them that the property is to be shared beneficially. The finding of an agreement or arrangement to share in this sense can only be based on evidence of express discussions between the partners, however imperfectly remembered and however imprecise their terms may have been. Once a finding to this effect is made, it will only be necessary for the partner asserting a claim to a beneficial interest against the partner entitled to the legal estate to show that he or she has acted to his or her detriment or significantly altered his or her position in reliance on the agreement in order to give rise to a constructive trust (*Lloyds Bank plc v Rosset* [1991] 1 A.C. 107).

In sharp contrast to this situation is the very different one where there is no evidence to support a finding of an agreement or arrangement to share, however reasonable it might have been for the parties to reach such an arrangement if they had applied their minds to the question, and where the court must rely entirely on the conduct of the parties, both as the basis from which to infer a common intention to share the property beneficially and as the conduct relied on to give rise to a constructive trust. In this situation direct contributions to the purchase price by the partner who is not the legal owner, whether initially or by payment of mortgage instalments, will readily justify the inference necessary to the creation of a constructive trust (*ibid.*). **10–025**

Where there have been direct contributions, but there is no direct evidence of intention, the court has to determine what proportions the parties must be presumed to have intended for their respective beneficial interests. The modern approach is for the court to undertake a survey of the whole course of dealing between the parties relevant to their ownership and occupation of the property and their sharing of its burdens and advantages. That scrutiny will not confine itself to the limited range of acts of direct contribution of the sort that are needed to found a beneficial interest in the first place. It will take into consideration all conduct which throws light on the question as to what shares were intended. If that search proves inconclusive, the court will fall back on the maxim that equality is equity (*Midland Bank plc v Cooke* [1995] 4 All E.R. 562). **10–026**

Where, however, there have not been direct contributions, a common intention to share ownership will not be inferred; it will have to be proved by express agreement (*Lloyds Bank plc v Rosset*, above, at 132). **10–027**

Secret trusts

Even if the will itself cannot be challenged, and its validity has to be accepted, equity may in certain circumstances by the application of the principle of secret trusts impress the dispositions made by the will with a trust for a third party. Secret trusts **10–028** are only one example of a wider category of case, such as mutual wills, in which equity will intervene to impose a trust. The principle of all these cases is that equity will not permit a person to whom property is transferred by way of gift, but on the faith of an agreement or clear understanding that it is to be dealt with in a particular way for the benefit of a third person, to deal with that property inconsistently with that agreement or understanding. If he attempts to do so after having received the benefit of the gift, equity will intervene by imposing a constructive trust on the property which is the subject-matter of the agreement or understanding. (*Re Cleaver* [1981] 1 W.L.R. 939).

10–029 Secret trusts may be either fully secret or half (or semi-) secret. A fully secret trust is a trust the existence of which is not apparent on the face of the will at all. A half-secret trust is a trust the existence of which is apparent on the face of the will, but the terms of which are not. Subject to one difference referred to below, at para. 10–039, the same principles apply to both. In both cases equity impresses property, the subject-matter of a valid disposition in a valid will, with a trust which then takes effect outside that will (*Re Young* [1951] Ch. 244).

10–030 Three requirements have to be satisfied in order to establish a secret trust:

(1) an expression by the testator of an intention to create over property given under his will to A a trust in favour of B;

(2) communication to A by the testator of this intention; and

(3) acceptance by A of the intended trust.

Intention to create a trust

10–031 The requirements for the creation of a valid trust apply equally to secret trusts as to any other trust. Accordingly, the three certainties must be satisfied, namely certainty of language in imperative form, certainty of subject-matter, and certainty of beneficiaries. Nothing less than a legally binding trust obligation is enough. Accordingly, a mere honourable engagement is not enough (*Lord Walpole v Lord Orford* (1797) 3 Ves. Jr. 402 at 419); nor is a mere moral or family obligation (*Re Snowden* [1979] Ch. 528 at 534). In the latter case, the testatrix, Mrs Snowden, made her will in the following circumstances. First, an attendance note of August 30, 1973 by S (her solicitor and executor) recorded that she was not clear how best to deal with things but thought the easiest way was to leave legacies to nephews and nieces, "leaving it to her brother to split up the remainder as he thought best". Secondly, on the morning of January 10, 1974, her brother, after speaking to the testatrix, gave S instructions over the telephone which appeared to have been carried out in the will as drafted. The brother further said that, as S knew, "she wants me [her brother] to deal with the final division for her". Thirdly, on the afternoon of January 10, 1974, the will was executed in the presence of two witnesses. S was unable to be present.

The evidence of those circumstances was the attendance note **10–032** of S dated August 30, 1973, a statement by S made in February 1974 amplifying that note, and affidavits of the two witnesses to the will, sworn in November 1977 and December 1977 respectively, in which they detailed the steps they took to ensure that the testatrix understood and approved the terms of the will. Asked whether she wanted the bulk of her estate to go to her brother instead of to a niece, she had answered "Yes". The statement by S of February 1974 recorded that she had wanted "to be fair to everyone", dwelling on what her brother had done for her and wanting the residue to be left to her brother to "look after the division for her". The court held in these circumstances that there was insufficient evidence to show that the testatrix intended to bind her brother by any legally enforceable trust as to the disposition of residue, and that there was no more than a moral obligation imposed on him to distribute it as she herself might have done; accordingly, he, and through him the first defendant, took the residue free from any secret trust. Sir Robert Megarry V.-C. put it thus:

> "He was her trusted brother, more wealthy than she, and a little older. There was thus no need to bind him by any legally enforceable trust; and I cannot see any real indication that she had any thought of doing this. Instead, she simply left him, as a matter of family confidence and probity, to do what he thought she would have done if she had ever finally made up her mind. In short, to revert to the language of Christian LJ., in *McCormick v Grogan,* 1 IR Eq 313, 328, I cannot see any real evidence that she intended the sanction to be the authority of a court of justice and not merely the conscience of her brother. I therefore hold that the brother took the residue free from any trust." (*ibid.* at 539c)

The court will in every case look closely at the whole course of **10–033** dealing leading up to the alleged expression of intention alleged to create the necessary legally binding trust obligation. In *Kasperbauer v Griffith* [2000] W.T.L.R. 333, the testator died on September 4, 1994 leaving a widow, Rosemary Griffith ("the widow"), and two adopted children of a former marriage,

Rhodri and Sian. The testator had been married twice before. His first wife, Margot, died in 1987 and his second marriage ended in divorce in 1990. He married the widow on January 7, 1993; at the time, he was aware that he was seriously ill with cancer. On April 18, 1990, after the breakdown of his second marriage, the testator made a will by which he gave the whole of the residue of his estate to Rhodri and Sian. In July 1991 the testator gave Rhodri £50,000, and in September of that year he took out a policy on his life, assuring £20,000 for the benefit of Rhodri.

10–034 On November 4, 1992, the testator instructed his solicitors to prepare a new will. He was to marry the widow on November 20 and he wanted to sign the will immediately afterwards. A draft was prepared, naming his sister and the widow as executors. It dealt with his personal chattels, gave Sian £50,000 to equal the £50,000 given to Rhodri earlier, and gave the residue to Rhodri and Sian. The solicitor noted that a pension would go to the widow and referred to the lump sum benefit under the pension scheme. A covering letter, enclosing the draft will for the testator's approval, advised him to contact the pension scheme trustees about whether he could direct payment of the lump sum benefit. The testator had a copy of the pension scheme booklet in his possession, which stated that the death benefit was payable to his surviving spouse, unless he filled in a form asking that the death benefit be paid into his estate.

10–035 The marriage was postponed until January 7, 1993. Eight days later, the testator telephoned his solicitor to have the draft will amended. On February 14, 1993, the testator held a family meeting at his house. Rhodri, Sian, her husband and the widow were present. He told them that he wished to take full advantage of the nil-rate band (which he believed to be the first £140,000 of his estate) by giving that to the children in equal shares, subject to adjustment to reflect the *inter vivos* gift of £50,000 which Rhodri had already received. He also said that the house and the death gratuity were to go to the widow, with the death gratuity (thought by the testator to be about £100,000) being used by her to discharge or reduce the mortgage, and that the house was to be sold within a year of the testator's death — on terms that the widow could buy it at a valuation — and the proceeds divided equally between Rhodri and Sian. Provisions were made for chattels. Rhodri expressed the view that it would be better if all were written down and the necessary tax paid, but the testator said that he did not want that, and that the widow "knew what she had to do". There followed many changes in instructions before the testator finally signed his will on April 27, 1993, but throughout it seems that the testator was adamant that things were to be arranged so that no tax would be paid. On April 28, 1993, the testator went into hospital for an operation, and while he was there the widow spoke to the solicitor, expressing her concern that there might be insufficient provision for Rhodri and Sian because of the large mortgage. It seemed then, and to the judge when hearing her evidence, that she did not fully understand the testator's scheme.

The testator died on September 4, 1993. As he had not 10–036 instructed the pension scheme trustees that the death benefit was to be paid into his estate, the widow took the benefit of some £113,000. The value of the house was £350,000, subject to the mortgage. The residuary estate after payment of unsecured debts amounted to £20,000, and was insufficient to discharge the mortgage debt or to meet the pecuniary legacies in full. Rhodri and Sian, in separate actions, claimed that the widow held the house and the death benefit as trustee on secret trusts, under which they were beneficiaries. The Court of Appeal held that the phrase which the testator repeated, that the widow knew what she had to do, was equivocal and was at least consistent with the belief and intention on the part of the testator that his expressed intentions imposed only a moral obligation on her; and the fact that the testator changed his mind in a number of important respects was also consistent with the view that the expression of his intentions at the meeting on February 14 was not intended to be a definitive instruction to the widow, presumptively intended to impose a legally enforceable obligation on her.

It is inherent in the concept of the creation of trusts generally 10–037 that the person who declares a trust affecting property must be the owner of that property. Accordingly, where a testator at the time he expresses an intention to create a secret trust does not own the property, nor have the power to bring it into his ownership, nor to dispose of it as he wishes, equity will not impose a secret trust (*Kasperbauer v Griffith* (above) at 343G *per* Peter Gibson L.J. and 347 *per* Harman J.). An example might be (as in that case) a death benefit under a pension scheme.

Communication of intention

The testator must communicate his intention in his lifetime (*Re* 10–038 *Cooper* [1939] Ch. 811). Nonetheless, it is sufficient communication if he hands over an envelope containing the trusts on the understanding that it will not be opened until after his death, provided that the recipient accepts the trusts by agreeing to carry them out whatever they are (*Re Keen* [1937] Ch. 237). Conversely, it is not sufficient communication if he merely hands over a sealed envelope and the recipient does not so agree.

Acceptance of the trust

10–039 The recipient must likewise accept the trust during the testator's lifetime (*Wallgrave v Tebbs* (1855) 2 K. & J. 313). However, a distinction must be noted here between acceptance of a fully secret trust and acceptance of a half-secret trust. A fully secret trust may be communicated and accepted after the will has been made (*Blackwell v Blackwell* [1929] A.C. 315). A half-secret trust, by contrast, must be communicated and accepted at the time the will is made (*Re Bateman* [1970] 1 W.L.R. 1463).

Burden of proof

10–040 It was formerly thought that establishing a secret trust required the same standard of convincing proof as is required for rectification (*Ottaway v Norman* [1972] Ch. 698). But it is now clear that that is not so. Apart from cases where fraud is alleged, the standard of proof is the ordinary civil standard of proof that is required to establish any trust (*Re Snowden* [1979] 1 Ch. 529 at 537).

Rectification

10–041 Since January 1, 1983 the court has had, by virtue of s.20 of the Administration of Justice Act 1982, power to rectify a will. Before that the equitable jurisdiction to rectify instruments did not extend to wills, whose provisions could be construed but not altered (subject only to a limited power to omit words from a probate). Section 20 is in the following terms:

> "(1) If a court is satisfied that a will is so expressed that it fails to carry out the testator's intentions, in consequence—
>
> (a) of a clerical error; or
> (b) of a failure to understand his instructions,
>
> it may order that the will shall be rectified so as to carry out his intentions.
>
> (2) An application for an order under this section shall not, except with the permission of the court, be made after the end of the period of six months from the date on which representation with respect to the estate of the deceased is first taken out.
>
> (3) The provisions of this section shall not render the personal representative of a deceased person liable for

having distributed any part of the estate of the deceased, after the end of the period of six months from the date on which representation with respect to the estate of the deceased is first taken out, on the ground that they ought to have taken into account the possibility that the court might permit the making of an application for an order under this section after the end of that period; but this subsection shall not prejudice any power to recover, by reason of the making of an order under this section, any part of the estate so distributed.

(4) In considering for the purposes of this section when representation with respect to the estate of a deceased person was first taken out, a grant limited to settled land or to trust property shall be left out of account unless a grant limited to the remainder of the estate has previously been made or is made at the same time."

In order to succeed in a claim for rectification under s.20, the first hurdle a claimant must surmount is to satisfy the court on the evidence that the will fails to carry out the testator's intentions. Although the standard of proof under s.20(1) is that the court should be satisfied on the balance of probability, the probability that a will which a testator has executed in circumstances of some formality does indeed reflect his true intentions is usually of such weight that convincing evidence to the contrary is necessary (*Re Segelman* [1996] Ch. 171). This mirrors the requirement of convincing proof under the Court's general equitable jurisdiction to rectify documents. However, the weight to be given to the terms of the written document may be diminished by difficulties of construction of the meaning of such terms; and in those circumstances it may be artificial to assume that the testator must have known what he was doing, if the effect of the words used cannot be ascertained without a decision of the court (*ibid.*). **10–042**

The second hurdle for a claimant to surmount is to establish that the failure to carry out the testator's instructions was in consequence of: **10–043**

(1) a clerical error; or
(2) a failure to understand his instructions.

The court has always given an expansive meaning to the expression "clerical error", even before s.20 came into operation. For example, in *Re Morris* [1971] P. 62, the mistake lay in a codicil by which, *inter alia*, the testatrix had revoked clause 7 of her will. It was clear from the evidence that the testatrix had never intended to revoke the whole of that clause but only to revoke the pecuniary legacy given by sub-clause 7(iv). The error was that of her solicitor in giving effect to her instructions. The court held that the introduction of the words "clause 7" instead of "clause 7(iv)" was *per incuriam*. The solicitor's mind was never applied to it, and he never adverted to its significance and effect. It was a mere clerical error on his part, a slip. He knew what the testatrix's instructions and intentions were; and what he did was outside the scope of his authority. In *Wordingham v Royal Exchange Trust Co Ltd* [1992] Ch. 412, the error with which the court was concerned lay in a failure to include in a new will made in 1989 a clause exercising a testamentary power of appointment in favour of her husband which had been conferred on the testatrix under the will of her father. The relevant clause exercising that testamentary power had been included in two earlier wills. The judge was satisfied that the testatrix intended that her 1989 will should include a provision precisely in the terms of the relevant clause in her immediately preceding will. He held that the draftsman's error in failing to include in the draft new will a paragraph following the provisions of the previous will was an error made in the process of recording the intended words of the testatrix and constituted a clerical error within s.20(1)(a). However, s.20(1)(a) is not limited to cases in which the intended words of the testator can be identified with precision. It also extends to cases where the relevant provision in the will, by reason of which the will is so expressed that it fails to carry out the testator's intentions, has been introduced, or has not been deleted, in circumstances in which the draftsman has not applied his mind to its significance or effect (*Re Segelman* above, at 186).

10–044 This expansive meaning given to the expression "clerical error" is wide enough to cover factual situations which involve the professional negligence of those involved in the error. It amounts to the negligent draftsman's charter. The facts which would support a successful negligence claim will normally be more than sufficient to support a successful rectification claim. In these circumstances the negligent draftsman can avoid the consequences of a damages claim against himself for professional negligence by obtaining rectification in proceedings in which he merely has to indemnify the claimant against the claimant's costs of obtaining such rectification. Indeed, on such facts his client has a duty to bring such proceedings pursuant to his duty to mitigate his damage, and failure to do so may result in his damages claim for professional negligence being dismissed (*Walker v Medlicott* [1999] 1 W.L.R. 727). The negligent professional draftsman is accordingly given considerable protection as a result of s.20, not only against claims by the personal representatives of the testator but also against claims by disappointed beneficiaries.

As appears from s.20(2), any application under s.20 must not be made more than six months after the grant of probate, except with the permission of the court. It has been held that the basis on which the court exercises its discretion to give permission is similar to that on which it exercises its discretion to give permission under s.4 of the Inheritance (Provision for Family and Dependants) Act 1975 when an application under that Act is made out of time (*Chittock v Stevens* [2000] W.T.L.R. 643). Guidelines for the giving of permission under that Act were laid down in *Re Salmon* [1981] Ch. 167, and are to the following effect:

10–045

(1) the discretion is unfettered, to be exercised judicially and in accordance with what is just and proper;

(2) the burden of proof is on the applicant, who must make out a substantial case for it being just and proper that time should be extended;

(3) consideration of how promptly and in what circumstances the applicant has sought permission after expiry of the period of six months, looking at the whole of the circumstances;

(4) the existence of negotiations;

(5) the relevance and importance of whether or not the estate has been distributed; and

(6) whether a refusal to extend time would leave the applicant without redress against his professional adviser.

But these guidelines are not exhaustive, and each case will depend on its own particular facts. The guidelines do not apply where a claimant has a full understanding of the nature and prospects of success of a claim available to him and decides not to pursue that claim, but later wishes to reverse that decision (*Escritt v Escritt* (1980) 3 F.L.R. 280).

Part II

Procedure

Chapter 11

The Rules as to Starting Claims

This Chapter looks at the way in which contested probate claims **11–001** may be started. Unlike other types of claim (*e.g.* over contracts, or land) there are some preliminary steps which may have to be taken before a claim is formally brought by the issue of a claim form. These preliminary steps (none of which are in fact mandatory) are looked at before the stage when the claim form is reached.

Caveats, citations and subpoenas

Caveats

What is a caveat?
Caveats are used to stop a grant from being taken out. The rules **11–002** governing the use of caveats are set out in rr.44, 45 and 49 of the Non-Contentious Probate Rules 1987 ("NCPR").

When will it be used or encountered?
It will invariably be the case that a caveat will be used or **11–003** encountered at the outset of a contested probate claim for the following reasons:

(1) the potential claimant wants to stop a grant being taken out in respect of a will which he thinks is invalid;

(2) the potential claimant wants to stop a grant of letters of administration from being taken out on the footing that the deceased died intestate and the claimant thinks there is a valid last will.

A caveat should *not* be used by those wishing to start claims under the Inheritance Act 1975. The Standing Search procedure under NCPR r.43 should be used to discover that a grant has been obtained. When it is, there will be notification under that procedure.

How can a caveat be issued?
11–004 The procedure for issuing caveats is as follows:

(1) The person wishing to prevent the grant from being taken out will complete Form 3 at either a probate registry or sub-registry, or send a completed Form 3 by post at his own risk to any probate registry or sub-registry. That person is called "the caveator". The fee payable is £15 (1999 Non-Contentions Probate (NCP) Fees Order, Sch. 1, item 4).

(2) the registry will send an acknowledgement to show that the caveat has been entered and this will show the date from which the six months will run during which the caveat will have validity. Note that until its appearance is entered (see below), the caveat must be renewed during the last month of the six-months period for a further six months (NCPR (r.44/3)). The fee on renewal is £15.

(3) The registry does not serve the caveat on anyone; it is simply entered on the computerised index record of caveats and will stop any grant from being taken out during the life of the caveat. The only exception to this is a grant *ad colligenda bona*, or a grant of letters of administration pending suit under s.117 of the Supreme Court Act 1981.

When will the caveat be discovered?
11–005 The person against whom a caveat is issued will discover the existence of a caveat in the following ways:

(1) by information from the caveator or his solicitor. This is often the case these days once it is clear that there is going to be a dispute over a will;

(2) by discovering the existence of the caveat when a grant is applied for.

Note that there is no formal requirement on the caveator or the registry to serve notice on anyone that a caveat has been entered.

What happens after the caveat has been discovered?
11–006 The person discovering it will have to "warn" the caveat by asking the probate registry to issue a "warning". This is done by the person who wants to warn the caveat completing Form 4

and sending it to the Leeds District Probate Registry, either by post or by DX. No other registry will accept requests to issue warnings. The present postal address is Leeds District Probate Registry, 3rd Floor, Coronet House, Queen Street, Leeds LS1 2BA; DX 26451 Leeds Park Square. However, an up-to-date check should be made to ensure that there has been no change to the address, or the DX number.

That person will warn the caveat for two reasons: **11–007**

(1) because he has an "interest" in the estate as a person entitled to an earlier, or later will than that which the caveator wants to prove — or the person warning seeks an intestacy; and

(2) because he is entitled to take a grant either as a person entitled to the grant as executor or as a person entitled to letters of administration.

There is no fee for issuing a warning.

The Form 4 must state what interest the person warning has **11–008** in the estate. For example:

"The person warning, namely AB, is entitled to share in the estate of the deceased under a will dated January 1, 2003, which is a valid later will than that put forward by CD"

or

"The person warning, namely AB, is one of the persons entitled to the estate of the deceased on an intestacy, the will dated November 1, 2002 being invalid".

or

"The person warning is entitled to a grant of probate of the will dated November 1, 2002 of the deceased as the sole executor named therein."

Leeds will then issue the warning by sealing it and sending it to the person warning the caveat. That person, having received it back from Leeds, must serve the Form 4 (as sealed) on the caveator (or his solicitor).

What must the caveator do next?
As can be seen from Form 4, he has a choice. He can either **11–009** "enter an appearance" or "issue and serve a summons for directions". He can also decline to enter an appearance,

because, for example, he has decided that he no longer wishes to oppose a grant.

11-010 If the caveator no longer wishes to oppose a grant, he can give notice in writing to the registry where he entered the caveat. He must also give notice of that desire to the person warning the caveat. This will have the effect (by means of the internal workings of the registry and the registry's notation on the Probateman computer system) that the caveat will cease to have effect (NCPR r.44(11)).

11-011 If the caveator wants either to enter an appearance or to issue a summons for directions, he must do one of these things within eight days of the date on which the warning was served on him. The eight days starts with the day of service and will include weekends and public holidays.

What should the caveator do?

11-012 The choice is a simple one. If the caveator wants to dispute the validity of a will, or disputes the distribution of the estate of the deceased on the basis of an intestacy, the caveator will have a "contrary interest". He must, therefore, *enter an appearance*. This will be the start of a contested probate claim, as we see below.

11-013 Alternatively, if the caveator does not challenge the validity of any will, or the fact that there is an intestacy, he has no "contrary interest". He must, therefore, *issue a summons for directions*. This is the proper course to take where, for example, he does not wish the person *prima facie* entitled to take a grant under the will or on the intestacy to do so, *e.g.* because that person would be dishonest, or incompetent, or would have a conflict of interest with the estate. It is usually the case that in such circumstances the caveator will issue the summons for directions (under NCPR r.44(6)) and seek an order under s.116 of the Supreme Court Act 1981 that a grant be issued to the person named in that application. The caveat may then be ordered to cease to have effect (NCPR r.44(7)). This book does not consider that type of application further as it is not a contested probate claim but rather an application under the non-contentious probate jurisdiction of the Family Division (see above, para. 1-003, for this distinction).

What must the caveator do to enter an appearance?

11-014 This requires the caveator to send Form 5 duly completed to Leeds District Probate Registry, and Leeds will issue that form by sealing it, to return it to the caveator. The caveator, having received it back from Leeds, must serve a sealed copy of it on the person warning — or his solicitor.

What happens after the caveator enters an appearance?
Two things will happen: **11–015**

(1) The caveat will remain in force until the commencement of the probate claim. (This also means that the caveat does not have to be renewed during the last month of the six-month period of validity under NCPR r.44(3).) The only exception to this is where the parties affected by the caveat agree that the caveat should be discontinued and on an application to the probate registry (which does not have to be Leeds) an order is made by a registrar or District Judge that the caveat will cease to have effect (NCPR r.44(13)). It is also possible that an application can be made by one party or the other (*i.e.* the caveator or the person warning) to have the caveat removed if, as sometimes happens, neither party has done anything after the caveat has been warned and an appearance has been entered to the warning. The estate is frozen, the caveat prevents any grant from being taken out and the caveator refuses to agree to have the caveat removed or to issue a claim form to start a contested probate claim. In such circumstances the registrar or District Judge will allow an application to discontinue the caveat. If the application is opposed on the footing that the caveator wants to issue a claim form, he may impose a tight timetable for that to be done, usually in "unless order" terms, failing which the caveat will cease to have effect (NCPR r.44(13)). Such an order was made in *Re Magson decd.* by D. J. White in the Principal Registry on October 14, 2003.

(2) Either the caveator or the person warning will issue a claim form and commence the contested probate claim. As to who should be claimant and such claims generally, see below, para. 11–047.

By NCPR r.45, following the issue of a probate claim form, **11–016** notice is given by the court in which the claim is issued to the senior district judge of the Family Division of that fact and he gives notice to all caveators (other than the claimant if he is a caveator) where their caveats are in force. Those issuing any caveats entered after the probate claim is started are also notified of that claim. Probateman is notated to record the issue of the claim form. Unless an order is made on a summons under the NCPR or unless the court who is entitled to a grant, no grant can issue after the probate claim form is issued. The only exception to this rule is a grant *ad litem* under s.117 of the Supreme Court Act 1981. See below, para. 11–042 as to when this type of grant may be necessary.

What happens if the caveat is not warned?

11–017 The caveat will remain in force and must be renewed for a further six months. The application to renew must be made during the last month of the six-month duration of the caveat under NCPR r.44(3). The renewal fee is £15 ((1999) NCP Fees Order, Sch. 1, item 4). It is possible for a contested probate claim form to be issued in such circumstances, and, if so, that will cause the caveat to continue to have effect until the court directs who is to take the grant (NCPR r.45(3)).

What happens if no appearance is entered to the warning?

11–018 Assuming this is not a case where the caveator decides to withdraw his caveat under NCPR r.44(11) but is a case where the caveator is simply refusing to do anything (or has not got round to doing it within the eight-day period), the person warning can apply for the caveat to cease to be effective (by filing an affidavit at Leeds District Probate Registry) stating that no appearance has been entered to the warning within the eight-day period. The caveat will then cease to be effective, and the person warning can obtain a grant (NCPR r.44(12)). The Probateman records are amended to reflect the caveat ceasing to be effective.

Citations

11–019 These may sometimes be encountered prior to a contested probate claim being brought.

By their nature, however, they are not often encountered, principally because the purpose of a citation is to act as the catalyst for a grant to be taken. The procedure for citations is set out in NCPR rr.46–49.

11–020 There are three types:

(1) a citation to accept or refuse a grant (NCPR r.47(1));

(2) a citation to take a grant (NCPR r.47(3)); and

(3) a citation to propound (*i.e.* to prove) a will (NCPR r.48).

The detailed analysis of citations are outside the scope of this book. The first two types of citation will be used depending on whether the person cited has taken steps in the administration of the estate ("intermeddled"), for if he has, only a citation to take a grant is appropriate.

11–021 The procedure for the first two types of citation is, in outline, as follows:

(1) The person wishing to cite under any of the three headings above must issue a caveat; the fee for that is

CONTENTIOUS PROBATE

currently £15 (see NCPR r.46(3) and 1999 NCP Fees Order, Sch. 1, item 4). This person is referred to as "the citor".

(2) The draft citation and the affidavit in support of it must be approved by the Probate Registry before service on the person cited. The fee for approval of each document is currently £10 (r.46(2) and 1999 NCP Fees Order, Sch. 1, item 11). Any wills referred to in the citation must be lodged with the registry; (r.46(5)), unless it is not in the citor's possession, or unless the registrar is satisfied that it is impracticable to lodge it. It is the practice to send the drafts for approval to the Principal Registry at First Avenue House, High Holborn, London WC1V 6NP.

The Principal Registry will accept applications for the issue of citations by post.

The procedure which should be adopted for the issue of probate citations by post is as follows:

1. Drafts of the citation and supporting affidavit should be sent for the citation to be settled to the Receiver of Papers, Principal Registry of the Family Division. First Avenue House, 42–49 High Holborn, London WC1V 6NP together with a photographic copy of any relevant will and codicil or the originals thereof. In the event of originals being sent, registered post should be used and the Registry will retain them unless their return is requested or necessary by reason of the intention to exhibit them to the affidavit.

2. After the citation has been settled the papers (but not original wills and codicils except in the circumstances set out in (1)) will be returned to the solicitor who should then, if he has not already done so, enter a caveat (by post to any Probate Registry with fee £15 payable to "H.M. Paymaster General" (H.M.P.G. is acceptable) if entered in the Principal Registry or to the District Registrar if entered elsewhere). The solicitor should return to the Principal Registry the settled draft citation, an engrossment of the citation, the sworn affidavit, any relevant original wills and codicil in the solicitor's possession at this stage and the receipt for entry of caveat. A cheque for £10, made payable to "H.M.P.G." should also be sent.

3. The engrossed citation will be returned to the solicitor after signature by the District Judge and sealing. The receipt for caveat will be returned at the same time.

4. After the citation has been served the necessary procedure to be followed, which involves amongst other matters the entry of an appearance by the citee or, in default search of the appearance book by the citor, must be carried out by personal attendance of the solicitor (Registrar's Practice Direction (Citation; Acceptance by Post) July 25, 1969 with revised fees).

(3) The citation and affidavit in support, once approved by the registry, must be served personally on the person cited. It may be necessary to effect service by some other means, such as by advertisement in a newspaper, where personal service is not practicable, *e.g.* where the person cited cannot be traced to a known address.

(4) The person cited has eight days (including the day of service) to enter an appearance to the citation (r.46(6)). This is done by completing Form 5.

(5) If no appearance is entered, the citor may apply for a grant to himself (in the case where the person cited has not intermeddled) or, in a case where the person cited has intermeddled, the citor may apply by summons for an Order that the person cited take a grant within a certain time as stated, or that a grant be issued to some other person, as specified in the summons (r.47(5)). The rule also provides for the citation of those to whom power has been reserved and who have not proved (see r.47(2) and (5)(b)).

(6) If an appearance has been entered but the person cited has not taken out a grant, the same routes are open to the citor as under (5) above (see r.47(7)).

Citation to propound a will

11–022 Where the citation is one under r.48 to propound a will, the procedure is as under (1)–(4) above, and the person cited must, therefore, enter an appearance to the citation and propound (*i.e.* prove) the will which the citor wishes to see proved. If the person cited neither enters an appearance within the eight-day period or, if having entered an appearance, fails with reasonable diligence to take a grant of the will, the citor can apply to the registry for one of the following:

(a) *If no appearance has been entered*

11–023 The citor can apply to obtain a grant as if the will is invalid, *i.e.* a grant of probate to the person entitled to an earlier will, or letters of administration on the footing of an intestacy. Proof of personal service of the citation is required (NCPR r.48(2)(a)).

(b) *If an appearance was entered, but no grant of representation has been taken within a reasonable time*

11–024 The citor can apply for an Order to the like effect as in (a) above. The summons must be served on the person cited who has entered an appearance (NCPR r.48(2)(b)).

11–025 Applications may be by summons under NCPR r.61(1).

A citation to propound a will may be a useful device to avoid **11–026**
a contested probate claim, as those cited may be holding a later
will which is plainly invalid, to the knowledge of the citor. The
citor will be able to clear that will off and obtain a grant.

It is important to note, however, that once a will has been **11–027**
admitted to probate in common form, the citation procedure
cannot be used to revoke that grant and a claim form must be
issued which complies with CPR r.57 for revocation of the grant
and solemn form proof of the valid will. See below, para.
11–046. Note, however, the procedure under s.121 of the
Supreme Court Act 1981 for calling in grants and revoking them
if it appears that they have been made in error, or if there are
errors in them. This jurisdiction is only used where it is plain
that the grant ought not to have been made, or that it contains a
clear error, such as to the identity of the executor. It has been
known for this jurisdiction to be used where the "deceased"
turns out to be alive after probate has been granted to his estate.

Subpoenas

What are they and what are they used for?
These are documents issued by the court in terms of an Order **11–028**
that the person served complies with the command in the
subpoena. For the forms of subpoena, see the Appendices. They
are still very much reminiscent of the form of writ in use up to
1980 and it can be seen that they have a certain "weight" which
usually leads to compliance.

Types
There are two types of subpoena which can be used: **11–029**

(1) the subpoena to produce a testamentary document (s.123 of the Supreme Court Act 1981); and

(2) the subpoena to require a person who has knowledge of a testamentary document to attend court and give evidence about it and be examined on that evidence; s.122 of the Supreme Court Act 1982.

Each subpoena can be used without the need for any claim form
to have been issued.

How to obtain a subpoena
If a subpoena under s.122 is required, an application by **11–030**
summons under NCPR r.61 is made for the issue of the
subpoena at the Principal Registry, or at a District Probate

Registry, and that summons is served on the person(s) required to attend to give evidence; NCPR r.50(1).

11–031 If a subpoena is required under s.123, the grounds of the application for the issue of the subpoena are made in an affidavit filed at the Principal Registry or at a District Probate Registry. It is open to the person served with that affidavit to reply by affidavit stating that he does not have the will in his possession, or control, but he is not bound to do so; NCPR r.50(2). Note, however, that if the person served with the affidavit stating that the will is in his possession, or control, chooses not to reply, it is preferable for the party applying to issue a summons for a subpoena under s.122 so that the person refusing to state whether he does or does not have the will can be examined as to the whereabouts of the will. This is preferable to an application to commit to prison for contempt.

11–032 There is no fee for issuing a subpoena.

When used?

11–033 The use of the subpoena procedure is recommended in the following circumstances:

(1) where it is clear that someone has the original last will but is refusing to hand it over, or lodge it at the registry: use a subpoena to bring it in under s.123;

(2) where there is doubt about due execution or compliance with s.9 of the Wills Act 1837: use the subpoena for examination of the attesting witnesses and any other person who can give evidence of execution under s.122;

(3) where a person has failed or refused to answer a subpoena to produce a will under s.123: the practice here is to subpoena him under s.122 to attend court and be examined about his knowledge. This is better than seeking to commit him to prison for failing to answer to the subpoena under s.123; see above, para. 11–029.

(4) where attesting witnesses have refused voluntarily to answer questions about the circumstances of execution, often having been required by a district judge, or registrar to provide such evidence of execution where there is doubt on the face of the will. They are witnesses of the court and can be compelled to give evidence. (*Re Fuld (No. 2)* [1965] P. 405 at 410).

11–034 In each case the use of the subpoena procedure may be a quick and relatively inexpensive procedure and an alternative to issuing a claim form in the Chancery Division. In most cases the issue of the validity of the will or its existence will be resolved quickly, one way or the other.

CONTENTIOUS PROBATE 109

The hearing after service of the subpoena and the submission of evidence

Section 122
In the case of subpoenas under s.122 for witnesses to the will to give evidence, there will be a hearing before the district judge or registrar, and he will decide whether or not the evidence can allow the will to be admitted to probate in common form. It will be so admitted if there is, on the balance of probability, no doubt about the validity of the will. **11–035**

Section 123
In the case of subpoenas under s.123, once the will has been brought in to the registry and examined, that is usually an end of the matter. However, if there is doubt about the validity of the will (*e.g.* doubt about execution, or attestation), it is open to the party concerned to issue a summons for a subpoena under s.122, and the hearing procedure described above will be followed. For obvious reasons the registry will not allow the will out of the building, and examination by, for example, handwriting experts can only take place under supervision. These are matters where the court may have to set out what is to happen or make an Order for inspection. **11–036**

Difficult cases
If after the hearing of the evidence under s.122 it appears that the formalities required under s.9 of the Wills Act 1837 have not been complied with, or that there is some other reason (*e.g.* possible forgery of the signature of the deceased) why probate cannot be granted of what appears to be the last will, the district judge or registrar will so rule and will not be able to grant common form probate of the will. It will then be for a party who seeks to propound that will to issue a claim form in the Chancery Division for proof in solemn form of that will; see the procedure under CPR r.57 below, para. 11–046. Failing that, an earlier will or an intestacy will prevail and a grant on that footing will be made in common form. **11–037**

If after the service of a subpoena under s.123, and at the hearing of the evidence in the affidavits served by the parties, it is clear that the original last will has been lost or accidentally destroyed, or, if destroyed, not destroyed in a manner to satisfy s.20 of the Wills Act 1837, the district judge or registrar may direct one of the parties to issue a claim form in the Chancery Division for proof of that will and its due execution. That will require admission of the evidence of the contents of the will (*e.g.* by a copy or by other evidence as to its terms) and of due execution; *e.g.* by examination of the attesting witnesses or **11–038** admission of their witness statements. (See the procedure under CPR r.57 below, para. 11–046).

Sugden v Lord St Leonards (1876) 1 P.D. 154 is an example of the admission of the oral evidence of the deceased's daughter who was able to give evidence of the contents of the deceased's will and of its execution and attestation. Notwithstanding his eminence and his office as Lord Chancellor, on Lord St Leonards' death his will could not be found. However, it was his frequent practice to read his will over to his daughter before retiring to bed and from that tradition she was able to recollect the terms of it. The daughter was a beneficiary under the will of which she gave evidence, but her evidence was not treated as self-serving.

Concerning the proof of contents of wills and their execution and attestation, and for the rebuttal of the presumption of revocation where the original was in the testator's custody, but cannot be found, see above, para. 9–017. That presumption will not, of course, apply where the original was held by the solicitor and it was lost or accidentally destroyed while in his custody. Proof of the execution and attestation of wills which were destroyed in the Blitz during the Second World War are now a great rarity. One of the authors does, however, recall one case in which he was counsel where the original will was lost accidentally while being sent by railway from the High Court in London to the Palatine Court in Manchester prior to the hearing of a contested probate action there. A short hearing took place before Blackett-Ord V.-C. at the conclusion of the contested probate action to prove the execution and attestation of the will in favour of which the court had declared, using a copy. Both attesting witnesses were able to give evidence to satisfy the court that the lost will had been executed and attested. The draft copy was admitted to probate. (*Re Kingsley dec'd* 1981).

The forms of summons, affidavit and subpoena are set out in the Appendices.

*When **not** to use the subpoena procedure*

11–039 The subpoena procedure is not appropriate where there is *already* doubt about the inherent validity of a will where the deceased may have lacked mental capacity or was subject to undue influence or did not know and approve of the terms of the will. In such cases the proper course is to consider a contentious probate claim in the Chancery Division under CPR r.57. (See below, para. 11–046).

The use of sections 122 and 123 after the contentious probate claim has started

11–040 Where a contentious probate claim has been commenced and it is necessary to bring in a testamentary document to the court, or for someone to attend court to give evidence during that claim, the procedure under ss.122 and 123 is governed by CPR r.57 PD, para.7. It is rare, but it sometimes occurs that during such a claim, there is a refusal (for example) to produce a testamentary document, in which case para. 7 of CPR r.57 PD allows the court to issue a witness summons under those sections. (Note: There is the general right to require an unwilling witness to turn up to give evidence, and a witness summons can be issued and served on that person under CPR r.34, so that person will be required to attend Court to give evidence). Under CPR r.57 PD, para. 7, an application can be made to a Master (in the Chancery Division), to a District Judge (where the contentious probate claim is in a Chancery district registry or in the county court) or to the trial judge. This is a specific right under ss.122 or 123 of the Supreme Court Act 1981. Such applications will usually be made in the early stages of the claim where the missing document or the witness has been identified and the need arises to examine a witness as to his knowledge of documents or events at that stage. It may be appropriate to issue any applications so as to be returnable on the hearing of the Case Management Conference ("CMC") and for directions to be given then on the hearing of the evidence.

Problem areas and special cases

Certain problems crop up fairly frequently after caveats have been entered, there has been a warning to it and the caveator has entered an appearance to the warning. These are: **11–041**

(1) where the caveator has entered an appearance but will not issue a probate claim form;

(2) where the caveator has entered an appearance but will not issue a probate claim form and where those *prima facie* entitled to take a grant are concerned about interest on unpaid inheritance tax or other problems created by a "foreign" estate; and

(3) where all the above factors are present and there may be some other need to take steps to administer the estate.

In these types of case there are a number of courses open. These are: **11–042**

(1) The party who wants to get a grip on the estate administration pending determination of any probate claim can apply for a grant *ad colligenda bona* under NCPR r.52 before a claim is issued. A grant pending suit under s.117

of the Supreme Court Act 1981 is only available once legal proceedings have begun, for under that section they must be "pending". NCPR r.44(1) allows such a grant to be taken notwithstanding the entry of the caveat. This will allow the getting in of assets for their protection, or their sale to pay inheritance tax and other debts and liabilities, but will not allow distribution; see also CPR r.57 PD, para 8. Note that the court may allow the administrator under a grant under s.117 to charge; s.117(3). It is suggested that the court has an inherent jurisdiction to allow fees to be charged in the case of a grant *ad colligenda bona*. (*Daniel v Abiola* [2003] EWHC Civ 1562).

(2) That party can apply under NCPR r.44(13) by summons for an order that the caveat cease to have effect, on the ground that the caveator has done nothing to progress his claim and that the caveat should be removed. (See also above, para. 11–024 where this point is made in the general context of events after an appearance has been entered to a warning). This application may have the effect of the caveator issuing a probate claim form or being required by the District Judge or Registrar to do so within a short time, failing which the caveat will cease to have effect. See *Re Magson* [2003] cited at 11–024.

(3) That party can end the stalemate and issue the probate claim form as a claimant. (See the "pros and cons" of this below, para. 11–047).

Costs in non-contentious probate business

11–043 Under NCPR r.63 the Probate Registrar or District Judge has power to determine by whom and to what extent the costs of any application dealt with by him on summons are to be paid. Applications by summons will include a summons for directions in respect of a caveat, a summons for an appointment of a personal representative under s.116 of the Supreme Court Act 1981, and applications by summons for production of documents or examination of witnesses under ss.122 and 123 of that Act.

11–044 Under NCPR r.60 the majority of the provisions of CPR rr.43, 44, 47 and 48 apply to costs in non-contentious probate matters, save as modified by that rule. NCPR r.60, as substituted by SI 2003/185 (L3); see Chapter 16 for the way in which the court determines costs under the CPR rules referred to. The discretion as to costs, whether indemnity costs are to be awarded, and assessment will accordingly be applied in this jurisdiction as in ordinary civil claims. The general rule that costs will follow the event will, therefore, be a warning to those with hopeless applications, or to those who use caveats improperly.

Appeals on costs matters in non-contentious probate matters from a district judge, a Costs Judge, or a Registrar, lie to a High Court Judge; (NCPR r.60(9)). The scale fees for the determination of costs will be as in the Supreme Court Fees Order 1999 (see NCP Fees Order 1999, Sch. 1, item 10).

Bringing a probate claim

A "probate claim" is defined in Pt. 57 r.1(2) as follows: **11–045**

1(2) In this Part:

    (a) "probate claim" means a claim for—

        (i) the grant of probate of the will, or letters of administration of the estate, of a deceased person;
        (ii) the revocation of such a grant; or
        (iii) a decree pronouncing for or against the validity of an alleged will;
        not being a claim which is non-contentious (or common form) probate business;
        (Section 128 of the Supreme Court Act 1981 defines non-contentious (or common form) probate business.) [See para. 1–003 above.]

    (b) "relevant office" means—

        (i) in the case of High Court proceedings in a Chancery district registry, that registry;
        (ii) in the case of any other High Court proceedings, Chancery Chambers at the Royal Courts of Justice, Strand, London WC2A 2LL; and
        (iii) in the case of county court proceedings, the office of the county court in question;

    (c) "testamentary document" means a will, a draft of a will, written instructions for a will made by or at the request of, or under the instructions of, the testator, and any document purporting to be evidence of the contents, or to be a copy, of a will which is alleged to have been lost or destroyed;

    (d) "will" includes a codicil.

The claim form

11–046 The formal requirements are in CPR r.57 and r.57 PD. The claim form must be in Form N1A.

Parties

Who should be claimant?

11–047 It is tempting for the person who has lodged the caveat and entered an appearance to the warning ("the caveator"; see above, para. 11–002 *et seq.* above) to be the claimant in the contentious probate claim. After all, he has asserted the invalidity of the will which would otherwise have been admitted to probate in common form. That person may also be inclined to "start the ball rolling" and may well be advised that, as a claimant, he will be in the driving seat, so it is better to start the claim than wait for it to be issued and served on him.

11–048 But there are some circumstances where it may be preferable to wait for the person warning the caveat to start the claim and for that person to be the claimant. These circumstances are: where the caveator has an interest in proving the will purely as a named executor, and has no beneficial interest (save possibly in a very small legacy — whether or not conditional on proving) in the deceased's estate under that will or any earlier disposition of the estate. Thus solicitors, accountants, banks and other professionals will only have an interest in the estate by virtue of proving. In the majority of cases, there is the expectation of the fees earned when administering the estate. The beneficiaries may, of course, press the named executor to take out the claim form and be the claimant. The named executor may have been a very close family friend and adviser. His bond with the deceased is translated into a firm bond of trust with the surviving spouse, children, or other friends and relations. But that named executor must consider the following before he embarks on a claim to prove the will in solemn form as a claimant:

(1) He is not obliged to prove the will; he can refuse if he wants to. See para. 16–018, for the extent to which he can seek the directions of the court as to what to do.

(2) What will happen if he loses? As is pointed out below, para. 16–002, he may have to pay the costs of all other parties, and his own costs in addition.

(3) If he is to prove the will and be claimant, has he got sufficient protection against any costs liabilities? Are

indemnities on offer from the beneficiaries? Are they worthless if those beneficiaries get nothing in the event of the claim being lost? If they are worth something in any event, how much will that be and how can that be enforced? Has the prospect of those beneficiaries seeking assessment of any costs for which they may be liable under an indemnity been considered? See s.71 of the Solicitors Act 1974.

(4) On what evidence will he rely?

(5) Is there a conflict of interest which makes it undesirable that he should take any active role to prove the will, for example where he, as the solicitor taking the deceased's instructions and arranging for execution, was possibly negligent in failing to ensure that the "golden if tactless rule" was complied with, or that the formal requirements of s.9 were complied with, without any room for doubt? In such a case it is preferable that the allegedly negligent solicitor should stand by and await the outcome of the claim. No doubt the solicitor will give assistance to those who will be seeking to prove the will and his insurers will expect him to do that. *Worby v Rosser* [1999] Lloyd's Rep. P.N. 972 is an example of a solicitor's negligent failure to check testamentary capacity where the will for which he was responsible was not admitted to probate and where a negligence claim followed. The loss to the beneficiaries was the costs of the claim which were not recoverable by the estate from the impecunious defendant who was found liable to pay those costs at trial but, being in receipt of Legal Aid, could not afford to pay them.

In all these cases the person entitled to take the grant should *not* be the claimant.

Consider also the following factors against being a claimant: **11–049**

(1) The lure of the fees to be earned once probate is granted should not allow the person entitled to the grant to be confused as to his responsibilities. It is often far better that the professional person should stand back, giving such assistance as may be appropriate, and await the order of the court. If the court pronounces in favour of that will, he will be able to take the grant and earn the fees. If the court decides otherwise, he will not get them, unless he proves an earlier will. In either case, the risk of an adverse costs order in the litigation is too great. Relevant evidence can still be given (*e.g.* as to the events surrounding the taking of instructions) by a named

executor, whether that person is a party or not. Such a party who is joined as a defendant can file a defence saying that he will take no part in the claim and abide by any order of the court. See below, para. 16–007.

(2) Where the use of the "notice to cross-examine" under CPR r.57.5 is open to a defendant; see below, para. 16–007, for details as to the use of this notice It is important to note that the use of the notice to cross-examine is available only to a defendant and *not* to a claimant.

As is explained below, para. 16–007 the advantage of the use of the notice to cross-examine is that even if the defendant using it loses, he will generally not have an order for costs made against him. So it offers huge protection against adverse costs orders — although the unsuccessful defendant will be left with his own costs to pay.

11–050 In considering who should be claimant, the use of the notice to cross-examine, available to defendants only, can make the decision whether or not to be the claimant an almost forgone conclusion *against* being the claimant. For example. Mr A, the deceased's solicitor, was responsible for the deceased's penultimate will, about which there is no doubt as to validity. The last will was a home made one, in very different terms to the earlier will, and it seems reasonable to suppose that s.9 may not have been complied with. There are statements from the attesting witnesses that one of them was paralytically drunk, after a drinking session with the deceased, at the time of execution and that his "signature" was in fact written by the other witness as "a lark".

11–051 If Mr A (supported by the beneficiaries under the penultimate will) is claimant, he will not only have no direct evidence to put to challenge the validity of the last will, but if he loses he will be potentially liable for his own costs and those of the successful defendants parties. However, If Mr A (or the beneficiaries under the penultimate will) are defendants, they will be able to use the notice to cross-examine. Moreover, Mr A can simply put in a formal defence stating that he will abide by any order the court may make. He will have no significant — if any — costs exposure or risk.

11–052 The conclusion is, therefore, that:

(1) claimants should only be those who *need* to bring the claim;

(2) they must understand the risks as to costs and the lack of any protection such as defendants may have under a notice to cross-examine;

(3) professionals named as executors should not be claimants — unless they are on "copper bottomed" terms such as indemnities; and

(4) in all cases *think* before being a claimant and avoid succumbing to pressure to be one.

See below, para. 16–018 as to how far directions can be sought by claimants who seek the protection of court Orders in probate claims. Intending claimants in such claims have to make up their own minds in most cases as to whether to bring the claim or not.

Who should be defendant?
As explained in detail below, at para. 11–055, those who should be defendants will be those who have a contrary interest to the claimant. They will, in general terms, be those entitled under a will which prevails if the claimant loses, or those entitled on intestacy if the will propounded by the claimant is not upheld, there being no other testamentary disposition, *i.e.* those with a "contrary interest" to the claimant. **11–053**

In practice this means: **11–054**

(1) Where the claimant asserts that the last dated will is the true last will, the defendants will be those entitled under the immediately preceding will, or if there is none (or so it appears), those entitled on intestacy.

(2) Where the claimant either asserts that a will which predates the last dated will is the true last will, or asserts an intestacy, the defendants will be those entitled under the last dated will.

(3) Where the claimant asserts that there is no valid will and asserts an intestacy, the defendants will be those entitled under any, or the last dated will.

(4) In revocation claims, those who have taken the grant which the claimant seeks to revoke *must* be the defendants; see CPR r.57.6(1). It is not thought necessary to join those to whom power has been reserved, or the principals under an attorney grant, or the minor under a minority grant. However, as the point may not always be clear, the court can be asked to deal with any such potential parties at the first CMC; see below, para. 12–024. It is also desirable to join those with a beneficial interest under the will, or entitled in accordance with the intestacy which has been the subject of the grant.

11–055 Join those with beneficial interests. They will be:

(1) Those who are residuary legatees — or the representatives of any estate taking such an interest

(2) Those with major, or significant legacies or devises — in form of size or value.

(3) Those who may be entitled to a grant if the claimant fails — although this is not required where a large potential class may be so entitled, such as the partners in a firm of solicitors.

(4) Where there are codicils, care must be given to analyse the effect of any codicil and to determine whether it is accepted as a valid testamentary document. The rules as to revival and republication under s.20 of the Wills Act 1837 may also have to be considered carefully. These principles, coupled with the effect of any codicils, may require additional defendants to be joined, or notified of the claim.

11–056 At para. 11–065 below, consideration is given to the representation of defendants, and notice to non-parties under CPR r.19; see also r.57 PD, para. 4 indicating that the first CMC is the time to sort out any points as to parties.

11–057 Having reached the stage of deciding that a probate claim has to be brought, the following stages are dealt with below:

Stage 1 — steps to be taken by a claimant when bringing the claim

Stage 2 — what a claimant must put in the claim form

Stage 3 — a claimant's statement of testamentary documents

Stage 4 — issuing and serving the claim form and statement of documents

Stage 5 — what a defendant must do when served with the claim form and statement of documents

Stage 6 — what a defendant must do if he has a counterclaim to make

Stage 7 — what a defendant must do if he has a claim against another defendant or any other person who is not already a party

Stage 1: steps to be taken by a claimant when bringing the claim

A claimant must decide in which Court he is going to bring his claim

High Court or county court?
CPR r.57 r.2 limits probate claims to: **11–058**

(1) the Chancery Division of the High Court; and

(2) County Courts where there is also a Chancery District Registry, *but nowhere else*.

That means (aside from the High Court in London) that probate claims can only be brought in the Chancery District Registries in Birmingham, Bristol, Cardiff, Leeds, Liverpool, Manchester, Newcastle upon Tyne and Preston, The Central London County Court — or in the County Courts there.

As the County Court limit is still £30,000 (being the value of the net estate — see s.32 of the County Courts Act and the High Court and County Courts Jurisdiction Order 1991), it is hard to imagine that many claims, if any, will now be brought in that court. The text below assumes that a claim will be issued in the High Court unless otherwise stated. **11–059**

It is also important to note the *very* important distinction between the *contentious* probate jurisdiction, which is in the Chancery Division of the High Court, and the *non-contentious* probate jurisdiction, which is in the Family Division (Probate) of the High Court. (See ss.25 and 128 of the Supreme Court Act 1981, and CPR r.57.1(2)(a) and r.57.2 for the definitions of which is which.) Within the financial limit set out above, the County Court has jurisdiction in contentious probate claims. There have been proposals from time to time to place the non-contentious probate business into the County Court system, at least outside London, but that has not found favour in a number of quarters, and "root and branch" reform of this aspect of the law is, at present, not under consideration. **11–060**

A claimant must pay the issue fee
This is currently £120. There is remission of the whole fee for those who are in receipt of a "qualifying benefit" and also remission of the whole or part of the fee where, owing to the exceptional circumstances of the case, payment of the fee would involve undue financial hardship. **11–061**

Stage 2: what claim form must be used in a probate claim and what must a claimant put in the claim form?

11–062 A claimant must use Form N2. He should follow the notes for the claimant in a probate claim set out in Form N2A. This is the form which is specially adapted for use in all probate claims. He must also serve Forms N2B (probate claim notes for the defendant) and N3 (acknowledgement of service form for probate claims), and lodge a completed form N205D (notice of issue). The court will serve Form N205D (notice of issue) after the court has issued the claim form, unless you have indicated that you will serve it. (See the Appendices for sample forms.) CPR r.7 will apply to all probate claims CPR r.57.3(b)). They are all assigned to the multi-track 2(4).

11–063 The Claimant must consider the following specific matters:

(1) the heading (see CPR r.57 PD, para. 2);

(2) the identity of the parties; and

(3) the interest which each party has.

11–064 Unique to probate claims is the requirement that the claimant and all other parties lodge with the court all testamentary documents and lodge and serve on all other parties a witness statement dealing with such documents, under CPR r.57.5 and CPR r.57 PD, para. 3. This is dealt with in detail below, at para. 11–077. It is vitally important that the rules as to lodging testamentary documents and lodging and serving statements relating to them are grasped at an early, pre-claim stage, as compliance is now required by the claimant on issue and on a defendant when he acknowledges service, unless the court otherwise directs. The policy behind the CPR requirements is to ensure that, *at the earliest possible stage,* all parties are aware of the state of the wills and documents. A failure to disclose them may cause major revisions to be made to claims at a late stage with heavy costs consequences for the defaulting party. The CPR rules in this respect represent a major shift in timing in terms of disclosure of the testamentary documents compared with the old rules in force before October 15, 2001. Paragraph 11–077 below considers this in detail.

11–065 As to the parties, the claimant (or claimants) will be those having an interest in seeking the relief claimed. As discussed above, para. 11–047, the claimant will usually have a financial interest in the outcome. A claimant (or claimants) will need to consider who must be joined as defendants. There are no hard and fast rules as to who they must be, but the general principles are as follows:

(1) Those who are entitled to the estate, or to take a grant to it, in default of the claimant being successful, must be defendants, but not, for example, small value legatees.

(2) If the class is very numerous, one member of the class can be joined and a representation order sought under CPR r.19.6. The first CMC is the time to seek this and the other orders referred to below at para. 12–004; CPR r.57 PD, para.4(1) specifically refers to this.

(3) If there are potential members of the class who are not ascertained (*e.g.* a large number of statutory next of kin entitled in the event of an intestacy) then an Order that one party represents that class can be made under CPR r.19.7.

(4) It may be necessary to consider whether the procedure under CPR r.19.8A should be used so as to avoid the need to join a large number of defendants at the initial stage. Once again, this point often arises where there are large numbers of persons potentially entitled on an intestacy, or where there are a large number of legatees under a will which is being challenged. This enables the court to direct that notice of the claim be given to a non-party with a request that such a person decides whether or not to acknowledge service and become a party to the claim, or does not do so and becomes bound by any judgment in the claim as if he was a party. (See CPR r.57 PD, para. 4 and s.47 of the Administration of Justice Act 1985; see also below, Appendix II).

(5) Those under a disability within the meaning of CPR r.21 (*i.e.* a child or a patient within the meaning of the Mental Health Act 1983) must be represented by their litigation friend.

The claim form will contain the standard question about whether the claim raises issues under the Human Rights Act 1998. Although proper thought must be given in all claims as to what answer should be given, in probate claims it invariably will be "no". The authors consider that contested probate claims are unlikely to raise questions under that Act, but that is not to say that there could be unusual claims when an issue under the Act could be said to arise. At present, that is speculation so no attempt is made here to outline any potential issues in this area. It is not thought, in particular, that the formalities of the Wills Act 1837, or any other statutory rules (*e.g.* under the NCPR) are incompatible with Convention rights.

11–066

The statement of case: What must go into the statement of case in the claim form?

11–067 CPR r.57.7 contains detailed provisions about what must go into the statement of case, and this will constitute the particulars of claim on the claim form. Reference must also be made to the CPR r.57 Practice Direction ("CPR r.57 PD").

11–068 As is stated above, CPR r.57.3(b) establishes that the CPR r.7 procedure applies to probate claims. Therefore, CPR r.7.4(1) applies and that states that the particulars of claim must be served either with the claim form, or within 14 days of service of the claim form if those particulars are not served with it. CPR r.7.5(2) states the general rule that the claim form must be served within four months after the date of issue.

11–069 There are three primary rules to observe when drafting the statement of case. These are:

> (1) That the interest of each party must be stated, with reasons. If there is a dispute about the interest of a party (as stated), the fact that it is disputed must be stated, with reasons (CPR r.57.7(1), (2).
>
> (2) That the grounds on which a will is alleged to be invalid must be set out (CPR r.57.7(3), (4)).
>
> (3) That a defendant can serve a notice with his defence that he will not raise a positive case and that, as he is insisting on solemn form proof, he will cross-examine the attesting witnesses; (CPR r.57.7(5). See also above, at para. 11–047, as to reasons for not being a claimant.

Taking each of the primary rules in turn, the analysis is as follows:

(1) A statement of the interest of each party

11–070 This means that the claimant must say in what capacity he is claiming, *e.g.* as the sole executor and residuary legatee of a will dated X, in respect of which solemn form proof is sought. The claimant must also say what interest the defendant(s) may have, *e.g.* on an intestacy, or under a different will. In a case where, for example, part of a will is in doubt (*e.g.* a page which the claimant alleges was inserted later and did not form part of the will on execution) the claimant will state that he is interested in the will dated X as the sole executor and sole residuary legatee, but without the additional page, and that solemn form proof is sought of the will, but without that page. There are many variations, including claims where the claimant is seeking to revoke an existing grant, or to challenge the right of a person who has entered a caveat claiming to be entitled to the estate on intestacy, and where that person's claim to an interest is denied, *e.g.* because there was no valid marriage between the caveator and the deceased, or that he was not a child of the deceased.

(2) Setting out the grounds on which the will is invalid
In each case where it is contended (or where a party wishes to contend): **11–071**

(a) that the testator did not know and approve of the contents of the will; or

(b) that the will was not duly executed; or

(c) that the testator lacked testamentary capacity; or

(d) that the execution of the will was obtained by undue influence or fraud,

the contentions must be set out, as must the particulars of the facts and matters relied on (CPR r.57.7(3), (4)).

It seems clear from the terms of CPR rr.57.7(3) and 57.7(4) that each contention must be supported by its own facts, which must be set out. It is equally clear that in some cases there may be an overlap between the facts which support (for example) a contention that there was want of capacity and those which support (for example) a contention that there was want of knowledge and approval. The same overlap may occur as between a contention of want of capacity and one of undue influence. **11–072**

The need for clarity
There is authority which makes it plain that the court will be alert to a party who sets out his contentions in such a way that, while he may be keen to assert his claim on one basis, he may be afraid to assert it on another basis; this is often referred to as "being willing to wound, but afraid to strike". This means that if a case is being put forward on the basis of want of knowledge and approval, the facts and matters set out in the claim form under *that* heading cannot be used in an *alternative* contention based on undue influence, without an express claim to that effect. See, for example *Re Stott* [1980] 1 W.L.R. 246. The rules then in force (RSC, Ord. 76, r.9(3), were in such terms that no allegation in support of a plea of want of knowledge and approval which would be "relevant in support of" a plea of want **11–073**

of due execution, of capacity, or of undue influence or fraud was to be made, unless that other allegation was also pleaded. The question in that case was whether the pleaded particulars in the plea of want of knowledge and approval were "relevant" to a plea of undue influence and should, therefore, be struck out. It was held by Slade J. that the particulars in the pleaded case before him were not in themselves sufficient to prove undue influence and accordingly would not be struck out. It was also held that the meaning of the words "relevant in support of" meant that the person pleading the case had to avoid making an affirmative allegation of undue influence (or want of due execution or of capacity) unless such an allegation was also expressly pleaded. Under CPR r.57.7 the wording of the rule is now different, but it is clear that the principle that the basis on which a contention as to invalidity of a will is made must be expressly stated with supporting particulars of the facts and matters relied on is still a good one and must be observed. The relevant rules were in fact drawn up with that case and the principle stated above in mind. Clarity of the claim being put forward is a vital element in litigation under the CPR and probate claims are an instance where the rules stress this.

11–074 The precedents in the Appendices show how the particulars under each claim may be set out. There is, of course, no reason why each contention as to invalidity should not be put in the alternative, with the facts and matters relied on under each contention set out and, if necessary, with cross-references to the facts and matters under other contentions. (Note that it is interesting to compare CPR r.57.7(3) with r.57.7(4), where the former begins with the words "Any party who contends . . ." that the testator did not know and approve of the contents of the will and the latter which commences "Any party who wishes to contend . . ." that the other grounds of invalidity apply. Quite why this difference is present is not clear and it may not be a significant one in practice.)

11–075 It would seem clear that the rules in CPR r.16 and CPR r.16 PD (as apply to statements of case and particulars of claim in all other claims) will apply to probate claims in any case. Thus in claims where there is a lack of testamentary intention (lacking, for example, in *Corbett v Newey* [1998] Ch. 57), where the document pretending to be a will was not one, or where the testator was not of age, particulars have to be given of the facts and matters relied on.

(3) Defendant's notice to cross-examine

11–076 This applies to defendants only but is mentioned here as part of the treatment of the rules which apply to the statement of case. (See also above, para. 11–049). This notice *must* be served with the defence, and is usually part of it. There is no power in the court to allow such a notice to be given later, although it is suggested that such a notice could be put in the defence by an amendment of that defence allowed under CPR r.17, on terms as to costs against the amending party.

The important consequence of using the notice to cross-examine will be that a defendant who uses it, even if unsuccessful, will not have an adverse costs Order against him (See below, Chapter 16, as to the principles relating to awards of costs in probate claims). The protection is lost if the court considers there was no reasonable ground for opposing the will; thus only in "hopeless" cases will a defendant be at risk of an Order for costs against him. The service of such a notice and the costs protection offers would not appear to extend to Orders for costs against the defendant's legal representatives under CPR r.48.7. The protection afforded by the notice to cross-examine is referred to as a specific example of an instance where the court may depart from the general rule that the unsuccessful party pays the successful party's costs in CPR r.44.3(2). See CPR r.44 PD 2, General Rules About Costs, s.8 para. 8.2; also see Chapter 16 on costs.

Stage 3: a claimant's statement of testamentary documents

CPR r.57.5 and CPR r.57 PD, para. 3
What are testamentary documents is defined by CPR r.57.1(2)(c). 11–077

> *"testamentary document" means a will, a draft of a will, written instructions for a will made by or at the request of, or under the instructions of, the testator, and any document purporting to be evidence of the contents, or to be a copy, of a will which is alleged to have been lost or destroyed.*

Note, however, the following:
(1) The width of the definition. All such documents must be lodged in original form (or, where copies only are in existence, in the "best copy" form). Copies of documents lodged must form the exhibits to the statement.
(2) The obligation on the maker of the statement to say who has possession or control of any document, if it is not with the maker. If he does not know that, he must say so; CPR r.57.5(3).

The obligation to lodge the testamentary documents and file the statement of documents is mandatory for *all* parties, unless the court gives permission for a party not to do so. If it does it will 11–078 expect compliance within a stated period of time. The usual ground for seeking further time is because that party needs to issue the claim form as a matter of urgency, and that it will take longer than anticipated to find the relevant documents, *e.g.* where a solicitor's will files have been mislaid. It may also be the case that there is an application under s.117 of the Supreme Court Act 1981 (grant pending suit; see above, para. 11–041) or pending application for delivery up of a will under s.123 of that Act, which means that not all the documents are to hand (see CPR r.57 PD, para. 3). Unless you have complied with the rules as to testamentary documents, you cannot inspect the other party's documents which have been filed, save with the leave of the court.

11–079 It is not generally possible to remove testamentary documents from the court once lodged until the end of the claim, and those needing to inspect them (*e.g.* handwriting experts) will need a direction from the Master or the District Judge of the court where the documents are lodged, so as to allow inspection under supervision of a court official, or for them to be released under strict conditions for examination, or analysis by such an expert. This rule also applies to a grant in a revocation action which under CPR r.57.6(2) must be lodged in Court.

11–080 On the commencement of a probate claim the court where the claim is issued sends a notice to the Leeds District Probate Registry requesting that all testamentary documents, grants of representation and other relevant documents (which may have been lodged at a probate registry) are sent to that court; CPR r.57 PD, para. 2.3. This ensures that the court has everything it needs and can at the first CMC (when all the testamentary documents not otherwise sent from Leeds should be in court), check what is and what is not in court. This is important if there are a number of wills potentially in issue.

11–081 The combined effect of NCPR r.45 and CPR r.57 PD, para. 2.4 is that the issue of a probate claim form has the effect that no grant (save under s.117 of the Supreme Court Act 1981 or a grant *ad colligenda bona*) can be issued without an order of the court; NCPR (r.44(1)). (See above at para. 11–016, for the effect of issuing a probate claim form and for s.117 grants.)

The Appendices contain a precedent of a statement of documents which must comply with CPR r.57.5 and CPR r.57 PD, para. 3.2. It is in the form of the annex to CPR r.57.

11–082 Finally, it is important to note that the statement about testamentary documents must be signed by the party *personally* or (if a child or patient) by his litigation friend and *not* by his solicitor, or other representative. (CPR r.57 PD, para 3.2(2)).

Stage 4: Issuing and serving the claim form, lodging the testamentary documents and filing the statement of documents

Revocation claims
Note the requirement to lodge the testamentary documents and file the statement of testamentary documents referred to above at para. 11–077. This must be done at the time of issue, unless the court has directed otherwise under CPR r.57.5, or under CPR r.57 PD, para. 3.3. **11–083**

Note also the requirement (in a claim to revoke an existing grant of representation) that the grant be lodged, if the claimant has it, when he issues the claim form; CPR r.57.6(2). The grant must be lodged at "the relevant office", which is defined in CPR r.57.1(2)(b) as either: (a) the registry of the Chancery District Registry in which the proceedings are issued (*e.g.* Birmingham; see above, para. 11–058); (b) in the case of any other High Court proceedings (*e.g.* those issued in the High Court in London), the Chancery Chambers at the Royal Courts of Justice, Strand, London WC2A 2LL; or (c) where the claim is issued in a county court, the office of the county court from which the claim form is issued. The same requirement to lodge the grant applies where the defendant has the grant and he must lodge it at the relevant office when acknowledging service; see below, para. 11–090. **11–084**

Issue of the claim form
See above, para. 11–058 for the relevant court offices from which a probate claim form can be issued, as defined by CPR r.7.1(2)(b). The current issue fee is £120; see above, para. 11–061. **11–085**

Service of the claim form

(a) *Within the jurisdiction*
CPR r.6 will apply to such service; see rr.1–5 thereof. Alternative service may be effected under r.8, *e.g.* an advertisement in a national, or local newspaper. This may be required in the case of next of kin entitled on intestacy whose last address has been lost. **11–086**

(b) *Outside the jurisdiction*
Where service outside the jurisdiction is required, CPR r.6.17ff. and the relevant Practice Direction apply. Probate claims fall within CPR r.6.20(13) and the permission of the court will be needed under that ground. Unlike the additional time allowed for a defendant to file an acknowledgement of service under CPR r.57.4(3) (see below, para. 11–092) there seems to be no **11–087**

additional period provided for a defendant who is outside the jurisdiction to file and serve his defence.

(c) Time for service from issue of the claim form

11–088 If within the jurisdiction, serve within four months of issue. If outside the jurisdiction, serve within six months of issue. The rules in CPR r.7.5 (time for service) and r.7.6 (extension of time for service) apply to probate claims.

Notice of issue

11–089 This is in Form 205D. If you (and not the court) are to serve the claim form and response forms on the defendant then you must effect service in accordance with the general rules in CPR r.6. (See the next stage where the acknowledgement of service requirement is dealt with). In probate claims, by virtue of CPR r.57.4(1), filing such an acknowledgement is *mandatory*; (*c.f.* CPR r.10.1(3)).

Stage 5: what a defendant must do when served with the claim form and statement of documents

File and serve the acknowledgement of service, lodge his testamentary documents and file his statement of documents

11–090 A defendant to a probate claim must use the special acknowledgement form, Form N3 (see below, Appendix I). He must also prepare and file his own statement of testamentary documents and lodge the documents referred to in it; CPR r.57.4(1) and r.57.5. (See above, para. 11–077 for what are testamentary documents). Any party who has not filed and served his own statement of documents will not be able to inspect the statement of documents and documents lodged under that statement by any other party. (CPR r.57.5(5)).

11–091 The court may give permission (under CPR r.57.5(5)) to relieve a party from this restriction, *e.g.* where a party may need to see what another party has filed before he can lodge his own documents and file his own statement, or where he is in some practical difficulty, such as where files have been mislaid and may not be recovered for some time. (See also CPR r.57 PD, para. 3.2).

11–092 He must file the acknowledgement of service form within 28 days from the date on which the claim form was served on him, (if it is contained the particulars of claim), or, if it is not and states that the particulars are to follow, he must do so within 28 days of the service of the particulars of claim; CPR r.57.4(2). CPR r.57.4(3) provides for an extra 14-day period for a defendant to acknowledge service beyond that specified in CPR r.6.22

or the relevant practice direction supplementing s.3 of CPR r.6. (See above, para. 11–087, for service out of the jurisdiction.) The extra time for acknowledging service is there to allow a defendant who is out of the jurisdiction time to find testamentary documents and make the statement about them, which must be filed on acknowledging service under CPR rr.57.5(2)(b) and r.57.5(4)(b). (See below, para. 11–095, about the lack of any extra time given by the rules for service of the defence.) In a claim to revoke an existing grant, if the defendant has the grant of representation, he must lodge it at the relevant office when he acknowledges service (CPR r.57.6(3); see also above, para. 11–058 and 11–084, as to what is the relevant office).

The acknowledgement of service form contains a "checklist" **11–093** which is designed to ensure that the defendant lodging it complies with the terms of CPR r.57.5 as regards testamentary documents.

Stage 6: what a defendant must do if he has a defence and/or a counterclaim to make

File and serve the defence and counterclaim
A defence (with or without a counterclaim) must be filed within **11–094** 28 days of the service of the particulars of claim. (CPR r.9 and CPR r.15.4(1)(b), as applied by CPR r.57.4(4)). Until particulars of claim are served on a defendant (where the claim form says they are to follow), he need not respond to the claim form until those particulars are served on him.

Where the defendant has been served out of the jurisdiction, **11–095** although he has the additional 14-day period in which to acknowledge service (see above, para. 11–092, the reason as stated there being that the defendant has to prepare his statement of documents and that may take longer when abroad, bearing in mind the need to communicate with persons in the UK or to arrange for searches of files, etc.), there appears to be no additional time given for that defendant to file his defence (and counterclaim) specifically in probate claims. Thus the usual rules set out by CPR r.6.23 and the accompanying Practice Direction will apply. The time allowed will depend on the country in which the defendant has been served (see CPR r.6.23). He may, of course, through his agents in the UK, apply for extra time. In complex claims, or where parties are in remote regions of the world, that will usually be given.

What must go into the defence?
A defence must comply with the terms of CPR r.57.7(3), (4) — **11–096** as explained above, para. 11–071 — if contentions are made about the validity of the will being claimed by the claimant. CPR

r.20 applies to counterclaims, save where CPR r.57 makes special rules. This means that if the counterclaim is served with the defence (which is usually the case), it can be served without the court's permission. If the counterclaim is served separately, permission will be needed, CPR r.20.4(2).

CPR r.57.8 contains special provisions about what a counterclaiming party must state in the counterclaim.

57.8 — Counterclaim

(1) *A defendant who contends that he has any claim or is entitled to any remedy relating to the grant of probate of the will, or letters of administration of the estate, of the deceased person must serve a counterclaim making that contention.*

(2) *If the claimant fails to serve particulars of claim within the time allowed, the defendant may, with the permission of the court, serve a counterclaim and the probate claim will then proceed as if the counterclaim were the particulars of claim.*

11–097 From CPR rr.57.7 and 57.8 it is important to remember that:

(1) A defendant must serve his notice to cross-examine with his defence if he is to fall within the costs protection of CPR r.57.7(5) (see above, para. 11–076, for the circumstances in which he may need to do this).

(2) A defendant who contends that he has any claim or is entitled to any remedy relating to the grant of representation in the estate must serve a counterclaim making that contention. This means that if a defendant wishes to claim, for example, that the true last will of the deceased was a later one than the claimant seeks to prove, or if a defendant wishes to claim that there should be an intestacy, he must make that contention in his counterclaim. It follows from this that a defendant must also make the necessary counter-assertion against the document which is put forward by the claimant.

(3) If the claimant fails to serve his particulars of claim within the time allowed, a defendant may obtain the permission of the court (on an application under CPR Pt 23) to serve a counterclaim, and the probate claim will then proceed as if the counterclaim were the particulars of claim; CPR r.57.8(2). CPR r.7.4(1) states that the particulars must be served either with the claim form or within 14 days of service if the claim form is not served with it. CPR r.7.5(2) states the general rule that the claim form must be served within four months after the date of issue.

CPR r.57.9 provides for what a defendant must do if he wants **11–098** to make a probate claim in other proceedings which are not in the nature of a probate claim. This rule has to be considered where, for example, a defendant in a claim which is not a probate claim (as defined by CPR r.57.1(2)(a)) wishes to bring a counterclaim which is in the nature of a probate claim *e.g.* where the claimant has issued a claim which seeks relief under the Inheritance Act 1975, or an estoppel interest in an estate, and the defendant wishes to contend that the last will (which may or may not have been admitted to probate) is not valid.

If such a counterclaim is made in claims which are not **11–099** probate claims, the claimant (*i.e.* the defendant to the counterclaim) can apply either to have the probate counterclaim dealt with in separate proceedings or to strike it out; the latter course might be proper not only where the probate counterclaim had no merits, but also where the probate counterclaim was quite inappropriate, having regard to the issues in the main claim. The party wishing to take advantage of these alternatives has seven days from the service of the probate counterclaim to do so; CPR r.57.9(4). If the court orders the probate counterclaim to be dealt with in separate proceedings, it will transfer the probate counterclaim to the Chancery Division, either to the High Court in London, to a Chancery District Registry, or to a County Court where there is such a registry, and that the court has jurisdiction there; CPR r.57.9(5).

If he does not make the application, or if the court refuses an **11–100** application to have the probate counterclaim dealt with in separate proceedings, or struck out, the court will do the following of its own motion:

(a) If the proceedings are not already in the Chancery Division it will transfer them to that Division, either in London, or a Chancery District Registry; CPR r.57.9(4)(a).

(b) If the County Court has jurisdiction, it will transfer the proceedings to a county court where there is a Chancery District Registry; (CPR r.57.9(4)(b).

It is clear from CPR r.57.9 that the court has a policy of **11–101** ensuring that probate counterclaims are kept within the right court and that they are managed at an early stage.

Once transferred with the main claim, or if treated as **11–102** separate proceedings, the court will be able to give directions under CPR r.3. This will include directions treating the probate counterclaim as the main claim, or that the hearing of the issues raised by the probate counterclaim are to be heard before the issues raised in the main claim. Where claims under the

Inheritance Act 1975 are being made this is often the proper course in view of the fact that the outcome of the probate counterclaim will determine the destination of the deceased's estate, and the 1975 Act claim comes after that is determined.

Reply and defence to counterclaim

(a) *Reply*

11-103 This is for the claimant to consider and is needed only if the defence raises an issue which cannot be dealt with under the general rule that there is an implied "joinder of issue" on the issues raised in the defence. The fact that a reply has not been served does not mean that the matters raised in the defence are admitted by the claimant; CPR r.16.7(1). CPR r.16.7(2) also provides that if a reply is served, which does not deal with a matter in the defence, the defendant still has to prove that matter. The effect of these rules is that, as most points raised in the defence will simply be either denials or non-admissions of the claimant's particulars of claim, there is no need to serve a reply to them. In such a case the claimant can simply dispute the defendant's version of events and put forward his own, as in the particulars of claim.

(b) *Serve a reply or amend the claim?*

11-104 Sometimes the defence will contain a new point. In probate claims that point will often relate to the circumstances in which the will in dispute was made; for example, the defendant may allege that the claimant exercised undue influence over the deceased, or the defendant will allege in his defence that there should be an intestacy against the will propounded by the claimant. If there is one, the claimant may then seek to propound an earlier will in the alternative. If that is so, the claimant should amend his claim (under CPR r.17) to bring in a new claim, as it is not usually appropriate to serve a reply setting out a new case. The amended claim may also be the occasion on which the claimant will want to raise the issue of revocation by a later will (raised by the defendant) being ineffective by reason of want of capacity. Or the claimant may want to allege that the will he seeks to propound was revived by a codicil, or some other instrument which satisfies s.22 of the Wills Act 1837 and which is later than the will which the defendant seeks to propound. In practice, such a need to amend would be rare in view of the fact that the claimant would in most cases have knowledge at an early stage of all the testamentary documents on which he will need to prove his claim. Under the general protocol, a protocol, or pre-claim letter should have "flushed out" any later codicils which might have declared an intention to revive an earlier revoked will. But the defendant's statement of documents can sometimes contain surprises which will force an amendment of the claimant's pleading. (See the notes in the White Book to CPR r.16.7 on the reply to a defence for details.)

11–105 It is important to note that the period for filing and service of a reply is geared by CPR r.15.8 to the claimant's filing of his allocation questionnaire, which will have been served on each party by the court earlier when a defendant files his defence; CPR r.26.3. The questionnaire, as completed, must be filed in court by the claimant with any reply to the defence; CPR. r.15.8. This must be done at least 14 days after it has been deemed to be served on him (under the provisions of CPR r.6.7) by the court; see CPR r.26.3(6). It is not possible for the parties to vary by agreement the time for filing the completed allocation questionnaire; see CPR r.26.3(6A). The court may, however, vary the time. Therefore, the reply must be filed at the same time as the completed allocation questionnaire, and within the 14-day period under CPR r.26.3(6). Although CPR r.57 probate claims are allocated to the multi-track (CPR r.57.2(4)) the practice of the court is to send out an allocation questionnaire. In any event the relevant form is Form N150 in Appendix I.

(c) *Defence to counterclaim*
11–106 This must be drawn, filed and served by a claimant whenever the defendant serves a counterclaim. It will often be preceded by a reply and the reply and defence to counterclaim should be in the same document; see CPR r.15 PD, para. 3.3 and CPR r.20 PD, para. 6.1. Save where CPR r.57 directs otherwise, CPR r.20 will apply to counterclaims in probate claims.

11–107 CPR r.57.7 will apply to the statement of case (and specific statements of the interest of parties in the estate) in the case of a defence to counterclaim, as it applies to statements of case in the claim form and by defendants in counterclaims.

11–108 Unless the defendant has raised a new allegation in his counterclaim (*e.g.* about a different will which has not been referred to in the claim form and particulars of claim), the claimant will simply repeat what his case is as set out in the claim form and particulars thereunder, by reference to that document. See below, para. 11–110, for what to do when a new point is made in a defence to counterclaim.

11–109 The period for filing and service of a defence to counterclaim is 14 days from service of the defence. (CPR r.15.4, as applied by CPR r.20.3 and CPR r.20 PD, para. 3).

(d) The counterclaiming defendant wants to raise a new issue in the light of the defence to counterclaim: what is the proper response from that defendant?

11-110 It is sometimes the case that the claimant's defence to counterclaim raises a new point to which the counterclaiming defendant will need to reply in accordance with the general rules governing a reply set out above. *E.g.* if the claimant's defence to counterclaim seeks to propound an alternative will, which the defendant now seeks to allege is also invalid. That defendant may need to file and serve a "reply to defence to counterclaim" and will need to set out the grounds on which he contends invalidity in accordance with CPR r.57.7. See the provisions about the reply above, para. 11-103. Alternatively, he may need to amend his counterclaim. See above, para. 11-104, where this is considered as an alternative to a reply. The preferable route is for the defendant to amend his counterclaim so that his entire claim is in that document. See CPR r.17 for rules about amendment.

(e) Further pleadings? None without leave

11-111 It is uncommon these days to need to consider any further pleadings by the parties to the claim. However, it is sometimes the case that a reply, whether to a defence, or to a defence to counterclaim, does raise a new issue with which the defendant should deal, which he cannot deal with by amendment of his defence. In such rare circumstances he will need to file and serve a "rejoinder". The leave of the court will be needed under CPR r.15.9.

Stage 7: what a defendant must do if he has a claim against another defendant or any other person who is not already a party?

CPR r.20 claims — claims against another defendant

11-112 See CPR r.20 and in particular r.20.5. The counterclaiming defendant will need to apply to the court for permission to add that defendant as a defendant to the counterclaim. The parties in the claim will then be as follows:

(1) AB claimant;

(2) CD, defendant/CPR r.20 claimant; and

(3) EF, CPR r.20 defendant.

(See also CPR r.20 PD, para. 7.1.)

These would be the parties, for example, if the facts were that AB wanted to prove will no. 1, and CD had a counterclaim for proof of will no. 2 against AB and EF.

CPR r.20 claims — claims against those who are not parties to the claim
See CPR r.20.5. As above, the leave of the court will be required. The parties to the claim will then be as follows: **11–113**

(1) AB, Claimant/CPR r.20 defendant;

(2) CD defendant/CPR r.20 claimant; and

(3) XY, CPR r.20 defendant.

(See also CPR r.20 PD, para. 7.2.)

These would be the parties, for example, if AB wanted to prove will no. 1 against CD and CD wanted to prove will no. 2 under which XY is entitled, but not AB.

It is uncommon for probate claims to raise issues where CPR r.20 claims have to be brought. **11–114**

If, for example, a party wishes to allege a solicitor's negligence in the preparation of a will and its execution, it is more appropriate to make that claim in separate proceedings.

It is beyond the scope of this book to analyse CPR r.20 claims in detail so reference should be made where necessary to CPR r.20 and to the notes in the White Book.

Other matters

(a) Non-availability of default judgment (CPR r.57.10)
Unlike most other CPR r.7 claims, r.7.10(1) prevents any party from getting judgment in default, under CPR r.12. But a claimant does have certain advantages where either one (or more) of several defendants fail to acknowledge service, or where no defendant acknowledges service or files a defence. In the former case the claimant can proceed as if the defaulting defendant has acknowledged service and can, therefore, await his defence. In the latter case the claimant can apply to the court for an Order that the claim is to proceed to trial. He must prove service of the claim form and any particulars of claim by filing written evidence of service. This situation allows the court to direct a hearing on written evidence only (CPR r.7.10(2), (3), (4), (5)). **11–115**

It is suggested that the court's case management powers under CPR r.3 are more than adequate to allow it to get to grips with a probate claim where any party is not prepared to file a defence. The rules above show how the court can, in effect, "fast **11–116** track" the claim where the claimant is faced with defendants who do not wish, or who are not prepared, to make their formal position clear.

(b) Defences stating that the defendant will simply abide by any Order the court may make

11–117 This is desirable where a defendant does not wish to take any active part in the claim, and can thereby avoid any costs Orders. The defendant who is only interested as a person to whom a grant can issue should adopt this position. (See above, para. 11–049, for "neutral" defendants.)

(c) Summary judgment under CPR r.25 and striking out under CPR r.3.4

(a) *Summary judgment for solemn form proof*

11–118 Under CPR r.57 this is permitted and there is no exclusion under CPR r.24.3(2). CPR r.57 PD, para. 5.1 allows an application for proof in solemn form on a summary judgment application, under CPR 24, provided that there is also written evidence proving due execution of the will which it is sought to prove. (Reference should be made to CPR r.24 and to the notes in the White Book for the practice in this area.) In a contested probate claim, in view of the threshold required for success in CPR r.24.2, it would have to be a plain case for proof in solemn form with no merit on the defendant's side. (Note the exclusion referred to above of any default judgment; see also CPR r.57.10.)

(ii) *Striking out*

11–119 It is also possible for a party in a probate claim to apply to strike out a claim under CPR r.3.4 in the circumstances listed there, including the absence of reasonable grounds for bringing or defending the claim, an abuse of process, or where there has been a failure (*inter alia*) to obey a court Order. In contested probate claims such applications are rare, particularly where a credible defence has been filed and served, for without a full trial it is usually impossible to assess the proper weight of the evidence on which the defence is based.

Where a defendant has served a notice to cross-examine under CPR r.57.7(5), the claimant's application for summary judgment is subject to the defendant's right to require the attesting witnesses to the will in question to attend court for cross-examination.

(d) Requests for further information

11–120 Reference should be made to CPR r.18 and to the notes in the White Book to the manner in which further information may be requested or ordered by the court. In view of the mandatory terms of CPR r.57.7 as to particulars of the case which will be relied on, it will be right that a CPR r.18 request should be made and complied with in any claim where the particulars do not contain the detail required under CPR r.57.7.

Limitation of claims
(a) Probate claims generally
There is no period of limitation of actions provided under the **11–121** Limitation Act 1980 for probate claims. Although such claims are not governed by the rules of equity, the principles which apply to equitable remedies where there is no specified period do, in effect, apply to probate claims. See *Snell's Equity* (30th ed.), 3–16 to 3–19. Thus, inexcusable delay, a substantial lapse of time (with knowledge of the potential claim) or acceptance of the benefit given under a will or an intestacy may all bar probate claims. See *Re Flynn* [1982] 1 W.L.R. 310 for an indication from the court that there is no defined period of time for the commencement of a probate claim. The court will have regard to whether it is possible to have a fair trial of the claim after many years' delay and whether the interest of justice would be served by allowing such a claim to go ahead. A *very* late claim may well be the justified object of an application to strike out under CPR r.3.4. In probate claims where testamentary capacity, or undue influence is in issue, it is hard to see how a claim could be dealt with justly when the evidence of witnesses and others was many years old, and where some crucial witnesses were dead without having left admissible statements. Equally, there may be very late discoveries of wills which will upset an existing grant and to which there can be no answer but to commence a claim for proof of that will.

Executors named in a will, potential administrators, or those **11–122** who have taken a grant may be entitled to tell a potential claimant to "put up or shut up" by a certain date, following which the personal representative will obtain a grant and distribute, assuming there is no caveat. In a matter where there is a revocation claim the personal representative with the grant may be more inclined to write such a letter giving such notice, as the estate may be ready for distribution. It may be that he should apply to the court for leave to distribute under CPR r.64. (See *Fitzhugh Gates v Sherman* [2003] EWCA Civ 886 and below, Chapter 12 at para. 12–026, on the directions which may be sought in advance of a claim being brought, or in advance of the full hearing.)

(b) Limitation problems applied to revocation claims in particular
Revocation claims pose particular problems in certain areas, **11–123** quite apart from the problems thrown up where the estate has already been administered.

(i) *Dealing with the estate during the claim*

11-124 As a general point, it should be noted that the commencement of a probate claim to revoke a grant does not cause the grant to cease to have effect. It is only revoked from judgment. It is valid until then, and anyone dealing with the personal representatives under it has the protection of s.204 of the Law of Property Act 1925 and also (subject to good faith in the party dealing with the personal representatives) ss.27 and 37 of the Administration of Estates Act 1925. (See Parry and Clark *The Law of Succession* (11th ed.), for the effect of revocation on transactions effected under a grant which is subsequently revoked, particularly in conveyancing and transfers of land. Where there is good faith the title will be safe, even in the event of a later revocation.) The fact that the grant may have to be lodged in the court under CPR r.57.6(2) does not affect its validity, and it may be possible for a copy to be issued with the leave of the court during the pendency of the claim, *e.g.* in the case of the need to produce it to sell shares in advance of a feared collapse in the market. In a case where the personal representatives are faced with a challenge to the validity of a grant and need to complete certain transactions, and where it may not be safe to rely on the protection of the statutory provisions set out above, they can apply to the court for an Order authorising those transactions. This may include payments to beneficiaries. But in general terms the scope of such an application, which can be made by application notice under CPR r.24 in the probate claim, should be limited to payments which would benefit the estate, whichever testamentary document or intestacy will control the estate after the claim is determined. (See below, Chapter 15, as to the comparison between common form and solemn form grants.) In *Daniel v Abiola* [2003] EWHC Civ 1562, Lawrence Collins J. made an order for the relief described in this passage.

(ii) *Revocation claims brought after Orders have been made in claims under Inheritance Act 1975*

11-125 One problem in particular arises where an Order has been made under the Inheritance Act 1975. A claim is then brought to revoke the grant which was current during the 1975 Act claim. The Order is endorsed on the grant under s.19(3) of the Act.

11-126 1975 Act claims, must be brought within the period of six months from the date of the grant under s.4. If later, they can be brought only with the leave of the court. It is vital not to confuse this period under the 1975 Act with the absence of any fixed period for probate claims. It may also be worth noting that there are certain fixed limitation periods in the Limitation Act 1980 for claims by beneficiaries for their share in an estate (12 years from the time when the right to the share accrued — s.22(1) —

noting the 6-year period for interest on a legacy by s.22(2)) and for an account, which may be either 6 or 12 years depending on the basis of the claim for an account. Other periods will apply to claims for possession of land under either the 1980 Act, or the Land Registration Act 2002.

With this in mind there are three points to bear in mind **11–127** where a revocation claim may have the effect (if successful) of altering the disposition of the deceased's estate, thereby casting into doubt the Order made under the 1975 Act, not only as a matter of jurisdiction, but also as a matter of overall justice. The three points are as follows:

(1) By s.19 of the 1975 Act the Order (if made) is retrospective for all purposes. Thus, even if the grant is revoked and another will is proved, or if there is an intestacy, the disposition of the deceased's estate will be subject to the Order under the 1975 Act. It is also not in doubt that the court (when making the Order in the 1975 Act claim) was entitled to treat the grant (and the will annexed) as regular and valid or in the case of an intestacy, as governing the disposition of the estate. (See above, para. 11–124.) So, as a matter of jurisdiction, it seems that the later revocation of that grant should not cast doubt on any Order made in reliance on its validity. However, there may be a restitutionary right to trace the estate into the hands of those who have received it, whether by the will or by Order under the 1975 Act. (See *Re Diplock* [1948] Ch. 465, and for a full explanation of the law relating to this right, see Parry & Clark, Ch. 25, paras. 25–36 to 25–46.)

(2) There may be circumstances in which the fundamental assumptions on which an Order was made (whether by consent or not) can change. (See *Edgar v Edgar* [1980] 1 W.L.R. 1410; *Barder v Caluori* [1988] A.C. 20; and *Tibbs v Dick* [1998] 2 F.L.R. 1118. See also Chapter 15, where Orders in probate claims are considered further.) One argument of substance, however, may be that as the 1975 Act claim was based on the premise that the estate was disposed of under the terms of the will or the intestacy then prevailing, if that proves false, why should not the Order (even if made by the court and not by consent) be set aside? This is a point which goes to the manner in which the estate was disposed of by the competing wills, or by the competing will and intestacy, and leads to the right of recovery against the beneficiaries. This argument may carry some weight where the claimant in the 1975 Act claim does better under the will, or the intestacy

which is the result of the revocation claim, than under the disposition of the estate believed to be correct for the purposes of the 1975 Act claim. Another beneficiary may feel aggrieved that he cannot receive his full share of the estate because part of it went to the claimant under the 1975 Act order, and that claimant has now got even more. It seems hard to satisfy the aggrieved beneficiary without revoking the Order in the 1975 Act claim and ordering the claimant to restore the fruits of the Order to the estate or bring into account what he gets under the 1975 Act Order against the new disposition of the estate. But what if the claimant has spent the award? To redetermine the claimant's requirement for reasonable financial provision (at the appropriate standard set by s.1(2) of the 1975 Act) might well be an impossible task. Why should the claimant in the 1975 Act claim have to go through that again? This may be one of those cases where the loss may have to lie where it falls. (The personal representatives will not be personally liable as they will have the protection of the Order made under the 1975 Act.)

If the old grant is revoked and a new one issued, there seems no reason why the six month period under section 4 of the 1975 Act should not start again.

(3) Finally, and this may in fact be the crucial factor, the resolution of the difficulties referred to above may turn on whether the claimant in the revocation claim was a party to the 1975 Act claim. If he was, and had the ability to bring a revocation at that stage, it may be harder for him to upset the effect of the 1975 Act Order, even though he may not be prevented by issue estoppel from bringing the revocation claim. If he was not a party, there may be no difficulty. An example shows how these factors could apply in practice:

(a) Under the will admitted to probate, the estate passes to a charity. The claim under the 1975 Act is made by the deceased's son, A, who obtains half the net estate, say £200,000.

(b) At a later date another child of the deceased (B) comes forward (not identified in the 1975 Act claim) and also seeks proof of a later will in which he is sole beneficiary. He can seek to revoke the original grant. The charity will have to disgorge its benefit under the will (£200,000), applying the principles in *Re Diplock* [1948] Ch. 465. A is, in theory, liable to disgorge his £200,000, but unless

his circumstances have changed for the better, B would be unwise in forcing A to do this as A would simply bring another 1975 Act claim.
(c) If B had been a party to the 1975 Act claim, whilst he might still be able to seek to revoke the grant and prove the later will, he would be met by issue estoppel arguments by A (if not the charity) if he sought to recoup the estate.
(d) If under the will proved in common form the beneficiary had not been a charity, but other children of the deceased, apart from A and B, nice questions will arise following revocation of the grant as to how far B can recover the estate from them, if it has been spent (see *Re Diplock* above) and whether those original beneficiaries might be able to bring their own 1975 Act claim against B.

Pre-claim protocols

At present there is no specific protocol which applies to contentious probate claims. Therefore, until a specific one is brought into force, the governing "protocol" is the Practice Direction — Protocols which, for convenience, is referred to as "the Protocol". **11–128**

The themes to be found in the Protocol and elsewhere (*e.g.* in the ACTAPS draft) and which represent the aims of the Protocol may be summarised by reference to the following points: **11–129**

(1) Disputes should be resolved without litigation, for that should be regarded as a last resort.

(2) There should be an early exchange of information and a "cards on the table" approach so that all parties can assess whether to settle before issuing a claim form. A joint approach should be made for certain information, *e.g.* health records.

(3) The early exchange of information should allow parties to apply a "cost benefit" analysis at an early stage to the potential dispute.

(4) With proper information to hand sensible offers can be made.

(5) If litigation is inevitable, the parties should be in a position to define the issues clearly at an early stage.

11–130 In probate claims the aims of the Protocol are met by additional sanctions and safeguards, which include:

(1) the requirements of disclosure as stated in *Larke v Nugus*; see below, para. 11–132;

(2) the obligation of the claimant to have his testamentary documents ready on issue; and

(3) the specific rules as to the particulars which must be given of the contentions as to invalidity of wills etc. in the particulars of claim required by CPR r.57.7; see above, para. 11–067.

All this means more work by way of obtaining evidence and conducting detailed investigations at an early stage, often prior to any claim being issued.

11–131 The following key points will have to be borne in mind if the Protocol is to be observed.

(1) Clients' instructions must be taken right at the outset and in detail, and this includes evidence which may have to go into a witness statement.

(2) Experts may have to be briefed early on in the claim — often so that a view can be taken on merits even before any claim form is drafted, *e.g.* as to testamentary capacity.

(3) The search for documents starts early — whether will files, or medical records.

(4) Key witnesses, such as witnesses to the will or medical witnesses, must be interviewed early, and inevitably (at least in the case of the witnesses to the will) their statements will form part of the *Larke v Nugus* disclosure; see below, para. 11–132.

(5) The guidance in the Protocol is only a *guide* and, as with all guides to best practice, slavish adherence is not required. Indeed, mechanical adherence to the terms of the Protocol is worse in some cases than non-adherence, just as much as the repetition (without any real intention to abide by its principles) of the need to observe the overriding objective in CPR r.1.1 can be a meaningless (and often patronising) feature of modern-day correspondence between advisers.

The principles of early disclosure as set out in *Larke v Nugus*

11–132 In *Larke v Nugus* [2000] W.T.L.R. 1033, CA, the Court of Appeal reaffirmed the Law Society recommendation as to what solicitors should do when wills they made were challenged. The decision dates from 1979, but was only fully reported in 2000. The recommendation in force in 1973 was as follows:

> "(a) **Where will in dispute**
> If the testator is dead, the solicitor must not disclose any information before probate is granted, except to the executors, without the consent of the executors. But this will not necessarily apply where a solicitor is asked to disclose information about a will which he has prepared and which is in dispute.
>
> Privilege cannot be claimed by one person claiming under a deceased testator's will as against another person having a similar claim in respect of matters communicated by the deceased to the solicitor during the lifetime of the deceased. The testator's solicitor could be compelled by the court under subpoena to answer questions directed to eliciting communications made to him by the testator in the course of preparing the will if put to him by either party.
>
> Where a serious dispute arises as to the validity of a will, beyond the mere entering of a caveat, and the solicitor's knowledge makes him a material witness, then the solicitor should make available a statement of his evidence regarding the execution of the will and the circumstances surrounding it to anyone concerned in the proving or challenging of that will, whether or not the solicitor acted for those who were propounding the will."

11–133 This recommendation was derived from an opinion given to the Law Society by Sir Edward Milner Holland Q.C. in the late 1950s.

In *Larke v Nugus* the Court of Appeal affirmed that principle in the following terms:

> "So far as the meaning and effect of the Law Society's recommendation is concerned, I would have no difficulty myself in interpreting it as covering the circumstances of the preparation of the will; but I am prepared to accept that the first plaintiff did not fully comprehend the effect of the recommendation. Nevertheless, it is necessary to consider, not only the recommendation itself, but the principle upon which the recommendation is based, and the duty of a solicitor when faced with matters of this kind. The recommendation is no doubt of importance, but even if it had not been made certain principles would apply to the matter, and in my judgment the principle which applied is that, when there is litigation about a will, every effort should be made by the executors to avoid costly litigation if that can be avoided

and, when there are circumstances of suspicion attending the execution and making of a will, one of the measures which can be taken is to give full and frank information to those who might have an interest in attacking the will as to how the will came to be made. In a case of this kind, where suspicion attaches to the will because certain persons, who have only recently come into the life of the testatrix, take a substantial benefit under the will, then clearly the circumstances in which instructions for the will were given are of the utmost importance, and it is information as to that matter, even more than information as to the formalities of attestation, that is needed. So I do not think the matter turns solely on the recommendation of the Law Society; I think it also turns on the principle that I have endeavoured to state." (*per* Brandon L.J.)

"The Law Society's recommendation in question is clearly concerned with problems arising out of the professional confidential relationship which has existed between the testator and his solicitor. In my view it is clear that the statement which the solicitor is recommended to make, where a serious dispute arises as to the validity of a will beyond the mere entering of a caveat and the solicitor's knowledge makes him a material witness, is a statement relating to such evidence as he himself can give.

In my opinion it is also clear that the statement is not intended to be confined to matters concerned with the execution of the will in the narrow sense of the term 'execution'. In my judgment it should extend to all matters surrounding the making of a disputed will which are relevant to the questions in the action and, in my view, should consequently extend to the circumstances leading up to the preparation and making of the will. I fully agree with what my Lord has said about the general principle which underlies the recommendation." (*per* Buckley L.J.)

11–134 The principles set out in *Larke v Nugus* are of vital importance and must be followed in all claims in which it applies.

11–135 A failure by a solicitor to respond properly to a letter written within the principle established by *Larke v Nugus* is not only a breach of professional duty, but will also be reflected in costs. Such failure may not only affect the Order as to costs as between the parties; it may also lead to a wasted costs Order against the firm who has failed to supply the information which has been sought under a request properly made within the principles of *Larke v Nugus*. See CPR r.48.7 for the jurisdiction to make wasted costs Orders; see also below, Chapter 16 on costs Orders in probate claims.

CONTENTIOUS PROBATE

The force of *Larke v Nugus* has been reinforced by the terms **11–136** of the general pre-action protocol referred to above (in particular, para. 4.1 thereof) by the terms of CPR r.44.3, and r.44.3(5). This concerns the extent to which the parties followed any pre-action protocol. It is also clear that "conduct of the parties" will include the way in which a party dealt with proper requests under *Larke v Nugus*.

The clearest warning is, therefore, that all parties and advisers **11–137** must observe *Larke v Nugus* and apply the principles of disclosure contained in it. (See *Buckenham v Dickinson* [2000] W.T.L.R. 1083, at 1099, for a recent warning in similar terms by H.H. Judge Roger Cooke, sitting as a deputy judge of the Chancery Division).

Thus, in practical terms, the advice is:

For potential claimants
  (1) send *Larke v Nugus* letters at the earliest appropriate **11–138** stage;
  (2) follow up replies; and
  (3) pay for reasonable copying charges — reasonable terms as to disclosure and use may be imposed.

For potential defendants/solicitors who were involved
  (1) reply to *Larke v Nugus* letters in proper terms promptly; **11–139**
  (2) the response should be accurate; and
  (3) files disclosed should be complete and not "filleted" save where contents are relevant to the claim.

See further below, Chapter 12 on disclosure of documents and pre-trial matters.

General Conclusions

The key to the successful conduct of contested probate claims **11–140** lies in the following areas:

  (1) Knowledge of the evidence required to maintain or defend a claim; *e.g.* medical evidence as to testamentary capacity; see below Chapter 12, on disclosure.
  (2) Use of the right machinery to obtain the relevant evidence, *e.g.* the *Larke v Nugus* letter; see above, para. 11–132, for *Larke v Nugus* principles.

(3) The correct assessment of the evidence obtained, and is there compliance with the civil standard of proof on the balance of probabilities?

(4) Disclosure of evidence at the right time, *e.g.* to show compliance with s.9 of the Wills Act 1837.

(5) An objective assessment of merits before commencing a claim, such an assessment to be continued throughout the claim until a final hearing. The same applies to defendants.

(6) A realistic approach to compromise; see below Chapter 14.

Chapter 12

Dealing with Claims Once Started: Pre-trial

The following topics arise under this heading: **12–001**

(1) the court's power to manage claims;

(2) the Case Management Conference ("CMC"); and

(3) the particular position of probate claims as CPR r.7 claims but automatically allocated to the multi-track by CPR r.57.2(4).

The court's power to manage claims

Probate claims will first come before the court by virtue of CPR **12–002** r.29, as multi-track claims allocated by CPR r.57.2(4). This means that the court will do the following:

(1) After the filing of the defence the court will send an Allocation Questionnaire ("AQ") to all parties (Form N150; CPR r.26.3 and CPR r.26 PD). This is done even though the claim is already allocated to the multi-track.

(2) Each party must complete and file his AQ within the time set out in it by the court.

(3) At the conclusion of that time limit the claim file will be put in front of the Master or (District Judge outside London). He will check the following:

 (a) Have the statements of testamentary documents been filed and have the documents referred to been lodged? (See above, para. 11–077 for this obligation on all parties.)

 (b) Have AQs gone out to all parties and have they been completed and filed?

If there is default in any of the above the Court will make an Order for compliance with a notified time limit. In all cases the Court will consider, in particular, what directions are proposed in the AQ (note box F on Form N150) and it will then decide what Order to make in terms of directions. In some cases, where the parties have worked together closely and the directions are agreed and acceptable to the court, the Master (or District Judge) will make the Order sought and there may be no need for a CMC. In other cases he will need to make an Order for a CMC to take place at the time and date specified in his Order to make the directions needed. (See below, para. 12–004, for what should be borne in mind in terms of directions and the conduct of the CMC.)

It is important to note that in *all* claims it is no longer the case (in view of the way in which the CPR work) that a claim can "go to sleep". The internal system of managing all claims is such that there will *always* be a date on the court file by which time the claim goes before the Master (or District Judge) who will check the progress of the claim. Probate claims share the same system, so the "bad old days" of allowing a file to moulder away in the hope that one party or another (if not the court) might forget about it have gone completely. There is, in effect, a "sell-by date" on all court files, and the court *will* manage the claims and not allow such Orders as "adjourn generally, liberty to apply" to be made any more. The court will always impose a timetable — even, quite sensibly, where the parties want some time to settle — with a "come back to court by" longstop date, allowing time for negotiations where requested.

(4) If the court has fixed a date for the CMC (CPR r.29.2(1)(b)) and notified the parties, it may send the parties a pre-trial checklist under CPR r.29.6. This must be completed and filed in court by the date fixed by the court. (For a sample form, see Form N170, Appendix I. It is sensible for all parties to exchange the completed checklists so that there is no unnecessary conflict between them. (See CPR r.29 PD, para. 8.1(5)). There is a strike out sanction for failure to file the completed checklist; CPR r.29 PD, para. 8.3.

12–003 For the full details of the procedure under CPR r.29 and CPR r.29 PD, see the White Book, Vol. 1. Only specific matters relevant to probate claims are referred to below. The full text of CPR r.29 and the accompanying Practice Direction *must* be consulted in advance of any claim which is about to come before a master or district judge on a CMC.

Preparation for the CMC hearing

It has already been pointed out that (in theory at least) the court will have been able to check that testamentary documents and statements of documents have been lodged. Thus, at the first hearing the court will be able to take stock of the claim in relation to the documents which have been lodged, and the pleadings will also tell their own tale. What the court will focus on will be the following matters, and, therefore, having regard to all the matters in CPR r.29 PD, para. 5, advisers must be prepared to deal with the following in particular: **12–004**

(1) Having the right parties before the court. The obligation to file testamentary documents will assist in ensuring that all those with an interest in the estate are either already parties or can be identified and, if necessary, joined or given notice under CPR r.19.8A; see above, para. 11–065 as to the choice of Orders the court can make under CPR r.19. Parties under a disability will need litigation friends under CPR r.21.

(2) Ensuring that all pleadings conform to CPR r.57.7. If they do not, the offending party will be ordered to amend, with the usual sanctions for non-compliance, including striking-out. Are there any other amendments needed? Is the case of each party clear?

(3) Making Orders for disclosure and inspection under CPR r.31. In probate claims disclosure is very important. (See below, para. 12–010, for specific issues which arise here.) This may require identifying specific files and documents relating to the will in dispute.

(4) Orders for expert evidence:
   (a) The identity of this expert and the purpose for which he will be called (*e.g.* to show lack of capacity) and how he is to give that evidence must be before the court at the CMC. (CPR r.29 PD, para. 5.5(1).)
   (b) Use of the single joint expert; (see CPR r.35.7).
   (c) CPR r.29 PD, para. 4.10(4) leans in favour of a single joint expert unless there is good reason not to do so. In probate claims, where the issue may be over testamentary capacity, it may be difficult for a

150 DEALING WITH CLAIMS ONCE STARTED: PRETRIAL

single joint expert to do justice to the evidence, and this may be an instance where there is a good reason for each side to have their own medical expert. However, there may be a costs risk in obtaining expert evidence before the CMC without getting a direction about that evidence; see CPR r.29 PD, para. 5.5(2). It is hard to see how this approach can be applied in practice in probate claims where there is invariably the need to obtain expert evidence (albeit not in the form of a final report) at a very early stage, usually before the pre-action letter under the Protocol referred to above, at para. 11–140. This is particularly so where forgery, or lack of capacity may be "in the frame" for investigation. Such evidence also will form the backbone of the particulars of claim directed by CPR r.57.7. It is suggested that there should be no costs penalties in getting (relevant) expert evidence early on.

(d) Consequential directions are made as to the exchange of reports and meetings to resolve matters of dispute and agree issues in accordance with CPR r.35.12; see CPR r.29 PD, para. 4.10(5), (6).

(5) Witness statements. See CPR r.32 for the formal rules.

12–005 In probate claims the focus will be on:

(1) Witnesses to the will — they are witnesses of the court and can be required to give evidence by any party, or the court, using s.122 of the Supreme Court Act 1981.

(2) Solicitors responsible for the preparation and execution of the will — see *Larke v Nugus* above, para. 11–132.

(3) Civil Evidence Act notices — see CPR r.33 for the rules on hearsay notices. Note the specific exception from the need to serve a hearsay notice in respect of any statement by the deceased in a probate action relating to his estate under CPR r.33.3(b).

12–006 In general terms and for guidance, see CPR r.29 PD, para. 5.3 as to the "topics" which the court will be likely to include at a CMC. See also the application form, Form PF 50, and the specimen Order to be made at a CMC below, Appendix I, PF 52.

12–007 Preparation for a CMC will require:

(1) In addition to the completed pre-trial checklist, if required filing a 500-word (maximum) case summary

CONTENTIOUS PROBATE 151

from all parties jointly which is agreed (so far as possible) as to the chronology of the claim, the issues of fact which are agreed or in dispute and the evidence needed to decide those issues which are in dispute. This must be lodged at least 24 hours before the hearing of the CMC; CPR r.29 PD, para. 5.7(1);

(2) attendance by a representative who is personally involved in the case and who has authority to deal with any issues that are likely to arise under CPR r.29.3(2) and CPR r.29 PD, para.5(2)). Inadequate representation (*e.g.* sending "the office junior" with no experience of the case, or any briefing) will lead to a wasted costs Order if there is an adjournment because of that person's inadequacy (CPR r.29 PD, para. 5.2(3));

(3) filing costs estimates of costs incurred to date and to be incurred (CPR r.43 PD, para. 6); and

(4) ensuring that any non-routine, or opposed applications (under CPR r.23) have been issued and served in time for the CMC; (CPR r.29 PD, paras 3.8 and 5.8).

Directions can and should, whenever possible, be agreed in advance under CPR r.29.4 and CPR r.29 PD, para. 4. The court encourages agreement; (CPR r.29 PD, para. 4.6). The court will, however, scrutinise the timetable to ensure that (*inter alia*) the date for the trial is no later than is reasonably necessary (CPR r.29 PD, para. 4.7(2)). **12–008**

Note also the following points: **12–009**

(1) As to venue, by CPR r.29 PD, para. 2.6(7), contentious probate claims are suitable for trial in the Royal Courts of Justice in London, unless the claim is in a Chancery District Registry.

(2) There is the right under CPR r.29.5 and CPR r.29 PD, para. 6 to seek the variation of any directions made or to appeal them.

(3) If a telephone, or video conference is thought desirable, or unavoidable, see CPR 23 PD, paras 6 and 7 for the arrangements that should be made prior to the CMC being held in this manner.

Disclosure of documents and inspection

Advisers should be familiar with the general principles of disclosure and inspection as provided for in CPR r.31 and the accompanying Practice Direction; What follows is a *summary* only. **12–010**

Thus in probate claims these principles are applicable as follows:

(1) Disclosure will be standard disclosure as follows within CPR r.31.6. This means that what is to be disclosed will be the party's own documents on which he relies and those which he has that may be adverse to his case. But documents which may be "relevant" in terms of background are not within the standard disclosure definition, nor are those which may lead to a train of inquiry enabling a party to advance his case; (see notes to CPR r.31.6 in the White Book). In probate claims it will often be necessary to consider a specific Order for disclosure at the CMC of documents which may well fall within the wider class of relevant or train of inquiry documents, *e.g.* documents relating to lifetime gifts, or the execution of an Enduring Power of Attorney at or about the time the will which is being challenged was made. (CPR r.31 PD, para. 1.)

(2) The duty to disclose carries with it a duty to make a reasonable search for documents within CPR r.31.6; (CPR r.31.7). Clients must be told, or reminded of this. (CPR r.31 PD, para. 2.)

(3) There is a right to inspect the documents disclosed (CPR rr.31.3 and 31.15). Copies may be taken on payment of reasonable copying costs (CPR r.31.15(c) PD, para. 7.)

(4) The court may order specific disclosure (CPR r.31.12). (CPR r.31 PD, para. 5). *Larke v Nugus* requires specific files to be disclosed.

(5) There is a right to pre-claim disclosure under CPR rr.31.16 and 31.17.

(6) The usual rules as to legal professional privilege and without prejudice communications will apply. But merely because a document is "confidential" does not mean that in general terms it should not be disclosed. In probate claims it is uncommon to find that documents may be protected from disclosure on the ground that not only are they confidential, but that they also protect the rights of a third party.

(7) A false disclosure statement may attract proceedings for contempt of court. (CPR r.31.23. PD, para. 8).

12–011 The general procedure for disclosure is in CPR r.31.10 and the form (which is in effect a list) for disclosure is Form N265. The form of disclosure statement must form part of the list. (See

CPR r.31 PD, paras 3 and 4, and the form in the Annex to that practice direction.

Specific issues which arise on disclosure in probate claims

(a) *Pre-claim disclosure under CPR r.31.16 and third party disclosure under CPR r.31.17*

12–012 This is often threatened where either a potential party (r.31.16) or a person not a party (r.31.17) has failed to make available a file which relates to the making of the will in question, or some other relevant document. Reference should be made to the requirements in rr. 31.16(3) and 31.17(3) to ensure that the application falls within the rule. The application should be made under CPR r.23, whether pre- or post-issue of the claim form. The threat of a r.36.16, or r.36.17 application will usually cause the relevant documents to be disclosed. It will be preferable to go by way of a subpoena under s.123 of the Supreme Court Act 1981 where wills are being called for; see above, para. 11–028.

(b) *Privilege questions*

12–013 As stated above, probate claims are no exception to the general rules which govern non-disclosure of documents which are covered by legal professional privilege. For the details of privilege, see the extensive notes in the White Book to CPR r.31.

12–014 In probate claims the usual claim to privilege will be made in respect of communications between the client (now deceased) and his solicitor, such communications being generally covered by privilege if the communications arose in the context of the client seeking to obtain legal advice from the solicitor acting in his professional capacity. *Three Rivers DC v Bank of England* [2003] EWCA Civ 474 contains a review of the law on the scope of legal advice privilege. In the context of making wills, the client's communications with his solicitor for the purpose of making a will, or receiving advice in connection with it usually come into existence otherwise than in the context of contemplated or pending litigation. The death of the client does not remove the privilege which attaches to those communications; *Bullivant v Att.-Gen.* of Victoria [1901] A.C. 196. The privilege will extend to communications to and from counsel. Communications with other professionals, or third parties will only apply if the communications arose when litigation is contemplated, or has arisen. The notes to r.31 should be studied for examples of exceptions to these general rules and for the circumstances of how privilege may be waived, or lost.

12–015 However, in the context of probate claims there is an exception to the rule that privilege may attach to the communications between the client and his solicitor. This concerns the

154 DEALING WITH CLAIMS ONCE STARTED: PRETRIAL

evidence surrounding the taking of instructions for and the making of the will which is in issue in the claim. If the solicitor has been instrumental in that context, then in accordance with the principles and rules of conduct derived from *Larke v Nugus* [2000] W.T.L.R. 1033 (see above, para. 11–132) neither that solicitor, nor any other party (*e.g.* those claiming to represent the estate whether pre-grant or post-grant) can claim the deceased's client's privilege in the documents leading up to the execution of the will. It is also the case that, as the attesting witnesses are witnesses of the court, any documents appertaining to the issue of attestation and execution will also be within the scope of disclosure notwithstanding their privileged character. (*Re Fuld* [1965] P. 405, at 410.) This obligation to disclose covers not only the original documents which the testator's solicitor may have retained, but also copies of such documents held by an attesting witness.

12–016 Note the following points:

(1) Where records which relate to the making of a will (and which fall within *Larke v Nugus*) are kept in electronic form, s.35(1) of the Data Protection Act 1998 will exempt those records from non-disclosure, either under the "rule of law" which *Larke v Nugus* establishes or, if an Order to disclose is made. Both of these exceptions to non-disclosure are set out in s.35(1).

(2) As stated above, it would seem to be clear that the principle established in *Larke v Nugus* (above) takes the documents within that principle outside the realm of privilege (*Re Fuld* above).

(3) There is no reason why the personal representatives (whether actual or potentially entitled) should not send a *Larke v Nugus* letter to the solicitors responsible for the will on their behalf and on behalf of the potential claimant.

(4) Reasonable copying costs (and other related costs) will have to be paid by those seeking them. Terms as to the use to be made of such documents and evidence may also have to be imposed, *e.g.* as to confidentiality and use only in the claim contemplated. *Larke v Nugus* is not to be taken to allow a general and wide-ranging "fishing expedition" in terms of seeking documents and files relating to the deceased's affairs.

(5) As stated above, at para. 11–033, attesting witnesses to the will are witnesses of the court and have a special role to play. They may be called by any party, or by the court (under s.122 of the Supreme Court Act 1981) and their

evidence is not privileged. *Re Fuld, (No. 2)* [1965] P. 405, at 410).

(c) *Medical records and the Access to Health Records Act 1990*
The position is not altogether clear, but it is suggested that medical records (*i.e.* notes maintained by the deceased's G.P., hospital notes, or notes maintained by consultants) should fall within the right of access to "health records" as defined by s.1 of the Access to Medical Records Act 1990 ("the 1990 Act"). Section 3(1)(f) gives the right of access to such records where the person seeking access (who may include the personal representative of the deceased) "may have a claim arising out of the patient's death". At first sight this provision may be thought to apply only where, for example, there is an allegation of medical negligence, and records are needed following the death of the patient to see if a claim can be made for damages. However, a probate claim where medical evidence is relevant to a plea of testamentary capacity may fall within this provision in view of the fact that, logically, the claim arises out of the patient's death. **12–017**

In practice few difficulties are caused by applications for health records. The following practical points arise when requests are to be made: **12–018**

(1) fees — it is usual to pay copying charges, (note the fee provisions in s.3(4) of the 1990 Act); and

(2) time — records may be sent to a central location after death from the deceased's local health centre, or from the hospital where he was a patient within a month or two from death, so this requires some speed in "chasing the files" before they get lost. See para. 12–020 below.

To avoid any difficulties about refusal to disclose, those representing the estate can apply. Records maintained by other organisations (Local Authority Social Services, etc.) will not fall within the terms of the 1990 Act and will have to be the subject of an application to produce them by the estate. **12–019**

(iv) *Medical ethics and patients' medical records*
As regards clinical practice, doctors typically delegate the obtaining of notes from other NHS institutions to the medical records officers of their own hospital. As regards notes from a private hospital, the clinician might well write a personal letter asking his private practice colleague to release copies of his notes to him. Once patients die, what happens varies in details as to whose notes are concerned. Wherever they are, the firm NHS requirement is for notes (not merely medical notes but **12–020**

also the nursing and paramedical notes and X-rays) to be kept to a minimum of eight years from the last clinical episode, in this case, the date of death. Private consultants would also observe this rule in regard to their personal records, not least for their own medico-legal protection. NHS Hospital notes are retained by the relevant medical records department; though "dead" notes may be stored off site or may be microfilmed rather than kept in original form. GP notes are a little different in that, because they are independent contractors, the notes are technically the property of what used to be called the Family Practitioner Committee but now Primary Health Care Trust holding their contract. So, at some variable time, usually a few months, from a patient's death, the GP will transfer the notes from his surgery to the care of the records department of the PHCT where they should similarly be retained for the minimum of eight years.

Witness statements

12–021 In probate claims the evidence may be from:

 (1) solicitors who prepared the will;

 (2) witnesses to the will;

 (3) lay witnesses generally;

 (4) expert witnesses; testing experts — assessing the weight of their evidence:

  (a) medical — did the doctor examine the deceased or is he relying on notes (*Richards v Allan*) [2001] W.T.L.R 1031;
  (b) handwriting — where forgery is at issue;
  (c) other specialisms — *e.g.* type fonts and paper dating;
  (d) impersonation — where identity is at issue;
  (e) parentage, DNA testing — where parentage is at issue.

12–022 With reference to (4)(d) above, the case of Annie Kay (who died in March 1997) is an example of impersonation of a testatrix, where simple precautions and checking the identity of a hitherto unknown client would have prevented what happened. In that case Mrs Kay had moved into a nursing home run by Mr and Mrs S, who persuaded her to move there. Mrs Kay had previously made a will through her solicitor leaving her estate (valued on her death at £1.8 million) to various charities.

After she entered the nursing home (which in fact was no longer licensed as such) Mr and Mrs S persuaded Mrs Kay to make a new will. Mr and Mrs S engaged a perfectly reputable will-writer to do this, and he agreed to meet Mrs Kay at her house. He was unaware that he was dealing with Mr and Mrs S's mother, Mrs R. In February 1997 the will-writer went to the house and saw a person he believed to be Mrs Kay, but who was in fact Mrs R. A "will" was made there and then, with a "signature" of Mrs Kay by Mrs R. The will-writer and his wife attested the will. It was only after the death of Mrs Kay that the penny dropped when the last "will" was compared with the earlier one, and it could be seen that in the last will the charities were cut out in favour of Mr and Mrs S with a legacy of £10,000 as the "reward" to Mrs R. Once a neighbour had stated that she never saw Mrs Kay return to her house after she moved to the home run by Mr and Mrs S, it was clear that there had been an impersonation.

It was also the case that Mrs Kay's signature was easy to forge. It will, inevitably, be a matter of judgment in individual cases, but some elementary precautions against impersonation ought to be considered where the circumstances warrant it. Production of a passport, a photocard driving licence or DSS card is not too difficult to arrange. In Europe, where a notarial system prevails, this is commonplace when executing legal documents, including wills. Note also the general rules as to the contents and form of witness statements and compliance with CPR r.32, and in probate claims in particular the need for relevant detail.

The question of detail is highly significant in probate claims. **12–023** This is because the crucial events may take place over only a very short period of time. For example, see *Re Parsons* [2002] W.T.L.R. 237 where the events which gave rise to the questions over the validity of the will, which included the examination of the testator by the consultant, the attendance by the licensed conveyancer with the previously prepared will, and the execution, all took place between 12pm and 1.15pm on March 27, 1998 at the hospital where the testator was an in-patient. The following practical tips may assist when assembling the evidence:

(1) preparing an overall statement of the facts which have to be proved in order for the claim to succeed, or for the defence likewise;

(2) identifying what each witness has to prove, *e.g.* the formalities under s.9 of the Wills Act 1837 or a lack of testamentary capacity;

(3) preparing witness statements with the two points above in mind — whilst also bearing in mind that it is the

158 DEALING WITH CLAIMS ONCE STARTED: PRETRIAL

witness's evidence which is being given and not the lawyer's version of it;

(4) preparing a schedule — in spreadsheet form if necessary — to link the various events and statements;

(5) when all parties' statements have been exchanged, using a witness summary to link those statements and salient points — with a spreadsheet format if necessary — *e.g.* as in *Re Parsons* (above) to link and contrast the location of various witnesses when they had arrived at the hospital, thereby identifying the location of one of the attesting witnesses who alleged that she had not been present during the execution of the will;

(6) using diaries and dates to create a calendar; and

(7) using investigation agencies — as in the case of Mrs Annie Kay, above — to question neighbours about the movement of people into and out of the deceased's house, *e.g.* where undue influence or impersonation is being alleged.

The orders the court can make on the CMC

12–024 A precedent of a Chancery Order in probate claims, Form PF 52, can be found in the Appendices. See also Appendix 6 to the Chancery Guide, reproduced in the Appendices.

Complying with orders

12–025 Carrying out what the court has ordered is important under the CPR regime. The courts will no longer allow parties and their representatives to get away with non-compliance. CPR rr.3.1 and 3.4 allow the court to strike out claims, or to make conditions as a term of being allowed to proceed within a defined time limit. Failure to comply with CMC directions is specifically governed by CPR r.29 PD, para. 7. Non-compliance can lead to the sanctions set out in CPR r.29 PD, para. 7.4. These are important and are set out here:

(1) The court will not allow a failure to comply with directions to lead to the postponement of the trial, unless the circumstances are exceptional.

(2) If it is practical to do so the court will exercise its powers in a manner that enables the case to come on for trial on the date, or within the period previously set.

(3) In particular the court will assess what steps each party should take to prepare the case for trial, direct that those

steps are taken in the shortest possible time and impose a sanction for non-compliance. Such a sanction may, for example, deprive a party of the right to raise, or contest, an issue, or to rely on evidence to which the direction relates.

(4) Where it appears that one or more issues are or can be made ready for trial at the time fixed while others cannot, the court may direct that the trial will proceed on the issues which are then ready, and direct that no costs will be allowed for any later trial of the remaining issues, or that those costs will be paid by the party in default.

(5) Where the court has no option but to postpone the trial it will do so for the shortest possible time and will give directions for the taking of the necessary steps in the meantime as rapidly as possible.

(6) Litigants and lawyers must be in no doubt that the court will regard the postponement of a trial as an order of last resort. Where it appears inevitable, the court may exercise its power to require a party as well as his legal represenatative to attend court at the hearing where such an order is to be sought.

(7) The court will not postpone any other hearing without a very good reason, and for that purpose the failure of a party to comply on time with directions previously given will not be treated as a good reason.

Interim remedies

In probate claims, as in all other litigation, advisers must keep a **12–026** "weather eye" on other claims which can be made in the estate and, in particular, must have regard to the need to protect the estate against dissipation. In revocation claims (where the grant has already been obtained and a title can be shown to assets in the estate) the need to preserve the estate is particularly important. The detail of how these remedies may be obtained is outside the scope of this book, but it is worth highlighting the following remedies which may have to be considered and, if necessary, sought at an interim stage of the probate claim — if not before it is brought.

(a) *Freezing Orders etc.*
These Orders are fully dealt within CPR r.25. Ancillary to such **12–027** applications may be an application for disclosure, with the jurisdiction under CPR r.31.16 in mind. Reference should be

made to the current White Book and other practice books for the full treatment of this topic. Applications for security for costs under CPR r.25.12 may also have to be contemplated where, for example, a defendant in the probate claim is faced with a non-resident claimant falling within CPR r.25.13. Reference to the White Book is essential here.

(b) *Applications for an administrator pending suit under s.117 of the Supreme Court Act 1981*

12–028 This can be made in the probate claim and does not have to be made in the Family Division (Probate), although once the Order is made the grant is actually issued out of the Principal Registry on production of the Order there. See above, para. 11–041, where grants under s.117 may also be needed to allow assets to be sold to pay inheritance tax, and see CPR r.57 PD, para. 8 for the procedure for making an application for the s.117 Order in the probate claim and the effect thereof.

(c) *Applications to register a unilateral notice under s.35 of the Land Registration Act 2002 at the Land Registry on property which may be within the scope of the claim*

12–029 The difficulty here is showing that the claim is one which relates to the land in question. However, if, for example, the claim is one to revoke the grant and the land is vested in the personal representative under that grant, it should be possible for the caution (or unilateral notice) to be entered. There *may* be standing to enter a restriction.

12–030 It is also important not to forget that requests to solicitors who are acting for parties who have the custody of estate assets, asking that those assets are not disposed of, is a pre-requisite in any application to freeze, or register a caution or notice. In most cases it is unusual to refuse such a request. To do so may provoke the application to freeze and the costs of that application will have to be paid by the refusing party.

(d) *Other applications in the probate claim*

12–031 In revocation claims, the grant is valid until and unless revoked by an Order of the court, and there is protection in favour of third parties who, in good faith, are relying on the grant under s.204 of the Law of Property Act 1925 and ss.27 and 37 of the Administration of Estates Act 1925. However, where there is knowledge in the third party of the probate claim, the personal representative may need to apply to the court (by a CPR r.24 application in the claim) for directions and Orders necessary to preserve the estate pending the final hearing of the revocation claim. This is a similar process to that which arises when there is no grant and there is a need for a grant pending suit under s.117, referred to at (b) above. In cases where it can be shown that payments and other steps should be taken to protect and preserve the estate, the court will make orders to give effect to that aim. (It did so, *per* Lawrence Collins J., in *Daniel v Abiola;* [2003] EWHC Civ 1562). See para. 11–124, above.

(e) *Inheritance Act 1975 claims*
These claims are always CPR r.8 claims (CPR r.57.16). They are **12–032** not the same as probate claims. Probate claims are not only governed by the procedural rules in s.1 of CPR r.57, but they are also CPR r.7 claims with a specific claim form (see above, para. 11–062). Furthermore, probate claims take effect as claims for, or against a will, for or against a grant of probate, or for letters of administration. It is not, therefore, appropriate or procedurally possible to have 1975 Act claims and probate claims in the same claim form.

Where a 1975 Act claim arises, it is suggested that the claim **12–033** (in CPR r.8 form) can be directed at the CMC to be heard with the probate claim and that the probate claim be heard first, or that the issues in the probate claim be resolved first, as fits the circumstances of the two claims. The court will have the power to manage the two claims sensibly together. Note, however, in the context of case management, the very limited jurisdiction of the county court in probate claims. The county court's jurisdiction is wider in 1975 Act claims. County courts have full jurisdiction in 1975 Act claims by s.25 of the County Courts Act 1984, and the Family Division of the High Court also has jurisdiction in those claims. In contrast, as is explained above, para. 11–058, in probate claims the jurisdiction of the county court is very limited, and probate claims are assigned to the Chancery Division only of the High Court and so must be commenced in that Division. This means that as part of case management, 1975 Act claims may have to be transferred to the Chancery Division.

As 1975 Act claims cannot usually be brought without a grant **12–034** having been issued, it is very rare for such claims to arise in the context of probate claims, save where the revocation of an existing grant is sought. See above at para. 11–012, for the problems created by revocation of grants where there has been an Order made in 1975 Act claims. For an unsuccessful attempt to challenge the validity of a will in a 1975 Act claim, see *Williams v Johns* [1988] 2 F.L.R. 475 at 488 per H.H. Judge Micklem. See also above, para. 11–096, for counterclaims in probate claims which are based on other types of claim.

Claims under the 1975 Act are not, therefore, the appropriate **12–035** forum in which to determine the validity of wills. Likewise, probate claims are not the appropriate forum in which to seek reasonable financial provision out of the deceased's net estate. It may be that the comparison between the matters which have to be proved in order to succeed in a probate claim will lead to the conclusion that the claimant will do better under the discretion contained in the 1975 Act, provided that the standards of eligibility and the proof of the failure to make reasonable financial provision can be met. But if both claims are to be run, the matters set out above have to be considered and dealt with.

Early disclosure of evidence

12–036 This requires compliance with the Protocol (see above, para. 11–128); see also the principles in *Larke v Nugus* [2000] W.T.L.R. 1033 as set out above, para. 11–132).

Preparation for the final hearing

Presentation of documents and bundles, etc. for the trial

12–037 For general practice, see the Chancery Guide. Compliance with the terms of the Guide is vitally important. Those parts which are of special application are Ch. 24 and Appendices 1–4 of this work.

12–038 The Order of the court on the CMC and any subsequent Order will set the timetable for exchange of witness statements and lists of documents and for any specific disclosure. The court will have given a "window" for the trial, and in London there will have been a direction as to attendance of counsels' clerks and/or solicitors on the Clerk of the Lists to fix the trial date(s). (See CPR r.39.4). This means that within a period of no later than eight weeks before the trial is due to start, attention must be given to the following matters. This eight-week period ties in with the pre-trial checklist which has to be completed (unless dispensed with) under CPR r.29.6; using Form N170. (See above, para. 12–002, for the CMC provisions under CPR r.29).

(1) The pre-trial checklist serves not just as an opportunity for the court to see that orders made on any CMC have been complied with, but also for the party completing it to check that there has been compliance. The checklist also leads to a trial date being given unless, as is usual in the Chancery Division in London, there has been an appointment to fix the date with the Clerk of the Lists as referred to above.

(2) Note that where a trial is estimated to last for more than ten days there may be a pre-trial review ordered (see

CPR r.29.7 and Chancery Guide, Ch. 3, para. 3.17). Lead times for hearing in the High Court in London (Chancery Division) are currently (September 2003) about six months from the application to fix a trial date hearing in the case of hearings estimated to last for two days or less, and almost nine months for those hearings estimated to last for five days. (Note, however, that times may vary). The old days when a claim could be allowed to slumber unnoticed in the corner of a room for about a year or more have gone.

Pre-trial preparation requires attention to be given to the following matters in particular: **12–039**

(1) bundles of documents (see Chancery Guide, App. 2. Compliance with the terms of this Appendix is vital. See also CPR r.39 PD, para. 3 for the way in which bundles are to be presented).

(2) attendance and availability of witnesses, especially experts;

(3) witness summonses (note in particular the time limits under CPR r.34.5 at least seven days before attendance is required) and the obligation to pay "conduct money" under CPR r.34.7;

(4) adequate time to confer with and brief counsel — with proper bundles of documents;

(5) preparation of skeleton arguments (see Chancery Guide, App. 3 for this in particular);

(6) checking that litigants in person have been fully "copied in" to correspondence, statements, bundles, etc.;

(7) checking that all matters within the scope of previous Orders have been complied with; and

(8) checking all without prejudice and CPR r.36 offers have been made, as instructed, and that those received have been replied to. (See under costs below, Chapter 16 and para. 14–013).

Presentation of evidence from witnesses

Evidence from witnesses taken by examiners, by the court at or near the witness' home, or at a county court near to it may be directed by the court if the witness is too ill or frail to come to **12–040** the trial court. The latter course was taken by Laddie J. when (in a High Court claim in London) he went to the Eastbourne County Court to hear the evidence from one of the attesting witnesses to a disputed will who was too frail to come to London and who lived in a home near Eastbourne. (*Re Chapman dec'd National Trust v RNIB*, unreported, January 24, 1999).

Skeleton arguments

12–041 See the Chancery Guide, App. II.

Client care

12–042 This requires a little thought as to not just the claim generally, but also as to how the client is likely to be feeling about the claim. The latter aspect is very important if you are new to the matter and have yet to develop a rapport with the client. In terms of modern litigation, because the lead time for hearings is now months and not years, you will invariably have only a short amount of time to prepare the claim, deal with compromise, instruct counsel and, most importantly of all, care for the client.

12–043 Some questions which can be usefully asked in this context are:

(1) Have I explained the claim fully to the client? This means that the client has to be able to understand by your explanation what the claim is about, what the risks are, and what the prospects of success are. Costs risks and amounts of costs — on all sides — must also be explained. In addition, all offers made or received must be explained so that the client understands them.

(2) Does the client understand what the claim is all about? This should follow from (1). But you need to satisfy yourself that this is the case.

(3) What does the client want to get out of the claim? This means testing the client's objectives. Is it money, particular property, clearing the good name of the deceased, or a matter of principle? How far does the client want to pursue the claim to the bitter end and, if so, can he afford to do that? Often clients will not have the stomach for a fight and want a quick settlement. If so, can you achieve that?

(4) Have you tested the claim against the most gloomy predictions?

(5) Have you explained the "batting order" at trial?

Most clients will never have been near, let alone in, a court before, save for jury service. This means that you need to show the clients where the court is situated. (The commonest mistake in London is to confuse the Old Bailey off Newgate Street in the City of London with the Royal Courts of Justice in the Strand.) In other cities confusion between court buildings can arise, *e.g.* in Manchester, the Chancery District Registry will not be in the same building as the Magistrates Court. Taxi drivers often have to be shown a map — so supply one to the client. Having explained, and if necessary demonstrated, location, take some time to show the client what the *inside* of the court is likely to look like. In London, as the hearing is probably going to take place in the Thomas More Building, which is modern (*i.e.* from the 1990's), show the client that area of the Law Courts in particular. Explain that there will be no jury. Explain the sort of judge who will hear the case. Explain that it is unlikely to look like anything seen on TV in the criminal dramas enacted there of the "Rumpole" variety. Explain that the hearing is likely to be a public one. Remind the client to get there in good time and show him how to get there and where to meet — if not at counsel's chambers. If the client is disabled, make enquiries of the court staff if there are special entrances for wheelchairs, etc. and find out where they are.

(6) Remind the client, if a witness, and all other witnesses of:
    (a) the time and place of their attendance;
    (b) the need to read their statements and reports and any other documents indicated within 24 hours of the time they are likely to have to attend and give evidence, ideally the night before. They will be asked if they have done so at the beginning of their evidence in chief, which will admit their statement formally into evidence. — ***This is a very important reminder;*** and
    (c) the need to bring reading glasses and any medication if they are to be there all day — which may often happen when waiting to give evidence.

Counsel instructed will often deal with much of this, but ensure, if instructing him, that he has time to confer with you and the client *before* the first day of the hearing.

Finally, Check *again* that you have complied with any Orders made on Case Management Conference and with the Chancery Guide, *e.g.* as to the time for lodging bundles, skeleton arguments and reading lists. Check also that the estimated duration

12–044

of the hearing has not altered (one way or the other); if it has or is likely to change, inform the Listing Officer in accordance with Ch. 6 of the Chancery Guide. Information as to the duration and whether the claim is likely to be dealt with in a summary way *must* be given by the claimant's solicitor seven days before the date for the hearing under para. 6.14 thereof.

Mediation and Alternative Dispute Resolution ('ADR')

12–045 All probate claims are susceptible to mediation with a view to a settlement of the claim. It is beyond the scope of this book to describe the mediation process, and the reader is recommended to consult the numerous specialist books on the subject for an overview if he is a stranger to this way of settling claims. There is formal mediation on the one hand, and an informal evaluation by a third party on the other hand. Between the two there are other ways of trying to reach agreement. All that can be said here is, provided all parties are prepared in a proper manner for a mediation, the cost of it is a small price to pay for the settlement of what will be an even more expensive trial.

12–046 A very important point in relation to mediation and ADR generally is that a failure to take part in mediation may lead to adverse costs consequences. The failure to comply with any direction as to mediation will certainly be taken into account in any Order for costs, even against a successful party. (See CPR r.44.3(5) and below, para. 16–009, under costs. See also *Dunnett v Railtrack* plc [2002] 2 All E.R. 850. (No Order for costs in favour of successful defendant who had refused to submit to ADR). Compare *Société International de Telecommunications Aeronautiques SC v Wyatt & Co. (UK) Ltd* [2002] EWHC 2401, where the successful defendants to a CPR r.20 claim who refused an offer of ADR three weeks prior to trial were not deprived of any part of their costs.

The circumstances and manner in which ADR is raised is relevant in respect of costs; see Pt 44 r.3(5) and Chapter 16.

Chapter 13

The Final Hearing

General observations

Probate claims are in many respects no different from other **13–001** types of civil claim. This means that the adversarial system will require all parties to put their own case forward so that the case is tested by the cross-examination of witnesses. The judge (who can always ask his own questions) can weigh the evidence he has heard, apply the relevant principles of law and determine the claim on the usual civil standard of proof, namely the balance of probabilities.

However, in probate claims, whilst the court has no *formal* inquisitorial function, the court is concerned to seek the truth as to whether a testamentary document should be admitted to probate. Admission to probate in solemn form means that the will so proved becomes not only the document which governs the disposition of the deceased's estate, but also a public document and, significantly, part of an Order of the court which is the grant of probate. The court has an obligation to do justice to the deceased as well as to the parties. Thus, the court may have an "inquisitorial" role (*e.g.* exercisable under s.122 of the Supreme Court Act 1981) to require attesting witnesses or others with knowledge of the will to give evidence before it. This means that the court will be concerned to exercise scrutiny over the testamentary documents before it and inquire whether they should be admitted to probate. The court will be *vigilant* to ensure that the deceased knew and approved of the terms of the relevant will where the circumstances in which it was made and its terms reasonably excite the suspicion of the court (see *Wintle v Nye* [1959] 1 W.L.R. 284; *Re Fuld* [1965] P. 405 at 410; *Re Fuld* [1968] P. 675 at 712; *Re Parsons, dec'd* [2002] W.T.L.R. 237 and *Fuller v Strum* [2002] 1 W.L.R. 1097; see also above Chapter 6, for the law on want of knowledge and approval). Therefore, while the principles of an adversarial trial will apply to the hearing of the claim, and it is for the parties to decide how they are to present their own case and to destroy, or weaken the other party's case, the court has an inquisitorial function to ensure that the solemn form proof of a will, or revocation of a grant, is the right Order to make.

The final hearing

13–002 Unless there are reasons to take the claim out of the general rule, the hearing of a probate claim will be in public (CPR r.39.2; see also Phipson, *Evidence* (15th ed.), para. 10–04).

Application will have to be made to the master in advance of the hearing if a private hearing of the claim is required. This is a matter which can be dealt with at the CMC. See para. 12–004, above.

The order of speeches

13–003 Subject to any specific direction made at the CMC (*e.g.* as to the hearing of a preliminary issue), it will be for the claimant to begin; Phipson, *Evidence* (15th ed.), para. 10–10. The exceptions to this general rule are:

(1) When the burden of proof lies on the defendant, *e.g.* where the claimant seeks proof of a will of the deceased which the defendant claims was revoked by a later will. There is no dispute about the validity of the will put forward by the claimant. The only issue is whether the later will put forward by the defendant is a valid revoking will. Hence, the burden and the right to begin is on the defendant.

(2) Where a party other than the claimant is putting forward allegations of fraud, undue influence, forgery, mistake, or misrepresentation against a will which appears to have been executed and attested in accordance with the Wills Act 1837.

13–004 The court, and the trial judge in particular, has a general discretion to determine in what order the parties are to present their case and bring on their evidence. Where there is a series of wills, to each of which a number of questions arise, there can be no hard and fast rule about the presentation of cases. It is invariably good practice for the advocates to agree this between themselves beforehand, subject, of course, to any views which the trial judge may have on the subject.

It is important to note that the standard of proof on all **13–005** matters in issue will be the usual civil standard, *i.e.* on the balance of probabilities (*Fuller v Strum* [2002] 1 W.L.R. 1097). Note also that the burden of proof is capable of "shifting" in a probate claim. For example, the *initial* burden of proof will always lie on the person seeking to put forward the claim based on want of capacity, or fraud, or want of knowledge. It is then for the party defending that claim to counter such evidence. Where a claim is based on want of knowledge and approval, the *ultimate* burden is on the person who has to dispel the suspicious circumstances (see *Wintle v Nye* [1959] 1 W.L.R. 284; see also above, para. 6–007, and *Re Fuld* [1968] P. 675 at 697–698).

Finally note that a defendant may also challenge the evidence **13–006** of the attesting witnesses by a notice under CPR r.57.7(5) and cross-examine them without calling any evidence of his own, thereby ensuring that the burden remains on the claimant to prove the validity of the will he seeks to propound. (See above, para. 11–076).

Evidence

Evidence in chief

This will be admitted under CPR Pt. 32 from the witness **13–007** statement(s) of the witness. There is only limited scope for additional oral evidence to be given. If there are errors, or points in the evidence which are not clear in the statement, the witness can give oral evidence about that after being sworn, or after giving the appropriate affirmation. The witness should always be asked to confirm the truth of his statement(s) and that he has read it within the past 24 hours; see above, para. 12–043 for preparation for this.

Experts who are giving evidence should always be asked to **13–008** confirm their reports and, if necessary, explain any points where it may be thought to be of assistance to the court; *e.g.* in the case of complex medical conditions where even the report, however clear, may require some explanation.

In probate claims it may be desirable for the court to hear the **13–009** oral evidence of a witness giving evidence in chief about a particularly significant event; *e.g.* the execution and attestation of a will. This should be done without the witness being able to read his statement. Accordingly, the advocate calling that witness must be prepared to conduct an "old style" examination in chief. The judge may well require this in order to see how the witness gives his evidence. Witnesses are usually allowed to remain in court during the evidence. However, it is open to a party to request that a witness remains out of court during the evidence, until it is that witness's turn to be called, where there is a risk that the witness may change his evidence to accord with that given. In view of the exchange of witness statements prior to the hearing, this risk may be harder to avoid. If the evidence of an attesting witness fails to prove due execution, invariably as a result of cross-examination, the party seeking to propound the will must still call the other attesting witness. Only if the evidence given by that witness is hostile to the case of the party calling him, should the witness be treated as such by the advocate calling him. As stated above, para. 11–033, attesting witnesses are witnesses of the court and may be called by any party, if not subpoenaed by the judge, and there can be a risk of such witnesses being shaken as to the evidence which may be in their witness statements. Any advocate conducting an examination in chief must, of course, *avoid leading questions*, particularly in respect of areas of evidence which are in contest. (The value of any evidence produced in reply to a leading question will be devalued.) In probate claims, where the evidence may turn on minutiae, this rule is a very important one.

Cross-examination

13–010 Any witness whose evidence is the subject of a witness statement which is to be relied on by the party calling that witness is to be regarded as available for cross-examination. The purpose of cross-examination in civil claims in general, and in probate claims in particular, is to ascertain the truth and in doing so to test the evidence which that witness has already given. Leading questions *are* permitted in cross-examination. Cross-examination should never be regarded as a bad-tempered exercise in putting questions to a witness with the sole aim (or so it would appear) of making that witness equally bad-tempered. In probate claims, where the issues may arise out of the course of events, such as the precise way in which execution and attestation occurred, the aim of cross-examination will often be to see if that witness's version of events may be regarded as faulty. In the case of expert witnesses, care will have to be taken when cross-examining them to ensure that the advocate conducting that cross-examination has the material to hand to enable him to do an effective job. This means not just a mastery of his own expert witness's report but also having his expert witness behind him in court so as to be there to deal with points as they arise.

Finally, as in all other claims, a party who has evidence which **13–011** is contrary to the evidence being put forward by the witness giving evidence (where such evidence is within the knowledge of that witness, or is something on which he can properly comment) must "put his case" to that witness in cross-examination. For example, conflicting versions of the events surrounding execution of the will must be put to the witness of those events. Likewise, conflicting medical evidence as disclosed in the reports must be put to experts. It is sometimes not necessary to put one's case down to every tiny detail, and advocates can agree with the judge that, although a point has not been put in cross-examination, that point is not necessarily conceded. But probate claims are, in the nature of all other civil claims, governed by English law and this means that the adversarial system of testing the evidence applies to them. The judge requires the evidence to be tested, and if it has not been, and unless there is an agreement or direction from the court that it did not have to be put, a party can make the point that the untested and contested evidence may not carry the weight it should do, or that it should be accepted if unchallenged. The only slight exception to the application of the adversarial nature of probate claims lies in the fact that the court will require evidence of formal execution and attestation in compliance with s.9 of the Wills Act 1837, or of revocation under s.20 if that is in issue. It is also the case that as attesting witnesses are witnesses of the court (*Re Fuld (No. 2)* [1965] P. 405, at 410), they are compellable by any party and potentially the object of a summons by the court under s.122 of the Supreme Court Act 1981. See above, para. 11–033.

Re-examination

Re-examination can be conducted by the advocate who has **13–012** called a witness who has been subject to cross-examination. Leading questions may not be put. Questions in re-examination are limited to those arising from the evidence given by that witness in cross-examination, unless the judge allows other questions to be asked. The purpose of re-examination is generally to clarify answers to questions put in cross-examination which may have been left unclear. Care should be taken when re-examining not to make the position of your witness worse than it was at the close of cross-examination. It is important in probate claims to remember that unless the evidence given by the witness in cross-examination is *very* damaging (in which case it will usually be too late to do anything about it), re-examination is usually not necessary, or prudent.

Releasing witnesses

13–013 It is important to remember that at the close of the evidence given by experts and in particular any witnesses who have been summonsed to attend under CPR r.34, the judge should be asked to release that witness from further attendance. This is because *unless* released they are bound to attend for the whole of the trial, even if adjourned. See CPR r.34.5 and note r.34.5.3.

Interposing witnesses

13–014 As stated above, there is no formal Order in which a party has to call his evidence in a civil claim, and this includes probate claims. The logical order usually dictates itself (*i.e.* attesting witnesses first) but there may have to be some interposition to allow, for example, for professional commitments by expert witnesses (see Phipson, *Evidence,* (15th ed.), para. 10–11).

Opening and closing speeches

13–015 The party with the obligation to begin will "open" the case. This is nowadays invariably quite short by comparison with an old-style opening. It is conducted with reference to the skeleton arguments and the trial bundles, which the judge will invariably have read. It is good practice to have a core bundle of, for example, the will(s) in dispute. The original testamentary documents should have been the subject of a request that they be in court before the start of the hearing and should be in court — but kept in a safe place and returned to the Master's or the District Judge's chambers at the end of the day's hearing.

13–016 At the close of the claimant's case the defendant will begin his case. He will probably have been asked to make a short "opening" at the start of the hearing after the claimant's opening so that the judge, with the aid of his skeleton, can understand what his case is all about.

13–017 At the close of the defendant's evidence the defendant will present his submissions to the judge. These are invariably oral but will nowadays be supplemented by written submissions; often a revised version of the skeleton prepared before the start of the hearing.

13–018 The claimant's reply will be limited to a reply on any law (or authority) which the defendant has referred to in his submissions. It is the invariable rule that the party with the obligation to begin and the ultimate burden of proof should have the "last word".

After judgment there will be submissions on the proper Order **13–019** as to costs, with reference to any CPR r.36 offer, or costs letters and any other material such as correspondence, which may be relevant to the conduct of the claim. This will also be the appropriate moment for any application for permission to appeal. In view of the nature of probate claims, unless they have been very straightforward, or dealt with in a very short time at the hearing, the court will direct a detailed assessment of costs under CPR r.44.7. Summary assessment may only be appropriate if the claim has gone short and lasted not more than one day, or where there is a discontinuance or some other compromise and the parties are prepared for a summary assessment to save the additional costs of a detailed assessment. (See CPR r.44 PD, para. 13). Costs statements must be exchanged in accordance with the terms of CPR r.44 PD, para. 13 whenever there is a risk of summary assessment. The time requirement is "as soon as possible" and in any event not less than 24 hours before the date fixed for the hearing. The unattractive habit of a statement of costs sent by fax to the opposing party at about 6.30 pm on the evening before the hearing is in breach of the Practice Direction, and para. 13.6 contains the sanctions which may be imposed for a failure to adhere to it. In some claims which have settled on all issues including who is to pay the costs, save the amount of those costs, the costs-only proceedings route under CPR r.44.12A may be appropriate. Note that detailed assessment is not stayed pending an appeal unless the court so orders (CPR r.47.2 and CPR r.47 PD, para. 29). Costs issues are dealt with below, Chapter 16.

Submission of no case to answer

It is rare for this to arise in probate claims, not only because the **13–020** lines of the dispute will have been well drawn from the outset, but also because, under the CPR, any weaknesses in the case of a claimant should have become apparent at a pre-trial hearing, such as the CMC, where an application to strike out should be considered. However, it is open to the defendant to submit at the close of the claimant's case that in effect there is no case for the judge to put to himself wearing his "jury hat". Such a submission requires the defendant to be put to his election as to whether he is going to call any evidence of his own, whatever the outcome of the submission, and the court will be reluctant to allow such a submission to be made without the defendant having accepted that he will not call any evidence, whatever the fate of his submission. The need to make such an election is the reason why this submission is so rarely made in a civil claim. (See CPR r.32.1 and the extensive notes at 32.1.6 in Vol. 1 of the White Book for a full treatment of the way in which recent authority has dealt with this submission and the need for an election not to call evidence.)

Chapter 14

Discontinuance and Compromise

Special rules apply to compromising probate claims. The application of those rules is dictated by the manner in which the parties want to bring the claim to an end by agreement. If termination is not agreed, one party may seek a discontinuance, and that may also be agreed, to which special rules also apply.

14–001

Where the parties agree to discontinue the claim, or where a party applies for such discontinuance

The rules about discontinuance set out in CPR r.38 do not apply to probate claims.

14–002

CPR r.57.11 sets out how a claimant (or a defendant who has acknowledged service) can apply to discontinue a probate claim. Unlike the procedure in CPR r.38, where a party wishing to discontinue simply files a notice of discontinuance (CPR r.38.2(1)) with certain automatic consequences as to costs (CPR r.38.6), under CPR r.57.11 the party wishing to discontinue must make an application to do so under CPR r.24.

It is for the court to make the Order "on such terms as to costs or otherwise as it thinks just". Therefore, unless the way in which costs are to be borne is agreed, the court has a wide discretion as to how the costs are to be borne and, unless all other terms are agreed, as to any other terms. (See CPR r.44.12A for costs-only proceedings).

14–003

Discontinuance under CPR r.57.11 will, therefore, arise:

14–004

(1) where such an Order is agreed; and

(2) where a party seeks such an Order, *e.g.* by a defendant because the claimant is not proceeding with his claim.

14–005 The order which the court will make on a discontinuance under CPR r.57.11 will depend on what has been agreed. If terms are not agreed, the court will make an Order that a grant *in common form* be made to the correct party "if entitled thereto". It is up to that party to satisfy the Probate Registry that he is entitled, on application for that grant (NCPR r.45(3)).

14–006 On a discontinuance, the court will *not* make a solemn form Order, as it has not heard any evidence from which it could make a finding as to validity (see s.49 of the Administration of Justice Act 1985 below, para. 14–009). If discontinuance occurs in a claim where there has been an appointment of an administrator pending suit under s.117 of the Supreme Court Act 1981 (see above, para. 11–041 for s.117 grants), and if the Order to discontinue is agreed in "Tomlin" form (*i.e.* the claim is merely stayed), the formal part of the Order must discharge that administrator. Otherwise, as that person's function will continue until the *end* of the claim (and will not cease on a mere stay of the claim) there may be difficulty in getting the common form full grant when applying to the probate registry. The jurisdiction to make an Order to discontinue, whether by consent or not, is exercisable by a High Court judge in all cases.

14–007 In cases where the Order is agreed but is subject to the court's approval because of the interest of a minor, or a patient, a Master (or District Judge outside London in the Chancery District Registry) will have jurisdiction if the interest of that person in the estate is less than £100,000 (CPR r.2, PD, B, para. 5.1(a)).

It should be noted that, apart from discontinuance under CPR r.57.11, there is no reason why a probate claim should not be struck out for want of prosecution or for non-compliance with orders of the court pre-trial, invoking CPR r.3. (See *Re Flynn* [1982] 1 W.L.R. 310, showing that mere delay in bringing a probate claim might not warrant striking it out; see also above, para. 11–121, on limitation). But under the CPR, delay in *getting on* with a claim — so far as the rules allow that state of affairs to exist — might well warrant a strike out.

Where there is a general compromise of the claim, parties may have a choice

A trial on written evidence only

14–008 This may be needed if, for example, the parties are agreed that a will which is earlier than the last dated will is to prevail. In such a case the court will have to be satisfied that, for example, the formalities under s.9 of the Wills Act 1837 were not complied with in respect of the last dated will. (But see s.49 of the Administration of Justice Act 1985 below, where a court can make an Order in favour of an earlier will by consent, without such a hearing). After the hearing and consideration of the written evidence the court can make an Order for solemn form proof of the will which the parties have agreed to admit to probate (see CPR r.57 PD, para. 6.1(1)). In view of the jurisdiction under s.49 of the Administration of Justice Act 1985 (as to which, see below), it is unlikely that this method of carrying out the terms of a compromise in favour of a particular will is going to be used — unless s.49 cannot be invoked because, for example, not all the relevant beneficiaries can consent, whether directly, or through a litigation friend. This problem can arise, for example, where a large class of those potentially entitled on intestacy cannot be found, and where CPR r.19.7 cannot be used to bind absent parties.

An Order under s.49 of the Administration of Justice Act 1985

The text of the section is as follows: 14–009

s.49 — Powers of High Court on compromise of probate action.

(1) Where on a compromise of a probate action in the High Court—

    (a) the court is invited to pronounce for the validity of one or more wills, or against the validity of one or more wills, or for the validity of one or more wills and against the validity of one or more other wills; and

    (b) the court is satisfied that consent to the making of the pronouncement or, as the case may be, each of the pronouncements in question has been given by or on behalf of every relevant beneficiary,

the court may without more pronounce accordingly.

(2) In this section—
"probate action" means an action for the grant of probate of the will, or letters of administration of the estate, of a deceased person or for the revocation of such a grant or for a decree pronouncing for or against the validity of an alleged will, not being an action which is non-contentious or common form probate business; and
"relevant beneficiary", in relation to a pronouncement relating to any will or wills of a deceased person, means—

(a) a person who under any such will is beneficially interested in the deceased's estate; and

(b) where the effect of the pronouncement would be to cause the estate to devolve as on an intestacy (or partial intestacy), or to prevent it from so devolving, a person who under the law relating to intestacy is beneficially interested in the estate.

14–010 Provided all "relevant beneficiaries" consent (whether directly, by a litigation friend, or by falling within an Order made under CPR r.19.7 and being bound by an Order of the court although absent), the court can make an Order in *solemn form* by consent in *favour of* any will. It can also make an Order by consent *against* the validity of a will. The court is not, therefore, constrained by the old law which prevented a Court from pronouncing against a will by consent or from granting proof in solemn form of a will, other than the last will, by consent.

14–011 Section 49 is, therefore, the means to achieve a solemn form grant without either a full trial, or a hearing on paper; see CPR r.57 PD, para. 6.1(3).

Note the following points:

(1) The form of Order is Chancery Practice Form No.CH38.

(2) Paragraph 6.1(2) indicates that application can be heard and the Order made by the Master or District Judge without any limit of jurisdiction, save that, if approved on behalf of a person under a disability, the limit on jurisdiction is £100,000 in respect of that person's share in the estate (CPR r.2 PD, B, para. 5.1(a), see above, para. 14–007).

(3) The written consents of the relevant beneficiaries (as defined by subsection (2)) or their litigation friends must be exhibited to a witness statement of one of the parties, or their solicitor, identifying each such relevant beneficiary. If an Order is made under CPR r.19.7, the compromise Order will bind all those represented (CPR r.19.7(6), r.19.7(7)). The same principle will apply where the Order is binding on persons notified under CPR r.19.8A; see CPR r.19.8A(6)).

(5) Compliance with the rules relating to testamentary documents under CPR r.57.5 (see above, para. 11–077) is necessary if an Order under s.49 is to be made; Part 57 PD para. 6.2. See Chancery Guide, Ch. 24, reproduced in the Appendices for what must be done in terms of lodging documents.

(6) A s.49 Order cannot be made in the rare event of a probate claim being in the County Court (CPR r.57 PD, para. 6.1). Such an Order can only be made in the High Court.

Note also the following: 14–012

(1) Where persons under a disability are parties and are represented by a litigation friend (as they must be under CPR r.21) good practice requires the filing of evidence that the litigation friend approves of the compromise. Also that person should exhibit instructions to counsel and counsel's opinion stating that the proposed compromise is for the benefit of the party under a disability.

If time does not allow this, for example where there is an agreement to compromise during a trial, counsel will, no doubt, be able to explain orally why the compromise is beneficial or prepare a short note to that effect. If the Court of Protection has approved the bringing or defending of the claim on behalf of a patient, it will be necessary to obtain the sanction of the Court of Protection before the receiver can ask the Chancery Court to approve the compromise of the probate claim. This may require an urgent *ex parte* application to the Court of Protection at Archway Tower; and the Official Solicitor should also be informed.

(2) Charity beneficiaries — If a charity beneficiary agrees to the compromise, that charity can agree to it through one of the officers of that charity and the Charity Commission need not be involved.

However, if there is an "absent" charity — *e.g.* where there is a gift for "charitable purposes only" and invariably a scheme is to be proposed, or if a named charity fails to appear, the Attorney-General (contactable through the Treasury Solicitor's office: (*www.treasury-solicitor.gov.uk*) should be joined as a party to the claim. If assenting, the Attorney-General will, by convention, in the form of the Order "consent" to the compromise of a claim by or against a named charity. But where there is no named charity (*e.g.* in the case of a gift for general charitable purposes only, as above) and the Attorney-General represents charity generally, the Order will state that it is the wish of the Attorney-General "not to object" to the compromise, or it is stated that the Attorney-General is "not objecting" to it.

(3) Section 49 can be used where it is agreed that an existing common form grant is to be revoked.

(4) It is permissible for the terms of compromise to be entered into in a form which contains not only the Order directing a solemn, or common form grant, but also terms in a schedule determining how the estate is to be distributed, if a variation has been agreed. Such a variation can only be agreed and regarded as enforceable if all relevant parties are party to such a variation and any parties affected who are under a disability, through their litigation friend, have satisfied the court that the compromise and variation is for their benefit; see above, as to what is required.

(5) A claim for revocation of a common form grant and solemn form proof of a will which has been admitted to probate under that grant may be needed where a party is asserting a claim against that common form grant without necessarily seeking to revoke it. The executors may want the finality of a solemn form grant (as opposed to a common form grant which is inherently revocable; see para. 15–002 below).

The use of CPR r.36 offers

Can they be used at all?

14–013 A probate claim is not a "money claim" within CPR r.36 so, therefore, payment into Court is not appropriate in probate claims. ("Money claim" is not defined by the text of CPR r.36 but clearly claims where there is a sum of money at issue, such as damages, or a claim to a debt, or a claim for a liquidated sum, fall within those words.) It is, however, possible in theory to use CPR r.36 offers in probate claims. But, as will be seen below, it is difficult to make *effective* CPR r.36 offers in this area of the law.

14–014 Reference should be made to the important and detailed terms of CPR r.36 for the way in which CPR r.36 offers should be made and their effect.

Why use them?

14–015 The overall purpose of making CPR r.36 offers will be to protect the party making the offer in terms of costs. Thus under CPR r.36.20, which applies to defendant's offers made to claimants, the claimant who has failed to obtain a judgment which is more advantageous than the defendant's offer will be ordered to pay the defendant's costs of the claim from the date when the offer could have been accepted without needing the court's permission. Only if it is unjust to make such an Order will the court make a different Order. In a case where the claimant has made an offer which is beaten, in the sense that the judgment against the defendant is more favourable to the claimant than the proposals in the claimant's offer, by CPR r.36.21, the costs effect will be the same, but with the added relish of indemnity costs. CPR r.36.20 does not mirror r.36.21 in terms of indemnity costs if a claimant fails to better a defendant's CPR r.36 offer. However, *Excelsior Commercial Holdings v Salisbury Hamer Aspden & Johnson* [2002] EWCA Civ 879 establishes that indemnity costs may be awarded if the circumstances of the case justify it. See also *Huck v. Robson* below at para. 14–017. See CPR r.44.4(3) and notes in the White Book as to the general principles applicable to indemnity costs orders. See also *All Rez-Delta Transport Co Ltd v United Arab Shipping Co (No.2),* unreported (*The Times,* July 4, 2003), which considers that the terms of CPR r.36 require a purposive approach to construction, as its aim is to encourage parties to accept reasonable offers and to save money and court time. Finally, see below, Chapter 16, on costs. (The power to award interest on any sum of money awarded under CPR r.36.21(2) is not relevant in a probate claim). What this means in simple terms is that in probate claims there may well be a need to consider what the likely outcome in financial terms will be, given the validity of the will, or wills in dispute.

Such offers are not, of course, disclosed to the trial judge until **14–016** all questions of liability have been decided, or where there is a stay following acceptance under CPR r.36.15. (CPR rr.36.19(2) and r.36.3(b)). This makes it vital to keep CPR r.36 offers and replies to them separate from the main correspondence files and to ensure that trial bundles do not contain CPR r.36 offers and replies by mistake. Care is needed at any CMC to avoid the risk of any CPR r.36 offers coming to the knowledge of the judge who may also be the trial judge. This is a particular risk outside London, where the "designated judge" may also conduct a CMC or pre-trial review if not being handled by the District judge; see notes to CPR r.36.19 in the White Book.

Pre-claim CPR r.36 offers (in the formal sense) cannot be **14–017** made (CPR r.36.2(4)). However, and this is very significant and a strong reason for making them pre-claim, the court *must* have regard to pre-claim offers when considering what Order to make about costs under CPR r.36.10. See also CPR r.44.3(4)(c), which is dealt with below, Chapter 16. For recent authority on the fact that pre-claim CPR r.36 offers will be taken into account when determining costs under CPR r.44, see *Huck v Robson* [2003] 1 W.L.R. 1340, where indemnity costs were awarded to the claimant who beat the pre-claim offer.

Special considerations present in probate claims

14–018 In the context of probate claims the following specific points should be borne in mind as regards making CPR r.36 offers.

(1) The purpose of making a CPR r.36 offer is to tempt the other party to accept that offer. That offer has to be a better one than the court will order, even if the party making the offer is successful at trial. Acceptance of the offer will usually have the consequence that, not only is the claim stayed, but also that the accepting party receives his costs up to the date of serving the notice of acceptance; see CPR rr.36.13 and 36.14. This assumes the offer is made not less than 21 days before the start of the trial under CPR r.36.11(1). If the offer is made within the period of 21 days of the start of the trial, unless the parties agree the liability for costs, the leave of the court will be needed for the acceptance of the offer; CPR r.36.11(2). Therefore, the CPR r.36 offer must be made no later than 21 days before the start of the trial and it must be attractive enough to merit consideration for acceptance.

(2) Thus, it is difficult, but not impossible in probate claims (when the claim is about documents and the effect of them), to use CPR r.36 offers to good effect. Unlike a claim which has a reasonably clear monetary value, the party wishing to make the offer, and the other party who will inevitably make a counter-offer, will try to assess what will be the practical effect of the court's Order.

(3) Where persons under a disability are parties to the claim, the approval of the court will be needed under CPR r.21.10; see CPR r.36.15(4). In addition, there will have to be compliance with CPR r.48.5 as to the costs of that party.

(4) It is at this stage, having regard to all the points above, that the problem of making effective CPR r.36 offers comes into play. In many respects probate claims will be "all or nothing" claims. To that extent, unless a party can beat what it is likely the court will Order in favour of the other party, there is little point in making a CPR r.36 offer. Thus if the claimant seeks to propound will A and the defendant will B, no CPR r.36 offer by the claimant which is made in terms of his will A being the one which the defendant ought to accept can really have any effect. If the claimant wins he should get his costs, and, if he loses, vice versa. No Order will be "more advantageous"

in such circumstances than any offer. But it is suggested that CPR r.36 offers can be made (for example) in terms whereby it is proposed by the claimant that the claim is settled on terms that will A is admitted to probate and that the offeror is prepared to allow the offeree a slightly greater interest in the estate than the defendant would have got had will B been proved. The words of CPR rr.36.20 and 36.21 which refer to "a judgment which is more advantageous" for or against a party, require a balanced consideration of who has won and who is, as a result, the unsuccessful party. If such an offer is made, it is clear that, even if the defendant wins, he has failed to obtain a judgment which is "more advantageous" than the offer. Such circumstances may be rare, but the message is that there is no reason why advisers should not *consider* whether CPR r.36 offers should not be made. The nature of such offers will vary from case to case, but the important point is that to be effective in costs terms the offer has to be better than the Order which the offeror is likely to get at trial. The difficult aspect of this analysis being put into practice in probate claims is in trying to achieve that. This is why some financial incentive may have to be offered, which, however unattractive as a concept, may at least save the costs of a trial.

Without prejudice offers

Such offers are protected from disclosure to the court at all times. They will not have any costs-saving consequences, but such offers may lead the parties to an agreement. They have their place in probate claims as in all other forms of civil claim and should not be ignored as a means of facilitating agreement and removing unnecessary barriers to dialogue. **14–019**

Without prejudice save as to costs, or "Calderbank" letters

Even though CPR r.36 is available, there is no reason why offers which are expressed to be "without prejudice save as to costs" should not be used. As in the discussion under CPR r.36 above, para. 14–013, probate claims, which are often "all or nothing in nature", do present a problem in terms of making an offer which is going to be effective in costs terms, and which cannot in effect be outbid by the court even if the court decides the claim **14–020** in favour of the offeror. Even an offer which in terms of the result may be "too close to call" may have an effect on the way in which costs are ordered. This was the effect of such an offer in a claim under the Inheritance Act 1975 in *Graham v Murphy* [1997] 1 F.L.R. 860, where the claimant was awarded provision which was very close to that made in a Calderbank offer by the estate. He only recovered one-third of his taxed costs out of the estate. In a probate claim, particularly where there are a number of wills in dispute, an offer which proposes a compromise based on the terms of a will which is "midway" in its financial effect between all the wills may cause the court not to award all the costs of the claim to the successful party if that party does less well or only marginally better than the terms of the offer. Certainly a party who offers such a compromise and who succeeds in proving a will which is more favourable than the terms of such an offer should get his costs against a party who has declined such an offer.

14–021 Such offers must be taken into account by the court in deciding what costs Order to make under CPR r.44.3(4)(c). Such offers do not, however, have the full effect of CPR r.36 offers if not beaten, such as in terms of indemnity costs. Any Calderbank offer should state terms as to the payment of the offeree's costs, if it is to be fully effective, but even if it does not, this does not mean that it should be rejected out of hand.

Open offers

14–022 These speak for themselves and are part and parcel of a pragmatic approach to a claim. It is sensible to consider open offers pre-claim when all the relevant evidence as to capacity or formal execution and attestation is to hand, and where such evidence discloses a clear case one way or the other.

Offers to mediate

14–023 As referred to above, para. 12–045, these can be very important in any consideration of Orders as to costs by the court. Because of the "all or nothing" nature of many probate claims and the difficulty of making effective CPR r.36 or Calderbank offers, such offers may have a greater significance than they may have at first glance. This is particularly so where the failure to agree to mediation may have a bearing on costs.

Taxation and the effect of orders made by consent in probate claims varying the disposition of the deceased's estate

Reference should be made to the textbooks on tax for a full consideration of the law relating to the fiscal effect of variations of estates after death. For example, see Dymond's *Capital Taxes,* Simon's *Direct Tax Service* and also James Kessler, *Drafting Trusts and Will Trusts,* (6th ed.). In addition, the Inland Revenue website (*www.inlandrevenue.gov.uk*) contains the text of the *Advanced Instruction Manual* (for inheritance tax) and the *Capital Gains Manual* (for capital gains tax). It also has other commentary on the effect for income tax purposes of post-death variations. Other websites, such as that maintained by James Kessler (*www.kessler.co.uk*) and STEP (*www.step.org*) are invaluable sources of information in this highly technical area of the law. What follows is only an outline of some relevant points. 14–024

Unlike s.19 of the Inheritance Act 1975, which treats Orders of the court made under s.2 of that Act as retrospective for all purposes, including that of inheritance tax, an order made in a compromise of a *probate claim* will not be so treated, to the extent that it varies the dispositions of the estate whether by the will, intestacy, or even any other manner by which property may pass on after death outside the grant, such as by survivorship. Clearly an Order of the court in a probate claim which makes no change to the dispositions (whether or not made by consent) will not have any tax effect in itself, as the estate will be administered without any variation. What may, however, be of concern in fiscal terms is when the compromise of a probate claim does cause a variation in the way in which the estate is going to pass. See above, para. 14–001, where Orders made on the compromise of probate claims are considered. Often the compromise will be in the schedule to the Order, frequently in the "Tomlin" form. To safeguard the fiscal position the compromise should oblige the parties to execute a deed of variation by a given date, if possible within the two-year period from the death, which allows the variation to be retrospective in theory for both inheritance and capital gains tax. Such variations may require the court to approve the terms of compromise on behalf of those under a disability within the meaning of CPR r.21; see above, para. 14–012, where this is referred to. In such cases there is no equivalent of s.19 of the 1975 Act, and if the compromise terms are to be retrospective, those terms, or a deed of variation executed in accordance with them, must be executed in accordance with s.142 of the Inheritance Tax Act 1984 and s.62 of the Taxation of Chargeable Gains Act 1992. In all cases the execution must take place within *two years of the* 14–025 *death* of the deceased whose estate is being varied. It is also important to check that there is no extraneous consideration being given by any party to the variation, which, if present, may affect the retrospective treatment of it. The parties may not want the variation to be retrospective, *e.g.* when redirecting property from a spouse, or a charity able to claim the exemption for inheritance tax to a chargeable beneficiary, or where it cannot be, as the variation is outside the two-year time limit.

In the former case great care must be taken to ensure that the benefit of exemptions is not lost. The danger may be that the compromise of the probate claim is treated as consideration which would take the variation out of the retrospective treatment for tax. This is a point which must be considered with tax specialists when a compromise is being discussed.

14–026 Therefore, in probate claims, even when merely contemplated, if there is likely to be a compromise which involves a variation of the dispositions of the estate, the two-year period from the death must be kept in mind with diary reminders during the unexpired part of that period.

14–027 It is important to note the following:—

(1) No attempt is made here to analyse the tax effect of an Order in a probate claim which revokes a grant and which has the practical effect of causing another will to be admitted to probate, or creating an intestacy, with a different beneficial entitlement. Such a change may well affect the exemptions and reliefs claimed when the first grant was taken, and will require the submission of new accounts to the Capital Taxes Office. In such cases refer to Dymond's Capital Taxes and the Advanced Instruction Manual on the Inland Revenue website, referred to above at para. 14–024.

(2) Variations must be considered very carefully where the incidence of IHT may be affected particularly in partly exempt estates.

(3) In all cases where the compromise of a probate claim will cause a variation of the dispositions of the estate, specialist tax advice must be sought.

Chapter 15

Orders which the Court Can Make

The Court may make an Order for a grant of probate of a will or letters of administration; this falls within the definition of a "probate claim" in CPR r.57.1(2)(a)(i). "The court" is used in this chapter to mean the High Court (Chancery Division) and includes the County Court where it has jurisdiction in probate claims. **15–001**

The effect of an Order for proof in solemn form

A grant in solemn form of probate of a will or other testamentary document can only be made as a result of an Order in a probate claim governed by CPR r.57.1(2). As has been pointed out above, para. 14–009, if an Order in solemn form is to be made by the court, whether or not by consent, the court is concerned to see that all parties who may have an interest in the claim are parties or have had the opportunity to be joined under CPR r.19.7, or are represented by a party under that rule, or have been notified of the claim under CPR r.19.8A. (Note the power to set aside a judgment or Order made in the absence of a person who did not attend under CPR r.39.3(3) and the remaining sub-rules of that r.39.3). Those who are aware of the claim may be obliged, if they are to protect their own interest, to apply to be joined as a defendant under CPR r.19.3; see above, para. 11–047 to 11–053, as to parties. Under old rules of procedure, a person who had an interest in the claim could issue a "citation to see" the proceedings; *i.e.* intervene in them. This is a term used in some of the old cases. In a probate claim the court will be reluctant to set aside an Order for probate in solemn form and will require a very strong indication of the merits of that party in being able to assert another will or an **15–002** intestacy so as to cause that Order to be set aside. (See below, para. 15–003).

15–003 Once the court has made the Order in solemn form it binds all those persons described above and those who can be shown to have been aware of their interest. That is why an Order in solemn form is often described as an Order made *"in rem"*, *i.e.* for a particular document and against all those with a claim against it. It is only if such a person did not know of his interest that he may be able to set aside the Order made. That is why it is so important that all those with a potential interest must be identified at an early stage (including, if necessary, the class entitled as next of kin on intestacy, which may require companies such as Title Research to conduct a kin inquiry) so that notification under CPR rr.19.7 and 19.8A can go out. Under NCPR r.45(1) and (2) the Principal Registry will notify caveators of the commencement of a probate claim (once it has been notified of the commencement seemingly under CPR r.57 PD, para. 2), and the Principal Registry will also notify the claim to any caveators who seek to enter a caveat after the claim has begun.

For authority on the effect of an Order for probate in solemn form as an Order *in rem* and binding all parties and those with knowledge of their interest and potential claim, see *Newell v Weeks* (1814) 2 Phillim. 224; *Ratcliffe v Barnes* (1862) 2 Sw. & Tr. 486; *Young v Holloway* [1895] P. 87; and *Re Langton* [1964] P. 163, at 175 *per* Danckwerts L.J.

15–004 A solemn form grant may be revoked by a later Order of the court where:

(1) *If subsequent to the solemn form Order, a later valid will is found.* In view of the modern procedural requirements as to statements of testamentary documents and disclosure, it is highly unlikely that this situation will occur. But in cases of fraud and suborned witnesses, later challenges may emerge.

(2) *If the Order has been obtained by fraud.* See, for example, *Birch v Birch* [1902] P. 60 and 130). In that case, following an Order made in December 1900 for proof in solemn form of a will, an attempt was made in June 1901 to set aside that Order on the ground that there had been fraud in obtaining that Order and that the will so proved was subject to tainted evidence. The Court of Appeal did not accept that the evidence before it was strong enough, or admissible to allow the claim to proceed. In *Sohal v Sohal* [2002] EWCA Civ 2002, CA the Court of Appeal held that "a fresh action should be brought to set the judgment aside." (See below, Chapter 19, for appeals in probate claims).

Orders for a grant in common form

15–005 Unlike a grant in solemn form, a grant in common form is inherently revocable. Such a grant is usually made under the non-contentious probate jurisdiction of the Family Division (Probate); see above, Chapter 1). In the context of a probate claim the court will normally make such an Order where the parties have consented to it, or as a result of a discontinuance or dismissal under CPR r.57.11. Because a common form grant is revocable, it may be the subject of a later revocation claim and that is why it is preferable to obtain a solemn form grant, with all interests represented or notified, to avoid this risk for the future.

15–006 It is important to bear in mind that a common form grant is valid until the court orders that it be revoked. Even though it has to be lodged in court in a revocation claim (CPR r.57.6(2)), it is still valid. The personal representatives may rely on it and third parties in good faith can also do so. (See above para. 12–026, under "interim remedies" for what may be done by personal representatives to preserve or protect the estate pending the determination of a probate claim where revocation of an existing grant is in issue. See also the authority of *Daniel v Abiola* [2003] EWHC Civ 1562, above, para. 11–124 and para. 12–031).

15–007 In the language used by lawyers in this context, the grant may be said to be voidable, and not void *ab initio*; *i.e.* from the outset even if the court so declares in an Order at a later date. (See Parry & Clark (11th ed.), for the effect of revocation of grant on transactions carried out in reliance on the (revoked) grant and before the Order to revoke). Section 204 of the Law of Property Act 1925 and ss.27 and 37 of the Administration of Estates Act 1925 confer extensive protection to third parties dealing in good faith and for valuable consideration with the grantee where the grant confers title on the grantee. But if a third party has an adverse claim which causes doubt as to the validity of the grant, he may not be in good faith and may only be prepared to deal with the personal representative after an Order of the Court has sanctioned the transaction. The personal representative may also require the protection of an Order, and will certainly be prudent in not paying legacies, etc. under the will or making payments to beneficiaries out of the estate to which the grant has been obtained and which is or is liable to be under attack (see *Daniel v Abiola* [2003], above, and *Guardian Trust Co v Public Trustee of New Zealand* [1942] A.C. 115). A personal representative may need to check that there will not be a revocation claim before he distributes if he has reason to believe that there may be one in the offing. He may seek the direction of the court before he does this; see *Fitzhugh Gates v Sherman* [2003] EWCA Civ 886. A common form grant may also be revoked, without a probate claim being commenced, where it has been obtained by a false statement, *e.g.* as to death, under NCPR r.41, or where the grantee becomes incapable, and if he disappears. See Parry and Clark, for examples and authorities. For revocation of such a grant on the basis of false statements made when it was applied for, see *Shephard v Wheeler* [2000] W.T.L.R. 1175. There is also the quite separate and wholly statutory jurisdiction to remove personal representatives under s.50 of the Administration of Justice Act 1985.

Revocation orders

15–008 The High Court may make an Order revoking an existing common form grant in a probate claim. Such relief falls within the definition of a "probate claim" in CPR r.57.1(2)(a)(ii).

15–009 The Probate Registry may also revoke a common form grant without the necessity for a probate claim to be brought. Under NCPR r.41 the Probate Registry also has jurisdiction to revoke a grant, but only in "exceptional circumstances" unless the grantee consents; (NCPR r.41(2)). Instances of this are where there has been impersonation, a mistake as to the death of the deceased, or capacity of the grantee to take the grant where there has been serious non-disclosure by the grantee about his fitness to take a grant (*Shephard v Wheeler* [2000] above). The grant will be revoked by the court of its own motion if there is evidence that it was issued in error, but where no person takes any step to seek revocation. (For a full account, see Williams, Mortimer and Sunnucks (18th ed.), paras 27–15 to 27–42.) As is pointed out above, at para. 11–121, there is no limitation period in respect of such a claim. In the circumstances set out above, para. 15–004, a grant in solemn form may also be set aside.

Declarations against the validity of an alleged will

15–010 This falls within the scope of a probate claim in CPR r.57.1; see r.57.1(2)(a)(iii). The court will make such a declaration if the burden of proof (to the civil standard of the balance of probabilities) is satisfied that the will cannot be admitted to probate as a valid will. Either it is formally invalid (for non-compliance with s.9 of the Wills Act, or as a revoked will under ss.18 or 20 of that Act) or it is inherently invalid on the grounds set out above in Chapters 3–8 above.

Carrying out the Order

Once the High Court (Chancery Division) has made an Order in a probate claim it is necessary to consider what is the next step to take, particularly from the point of view of the party who will have the right to the grant. In summary, the position is as follows: **15–011**

(a) *In all cases where the court has made an Order which determines a contested probate claim*
  (1) The Chancery Division court clerk will send a copy of the Order made by the Court, any grant lodged and all testamentary documents which will have been lodged with the Court, to Leeds District Probate Registry; ("Leeds"). Leeds is the nominated registry for receipt of all papers at the conclusion of a probate claim. Note that the Principal Registry, at First Avenue House, 42–49 High Holborn, London WC1, no longer receives these documents. **15–012**

  (2) Leeds will note the Order against any caveats. Since the Probateman computer record system came online in November 1998, all caveats are on that system, but any manual entries will also be checked; and if the Order directs, or has the effect of causing a caveat to cease to have effect, Leeds will give effect to that.

The next stages will vary according to the Order made.

(b) *Where the original grant is confirmed*
  (1) In the case of a grant of probate the Chancery Court staff will notate the grant as follows: **15–013**

  > "The force and validity of the will a copy whereof is hereunto annexed, was pronounced for in a claim entitled [short title of the claim] on [date of judgment or order]"

  (2) Leeds will notate the probate records held to confirm the effect of the Order. In the case of grants made since November 1998, as the Probateman system will have them on file, this is all that needs to be done, apart from the marking referred to above.

  (3) The copy grant will be released to the extracting solicitor usually direct from the Chancery Court. Only if there needs to be any notation made to the original contents of the probate registry records will it be returned to Leeds and released from there.

(c) *Where the grant is revoked*

15–014 On the commencement of the Probateman computer system in November 1998, all contentious matters pending in the Chancery Courts, together with caveats, warnings and appearances, were transferred into that system.

> (1) Leeds will notate the Probateman computer record that the case has been determined and that the grant has been revoked by an Order of the court, reciting the formal parts of the Order the claim reference and the date of the order.
>
> (2) Leeds will then send the grant and Order to the registry where the grant was issued. That registry will then check that the Probateman computer has on it the record of the Order to revoke that grant, and then an officer will cut a slice out of the seal on the grant and keep the original grant as notated and mutilated on file.
>
> (3) Probate registries now only maintain file records for the last two years preceding the current year. Earlier files are kept at the Probate Record Centre. If the file has been transferred to the Probate Record Centre, Leeds will send the grant and Order to Birmingham District Probate Registry, which notates the paper records held at the Probate Record Centre and sends the revoked grant and Order for filing there.
>
> (4) It will be for the party in whose favour the new grant is ordered to be taken to apply for that grant. This will require the completion of the form of oath applicable following a revocation, and the payment of probate fees. (There is no refund of fees paid on the occasion of the application for the grant which has been revoked.) Additional inheritance tax will be payable if, for example, the grant is of a will, or is in respect of an intestacy, where the benefit of exemptions or reliefs for inheritance tax have been lost.

(d) *Other points which will arise after the Order is made*

15–015 (1) In cases where the court has pronounced in favour of a will or an intestacy and directs that a person take a grant (sometimes with the words "if entitled thereto"), when Leeds receives the Order and scripts from the Chancery Court it will check Probateman to see if there is a pending application for a grant at any registry. If the grant application was made by or on behalf of the same person who is directed to take the grant by the court (but which has been held up by a caveat and the issue of the probate claim form), it will send the papers to the registry where that application was made. That registry will check with the solicitor who made the original application to ensure names, addresses and estate values appearing in the past have not changed, and the registry will then proceed to issue the grant.

(2) A variation on (1) above can arise if the person to whom the Order of the Chancery Court is made is different from the person who was to take the grant under the original application, as discovered by Leeds. Leeds will retain the papers until the registry where the new application is made calls for the papers from it. The registry where the new application is made will have searched Probateman and found that Leeds is retaining the papers.

In all cases of doubt, solicitors should contact Leeds District Probate Registry if they are seeking to trace papers, or their local probate registry to seek advice. The staff and registrars there are unfailingly helpful and will explain what should be done.

15–016 The authors wish to acknowledge the great assistance provided by Mr Keith Biggs Registrar of the District Probate Registry at Winchester in providing the explanation of the inner workings of the system once the Chancery Court has made the Order determining a probate claim, and also in explaining what happens when orders are made to rectify wills. The system described is of the practice in force in July 2003 and it is pointed out that changes may occur during the lifetime of this book. Hence the invariable advice to ask the appropriate registry in any case of doubt.

Chapter 16

Costs

The general rule

The general principles which determine how the court should exercise its discretion over costs are set out in CPR r.44.3. These principles apply with equal force to probate claims as they do to other types of civil claims. The principles set out in this rule are so important that the rule is set out in full here. **16–001**

r.44.3—Courts discretion and circumstances to be taken into account when exercising its discretion as to costs:

(1) The court has discretion as to—

(a) whether costs are payable by one party to another;
(b) the amount of those costs; and
(c) when they are to be paid.

(2) If the court decides to make an order about costs—

(a) the general rule is that the unsuccessful party will be ordered to pay the costs of the successful party; but
(b) the court may make a different order.

(3) The general rule does not apply to the following proceedings—

(a) proceedings in the Court of Appeal on an application or appeal made in connection with proceedings in the Family Division; or
(b) proceedings in the Court of Appeal from a judgment, direction, decision or order given or made in probate proceedings or family proceedings.

(4) In deciding what order (if any) to make about costs the court must have regard to all the circumstances, including—

(a) the conduct of all the parties;
(b) whether a party has succeeded on part of his case, even if he has not been wholly successful; and
(c) any payment into court or admissible offer to settle made by a party which is drawn to the court's attention (whether or not made in accordance with Part 36).
(Part 36 contains further provisions about how the court's discretion is to be exercised where a payment into court or an offer to settle is made under that Part)

(5) The conduct of the parties includes—

(a) conduct before, as well as during, the proceedings and in particular the extent to which the parties followed any relevant pre-action protocol;
(b) whether it was reasonable for a party to raise, pursue or contest a particular allegation or issue;
(c) the manner in which a party has pursued or defended his case or a particular allegation or issue; and
(d) whether a claimant who has succeeded in his claim, in whole or in part, exaggerated his claim.

(6) The orders which the court may make under this rule include an order that a party must pay—

(a) a proportion of another party's costs;
(b) a stated amount in respect of another party's costs;
(c) costs from or until a certain date only;
(d) costs incurred before proceedings have begun;
(e) costs relating to particular steps taken in the proceedings;
(f) costs relating only to a distinct part of the proceedings; and
(g) interest on costs from or until a certain date, including a date before judgment.

(7) Where the court would otherwise consider making an order under paragraph (6)(f), it must instead, if practicable, make an order under paragraph (6)(a) or (c).

CONTENTIOUS PROBATE

(8) Where the court has ordered a party to pay costs, it may order an amount to be paid on account before the costs are assessed.

(9) Where a party entitled to costs is also liable to/pay costs the court may assess the costs which that party is liable to pay and either—

  (a) set off the amount assessed against the amount the party is entitled to be paid and direct him to pay any balance; or
  (b) delay the issue of a certificate for the costs to which the party is entitled until he has paid the amount which he is liable to pay.

It is, therefore, important to remember that, as a general rule, the Order for costs in probate claims will follow the event. 16–002

The "myth" which is sometimes perpetuated is that all parties, even unsuccessful ones, will have their costs out of the estate. *This is wrong. The advice to every client, at the outset of any claim, is that the client must be prepared to pay not just his own costs, but also the costs of the successful parties in the event of failure of the client's case.*

The principle that costs follow the event as between the parties was followed in a post-CPR decision of Hart J. in *Rice-Hunt dec'd; Isaac v Kenny,* (unreported February 16, 2000), where he ordered the beneficiary who lost his claim to pay the costs of the successful beneficiary. The unsuccessful claimant, who was named as executor in the disputed last will of the deceased (which the defendant succeeded in overturning in favour of an earlier will), was not allowed his costs out of the estate, and bore his own costs. The claimant did in fact have the benefit of an indemnity from the unsuccessful beneficiary, and the claimant was eventually paid his assessed costs under that agreement. 16–003

The power to order costs will include the power to apportion costs, to order that there be one set of costs between more than one party, and to order that the costs of certain issues be treated separately from other issues. In probate claims the last point may be significant where there can be success on some parts of the claim (*e.g.* want of knowledge and approval) and failure on another (*e.g.* want of capacity). The modern approach to the exercise of discretion on costs is now often "issue" related. 16–004

Exceptions to the general rule

(a) *Where the claim is in some way the fault of the deceased*
Examples will include a muddle left by the deceased in respect of his papers, or a muddle created by him in terms of the events at the time when he gave instructions or executed the will 16–005

(*Spiers v English* [1907] P. 122; *Re Good* [2002] W.T.L.R. 801 *per* Rimer J.; [2002] W.T.L.R. 1311, CA.)

(b) *Where the claim is in some way the fault of a beneficiary*

16–006 Examples will include failure to produce the valid last will, or suspicious conduct in the preparation of the will. Note that in this and the preceding class of case, where costs may not follow the event, the modern procedures of case management should reveal at an early stage what is the true position as to the evidence surrounding the wills in issue. This means that those who do not "place their cards on the table" at an early stage are at a much greater risk of adverse costs Orders, or may not get all their costs out of the estate, even if ultimately successful.

(c) *Where there were reasonable grounds for opposing a grant of probate to a will*

16–007 This argument may prevail where, for example, there is conflicting evidence over whether the formalities set out in s.9 of the Wills Act 1837 were complied with, and it is only at the trial that such an argument could be resolved. Want of knowledge and approval claims may be an example when this contention may succeed. Until the suspicion is dispelled, it may be impossible for the party who has raised it, or the court, to accept that the will is valid. But the grounds for opposing the will must be sufficient and reasonable ones. In *Re Parsons* [2002] W.T.L.R. 237, the court made no Order as to the costs of the parties who lost the claim and who had raised the question (*inter alia*) whether s.9 of the Wills Act 1837 had been complied with. They had been faced with conflicting and unsatisfactory evidence before the hearing, and that state of affairs was partly due to the conduct of the first defendant who had taken instructions for the will in dispute. In *Buckenham v Dickinson* [2000] W.T.L.R. 1083, the court made no Order as to the costs of the defendants who lost, treating this as a claim where there was reasonable cause for investigation; see the report at 1099–1100. In *Re Good* [2002] W.T.L.R. 801; [2002] W.T.L.R. 1311, A, an unsuccessful defendant in a claim based on undue influence was ordered to pay only half the successful claimant's costs where there had been reasonable grounds to suspect undue influence; see *Spiers v English* [1907] P. 122, applied in *Re Good*, above.

(d) *Where a defendant has served a notice to cross-examine under CPR r.57.7(5)*

16–008 This rule states:

(a) A defendant may give notice in his defence that he does not raise any positive case, but insists on the will being proved in solemn form and, for that purpose, will cross-examine the witnesses who attested the will.

(b) If a defendant gives such a notice, the court will not make an order for costs against him unless it considers that there was no reasonable ground for opposing the will.

This important protection against an adverse costs Order is important and only available to defendants. Note the limitation that it only protects against an adverse Order — so the defendant within this provision may still be liable for his own costs — and the further limitation that the defendant must have had reasonable grounds to oppose the will; see above, para. 11–076, for how to use it.

(e) *Where the conduct of a party, whether prior to or after the claim has been commenced, is such that a different Order should be made than one which gives that party his costs out of the estate or condemns him to bear other parties' costs*

This is just one example of the general discretion which the court has in respect of costs. Any Order the court makes must be made having regard to CPR r.44.3 and the general power to determine by whom and to what extent costs are to be paid under s.51 of the Supreme Court Act 1981. For the full discussion of the effect of this section, see the notes to it in Vol. 2 of the White Book. Litigators and parties must watch how they proceed both before as well as during the claim in view of the factors which affect the general costs discretion and the rule that costs will "follow the event". A classic example of the application of the general principle stated in the sub-heading is where a party has failed to comply with a *Larke v Nugus* request (see above, para. 11–132) or with Orders made at a CMC, or has failed to agree to mediation (see *Dunnett v Railtrack* [2002] 1 W.L.R. 2434). The issue related approach to costs is also relevant here. Not just any degree of success is always enough for a full costs award in one's favour.

16–009

Some "special rules"

(a) *Where the claim has been the subject of an appeal to the Court of Appeal*
In the Court of Appeal, CPR r.44.3(3)(b) specifically takes probate claims out of the general rule that costs follow the event (see "Appeals", Chapter 19, below). The Court of Appeal has a "free hand", although in practice the Order which that Court will make will invariably follow the outcome of the appeal, both as to the costs of the appeal and below.

16–010

(b) *Where an executor who is a party to the claim proves the will in solemn form, whether as a claimant or a defendant*

16–011 In such a case he can claim his costs out of the estate and does not have to apply to the court to claim those costs and have them paid to him. The same applies to a creditor who takes a grant. There is a suggestion in one old case that such a personal representative may be better off without an Order for costs in view of the fact that this would entail assessment of his costs. However, it is suggested that it is open to the court to make an Order in terms that the costs of the personal representative be raised and paid out of the estate in due course of administration, such costs to be assessed on the *indemnity* basis (CPR r.44.4), if not agreed. The case is *Re Cole dec'd* (1962) 106 Sol. 837. A beneficiary now has the right to seek assessment of costs under s.71 of the Solicitors Act 1974.

(c) *Where a party pleads undue influence, fraud or want of capacity and fails to succeed on that plea he will be ordered to pay the costs of the other parties unless he can fall within para. 8.2(c) above*

16–012 The escape from the usual consequence of failure to succeed will be rare and exceptional. The same principle will apply where a party disputes the interest of another party (*e.g.* to take as a child of the deceased on intestacy on the ground that he was not a child of the deceased) and loses. (See *Re Good* above where there were reasonable grounds to suspect undue influence, so the unsuccessful defendant only had to pay half the claimant's costs.) In *King v Bonnar* (1998) LTL, Court of Appeal, June 22, 1998, an adverse costs order was made where a plea of undue influence and fraud failed.

(d) *The costs of a party who has had to apply for a grant* pending suit *under s.117 of the Supreme Court Act 1981 should be allowable out of the estate at the conclusion of the probate claim when the functions of the administrator appointed under s.117 cease*

16–013 See above, Chapter 11, as to appointments under s.117; his right to charge fees should be part of the Order on appointment.

(e) *Where a party has public funding and the benefit of costs protection, any Order that he pay costs must be expressed to direct assessment under the Legal Services Commission ("LSC") Costs Regulations, and any enforcement is subject to the costs protection under s.11 of the Access to Justice Act 1999*

16–014 See below, para. 18–003, where LSC funding is considered.

Taking indemnities

16–015 There is no reason why any party should not take an indemnity as to costs from any other party or a person outside the claim. The indemnifier has the right to have any costs for which he is liable to the indemnified party assessed under s.71 of the Solicitors Act 1974.

Assessment of costs

16–016 For the detailed law and practice on the assessment of costs, see CPR rr.44–48 and associated Practice Directions. This topic is beyond the scope of this book.

16–017 Assessment on the standard basis is the rule in probate claims. Assessment on the indemnity basis will, however, be directed where:

(1) An offer under CPR r.36 has not been beaten and indemnity costs are payable under CPR r.36.21; see above, para. 14–015.

(2) Where the court orders indemnity costs under CPR r.44.4 because of the way in which the party who is liable to pay those costs has conducted himself, or there are other circumstances which warrant such a basis of assessment. Indemnity costs may be awarded in a claim where a party has Legal Services Commission funding, if appropriate in favour of that party, and if against that party subject to the costs protection of the Access to Justice Act 1999. (See *Brawley v Marczynski* [2003] 1 W.L.R. 813). For the full treatment of this complex topic, see the notes to CPR r.44.4 in the White Book.

(3) A successful proving personal representative should be entitled to his costs on the indemnity basis under CPR rr.44.4(3) and r.48.4. See above, Chapter 11, for the discussion of the question whether a professional should be the claimant or take some other active role in a probate claim, where he is simply interested as a person who may be entitled to a grant. It is thought that in such a case, this type of person proceeds in terms of active engagement in the claim at his peril. A probate claim is *not* one where a "Beddoes" application can or should be made, nor is such a person likely to get an Order for his costs out of the estate in any event on a pre-emptive costs application. If he wants his costs secured he should get the beneficiaries who are concerned financially in the

outcome to indemnify him; see below, para. 16–018, for details.

(4) Parties who are beneficially interested in the claim and who may have an inherent "special status", such as charities, the Official Solicitor and the Treasury Solicitor (on behalf of the Crown in estate which may be *bona vacantia*), should not be in any different position as regards costs Orders from other parties without any special status.

The position of the "neutral" personal representative

16–018 As has been discussed above, at Chapter 11, under the topic of who should be claimant, whilst there may be a general principle that a person named as executor in a will may have a general duty to propound it, that duty falls away when there is compelling evidence that the will may not have been the true last will of the deceased. He is not obliged to seek to prove a will where he is aware of some reason why it could not be admitted to proof. This means that a person named as executor (or a person with a *prima facie* right to a grant of letters of administration) has no right to his costs out of the estate if he fails to prove the will or his right to letters of administration. This is all the more so when he is also a beneficiary in the estate.

16–019 Such a person, therefore, has to decide, at an early stage, whether there is compelling evidence which would lead to his position being challenged. If that is the case, he should indicate to those beneficially interested in the estate that he does not wish to take an active role in the dispute. That is the correct thing to do where there are beneficiaries who can argue the claim between themselves; see *Alsop Wilkinson v Neary* [1996] 1 W.L.R. 1220 at 1225. This view is still the correct one since the introduction of the CPR and the costs rules in r.44.3 — for probate claims are hostile litigation and it is difficult to see why a neutral potential personal representative should be involved in such litigation. Whilst it may not be proper for those potentially entitled to take a grant to issue a claim seeking the direction of the court (*e.g.* as to whether they should be claimants or what they should do if joined as defendants), there may be something to be said for a personal representative *holding a grant* and wishing to distribute the estate seeking the directions of the court where he is being threatened by a claim to revoke that grant, but where the potential claimant is unwilling to make the challenge by issuing a claim form. In such cases, quite apart from a letter in terms warning the potential claimant to "put up or shut up", the personal representative should seek the directions of the court to the effect that, after a defined time limit within which the potential claimant is to issue the claim form, he is free to distribute the estate; see *Fitzhugh Gates v Sherman* [2003] EWCA Civ 886 at [57]–[58].

For the details of the law in relation to pre-emptive costs applications and other types of Order which "neutral" parties may seek, see Lewin, *Trusts,* (17th ed.), paras 21–106ff., CPR r.64 and CPR r.64 PD, and *D'Abo v Paget* [2000] W.T.L.R. 863. This is an area of the law where each case may require a different approach. There *may* be probate claims which can present unusual features (*e.g.* where beneficiaries are abroad) where the potential personal representative may need to seek the directions of the court, for example as to who is to represent a large class of beneficiaries who are abroad, or to represent the interest of a foreign religious charity which seems to have no obvious "leader". 16–020

There is no reason why a neutral potential personal representative should not take an indemnity as to his costs from any other party. It will be a matter for the indemnified to assess the worth of that indemnity. As has already been stated, at 11–047, 11–048 and 16–015 the indemnifier has the right to have the costs which he has to pay to the indemnified under the indemnity assessed under s.71 of the Solicitors Act 1974. It is not clear, but it would seem that for public policy reasons to be the case that this right to have the costs assessed cannot be excluded by agreement of the parties. 16–021

Wasted costs orders, etc.

In probate claims, as in other claims, the court has the power to make orders in appropriate cases under the following rules: 16–022

(1) CPR r.48.2 against non-parties, *e.g.* "maintainers" — This is an exceptional jurisdiction derived from s.51(3) of the Supreme Court Act 1981, and is exercised with considerable caution. "Pure" funders (*i.e.* those who have no interest in the outcome of the claim) are generally exempt from Orders that they pay any of the costs of the successful party. See *Hamilton v Al Fayed (No.2)* [2003] 2 W.L.R. 128 for a full review and statement of the law in this field.

(2) CPR r.48.7 against legal representatives ("wasted costs orders") — See *Fitzhugh Gates v Sherman,* above for an unsuccessful attempt to seek such an Order in the context of a probate claim.

(3) CPR r.48.6 — Costs Orders in favour of litigants in person and the determination of how much can be recovered by such litigants.

In all three cases, reference should be made to the detailed notes in the White Book for the law and practice.

Costs-only proceedings and claims which have been settled save as to the costs

16–023 It is open to the parties to agree all matters in the potential claim save that of costs and to bring a CPR r.8 claim on the question of costs only (CPR r.44.12A). In claims where the parties have come to terms and settled the litigation with the sole exception of the costs, the court can and will look at which party would have won had the parties not settled. Where this is not clear, it will conduct a limited inquiry into the issues in the case, the amount of costs, the conduct of the parties and the circumstances of the case, and will make an appropriate Order as to costs. The fall-back is to make no Order as to costs, but there is no convention that this is the proper order (*Brawley v Marczynski (Nos 1 and 2)* [2003] 1 W.L.R. 813). It is ordinarily irrelevant that a party is publicly funded.

Chapter 17

Enforcement of Orders and Terms of Settlement

Enforcement of Orders

It is rarely the case that in probate claims (unlike, for example, **17–001** claims for the payment of money) there will be problems encountered in the carrying out of the terms of the Order after the judgment. The person with the right to the grant has the benefit of the Order and takes the grant out from the Principal Registry; see above, para. 15–011, for how this is done.

This book does not consider post-grant remedies, such as **17–002** seeking an account of the estate in administration or removal of the personal representative under s.50 of the Administration of Justice Act 1985, or the other remedies, such as claims under the Inheritance Act 1975. For the rare case where enforcement of an Order is required out of the jurisdiction, see CPR r.74 and Dicey and Morris, *The Conflict of Laws,* (13th ed.). The final Order will be the end of the claim, subject to any appeal and the payment of costs, as ordered. If enforcement questions arise, as a precondition to any application to enforce, it is assumed that the Order made is clear, and that if it is by consent, terms of the order and any terms in a schedule are properly drawn. Care must be taken to ensure not only that the terms are clear, but also that there has been no pressure on any party to agree to a consent Order, and that the court's approval has been obtained for any person affected who is under a disability within CPR r.21. For instances where the court may not uphold and may even set aside consent Orders which have been invalidated by pressure, or for some other reason, see the "classic" statement in *Edgar v Edgar* [1980] 1 W.L.R. 1410, at 1417. It may also be the case that a consent Order is liable to be set aside by some event altering the fundamental assumptions on which the Order was agreed and made. In a probate claim this may be the discovery of another will before a grant is taken out under that

Order. See *Barder v Caluori* [1988] A.C. 20 for a tragic case in the matrimonial jurisdiction where a consent Order for ancillary relief was set aside. See also above, Chapter 15 for the circumstances in which a grant of probate, whether in common form or in solemn form, may be revoked.

17–003 However, if there is a failure to perform the terms of any Order made in a probate claim, what follows is an outline of the way in which a party can obtain redress against the defaulting party:

(1) Correspond with the solicitors who are acting for the defaulting party. Why is there a delay in taking out the grant?

(2) Go back to court and seek the directions of the court, particularly if the claim has been stayed on Tomlin terms.

(3) Commit for breach of the Order under what are still RSC Ords 45 and 52. This is usually the last resort, as a person entitled to take a grant who is in prison is no help to anyone.

(4) More constructive than committal, apply under s.116 of the Supreme Court Act 1981 on the ground that the failure to comply with the Order in the probate claim is a special circumstance which makes it "necessary or expedient" to pass that person over and appoint someone else to take the grant. The authors consider that a person in whose favour an Order has been made, but who has not applied for a grant, may not have intermeddled. He may be entitled to renounce, and may be cited to decide whether to take or renounce a grant under NCPR r.47. However, the simpler course is to apply under s.116 in view of the failure to carry out the terms of the Order in the probate claim without any prior need to cite him.

It is important to observe the legal principle of full disclosure of all relevant circumstances when making an application under s.116 (*Shephard v Wheeler* [2000] W.T.L.R. 1175).

(5) Enforcement of *undertakings* given by solicitors may be made summarily under s.50 of the Solicitors Act 1974.

Enforcement of Tomlin Orders: applying to lift the stay

17–004 In cases where the probate claim has been stayed on terms (usually in a "Tomlin" form of Order, it may be necessary to apply to the court to lift the stay, *e.g.* where the terms of the

Order or of the schedule to the Order have not been complied with or performed. In such a case (on an application under CPR r.24) the court may lift the stay and the claim may be re-opened. The court is usually reluctant to do this, but in a probate claim where, for example, a claimant had not observed the terms set out in the schedule to the Order to take out a common form grant and to distribute the estate in a certain way, the court may be faced with no choice but to hear the claim in full. In most cases, of course, the parties never want to get that far and the mere threat of an application to go back to court will cause good sense to prevail. If there has been a failure to observe the terms of the schedule to the Order it is important to remember that an application to enforce them may be made in the original claim and there is no need to start a fresh claim. (See the notes to s.49(2) of the Supreme Court Act 1981 in Vol. 2 of the White Book at 9A–160ff. on this topic, and the authority of *Wagstaff v Colls* [2003] EWCA Civ 469 for a review of the authorities on the jurisdiction to lift the stay on the claim.)

Problems post-grant

Reference has already been made above, para. 17–003, to the matters which can arise in the administration of the estate post-grant, such as a failure to supply accounts, to pay legacies and to sell property, and the myriad of other questions which can bedevil the life of a personal representative as well as the beneficiary who may be unhappy with the administration of the estate. The reader is referred to textbooks which deal with these topics such as Williams and Mortimer, *Executors Administrators and Probate,* and Lewin, *Trusts,* for full treatment of this area of law which lies beyond contested probate.

17–005

Chapter 18

Funding Probate Claims

Private funding

Probate claims are no different from other civil claims in terms **18–001** of contentious business agreements and compliance with Law Society rules for the recovery of costs from a client, and the reader is referred to the textbooks and guides on the subject if he is in any doubt; See, in particular, Cordery, *Solicitors* (two Volumes), *The Professional Conduct of Solicitors* (published by the Law Society and available on www.guide-on-line.lawsociety.org.uk), and Lesley King, *The Probate Practitioner's Handbook*, (4th ed.), Law Society, 2003. This book does not touch upon those matters.

In probate claims the following reminders may be worth **18–002** keeping to hand when funding on a private basis is being contemplated:

(1) Having regard to the effect of the bereavement on the client's state of mind, has proper care been taken in writing, as well as at meetings, to explain:

(a) the overall likely cost of the claim to the client — with the additional element of VAT at the current rate;
(b) the rule that costs will generally follow the event — thereby adding the other party's costs to the client's own bill (see above, Chapter 16);
(c) the rules as to third party liability as "paymasters" under CPR r.48 (see above, Chapter 16);
(d) that costs estimates are only estimates; and
(e) that the other side can always be asked to provide an assessment of their own costs and that this may be disclosed at a CMC (see above, para. 12–007(3).

(2) Where likely costs estimates are being discussed, do not forget to take into account experts' fees and always take the advice of those who have first-hand experience of litigation and the likely scale of costs which will be awarded on assessment on the standard basis — if not on the indemnity basis.

(3) A realistic approach to the merits and the way in which the claim may settle is an essential tool when considering costs and funding at an early stage.

Legal Services Commission funding

18–003 Reference should be made to the three-volume *Legal Services Commission Manual* for up-to-date guidance on the availability of Legal Services Commission ("LSC") funding in contentious probate claims. At the time of writing, the position is as follows:

(1) Contentious probate claims are within the "residual list" for which LSC funding is available. Therefore, firms with a civil or family contract are able to offer clients LSC funding for these claims (see *LSC Manual* Vol. 3, ref. 3E–028).

(2) The standard financial criteria and funding code criteria will apply to such claims. There are no specific criteria at the time of writing which apply to these claims (see *LSC Manual,* Vol. 3, refs 3C–029 to 3C–038 and 3C–063 to 3C–078 for the Funding Code standard criteria).

18–004 It is also important to note the following points:

(1) Disputes about trusts arising on an intestacy, or where implied resulting or constructive trusts are at issue, or where there is a dispute over the trust of land affecting the client's home under s.14 of the Trusts of Land, etc. Act 1996 are within the scope of LSC funding by authorisation of the Lord Chancellor (Funding Code, *LSC Manual* ref. 3C–020.1, para. 14, under "Excluded Work"). Note also that LSC funding is available for claims under the Inheritance Act 1975. Such claims fall within the definition of "Family Proceedings" as defined by para. 2.2 of the Funding Code.

(2) The position as to availability of LSC funding is not made very clear by the terms of the *primary legislation*. Under Sch. 2, para. 1(d) to the Access to Justice Act 1999, the provision of help (beyond the provision of

general information about the law the legal system and the availability of legal services) in relation to "the making of wills" is excluded from LSC funding. (s.4(2) of that Act sets out what falls within the various categories of the services which the LSC provides, and "help" in this context would seem to refer to that sub section). The LSC does not, however, regard this exclusion as applying to contentious probate claims.

There is a limited provision for legal help in connection with the *making* of wills where the client is aged 70 or over, or is a disabled person within s.1 of the Disability Discrimination Act 1995, or is the parent of such a disabled person who wishes to provide for that person in his will, or where the client wishes to appoint a guardian for a minor in a will and where the parent of the minor is living with the minor but not with the other parent; see Funding Code, *LSC Manual,* ref. 3C–016, para. 4; see also Lord Chancellor's authorisation under s.6(8) of the Access to Justice Act 1999.

(3) In any claim where LSC funding has been provided, the client must be made aware of the effect of the statutory charge under s.10(7) of the Access to Justice Act 1999, and the scope of the costs protection under s.11 thereof. (See CPR r.44 Costs PD, paras 22 and 23 for the manner in which liability of an LSC-funded person is to be determined).

Funding from insurance policies

Little can be said in terms of this method of funding other than to observe: **18–005**

(1) that the existence of such a funding arrangement must be disclosed to the other parties under CPR r.44.15 and CPR r.44 PD;

(2) that the premium may be recoverable as part of an award of costs under s.29 of the Access to Justice Act 1999; and

(3) that insurers will usually require counsel's opinion with a high prospect of success before agreeing to accept risk and issue cover for a pre-agreed amount of costs. This is true as regards both after-the-event insurance as well as the cover provided by certain legal expenses insurance policies in force before the claim is brought.

Conditional fee agreements

18-006 Probate claims are within the scope of conditional fee agreements (CFAs) as defined by ss.58 and 58A of the Courts and Legal Services Act 1990 (as amended). Those advising clients who are prepared to consider entering into such CFAs must obtain the following documents before giving advice on the terms and effect of any CFA and deciding how the CFA will work in the claim:

(1) the *current* Law Society CFA which complies with the current regulations. The current regulations are the Conditional Fee Agreements Regulations 2000 (SI 2000/692, as amended by SI 2003/1240; and

(2) the *current* Chancery Bar Association terms of engagement for CFA cases and the terms of engagement for preliminary work where a CFA is contemplated.

18-007 Great care should be taken in defining "success", which must be common to both the solicitor/client agreement and the solicitor/counsel agreement if counsel is instructed. Only practitioners with experience in working with CFA claims should conduct probate claims in which they are used.

18-008 It is also necessary to bear in mind that the decision of the Court of Appeal in *Hollins v Russell* (and conjoined appeals in other cases) is of crucial importance. It stresses the need to comply with the CFA Regulations and also contains important observations regarding the disclosure of CFAs at the assessment of costs stage. (*Hollins v Russell* [2003] EWCA Civ 718). The *current* costs rules and related Practice Directions in the CPR must be consulted in view of the changes which are frequently made to them, and which no doubt will continue to be made, in the light of developments in this area of funded litigation.

Chapter 19

Appeals

The route of appeals

From the first-instance *final decision* at trial in all contentious probate claims the appeal is to the Court of Appeal. (Art. 4 of the Access to Justice Act 1999 (Destination of Appeals) Order 2000 (SI 2000/1071), para. (b), as amended by SI 2003/490 art. 2; ("Destination of Appeals Order"). Probate claims are within section (I) of CPR r.57 (see also CPR r.52 PD, para. 2A.1 and 2A.2). Thus appeals in hearings before a county court judge or a judge of the High Court (wherever sitting) which have led to a final decision by the judge of that court will lie to the Court of Appeal. **19–001**

A *final decision* means a decision of the court that would finally determine (subject to any possible appeal or detailed assessment of costs) the entire proceedings, whichever way the court decides the issues before it; Destination of Appeals Order, art. 1(2)(c); see also CPR r.52 PD, para. 2A.3 and 2A.4. **19–002**

Permission to appeal will be required in *all* cases from the trial judge, and in the event of a final decision being given by a master or district judge (exceptional). Permission must be sought if the party who has lost gives instructions for that to be done. Invariably, permission should be sought at the end of the judgment and any Order for costs. Otherwise there will have to be an application back to the trial judge, and in view of the time limits under CPR r.52 this is not recommended. But, in view of the terms of CPR r.52.3(2), it is open to a party who has failed to seek permission from the lower court to go to the higher court and ask for it. In view of the fact that it costs nothing to make the application at the end of the final hearing, and that nothing is lost if it fails, the better course is to apply at that stage rather than leave it to a later application to the higher court; see CPR r.52 PD, para. 4.6 and 4.7. If that is refused, permission must be sought from the Court of Appeal, CPR r.52.3. **19–003**

19–004 It should be noted that the route described above applies in the case of *final decisions* only, as defined above. Where pre-trial or interim Orders (*e.g.* those made at a CMC) are made, which are *not* final decisions as defined above, the appeal will be to the next tier of judicial officer. Thus an appeal lies from a District Judge to the Circuit Judge and thence to the High Court judge, or from a Master to the High Court judge, with all in turn leading from the High Court judge to the Court of Appeal; See CPR r.52 PD, paras 2A.1 and 2A.2.

Appeals are *not* favoured from CMC and other directions Orders; see CPR r.52 PD, paras 4.4 and 4.5.

The relevant rules which apply to appeals

19–005 These are CPR r.52 and CPR r.52 PD. The up-to-date version of these rules must be consulted in all cases where an appeal to the Court of Appeal is contemplated. There are frequent changes to the rules and associated Practice Directions which mean that a detailed account of procedure is not set out here in view of the limited "shelf life" of such an account.

Deciding whether to appeal or not

19–006 Unless the court orders otherwise (*i.e.* the court below, or the court to which the appeal is being made), an appeal does not operate as a stay of any Order or decision of the lower court; CPR r.52.7. Thus an Order to take a grant, etc. may still be carried out pending an appeal, unless there is a contrary order. A s.117 grant may be needed in the intervening period.

19–007 The decision to appeal should be taken after proper reflection. Although 14 days may not be a long time, it should be clear one way or the other within a day or two of the decision and upon proper reflection whether an appeal has merit. In any event, the lodging and serving of a notice of appeal may always be withdrawn, and the costs consequences at the early stage of such an early withdrawal should be minimal.

The time limit for filing a notice of appeal

19–008 This is 14 days from the date of the decision which the appellant wishes to appeal, unless the lower court states that a longer period is given. (See CPR r.52.4 and CPR r.52 PD for what has to be filed and served. Form N161 is the prescribed form of notice for both leave to appeal and the appeal itself). Note, however, that this time runs from the date *when the decision is given* and *not* from the (later) date when an Order is drawn up.

19–009 The notice of appeal must not only be filed at the Civil Appeals Office but must also be served on each respondent as soon as practicable and in any event not later than seven days after it is filed. (CPR r.52.4). "Days" will include any weekends and statutory holidays in view of CPR r.2.8. The intervention of statutory holidays during the 14-day period may be a good reason for seeking a modest extension of time from the trial judge when leave is being sought.

19–010 If a respondent wants to support the decision of the court which is the subject of the appeal on different grounds he must file and serve a respondent's notice within the period specified in CPR r.52.5, *i.e.* generally within 14 days of the date when he is served with the appellant's notice of appeal, or from the date when he is served with notice that the Appeal Court has given permission to appeal.

How can permission to appeal be obtained and when will it be given?

How and when?

19–011 The form for application is Form N161. See above, para. 19–003 for the desirability of applying for permission at the end of the hearing before the lower court. The initial application is, therefore, made on paper, together with the documents listed in CPR r.52 PD, para. 5.6. Significantly, this will include the skeleton argument stating in concise terms what points are raised on the appeal and, if necessary, why permission should be given; r.52 PD, para. 5.10/11. A copy of the judgment or an agreed note or transcript should also be lodged; r.52 PD, para. 5.12. The same applies to notes of evidence; r.52 PD, para. 5.15/16.

Criteria

19–012 It is rare for the lower court judge to give permission unless he has already decided that the case raises questions which ought to go to a higher court. Therefore, permission will have to be sought, and the burden will be on the appellant to show:

(1) either that the appeal would have a real prospect of success; or,

(2) there is some other compelling reason why the appeal should be heard (CPR r.52.3(6)).

This means that in terms of (a) there must be a realistic, as opposed to a fanciful, prospect of success. In terms of (b), which is a more difficult concept to analyse, it is necessary to show some public interest in the outcome of the appeal, or that an important question of law arises which needs sorting out. In *Re Good* [2002] W.T.L.R. 1311, the Court of Appeal refused leave to appeal from the judgment of Rimer J. in that case reported at [2002] W.T.L.R. 801, holding that the last will of the deceased be admitted to probate on the ground that the appeal would have no prospect of success. The finding of Rimer J. that the deceased knew and approved of the contents of the will was "unimpeachable".

In this context it may be worth noting that contested probate claims are unlikely to raise issues under the Human Rights Act 1998, nor are they likely to raise important questions of law in such a settled area of law, so it is usually ground (a) which is going to be relevant.

Thus a real prospect of success is the key.

19–013 In the rare event of an appeal from a CMC Order, the court will need to be satisfied that the higher threshold stated in CPR r.52 PD, para. 4.5 is met; *i.e.* that the issue is significant enough to justify the costs of an appeal. This would appear to be an additional hurdle to the need to show "a real prospect of success".

What should the respondent do when served with the appeal notice and other documents on an application for leave?

19–014 He should address only the questions raised under CPR r.52.3(6), above, and can do so in a short written submission initially. He should not engage in an argument over the merits of the proposed appeal generally.

19–015 He is not bound to send in a written submission, as the application for permission is really an occasion for the appellant to show his mettle. If permission is given, the respondent will have a full opportunity to lodge and serve his own documents under CPR r.52.5. But no prejudice can be caused by a short statement in writing showing why permission should not be granted, addressing the "real prospect of success" test referred to above, and this is so particularly in a clear case. It is not a mark of prejudice if no statement is made at this stage.

How will the appeal court deal with the application for permission?

Generally it will deal with it on paper without any appearance by the appellant. Only if the Appeal Court is having difficulty making up its mind, or for some other reason, will it require attendance by the appellant. It may not always call for the respondent's attendance — indeed, he may never be informed of any such hearing — but any written submissions will be taken into account, and he may be required to attend if, for example, the case is very difficult or if the appellant wants some remedy against the respondent pending the appeal being determined; *e.g.* a stay on a grant being obtained; see CPR r.52 PD, para. 4.15 and 4.16. If permission is granted he will be notified and he has 14 days from the date when he is served with that decision to file and serve his own respondent's notice, if any; CPR r.52.5. **19–016**

What if permission is refused on paper?
The appellant is entitled to ask for an oral hearing so the decision can be reconsidered; CPR r.52.3(4). This is what happened in *Re Good* above. This must be asked for within seven days of the service of the notice of the refusal to give permission. If there is still a refusal to give permission, that is the end of the road for the appellant. **19–017**

Costs of the application for permission

(1) The Appeal Court may order that the appellant will have to provide security for the costs of an appeal; see CPR r.25.15 and CPR r.25.13 generally for the factors which the court must apply. It is considered that in probate claim appeals, this is not an order the Court will make frequently. **19–018**

(2) If permission is refused, the Appeal Court may award costs to the respondent. It may limit those costs to the written submissions; (*Jolly v Jay* [2002] EWCA Civ 277).

(3) If permission is granted, conditions may be imposed as terms of allowing the appeal to be made; *e.g.* in probate claims, that a s.117 grant be taken out by a party pending the determination of the appeal.

(4) If permission is granted, the appellant must serve his appeal documents on the respondent under CPR r.52 PD, para. 6 within seven days after receiving the Order giving permission to appeal. The respondent then has 14

days to lodge and serve his respondent's notice under CPR r.52.5. (He may not, of course, need to do this if he is content to uphold the lower court's decision for the same reasons given.) He may need leave to appeal himself and in such a case he will have to make the same application as the appellant, as described above.

The principles on which an Appellate Court will act

19–019 All appeals are limited to a review of the decision below, unless the court considers that there should be a rehearing; the latter is a rare event in view of the costs involved. This means that the appellate court will take a retrospective look at the case in order to decide whether the decision of the lower court was wrong. (See CPR r.52.11 and *Assicurazioni Generali SpA v Arab Insurance Group* [2003] 1 W.L.R. 577).

19–020 In probate claims the appellate court will allow the appeal where the lower court's decision was "wrong" within CPR r.52.11(3)(a) or, in very rare cases, where the lower court has committed a procedural irregularity within para. (3)(b) thereof. The vast majority of appeals in these claims will fall within para. (3)(a), so the alternative is not considered further.

19–021 It is rare for the Court of Appeal to admit fresh evidence on an appeal. (See CPR r.52.11(2) and notes to that rule in the White Book. Only if the evidence could not have been obtained at the trial will the appellate court look at it. *e.g.* where there is new evidence from witnesses as to the execution of the will. (See *Sohal v Sohal* [2002] EWCA Civ 1297; *Ladd v Marshall* (1954) 1 W.L.R. 1489).

19–022 What does "wrong" mean? It can mean:

(1) an error of law; or

(2) an error of fact; or

(3) an error in the exercise of a discretion.

In probate claims the appellate court will really be concerned to see if there has been an error either in applying the law, or in applying facts, or, in the case of the latter, in applying inferences from them. Probate claims (unlike claims under the Inheritance Act 1975) do not leave the court with any discretionary function.

19–023 In the case where a discretion has been exercised and is under attack on the appeal, or even where the appellate court is being asked to review inferences from finding of fact, this means that the appellate court will only interfere when it considers:

"that the judge of first instance has not merely preferred an imperfect solution which is different from an alternative imperfect solution which the Court of Appeal might or would have adopted, but has exceeded the generous ambit within which a reasonable disagreement is possible". (*per* Lord Fraser in *G v G (Minors: Custody Appeal)* [1985] 1 W.L.R. 647 at 652). (See also the *Assicurazioni Generali* case above, para. 19–019, at 584E–G *per* Ward L.J.)

Because in probate claims there is no real element of discretion, **19–024** the appellate court will only interfere where the review of the trial judge's decision produces the descriptive adverbs of "clearly" or "plainly" or "blatantly" or "palpably" wrong as a result of the following:

(1) A failure to apply a relevant principle of law, *e.g.* as to the burden and standard of proof in want of knowledge and approval claims, and the burden of dispelling the suspicion, (as occurred in the case of *Fuller v Strum* [2002] 1 W.L.R. 1097. Here the appellate court will be prepared to find that the lower court has got the law wrong.

(2) A failure to come to the right conclusions in making primary findings of fact from the evidence. In this respect the appellate court is often reluctant to interfere, as it will not have seen the witnesses, including the observation of their demeanour. That gives the trial judge an advantage which the appellate court will rarely set to one side. (See the *Assicurazioni Generali* case above, para. 19–019, at 584D *per* Ward L.J.).

(3) A wrong inference or deduction from such primary facts. Here the appellate court can and will readily decide whether the lower court was right or not, albeit that weight will be given to the trial judge's opinion.

"Personal unease" is not enough to allow an appeal to succeed, **19–025** nor does the decision have to be "perverse". For a fairly recent example of a claim where the Court of Appeal refused to interfere with the judge's findings that the testator lacked capacity, and the finding that the onus of establishing it had not been discharged by those taking under the will, see *Wood v Smith* [1993] Ch. 90.

Retrials in probate claims

Where the application for leave to appeal or the appeal itself is **19–026** based on evidence which suggests that the judgment below (*e.g.* for a solemn form grant) may have been obtained by fraud, the

Court of Appeal has recently indicated that the person seeking to set that judgment aside should bring a fresh claim for revocation of that grant. A retrial of the original claim is not thought appropriate. (*Sohal v Sohal* [2002] EWCA Civ 1297, noted in *Civil Procedure Practice News,* November 18, 2002).

Costs of appeals

19–027 These will usually follow the event, and the appellant will have the costs of the appeal and the costs of the lower court if he is successful; likewise the successful respondent. However, appeals in probate matters to the Court of Appeal are taken out of the general rule that the costs will follow the event and the Court of Appeal is not bound to apply the general rule in view of the specific exception in CPR r.44.3(3)(b). In theory this gives the Court of Appeal a freer hand, but in practice it is hard to see why the principle that the costs of the appeal (and below) will follow the event should not apply in appeals in probate claims.

19–028 CPR r.36 offers made below must not be disclosed to the Court of Appeal until all questions relating to the appeal have been determined. This principle does not apply where the CPR r.36 offer is relevant to the substance of the appeal or to the matter to be decided. (CPR r.52.12).

Appeals to the House of Lords from Court of Appeal

19–029 These are extremely rare in contentious probate claims. To the authors' knowledge, the last contested appeal heard by the House of Lords in such a claim was the appeal in *Wintle v Nye* [1959] 1 W.L.R. 284, heard in November 1958. In a case where an appeal to the House of Lords is contemplated, reference should be made to the Practice Direction and the Standing Orders which govern appeals in civil cases to the House of Lords. Permission must first be sought from the Court of Appeal. It is not thought that a contentious probate claim would raise an issue worthy of a "leapfrog" appeal from a decision of the High Court (Chancery Division) direct to the House of Lords under s.12 of the Administration of Justice Act 1969. (For such an appeal to be considered, there would have to be a point of law of general public importance involved and that there is a decision of the Court of Appeal or the House of Lords which is binding on the High Court judge.)

19–030 The material which must be considered in any appeal to the House of Lords is at s.4 of Vol. 2 of the White Book. In view of the rarity of such appeals they are not considered further in this book.

Chapter 20

Claims to rectify wills

Introduction

The law relating to the rectification of wills is dealt with in **20–001** Chapter 10 above. As a brief reminder, the grounds on which rectification of a will can be sought are:—

(a) That the claim falls within s.20 of the Administration of Justice Act 1982; *i.e.* that there is either a clerical error in the will, or that there has been a failure to understand the testator's instructions. A "clerical error" can be one made by the testator himself and not just one made by a solicitor, clerk, or will-writer who drew the will; *Re Williams* [1985] 1 W.L.R. 905. "Will" in this context includes a codicil, or other testamentary document. It is an open question whether a secret, or half secret trust could be rectified under s.20, but is thought that as such trusts operate outside the will, even if incorporated by reference, they are not within the terms of s.20. If in writing, the terms of such trusts may be rectifiable under the general jurisdiction in equity to rectify trust documents; see Parry & Clark, *The Law of Succession*, (11th ed.), paras 6–17—6–20, for further analysis of the nature of such trusts. Agreements, if in writing, to make mutual wills may also be rectifiable under the jurisdiction in equity. The wills themselves, made under an agreement to make mutual wills, are within the jurisdiction to rectify under s.20. A declaration in writing within s.20 of the Wills Act 1837 which declares an intention to revoke a will (or a codicil) and executed and attested is not within s.20 as a "will" and is thought to be subject to the jurisdiction in equity to rectify it, for example if such a revoking instrument declared in error (*e.g.* as to dates) that the wrong will or codicil was to be revoked. In addition it would be open to a party to bring a probate claim seeking to set aside such an instrument on the ground of want of knowledge and approval; see Chapter 6 above.

(b) That the claim is one under the inherent jurisdiction of the Court with power to omit words where the testator did not know and approve of them. (*Re Morris* [1971] P. 62; *Re Reynette-James* [1976] 1 W.L.R. 161). It was the limit on this power to omit words which led to the wider statutory power to rectify, which includes the ability to add words, under s.20 referred to above, in respect of deaths after December 31, 1982.

(c) Where words in a will have been obtained by fraud the Court would not only have power to omit them, but also, if appropriate, to set aside the whole will. See Chapter 8 above on fraud.

20–002 *Note:*

(1) That the power of the Court to rectify a will is different from the power of the Court to construe the words in a will. The process of construction requires the Court to look at the words which are there, and it is rare that a Court would insert words. It is also important to remember that rectification is not the remedy where words have been used in the wrong way, either because the testator failed to appreciate their legal effect, or because they are uncertain in their context. The remedy where questions of construction arise is to issue a Part 8 Claim Form, following the procedural rules in CPR r.64. Evidence of the testator's intention can be admitted under s.21 of the Administration of Justice Act 1982.

(2) The Court can be asked to authorise the personal representatives to administer the estate in reliance upon counsel's opinion (counsel to be of at least 10 years standing) where a question of construction of a will has arisen, under s.48 of the Administration of Justice Act 1985.

(3) These remedies are not contentious probate claims so they are outside the scope of the book and the reader is referred to textbooks on the law of the construction of wills for further details when such questions arise.

20–003 The practice and procedure described above in probate claims applies to a large extent in claims to rectify wills. The major differences are as follows:—

(a) A claim for rectification of a will is NOT a "probate claim" within the definition in Pt 57, r.1(2). This means that the detailed procedure set out in s.1 of Pt 57 does not apply to these claims. In particular, there is no requirement to lodge testamentary documents, or to lodge and serve statements of such documents in rectification claims.

(b) Section 2 of Pt 57 applies to rectification claims. Although it does not expressly say so, this section would appear at first sight to apply to claims both under s.20, as well as claims under the inherent jurisdiction of the Court. However, as the latter are likely to be based on want of knowledge and approval of the words to be omitted, or on fraud, such a claim might well fall within s.1 of Pt 57. It is also thought that such claims based on the inherent jurisdiction are rare, and it is also only in an unusual case that the Court will refuse to admit part only of a will; see *Fuller v Strum* [2002] 1 W.L.R. 1097. For these reasons the remainder of this Chapter will only deal with the procedure in claims to rectify under s.20. In other claims it is likely to be the case that the claim will be a "probate claim" within s.1 of Pt 57, *e.g.* a fraud case. In the case of a claim for the omission of a word formerly arising under the inherent jurisdiction (and now falling within s.20) the procedure will be under s.2.

(c) Pt 57, s.2 and the related PD contains some specific procedural requirements. These are referred to below.

(d) LSC funding for claims to rectify wills is available subject to compliance with the rules relating to such funding; see LSC Manual at 3E–028 where all proceedings under the heading of "contentious probate" are within the residual list of matters for which LSC funding may be available. It is suggested that rectification of wills falls within this category. It seems that LSC funding is available for these claims whether brought in the Chancery Division, or under NCPR, r.55, in the Family Division (Probate).

(e) There is a simple form of application which can be made in the Family Division (Probate) to rectify a will where the claim is unopposed under NCPR, r.55; see para. 20–034 below.

Time limits

All claims under s.20 **must** be brought within "six months of the date on which a grant of representation was taken out to the estate, unless the leave of the Court is obtained;" s.20(2). The

20–004

grant referred to is generally understood, in line with claims under the Inheritance Act 1975, to mean a full grant and not, for example, a limited grant pending suit, or one *ad colligenda bona*. Section 20(4) specifically excludes other forms of limited grant from the running of time; *e.g.* grants limited to settled land, or trust property.

20–005 The Court has a wide and unfettered discretion to extend the time for issuing a claim under s.20. This must, however, be exercised judicially and this means having regard to what is just and proper. In line with claims under the Inheritance Act 1975 the Court will have regard to all the circumstances, including the length of time itself, the reasons for the delay, how promptly the application has been made for leave once the right to claim has been discovered, whether there have been negotiations within the time limit and whether there has been distribution of the estate. The last factor is particularly important. The Court will also have regard to the overall merits of the claim to rectify. (See *Chittock v Stevens* [2000] W.T.L.R. 643, applying the principles set out in *Re Salmon* [1981] Ch. 167 in claims under the Inheritance Act). The emphasis on merits is consistent with the modern approach of the Courts in *Re Dennis* [1981] 2 All E.R. 140, and *Re McNulty* [2002] W.T.L.R. 737 in 1975 Act claims. This element in the exercise of the discretion is also consistent with the overriding objective in the CPR as set out in Pt 1, r.1. There is no point in granting leave in a hopeless claim where the evidence at the stage at which leave is sought fails to come within either of the grounds in s.20. It is important to bear in mind that, as in 1975 Act claims, there is no time delay "tariff". Each claim is looked at on its own merits.

20–006 One area of controversy is how far the Court should take into account the availability of a remedy against another party when deciding whether or not to grant leave. The weight of that factor may well depend on how strong is the claim. For example, is there a strong claim in negligence against the solicitor who drew the will containing the error? The unreported decision of the Court of Appeal in *Adams v Schofield* (1981) (a claim for leave to apply out of time under the Inheritance Act 1975) indicates that this factor will only have weight where there is a strong *prima facie* claim against the negligent solicitor. It is also relevant to note that the bringing of a claim to rectify under s.20 may be a necessary step in mitigation of loss where there has been a negligent failure by the solicitor to draw the will correctly. But there is some conflict between the authorities on this point in respect of whether it is necessary to start a s.20 claim as a matter of mitigation; in particular where the error may be on the borderline of being rectifiable within s.20. Compare *Walker v Medlicott* [1999] 1 W.L.R. 727 (a failure to bring a s.20 claim amounted to a failure to mitigate loss) with

Horsfall v Haywards [1999] 1 F.L.R. 1182 (no failure to mitigate unless there is a clear s.20 claim). See also *Re Grattan* [2001] W.T.L.R. 1305, where a s.20 claim was brought together with a claim under the Inheritance Act 1975. The former claim failed, but the latter succeeded.

20–007 It is, therefore, important to consider how far a s.20 claim should be brought in conjunction with other claims; *e.g.* negligence claims and Inheritance Act 1975 claims. In the case of negligence claims it is essential that the insurers to the solicitors against whom the negligence claim may be brought, are involved in any consideration whether a s.20 claim should be commenced by way of mitigation. (The insurers will have been notified by the solicitor against whom negligence is alleged.) The insurers may be willing to bear the costs of such a claim on terms that they are fully consulted about the merits and conduct of it. The detailed aspects of the law and practice in such cases is beyond the scope of this book and specialist works on professional negligence should be studied when such issues arise.

20–008 If an application for leave has to be made (at the CMC stage), the Court may well direct that the application for leave should be heard at the start of the hearing of the substantial issues arising under the s.20 claim. This is the right order to make where the delay is a short one, or where it is plain that the claim has some substance, or where the defendant is content that all the issues on the claim should be heard at one hearing.

20–009 To avoid unnecessary costs being incurred in applications for leave to bring a s.20 claim out of time, parties can sensibly agree that no point will be taken on an application for leave to bring the claim out of time, while negotiations are carrying on. A "longstop" date is a desirable feature in such agreements so that negotiations do not drag on and so that the personal representatives can start distributing the estate once the agreed extension has passed without a claim being brought under s.20.

20–010 To ensure that the six month time limit is not missed, a request should be made to the solicitor or party who is going to extract, or take the grant, to send a copy once the grant is issued. A Standing Search under NCPR, r.43 is also prudent. The entry of a caveat under NCPR, r.44 is NOT appropriate as it frustrates the start of the running of time. As in claims under the Inheritance Act 1975, the six month period in rectification claims under s.20 is regarded as the *maximum* time for the commencement of a claim. Under the CPR, it is now the responsibility of those representing claimants and other parties to litigation to get on with claims. This means that, unless the parties are amenable to discussion for settlement, they must issue claims promptly and well within the six month period and not leave it to the last moment.

20-011 Although there is sometimes controversy in Inheritance Act claims as to whether a grant is a prerequisite to issuing a claim, the authors prefer the view that such a grant is needed. In the case where there is no grant, either a grant *ad litem,* or as a last resort (in default of any person being able to take a grant) a grant taken by the Official Solicitor, is necessary to allow the claim to be brought.

Procedure in s.20 claims generally

20-012 This is governed by s.2 of Pt 57 and s.2 of the Pt 57 PD. Unlike Pt 57, r.2(2) which assigns probate claims to the Chancery Division of the High Court, rectification claims are not expressly assigned by that rule to that Division. However, in view of the nature of the claim and the terms of Sch. 1 to the Supreme Court Act 1981, para. 1(g), claims for the rectification of wills are assigned to the Chancery Division of the High Court. The County Court would not appear to have jurisdiction in claims to rectify wills under s.20. (A rectification claim — which is not a probate claim to omit words on the ground of want of knowledge or fraud — will not fall within s.32 of the County Courts Act 1984. Nor is a rectification claim under s.20 within the definition of the equity jurisdiction in s.23(a), (d) or (g) of that Act, nor is a claim under s.20 within the jurisdiction conferred on the County Court by the High Court and County Courts Jurisdiction Order 1991 (SI 1991/724). See Pt 9B, para. 138 of the White Book, Vol. 2.) The natural home for these claims will, therefore, be the Chancery Division, and this will include claims issued out of the Chancery District Registries. District Judges or Masters of the Chancery Division do not have jurisdiction to make orders under s.20, save where they are approving compromises of claims on behalf of those under a disability where the interest of that person in a fund or the amount of the claim does not exceed £100,000; CPR, r.2, PD B, para. 5.1(a). But note the jurisdiction in the Family Division (Probate) in unopposed applications under s.20 to rectify wills under NCPR r.55; this method of application can be used before the grant is taken out.

20-013 No Claim Form is specified but it is suggested that a Pt 7 Claim Form (N1) should be used. There will invariably be a dispute over the facts, so Pt 8 is not appropriate. However, in claims where a claim under the Inheritance Act 1975 is being brought alongside a rectification claim (as it was in *Re Grattan* [2001] W.T.L.R. 1305 — where the rectification issue was decided before determination of the 1975 Act claim) a Pt 8 claim form may have to be used for the rectification part of the claim, as a Pt 8 Claim Form is mandatory for 1975 Act claims; see Pt 57, r.16(1). If necessary, points of claim in the rectification claim can be an agreed way of stating the issues between the parties, or can be directed by the Court.

The Part 7 Claim Form will require particulars of claim to be endorsed on it, or served with it. **20–014**

Although not automatically assigned to the multi-track, a rectification claim is invariably going to be allocated to the multi-track in view of either the financial values at stake (*e.g.* a very large legacy or devise where there has been an error, or the destination of a large residuary estate) or because of complex questions of fact and/or law; see Pt 26, r.8. On the Allocation Questionnaire the claim should, therefore, be indicated as one for the multi-track. **20–015**

Every personal representative must be joined as a party; Pt 57, r.12(2). It is not thought that this rule extends to those to whom power has been reserved, or minors in the case of grants during their minority, or principals under attorney grants. If there is doubt, an order as to who should be joined should be sought at the CMC. **20–016**

The claimant must lodge the grant with the Court when he issues the claim form seeking relief under s.20; Pt 57 PD, para. 10(1). If the defendant has the grant he must do this within 14 days after the service of the claim form on him. It is often the case that the personal representative will be a defendant and will be holding the grant; Pt 57 PD, para. 10(2). In either case the Court may order otherwise; *e.g.* where the grant cannot be found, or is currently with share registrars. Unlike Inheritance Act 1975 claims there is no obligation on a claimant to file an official copy of the grant with the witness statement filed and served with the claim form. Presumably Court Staff will be alert to any date stated in the claim form as to when probate was granted, but there seems to be no system in the rules to force the disclosure of the grant, or a copy of it when the claim form is issued. **20–017**

The rules and principles relating to case management apply to the same extent to s.20 rectification claims as they do to probate claims. Certain points do emerge in these claims which may be worth emphasising: **20–018**

(a) Where a rectification claim is contemplated, the firm of solicitors who were responsible for taking instructions for and drawing the will and obtaining its execution must release a copy of the relevant file. A statement of the solicitor or clerk responsible should also be supplied.

(b) If there is any conflict of evidence about what instructions were given, this should be identified early in the potential claim.

(c) The potential claimant must send a letter before claim to the personal representatives at the earliest possible stage identifying the issue which the claimant says requires rectification. This is crucial where there is about to be a distribution.

(d) Because of the six month time limit from the date of the grant for the issue of the claim under s.20, solicitors acting for claimants must ensure that the date is diarised with warning dates no later than four clear weeks before the expiry of the period. Holiday periods and other dates when Court offices may be closed must also be carefully marked if they are near to the end of the period. Good practice in Inheritance Act 1975 claims in respect of dates applies to rectification claims under s.20. **File covers and computer records must be marked with these dates.**

Other procedural features of rectification claims

20–019 The standard of proof in a rectification claim is the usual civil standard, namely that the court should be satisfied on the balance of probabilities that a rectifiable error occurred within one of the grounds in s.20. In inherent jurisdiction cases, the Court has to be satisfied, on the same standard, that a word, or words should be omitted from a will when it is alleged that the testator did not know or approve of them. However, because a will is executed in circumstances of some formality, the probability that it reflects his intentions is usually of such weight that convincing evidence to the contrary is necessary. The words "convincing evidence" are important and are an echo of the same words when used in claims based on the jurisdiction (founded in equity) to rectify other documents such as contracts and deeds. The archaic phrase "strong irrefragible evidence" may now be abandoned in favour of the more modern words "convincing evidence". It is also important for the claimant to bear in mind that the burden is on him to satisfy the court that such convincing proof of either a clerical error, or of a failure to understand the testator's intentions, exists under s.20. Extrinsic evidence (*i.e.* outside the terms of the will) is required to prove this. See *Re Segelman* [1996] Ch. 171, applied in *Walter v Medlicott* [1999] 1 All E.R. 685 at 690; *Re Grattan* [2001] W.T.L.R. 1305. Speculation about the testator's intention will not be enough: *Re Bell dec'd* (Blackburne J.) [2002] [E.W.H.C.] 1080. See also, *Snell's Equity,* (30th ed.) at Chapter 43 for the principles which apply to the equitable remedy to rectify contracts, deeds and other *inter vivos* transactions.

In view of the fact that the burden is on the claimant to prove **20–020** the claim that the will should be rectified it is for the claimant to open the claim at any hearing, and he will have the final right of reply. The exception to this general rule may arise in a claim to omit words on the basis of want of knowledge and approval. There the burden may be on the party propounding the will with the disputed words in it, to dispel the suspicion that the testator did not know and approve of them.

The effect of an order for rectification under s.20, or under the inherent jurisdiction

An order for rectification of a will is one which relates back to **20–021** the date of the death, if not to the date of the will, in view of the fact the Court is correcting the will to accord with the testator's intentions. For tax (*i.e.* Inheritance Tax ('IHT') and Capital Gains Tax ('CGT')) purposes the estate must, therefore, be administered and assessed to tax on the basis of the will as rectified by the Order. This may require a reconsideration of exemptions and reliefs for IHT purposes, where, for example, the effect of the order for rectification is to cause property to go to an exempt beneficiary such as the surviving spouse, or a charity. In cases where the estate is partly exempt, care must be taken to ensure that the effect of any rectification order is not such as to create problems with IHT where the effect of the partial exemption requires reconsideration of how interests in the estate are to bear the IHT; see *Re Ratcliffe* [1999] S.T.C. 262. Specialist tax advice should be taken here.

It is important to distinguish an order rectifying a will under **20–022** s.20 (or under the inherent jurisdiction to omit words) from a Deed of Variation, or an order under the Inheritance Act 1975. Deeds for orders in the latter class may have certain fiscal advantages and may be treated as retrospective to the moment before the death of the deceased for IHT and CGT purposes, if they satisfy certain strict conditions, but they must not be confused with orders to rectify a will. (See Francis, "Inheritance Act Claims, Law Practice and Procedure", Chapter 14 for a full treatment of the tax effect of variations of the dispositions in an estate whether by Deed of Variation, or under the Inheritance Act 1975. See also para. 14–024 above.)

There is no reason why an order made under s.20 should not **20–023** be made by consent of the parties, and such an order will have the same effect as one made after a full hearing without any party consenting to it. There would seem to be no reason why a rectification claim under s.20 (but not one which is in effect a probate claim where want of knowledge and approval is alleged so as to omit words) should not be within the general rules as to discontinuance (CPR, Pt 38) and the compromise of claims generally. The Court may, however, be reluctant to make an order by consent under s.20 where children or patients are parties (within CPR, Pt 21) or where parties with an interest in the claim are for some reason not before the Court, without full consideration of the evidence and being satisfied that the order to rectify should be made.

20-024 Section 20(3) protects personal representatives who make distributions of the estate after the expiry of the six months period from the grant. This is in similar terms to s.20(1) of the Inheritance Act 1975. But the right to recover any distribution made after the end of the six months period is preserved. In practice, as in cases where Inheritance Act 1975 claims are feared, personal representatives should warn those who may have threatened to bring a claim to rectify the will, but who have not done so within the six month period from the date of the grant, that they will make the relevant distribution within a stated time. In cases of doubt the personal representatives may need to seek the directions of the Court under CPR, Pt 64.

Recording the Order of the Court

20-025 Part 57 PD, para. 11.1 requires a copy of the order to rectify the will to be sent to the Principal Registry of the Family Division for filing, and for the order to be endorsed on, or permanently annexed to the grant under which the estate is administered. These last words mean that the endorsement or annexation of the Order is on the "full" grant and not any limited grant which may have issued in the past.

20-026 In practice the Court will send the Order and the grant (already lodged with the Court under Pt 57 PD, para. 10) to the Probate Registry which issued the grant. That Registry will make the following endorsement on the grant (down the right hand margin:—

> "Memorandum of an Order dated [ ]. Pursuant to the Order of [name of judge/Master/District Judge] of the Chancery Division of the High Court of Justice at [place at which the Court sat] pursuant to s.20(1) of the Administration of Justice Act 1982 it was ordered that the Will dated [ ] of [ ] deceased be rectified in accordance with the Order annexed hereto"

> Signed by the District Judge or Registrar of the Probate Registry.

The Registry then annexes the Order to the grant with **20–027** machine-inserted brass eyelets. As a matter of internal discretion a note of the Order may be put on the Probateman computer record by the District Judge or Registrar. The original grant with the order endorsed on and attached to it is then retained in the Registry files, if the grant was issued by that Registry within the past two years. If it was issued more than two years ago, the Registry will send the original grant with the Order to the Probate Record Centre for permanent filing. In all cases the Registry sends an official (sealed) copy of the grant with the order endorsed and annexed to the solicitors or person who extracted it. If the Order to rectify is made under NCPR, r.55 at the Registry which issued the grant, the endorsement and the other tasks referred to above will be made there.

Costs in rectification claims

The terms on which orders for costs are made in claims to **20–028** rectify wills attract the same principles as apply in probate claims. That is to say that Pt 44, r.3 applies so as to determine how the Court should exercise its discretion, with the general rule that the losing party pays the successful party's costs being paramount. Most rectification claims will fall within this principle. It is a hostile form of litigation. (See *Re Grattan* [2001] W.T.L.R. 1305, where at p.1324E, the Court treated the claimant's failure in her rectification claim as disentitling her to half of her costs of the whole claim, she having succeeded in her claim under the Inheritance Act 1975). The costs of an application for leave to apply out of time may well be borne by the solicitor who failed to make that application in time.

Where it is plain from the outset that a clerical error was **20–029** made, or that there was a failure to understand instructions within s.20(1)(a) or (b), and where the parties simply want an order to rectify, the costs may be ordered to come out of the estate. There may be an issue between the parties as to whether those costs should be borne by those whose interests are affected by the order and not by those who are not so affected. It would seem right that those whose interests are affected should exonerate the others who are not from any costs. The solicitors, or their insurers may well be paying the costs in any event.

In line with the advice given to personal representatives **20–030** contemplating being claimants in probate claims, such personal representatives should not be claimants in a rectification claim without an indemnity for any costs for which they may be liable from the beneficiaries with a financial interest in the outcome.

However, unlike probate claims, rectification claims may be a proper occasion for a personal representative who is faced with a plain error to seek the directions of the Court under CPR, Pt 64, and if necessary an order that he is entitled to his costs of the claim out of the estate, if there are beneficiaries unwilling to bring the claim. Unlike a probate claim, in a rectification claim there is a will which has been proved and which, it is alleged, contains a rectifiable error. This means that there may be a case to be made for a personal representative faced with unwilling beneficiaries, to seek the directions of the Court as to whether he should bring the claim, and if possible, seek some protection as to his costs; see *Alsop Wilkinson v Neary* [1996] 1 W.L.R. 1220 and *D'Abo v Paget* [2000] W.T.L.R. 863. Neutral personal representatives who are joined in claims under s.20 (as they must be under Part 57, r.12(2)) should not be involved in the merits of the claim, save to the extent that they may have relevant evidence to give. Any defence filed and served by such parties should state in simple terms that they will abide by any order of the Court and take no active role in the claim.

20–031 Where the personal representative is the person responsible for the error (or where, for example, his firm took the instructions for the will which are the source of the claim), he may have to consider how far there is a conflict between his role as personal representative and as the person who directly, or indirectly is responsible for the claim. No doubt he will be in touch with his, or his firm's insurers. He will need to take separate advice about the negligence implications of the claim. In extreme cases an application may be made under s.50 of the Administration of Justice Act 1985 for that person to be removed as personal representative. That is an extreme move and may only be necessary where the only person who represents the estate is responsible for the error and the beneficiaries consider that a neutral personal representative is required to ensure proper administration of the estate. If such problems are apprehended *before* any grant is taken there may be a renunciation, a non-appearance to a citation to take or renounce a grant, or an order under s.116 of the Supreme Court Act 1981 can be made, so that a neutral person takes the grant.

20–032 The principles which apply to Pt 36 offers, and other forms of offer, and offers to mediate apply to rectification claims as they do to probate claims.

Appeals in rectification claims

20–033 The same routes of appeal apply to rectification claims as they do to probate claims, and the factors in whether or not to grant leave to appeal, and whether an appeal would be allowed also apply here, as they do in probate claims. The one variant is that rectification claims will invariably turn on questions of fact. So, unless the lower court has got the primary facts wrong, or made wrong deductions from them, the higher court will not interfere. The law in rectification claims is clear and at least under s.20 the lower court is highly unlikely to get it wrong. (In *Re Grattan*, above, leave to appeal was refused as the questions arising on the rectification claim were ones of fact; see p.1324G of the report).

Unopposed applications to rectify in the Probate Registry under NCPR, r.55

Applications to rectify may be brought under NCPR, r.55 before a District Judge or Registrar of a Probate Registry and if the application is unopposed, an order to rectify may be made under s.20. (Note: the CPR do not apply to contentious probate business so the NCPR will apply to govern the procedure and the forms of application; see CPR, Pt 2, r.2(2) Table Pt 2). **20–034**

The text of r.55 is as follows: **20–035**

55.—(1) An application for an order that a will be rectified by virtue of section 20(1) of the Administration of Justice Act 1982 may be made to a district judge or registrar, unless a probate action has been commenced.

(2) The application shall be supported by an affidavit, setting out the grounds of the application, together with such evidence as can be adduced as to the testator's intentions and as to whichever of the following matters as are in issue:—

(a) in what respects the testator's intentions were not understood; or

(b) the nature of any alleged clerical error.

(3) Unless otherwise directed, notice of the application shall be given to every person having an interest under the will whose interest might be prejudiced or such other person who might be prejudiced by the rectification applied for and any comments in writing by any such person shall be exhibited to the affidavit in support of the application.

(4) If the district judge or registrar is satisfied that, subject to any direction to the contrary, notice has been given to every person mentioned in paragraph (3) above, and that the application is unopposed, he may order that the will be rectified accordingly.

This is a very useful and inexpensive way of rectifying wills under s.20 where all persons having an interest under the will (or otherwise — *e.g.* on partial intestacy) whose interests might **20–036** be prejudiced, have been notified and do not oppose the order sought. It is the route to be chosen where, for example, there are typing errors (often in the amount of pecuniary legacies) which are accepted by all parties as such. The use of r.55 clearly avoids the cost of a Pt 7 claim form in the Chancery Division. Rule 55 cannot be used where a probate claim has been commenced; see the words at the end of r.55(1). As the rule indicates (para. 2) the application is made by an affidavit setting out the matters required by that paragraph of r.55. The final paragraph of the affidavit should set out what Order is sought. Notice of the application must be given to all persons having an interest which might be prejudiced by the rectification of the will as applied for. Such persons may be not only those interested under the will, but also those interested on a partial intestacy, if rectification of the will is ordered. It will have been prudent to advise all such parties in advance of the application to see if it can be treated as an unopposed one. The comments of those with an interest must be exhibited to the affidavit in support of the application; r.55(3). Where persons with an interest are under a disability, or are unascertained, or unborn, it may be impossible to use the r.55 procedure unless the Court accepts representation on their behalf. In such cases it may be safer to use the Pt 7 procedure in the Chancery Division. In cases where there may be difficulties about notifying all interested parties, or where it is uncertain who is, or who is not opposing the rectification sought, the District Judge or Registrar will usually set a date for a preliminary hearing to take stock of the application and make any necessary directions as to how it is to proceed. In some cases he may direct that the application proceeds by the issue of a summons under r.61 and service on those with an interest. (Service is governed by NCPR, r.66 with a general requirement for at least two clear days service before the date of a hearing). The District Judge or Registrar may refer the application to a Family Division Judge in difficult cases; NCPR, r.61(1).

20–037 Costs in such applications fall within the discretion in NCPR, r.63 and the terms of rule 60. It is suggested that in applications made under r.55 which are successful the costs will come out of the estate, although in practice they will be ultimately borne by the solicitor, or other party who has drawn the will and made the error. Where a r.55 application is made but there is dissension so that an order cannot be made, the costs may follow the event under the application of CPR, Pt 44 by virtue of NCPR, r.60. This means that the party making the application pays the costs.

20–038 Appeals from orders of a District Judge, or Registrar under r.55 are to the Family Division Judge under NCPR, r.65. The summons must be issued within seven days of the decision complained of and served on the respondents to the application.

In the case of an unsuccessful application under r.55, a **20–039**
disappointed party may want to bring a Part 7 claim in the
Chancery Division

An application under r.55 can be and is often made before **20–040**
the grant is taken out; *e.g.* to rectify obvious and agreed typing
errors. If a grant has been taken out, the six month period for
claims under s.20 applies to applications under r.55. The same
factors as to whether leave should be given will also apply,
although where the application is unopposed, no point will be
taken by the parties on the question of time. But the terms of
r.55(4) do give the District Judge or Registrar a discretion, so he
has to be satisfied that the Order, albeit unopposed, is a proper
one to make.

Note that the jurisdiction under r.55 is not the same as the **20–041**
Probate Registrar's jurisdiction to omit words from wills when
they have been inserted after execution and are unexecuted and
unattested, or where the words are offensive, libellous or
blasphemous.

Appendix I

Forms and Precedents

Form 1

Rule 42 Certificate of Delivery of Inland Revenue Affidavit

And it is hereby certified that an Inland Revenue affidavit has **A–001** been delivered wherein it is shown that the gross value of the said estate in the United Kingdom (exclusive of what the said deceased may have been possessed of or entitled to as a trustee and not beneficially) amount to £........................ and that the net value of the estate amounts to £........................

And it is further certified that it appears by a receipt signed by an Inland Revenue officer on the said affidavit that £.................... on account of estate duty and interest on such duty has been paid.

Form 2

Rule 43(1)   **Standing Search**

In the High Court of Justice   **A–002**

Family Division

The Principal [*or* ....District Probate] Registry

I/We apply for the entry of a standing search so that there shall be sent to me/us an office copy of every grant of representation in England and Wales in the estate of—

Full name of deceased: ....

Full address: ....

Alternative or alias names: ....

Exact date of death:

which either has issued not more than 12 months before the entry of this application or issues within 6 months thereafter

Signed ....

Name in block letters ....

Full address ....

Reference No. (if any) ....

Form 3

Rule 44(2)   **Caveat**

A–003   In the High Court of Justice

Family Division

The Principal [or .... District Probate] Registry
   Let no grant be sealed in the estate of (*full name and address*) deceased, who died on the day of 20............ without notice to (*name of party by whom or on whose behalf the caveat is entered*).
Dated this .... day of .... 20..............
(*Signed*)   (*to be signed by the caveator's solicitor or probate practitioner or by the caveator if acting in person*)

Form 4

Rule 44(5)   **Warning to Caveator**

In the High Court of Justice   A–004

Family Division

(*The nominated registry as defined by rule 44(5)*]

To .... of ....a party who has entered a caveat in the estate of .... deceased.

You have eight days (starting with the day on which this warning was served on you):

(i) to enter an appearance either in person or by your solicitor or probate practitioner, at the [*name and address of the nominated registry*] set out what interest you have in the estate of the above-named of deceased contrary to that of the party at whose instance this warning is issued; or

(ii) if you have no contrary interest but wish to show cause against the sealing of a grant on such party, to issue and serve a summons for directions by a district judge of the Principal Registry or a registrar of a District Probate Registry.
    If you fail to do either of these, the court may proceed to issue a grant of probate or administration in the said estate notwithstanding your caveat.

Dated the .... day of 20............

Issued at the instance of ....

[*Here set out the name and interest (including the date of the will, if any, under which the interest arises) of the party warning, the name of his solicitor or probate practitioner and the address for service. If the party warning is acting in person this must be stated.*]

                                                      Registrar

Form 5

Rules 44(10), 46(6) Appearance to Warning or Citation

A–005 In the High Court of Justice

Family Division

The Principal [*or* .... District Probate] Registry

Caveat No. .... dated the ....
day of .... 20............

[Citation dated the ....day of .... 20............]

Full name and address of deceased ....

Full name and address of person warning [*or* citor]: ....
(*Here set out the interest of the person warning, or citor, as shown in warning or citation.*)

Full name and address of caveator [or person cited.]

(*Here set out the interest of the caveator or person cited, stating the date of the will (if any) under which such interest arises.*)

Enter an appearance for the above-named caveator [*or* person cited] in this matter.

Dated the .... day .... 20............

(*Signed*)

whose address for service is:
        Solicitor or probate practitioner (*or* 'In person').

Annex

A form of witness statement or affidavit about testamentary documents (CPR rule 57.5)

(*Title of the claim*)

A–006 I [*name and address*] the claimant/defendant in this claim state [on oath] that I have no knowledge of any document—

CONTENTIOUS PROBATE 241

(i) being or purported to be or having the form or effect of a will or codicil of [*name of deceased*] whose estate is the subject of this claim;

(ii) being or purporting to be a draft or written instructions for any such will or codicil made by or at the request of or under the instructions of the deceased;

(iii) being or purporting to be evidence of the contents or a copy of any such will or codicil which is alleged to have been lost or destroyed,

except .... [*describe any testamentary document of the deceased, and if any such document is not in your control, give the name and address of the person who you believe has possession or control of it, or state that you do not know the name and address of that person*] . . .

[I believe that the facts stated in this witness statement are true] [or *jurat* for *affidavit*]

(*NOTE:* '*testamentary document*' *is defined in CPR rule 57.1*)

SUBPOENA to bring in a script: contentious proceedings:[1]

(Royal Arms)

Claim form

In the High Court of Justice **A–007**
Chancery Division
[............District Registry]
Claim No. HC ....

In the estate of (*name*) deceased (Probate)
Claimant   A. B.
(*address*)
and

---

[1] Supreme Court Act 1981, s.123. Adapted from Chancery Masters' Practice Forms No. 35.

Defendants   (1) C. D.
                              (address)
                              (2) L. M.
                              (address)

Issued pursuant to the authority of [Master or District Judge ....] dated........................ 20............

Disobedience to this subpoena would be a contempt of court punishable by imprisonment[2]

ELIZABETH THE SECOND, by the Grace of God, of the United Kingdom of Great Britain and Northern Ireland and of Our Other Realms and Territories Queen, Head of the Commonwealth, Defender of the Faith

To C. D. of (address):

WHEREAS it appears by an [affidavit or witness statement] of A. B. filed on .... 20............ in the Chancery Division of the [High Court of Justice or .... District Registry], that a certain original paper or script, being or purporting to be testamentary, namely the [last will and testament dated .... 20............ of X. Y. deceased of (address) who died on .... 20............] is now in your possession, within your power or under your control.

WE COMMAND YOU that, within eight days after service hereof on you exclusive of the day of such service, you do bring into and leave with the proper officer in [Chancery Chambers, Room TM7.09, Thomas More Building, Royal Courts of Justice, Strand, London WC2A 2LL, or the .... District Registry at (address)] the said original paper or script now in the possession, within the power and under the control of you the said C. D.

WITNESS, the Right Honourable .... Lord High Chancellor of Great Britain, on .... 20............ .

                              (Signature)
                              [Master of the Supreme
                              Court or District Judge]

Subpoena to bring in a script issued by E. F. & Co. of (address), Solicitors

---

[2] See CPR, Sch. 1 RSC Ord. 45, r.7(4). This notice should be indorsed prominently on the front of the document served.

PF36CH

Order Appointing Administrator pending determination of Probate Claim

IN THE HIGH COURT OF JUSTICE
CHANCERY DIVISION

In the estate of AB deceased   A–008

Claim No.

Before   Master

Claimant

Defendant

An application by notice dated ( ) was made on   (*date*) by [counsel] [solicitor] for   [*party*] and was attended by (   ).

The Master heard [counsel] [solicitor] for   [*party*]
[**The Master** read the evidence filed]

The court appoints CD of   administrator of the estate of the deceased pending the determination of this claim
CD has given security of £   to the satisfaction of the court

IT IS ORDERED that a grant of administration pending determination of this claim under section 117 of the Supreme Court Act 1981 be made to (*AB*)
And it is ordered that (*AB*) pass his accounts as the court from time to time

---

*Where there is more than one claimant/defendant, the parties should be described as follows:

(1) AB
(2) CD
(3) EF   Claimants

    and

(1) GH
(2) IJ
(3) KL   Defendants

PF38CH

Order in Probate claim involving compromise

IN THE HIGH COURT OF JUSTICE
CHANCERY DIVISION

A–009 **In the estate of AB** (*deceased*)

Claim No.

Before Master

Claimant*

Defendant*

An application by notice dated   was made on   [*date*] by [*counsel*] [*solicitor*] for   [*party*] and was attended by

The Master heard [*counsel*] [*solicitor*] for   [*party*]
[The Master read the evidence filed]

Probate of the alleged last will and testament of   (*deceased*) dated   was granted on   [*date*] to
The court is satisfied that:

(1) consents by or on behalf of every relevant beneficiary (as defined by s.49 of the Administration of Justice Act 1985) have been given to the making of this order; and

(2) the order is for the benefit of those relevant beneficiaries who are children.

*Where there is more than one claimant/defendant, the parties should be described as follows:

(1) AB
(2) CD
(3) EF   Claimants

     and

(1) GH
(2) IJ
(3) KL   Defendants

The Court pronounces for/against the force and validity of the last will and testament of the deceased a completed copy of which is the script dated and marked exhibit [   ] referred to in the [witness statement] [affidavit] of scripts of [*name*] sworn on [*date*] and against the force and validity of the last will and testament of the deceased a completed copy of which is the script dated   and marked exhibit [   ] referred to in the [witness statement] [affidavit] of scripts of   [*name*] sworn on   [*date*]

It is ordered that

(1) this claim [and counterclaim] be discontinued
( ) the [probate] [letters of administration] be revoked
( ) the terms set out in the Schedule be carried into effect
( ) [probate of the will] [and   codicil] [letters of administration of the estate] of AB deceased late of   [*address*] be granted to [the claimant] [the defendant]
[   ] named as executor if entitled thereto
( ) on application for such a grant the caveat numbered [   ] and entered on   [*date*] do if still subsisting cease to have effect
( ) there be assessed if not agreed

   (a) the costs of this claim [and counterclaim] of the claimant/defendant [   ] the executor named in the will

   (b) the costs of this claim [and counterclaim] of the claimant/defendant [   ] and [   ]

   (c) the costs of the claimant/defendant under the Legal Aid Act 1988 ( ) the costs specified in (a) and (b) above be paid out of the estate of the deceased in the due course of administration.

Schedule

[*Set out the agreed terms*]

APPENDIX I

A–010

Claim Form

In the	

	for court use only
Claim No.	
Issue date	

Claimant(s)

Seal

Defendant(s)

Brief details of claim

Value

Defendant's name and address

	£
Amount claimed	
Court fee	
Solicitor's costs	
Total amount	

N1 Claim form, general.

Claim No.	

Does, or will, your claim include any issues under the Human Rights Act 1998? ☐ Yes ☐ No

Particulars of Claim (attached) (to follow)

Statement of Truth
*(I believe) (The Claimant believes) that the facts stated in these particulars of claim are true.
*I am duly authorised by the claimant to sign this statement

Full name _____

Name of claimant's solicitor's firm _____

signed _____ position or office held _____
*(Claimant) (Litigation friend) (Claimant's solicitor)
(if signing on behalf of firm or company)

*delete as appropriate

Claimant's or claimant's solicitor's address to which documents or payments should be sent if different from overleaf including (if appropriate) details of DX, fax or e-mail.

APPENDIX I

Claim Form
(probate claim)

In the
Claim No.

In the estate of   deceased (Probate)

Seal

Claimant(s)

Defendant(s)

Brief details of claim

Defendant's
name and address

Court fee	
Solicitor's costs	To be assessed

Issue date	

N2 Claim form probate (10.01)

|Claim No.||

Does, or will, your claim include any issues under the Human Rights Act 1998? ☐ Yes ☐ No

Particulars of Claim (attached) (to follow)

Statement of Truth
*(I believe) (The Claimant believes) that the facts stated in this claim form are true.
*I am duly authorised by the claimant to sign this statement

signed _____ date _____
*(Claimant) (Litigation friend *(where claimant is a child or a patient)* (Claimant's solicitor)
*delete as appropriate

Full name _____

Name of claimant's solicitor's firm _____

position or office held _____
(*if signing on behalf of a company*)

Claimant's or claimant's solicitor's address to which documents or payments should be sent if different from overleaf including (if appropriate) details of DX, fax or e-mail.

Probate Claim

Notes for claimant on completing a claim form

A–011　Please read all these guidance notes before you begin completing the claim form. The notes follow the order in which information is required on it.

Court staff can help you fill in the claim form and give information about procedure once it has been issued. But they cannot give you legal advice. If you need legal advice, for example about the likely success of your claim, you should contact a solicitor or a Citizens Advice Bureau.

If you are filling in the claim form by hand, please use black ink and write in block capitals.

The claim form and all subsequent court documents relating to the probate claim must be marked at the top:

'In the estate of *[name]* deceased (Probate)'

Copy the completed claim form and the defendant's notes for guidance so that you have one copy for yourself, one copy for the court and one copy for each defendant. Send or take the forms to the court office with the appropriate fee. The court will tell you how much this is.

You must fill in the heading of the form to indicate the court where you want the claim to be issued. In London, you can issue your claim at the Royal Courts of Justice. The heading will be:

'In the High Court of Justice Chancery Division'

Outside London, you can only issue your claim in Birmingham, Bristol, Cardiff Leeds, Liverpool, Manchester Newcastle upon Tyne or Preston. This will be either in the District Registries; the heading will be:

'In the High Court of Justice Chancery Division
　　　　　　　　　　　　　　　　　　　District Registry'

or

in the county court: the heading will be:

'In the　　　　　　　　　　　　　　　　　County Court'

As the person issuing the claim, you are called the 'claimant'; the person you are suing is called the defendant'.

CONTENTIOUS PROBATE

Claimants who are under 18 years old or patients within the meaning of the Mental Health Act 1983, must have a litigation friend to issue and conduct court proceedings on their behalf Court staff will tell you more about what you need to do if this applies to you. You must provide the following information about yourself and the defendant according to the capacity in which you are claiming and in which the defendant is being sued. When claiming or being sued as:—

An individual

All known forenames and surnames, whether Mr, Mrs, Miss, Ms or other (*e.g.* Dr) and residential address (**including** postcode, telephone and fax number or e-mail address) in England and Wales.

Where the individual is Under 18 write '(a child by "Mr Joe Bloggs" his litigation friend)' after the child's name. If the child is conducting proceedings on their own behalf write '(a child)' after the child's name.

A patient within the meaning of the Mental Health Act 1983 write '(by "Mr Joe Bloggs" his litigation friend)' after the patient's name.

Where your claim seeks revocation of a grant of probate or letters of administration, every person who is entitled to, or claims to be entitled to, administer the estate under the grant, must be made a party to the claim.

Claim form

- The claim form must contain a statement of the nature of the interest of the claimant and of each defendant in the estate.
- If you dispute another party's interest in the estate you must state this and set out your reasons.
- If you contend that
  — at the time when a will was executed the testator did not know of and approve its contents,
  — a will was not duly executed; or
  — at the time of the execution of a will the testator was not of sound mind, memory and understanding; or
  — the execution of a will was obtained by undue influence or fraud,

you must set out the contention specifically and give particulars of the fasts and matters relied upon.

Statement of truth

This must be signed by you, by your solicitor or your litigation friend as appropriate. Proceedings for contempt of court may be brought against a person who signs a statement of truth without an honest belief in its truth.

Address for documents

Insert in this box the address at which you wish to receive documents if different from the address you have already given under 'the heading Claimant',The address must be in England and Wales.

If you are willing to accept service by DX, fax or e-mail, add details.

Documents to be filed

You must file any testamentary document of the deceased person which you have in your possession or control **with** your claim form.

A testamentary document means a will, a draft of a will, written instructions for a will made by or at the request of, or under the instructions of the testator and any documents purporting to be evidence of the contents, or to be a copy, of a will which is alleged to have been lost or destroyed.

In addition you must file written evidence about the documents which should be in the form annexed to the Practice Direction to Part 57. It must be signed by you personally (and not your solicitor) or by your litigation friend,

You may only file your claim form without the testamentary documents or evidence about them if the court gives permission. It will normally do this only in cases of urgency. For example, where you wish to apply for the immediate appointment of an administrator pending the determination of your claim and it is not possible to obtain the documents immediately.

If the court gives permission it will expect you to give an undertaking to lodge the documents by a specific date.

Inspection of testamentary documents

Except with the permission of the court, no party is allowed to inspect the testamentary documents or written evidence lodged or filed by another party until they have lodged their testamentary documents and filed their evidence.

N2A Notes for claimant on completing a claim forn (10.01)

Probate Claim

Notes for the defendant

Please read these notes carefully they will help you decide what to do about this claim. If you need legal advice, you should contact a solicitor or Citizens Advice Bureau immediately.

A–012

You have 28 days from the date on which you were served with particulars of claim in which to respond. Particulars of claim may be contained in the claim form itself or served separately. You should respond by completing and returning the acknowledgment of service enclosed with this claim form.

Court staff can help you complete the form and tell you about procedures but they cannot give you legal advice.

RESPONDING TO THIS CLAIM

Acknowledgment of Service

Whether or not you wish to defend the claim, you must file an acknowledgment of service. The period for filing the acknowledgment of service is:

- if you have been served with a claim form which states that particulars of claim are to follow, within 28 days after you have been served with the particulars of claim;
- in any other case, 28 days after you have been served with the claim form.

Defence/Counterclaim

If you wish to defend the claim you must file a defence (and or a counterclaim). The period for filing it (them) is the same as the period for filing an acknowledgment of service set out above.

Failure to acknowledge service

If you fail to acknowledge service, the claimant may, after the time for acknowledging has expired, ask the court to proceed with the claim.

Documents to be filed with the acknowledgment of service

When you file your acknowledgment of service with the court you must also lodge any testamentary documents of the deceased person that are in your possession and control.

A testamentary document means a will, a draft of a will, written instructions for a will made by or at the request of or under the instructions of the testator and any documents purporting to be evidence of the contents, or to be a copy, of a will which is alleged to have been lost or destroyed.

In addition you must file written evidence about the documents which should be in the form annexed to the Practice Direction to Part 57. It must be signed by you personally (and not your solicitor) or by your litigation friend.

Non inspection of testamentary documents

A party is not, unless the court gives permission, allowed to inspect the testamentary documents or written evidence lodged or filed by any other party until they have lodged their testamentary documents and filed their evidence.

Counterclaim

If you believe that you have a claim or are entitled to a remedy relating to the grant of probate of the will, or letters of administration of the estate of the deceased person, you must serve a counterclaim.

If the claimant fails to serve particulars of claim within the time allowed, you may ask the court's permission to serve your counterclaim, If permission is granted, the claim will then proceed as if your counterclaim were the particulars of claim.

Acknowledgment of service
(probate claim)

In the   Claim No. **A–013**

Claimant(s)

Defendant(s)

In the estate of   deceased (Probate)

You should read the 'notes for the defendant' attached to the claim form before you complete this form.
Tick the appropriate box

☐   I intend to defend this claim and attach my defence (and counterclaim).

☐   I *do not* intend to defend this claim.

Testamentary documents of the deceased

☐   Testamentary documents are described in the attached witness statement or affidavit. [The documents are also attached for lodging].

☐   I do not know of any testamentary documents — see attached witness statement or affidavit.

Revocation of existing Grant

Do not complete this part unless the claimant is seeking revocation of a grant of probate or letters of administration, and the grant has not *already been lodged in court.*

☐   I do not have the [probate] [letters of administration] under my control.

☐   I do not have the grant of [probate] [letters of administration] under my control. [I am lodging it with this acknowledgment of service.]

Signed   **Position or office held (if signing on behalf of a company)**

(Defendant) (Defendant's Solicitor)
(Litigation friend *(where defendant is a child or a patient)*)

This acknowledgment is filed on behalf of the _____ Defendant
(Please state whether 1st, 2nd, 3rd etc. as appropriate)

Address to which documents about this claim should be sent

		if applicable
	fax no.	
	DX no.	
	e-mail	
Tel. no. Postcode	ref no.	

N3 Acknowledgment of service (10.01)

APPENDIX I

Notice of issue
(probate claim)

A–014 In the Claim No.

 Claimant(s)

 Defendant(s)
 Issue fee

In the estate of deceased (Probate)

Your claim was issued on [ ]

[The court sent it to the defendant(s) by first class post on [ ]
and it will be deemed served on [ ]].

[The claim form (which includes particulars of claim) is returned to you, with the relevant response forms, for you to serve them on the defendant(s)]

Notes for guidance
The claim form and particulars of claim, if srved separately, must be served on the defendant within 4 months of the date of issue (6 months if you are serving outside England and Wales. You may be able to apply to extend the time for serving the claim form but the application must generally be made before the 4 month or 6 months period expires.

You must inform the court immediately if your claim is settled.

The defendant must file an acknowledgment of service and defence within 28 days of service of the Particulars of Claim (whether they are served with the claim form or separately). A longer period applies if the defendant is served outside England and Wales.

Default judgment **cannot** be obtained in a probate claim.

If no defendant acknowledges service or files a defence, and the time for doing so has expired, you may apply to the court for an order that the claim proceed to trial.

To

Ref.

N205D Notice of issue (probate) (10.01)

CONTENTIOUS PROBATE

Appellant's Notice

In the ☐

Notes for guidance are available which will help you complete this form. Please read them carefully before you complete each section.

A–015

For Court use only	
Appeal Court Reference No.	
Date filed	

Seal

Section 1: Details of the claim or case

Name of court

Case or claim number

Names of claimants/ aplicants/ petitioner

Names of defendants/ respondents

In the case or claim, were you the *(tick appropriate box)*
- ☐ claimant
- ☐ defendant
- ☐ applicant
- ☐ respondent
- ☐ petitioner
- ☐ other *(please specify)* _____

Section 2: Your (appellant's) name and address

Your (appellant's) name _____

Your solicitor's name _____
(if you are legally represented)

Your (your solicitor's) address

reference or contact name

contact telephone number

DX number

N161   Appellant's Notice (10.00)

Section 3: Respondent's name and address

Respondent's name _____

Solicitor's name _____
(if the respondent is legally represented)

Respondent's (solicitor's) contact address

	reference or contact name	
	contact telephone number	
	DX number	

Details of other respondents are attached ☐ Yes   ☐ No

Section 4: Time estimate for appeal hearing

Do not complete if appealing to the Court of Appeal

	Days	Hours	Minutes
How long do you estimate it will take to put your appeal to the appeal court at the hearing?			

Who will represent you at the appeal hearing? ☐ Yourself ☐ Solicitor ☐ Counsel

Section 5: Details of the order(s) or part(s) of order(s) you want to appeal

Was the order you are appealing made as the result of a previous appeal?
Yes ☐   No ☐

Name of Judge

Date of order(s)

If only part of an order is appealed, write out that part (or those parts)

Was the case allocated to a track?   Yes ☐   No ☐
If Yes, which track was the case allocated to?
  ☐ small claims track ☐ fast track ☐ multi-track
Is the order you are appealing a case management order?   Yes ☐   No ☐

Section 6: Permission to Appeal

Has permission to appeal been granted?

    Yes ☐   complete box **A**   No ☐   complete box **B**
                                                                                if you are asking for permission or it is not required

A	**B**
Date of order granting permission	☐ I do not need permission
Name of judge _____	☐ I _____ appellant('s solicitor) seek permission to appeal the order(s) at **section 5** above.
Name of court _____	

Are you making any other applications? Yes ☐   No ☐
If Yes, complete section 10

Is the appellant in receipt of legal aid certificate or a
community legal service fund (CLSF) certificate?   Yes ☐   No ☐

Does your appeal include any issues arising from the Human Rights Act 1998?
                                      Yes ☐   No ☐

Section 7: Grounds for appeal

> I (the appellant) appeal(s) the order(s) at **section 5** because:

Section 8: Arguments in support of grounds

My skeleton argument is:

☐ set out below ☐ attached ☐ will follow within 14 days of filing this notice

I (the appellant) will rely on the following arguments at the hearing of the appeal:—

Section 9: What decision are you asking the appeal court to make?

I (the appellant) am (is) asking that:—

(tick appropriate box)

☐ the order(s) at **section 5** be set aside

☐ the order(s) at **section 5** be varied and the following order(s) substituted:—

☐ a new trial be ordered

☐ the appeal court makes the following additional order:—

Section 10: Other applications

I wish to make an application for additional orders ☐ in this section

☐ in the Part 23 application form (N244) attached

PART A
I apply (the appellant applies) for an order (a draft of which is attached) that:—

because:—

PART B
I (we) wish to rely on:—

☐ evidence in Part C
☐ witness statement (affidavit)

PART C
I (we) wish to rely on the following evidence in support of this application:—

Statement of Truth
I believe (the appellant believes) that the facts stated in Section 10 are true.

Full name _____

Name of appellant's solicitor's firm _____

signed _____ position or office held _____
Appellant('s Solicitor)   (if signing on behalf of firm or company)

Section 11: Supporting documents

If you do not yet have a coument that you intend to use to support your appeal, identify it, give the date when you expect it to be available and give the reasons why it is not currently available in the box below.

Please tick the papers you are filing with this notice and any you will be filing later.

- ☐ Your skeleton argument *(if separate)*
- ☐ A copy of the order being appealed
- ☐ A copy of any order giving or refusing permission to appeal together with a copy of the reasons for that decision
- ☐ Any witness statements or affidavits in support of any application included in this appellant's notice
- ☐ A copy of the legal aid or CLSF certificate *(if legally represented)*
- ☐ A bundle of documents for the appeal hearing containing copies of your appellant's notice and all the papers listed above and the following:—

    - ☐ a suitable record of the reasons for the judgment of the lower court;
    - ☐ any statements of case;
    - ☐ any other affidavits or witness statement filed in support of your appeal;
    - ☐ any relevant transcript or note of evidence;
    - ☐ any relevant application notices or case management documents;
    - ☐ any skeleton arguments relied on by the lower court;
    relevant affidavits, witness statements, summaries, experts' reports and exhibits;
    - ☐ any other documents ordered by the court; (give details)

    - ☐ in a second appeal, the original order appealed, the reasons given for making that order and the appellant's notice appealing that original (first) order
    - ☐ if the appeal is from a decision of a Tribunal, the Tribunal's reasons for that decision, the original decision reviewed by the Tribunal and the reasons for that original decision

Reasons why you have not supplied a document and date when you expect it to be available:—

Signed _____ Appellant('s Solicitor)

PF50

Application for case management directions in the multi-track (Part 29)

Use Form PF244/N244 attaching the whole of Form PF52 as a **A–016** draft Order (with double spacing between the lines),
1. completing those paragraphs or parts of paragraphs, for which an Order is sought, as appropriate, and
2. marking those paragraphs or parts of paragraphs for which an order is not sought, by striking through the paragraph or sub-paragraph **number** only.

PF 52

Order for case management directions in the multi-track (Part 29)

IN THE HIGH COURT OF JUSTICE **A–017**
[CHANCERY]
[DISTRICT REGISTRY]
[IN THE   COUNTY COURT]

Claim No.

Before *(Master or District Judge)* [sitting in Private]

Claimant

Defendant

An application was made by [application notice/letter] dated *(date) or* by [Counsel] [solicitor] for *(party)* and was attended by ( )

The Master [District Judge] read the written evidence filed

[**The parties** having agreed the directions set out in paragraph(s) ( ) below which are made by consent],

IT IS ORDERED that:

1. ALLOCATION
   the case be allocated to the multi-track.

2. TRANSFER
   (1) the claim be transferred to;

       (a) the ( ) Division of the High Court,
       (b) the ( ) District Registry [Mercantile List], or
       (c) the ( ) County Court [Chancery List] [Business List],

   (2) the issue(s) (*define issue(s)*) be transferred to (*insert one of (a) to (c) above*) for determination.
   (3) the (*party*) apply by (*date*) to a Judge of the Technology and Construction Court [or other Specialist List] for an order to transfer the claim to that court.
   (4) the claim (*give title and claim number*) commenced in the (*name*) County Court be transferred from that court to the [Chancery] [Queen's Bench] Division of the High Court.

3. ALTERNATIVE DISPUTE RESOLUTION
   the claim be stayed until (*date*) while the parties try to settle it by mediation or other means. [The parties shall notify the Court in writing at the end of that period whether settlement has or has not been reached, and shall submit a draft consent order of any settlement]. The claim will be listed on (*date*) for the court to make further directions unless;

       (a) the claim has been settled and the claimant advised the court of the settlement in writing and files a draft consent order,
       or
       (b) the parties apply not later than 3 days before the hearing for further directions without a hearing, or
       (c) the parties apply for an extension of the stay and the extension is granted, upon which the hearing will be relisted on the date to which the extension is granted.

4. PROBATE CASES ONLY
   the [Claimant] [Defendant] file his witness statement or affidavit of testamentary scripts and lodge any testamentary

CONTENTIOUS PROBATE

script at Room TM7.09 Thomas More Building, Royal Courts of Justice, Strand WC2A 2LL [District Registry/ County Court, at (*address*)] by (*date*).

5. CASE SUMMARY

   the (*party*) (*date*) prepare and serve a Case Summary [not exceeding ( ) words] on all other parties, to be agreed by (*date*) and filed by (*date*) and if it is not agreed the parties by that date file their own Case Summaries.

6. CASE MANAGEMENT CONFERENCE, etc.

   [(*a*) there be a [further] Case Management Conference/Listing Hearing before the Master/District Judge in [Court/Room No.] [[Thomas More Building] Royal Courts of Justice] [Court (trial centre)] on (*date*) at (*time*) of hours/minutes duration.]

   or

   [(*b*) there be a Case Management Conference/Listing Hearing of hours/minutes duration. In order for the Court to fix a date the parties are to complete the accompanying questionnaire and file it by (*date*).] *or*

   [(*c*) the (*party*) apply for an appointment for a [further] Case Management Conference/Listing Hearing by (*date*).]

   At the Case Management Conference, except for urgent matters in the meantime, the Court will hear any further applications for Directions or Orders and any party must file an Application Notice for any such Directions or Orders and serve it and supporting evidence (if any) by (*date*).

7. AMENDMENTS TO STATEMENTS OF CASE

   (1) the (*party*) has permission to amend his statement of case in accordance with the attached draft initialled by the [Master][District Judge].

   (2) the amended statement of case be verified by a statement of truth.

   (3) the amended statement of case be filed by (*date*).

   (4) the amended statement of case be served by (*date*) *or* service of the amended statement of case be dispensed with.

   (5) any consequential amendments to other statements of case be filed and served by (*date*).

   (6) the costs of and caused by the amendment to the statement of case be (*party*) in any event *or* are assessed in the sum of £ and are to be paid by (*party*).

8. ADDITION OF PARTIES
   (1) the (*party*   ) has permission;
       (a) to [add] [substitute] [remove] (*name of party*   ) as a (*party*   ), and
       (b) to amend his statement of case in accordance with the attached draft initialled by the [Master] [District Judge].
   (2) the amended statement of case be verified by a statement of truth.
   (3) the amended statement of case be;
       (a) filed by (*date*   ) and
       (b) served on (*new party, existing parties or removed party, as appropriate*   ) by (*date*   ).
   (4) a copy of this order be served on (*new party, existing parties or removed party, as appropriate*   ) by (*date*   ).
   (5) any consequential amendments to other statements of case be filed and served by (*date*   ).
   (6) the costs of and caused by the amendment to the statement of case be (*party*   ) in any event *or* are assessed in the sum of £   and are to be paid by (*party*   ).

9. CONSOLIDATION
   this claim be consolidated with claim number (*give number and title of claim*), the lead claim to be claim number (*give number*). [The title to the consolidated case shall be as set out in the Schedule to this order.]

10. TRIAL OF ISSUE
    the issue of (*define issue*) be tried as follows;
    (1) with the consent of the parties, before a Master
        (a) on (*date*   ) in Room (   ) at the Royal Courts of Justice,
        (b) with an estimated length of hearing (   ) hours,
        (c) with the filing of listing questionnaires dispensed with, *or*
    (2) before a Judge
        (a) with the trial of the issue to take place within (*period*   ) after (*date*   ) ("the trial window")
        (b) with the (*party*   ) to apply to the Clerk of the Lists at Room [W14] [W15] by (*date*   ) for a trial date within the trial window

(c) with the issue
- (i) to be entered in the [Jury List] [Trial List] [General List] category "A" "B" or "C", with a time estimate of (*specify number of days/weeks*   ), and
- (ii) to take place in London (*or identify venue*)

[(d) the filing of listing questionnaires be dispensed with [unless directed by the Clerk of the Lists] *or* each party file his completed listing questionnaire by (*date*   )], *or*

(3) before a [District Judge, with the consent of the parties] [Circuit Judge] [High Court Judge] [listing category [A][B][C]], at a hearing details of which [accompany this order] [will be sent shortly] with an estimated length of hearing (   ) hours.

11. FURTHER INFORMATION

(1) the (*party*   ) provide by (*date*   ) the [further information] [clarification] sought in the Request dated (*date*   ) attached and initialled by the [Master] [District Judge].
(2) any request for [further information] [clarification] be served by (*date*   ).

12. DISCLOSURE OF DOCUMENTS

(1) no disclosure is required.
(2) each party give by (*date*   ) standard disclosure to every other party by list [by categories].
(3) the (*party/parties*) give specific disclosure of documents [limited to the issues of (*define issues*)] described in the Schedule to this order [initialled by the Master/District Judge] by list [by categories] by (*date*   ).
(4) the (*party*   ) give by (*date*   ) standard disclosure by list [by categories] to (*party*   ) of documents limited to the issue(s) of (*define issues*) by list.

13. INSPECTION OF DOCUMENTS

Any requests for inspection or copies of disclosed documents shall be made within   days after service of the list.

14. PRESERVATION OF PROPERTY

the (*party*   ) preserve (*give details of relevant property*) until trial of the claim or further order *or* other remedy under rule 25.1(1).

15. WITNESS STATEMENTS

(1) each party serve on every other party the witness statement of the oral evidence which the party serving the statement intends to rely or in relation to [any issues of fact][the following issues of fact (*define issues*)] to be decided at the trial, those statements and any Notices of intention to rely on hearsay evidence to be

    (a) exchanged by (*datee*) *or*
    (b) served by (*party*   ) by (*date*   ) and by (*party*   ) by (*date*   ).

(2) the (*party*   ) has permission to serve a witness summary relating to the evidence of (*name*) of (*address*) on every other party by (*date*   ).

16. NO EXPERT EVIDENCE

(1) no expert evidence being necessary, [no party has permission to call or rely on expert evidence] [permission to call or rely on expert evidence is refused].

17. SINGLE EXPERT

(1) evidence be given by the report of a single expert in the field of (*define field*), instructed jointly by the parties, on the issue of (*define issue*) [and his fees shall be limited to £   ].

(2) the claimant advise the court in writing by (*date*   ) whether or not the single expert has been instructed.

(3) if the parties are unable to agree [by that date] who that expert is to be and about the payment of his fees any party may apply for further directions.

(4) unless the parties agree in writing or the court orders otherwise, the fees and expenses of the single expert shall be paid to him [by the parties equally] (*or as ordered*).

(5) each party-give his instructions to the single expert by (*date*   ).

(6) the report of the single expert be filed by (*date*   ).

(7) the evidence of the expert be given at the trial by written report/oral evidence of the expert.

18. SEPARATE EXPERTS

[(1) each party has permission to adduce [oral] expert evidence in the field of   [limited to   expert(s) [per party] [on each side]].

(2) the experts reports shall be exchanged by (date   ).
(3) the experts shall hold a discussion for the purpose of:

    (a) identifying the issues, if any, between them; and
    (b) where possible, reaching agreement on those issues.

(4) the experts shall by [*specify date after discussion*] prepare and file a statement for the Court showing:

    (a) those issues on which they did agree; and
    (b) those issues on which they disagree and a summary of their reasons for disagreeing.

(5) no party shall be entitled to recover by way of costs from any other party more than £   for the fees or expenses of an expert.]

[(1) the parties (*party*   ) have permission to rely on expert evidence as follows:

Party	Identity of Expert	Field of Expertise	Issue to be addressed
Claimant			
Defendant			
(*other parties*)			

(2) the number of expert witnesses in each field be limited to [one] for the (*party/parties*) and to [one] for the (*party/parties*).

[(3) the amount of the fees and expenses of the experts in the field[s] of (*define field(s)*) that the (*party/parties*) may recover from the (*party/parties*) be limited to £   ].

(4) the experts in the field(s) of (*define field(s)*) prepare reports which are to be served as follows:

    (a) by simultaneous exchange by (*date*   )
    (b) by (*party/parties*) by (*date*   ) and by (*party/parties*) by (*date*   ).

(5) the reports be agreed if possible by (*date*   ).

(6) (a) if the reports are not agreed by that date, then the experts in the same field(s) shall, by (*date*   ), seek to identify, by "without prejudice" discussion, the issues between them and, where possible, to reach agreement on all/any issue(s),

   (b) the experts shall by (*date*   ) prepare and file a statement showing those issues on which they are agreed, those issues on which they disagree and a summary of their reasons for disagreeing.

(7) the expert evidence relied on by the (*party/parties*) in the field of (*define field(s)*) be given at the trial by written report(s)/written summary of agreement/oral evidence of the expert(s).

(8) no party shall be entitled to recover by way of costs from any other party more than £   for the fees or expenses of an expert.]

19. TRIAL AND LISTING QUESTIONNAIRES

(1) (a) the trial of the claim/issue(s) take place [within (*period*   ) after (*date*   )] [between (*date*   ) and (*date*   )] ("the trial window").

   (b) the (*party*   ) make an appointment to attend on the Clerk of the Lists/Listing Officer at Room [W14] [W15] in order to fix a trial date within the trial window, such appointment to be [within 14 days after] [on] [not later than] (*date*   ) and give notice of the appointment to all other parties.

   (c) the claim

   (i) be entered in the [Jury List] [Trial List] [General List] category "A" "B" or "C", with a time estimate of (*specify number of days/weeks*), and

   (ii) take place in London (*or identify venue*), or

(2) (a) Trial Date the trial take place [on (*date*   )] [on   a date to be fixed], a Notice of Hearing [accompanies this order] [will be sent shortly], at [Court] [a venue to be notified], *or*

   (b) Trial Window — the trial take place during the period beginning on (*date*) and ending on (*date*) at a venue to be notified,

(c) the present estimate of the time to be allowed for the trial is (*specify number of days/weeks*).

(3) Listing Questionnaires—

[(a) the filing of listing questionnaires be dispensed with [unless directed by the Clerk of the Lists/Listing Officer]], *or*

[(b) each party file his completed listing questionnaire by [4.30pm] [4.00pm] on (*date*   )],

(4) the parties inform the Court forthwith of any change in the trial time estimate.

20. PRE TRIAL REVIEW

[[The trial being estimated to last more than 10 days], There be a Pre Trial Review on a date to be arranged by the Clerk of the Lists/Listing Officer in Room [W14] [W15]] [there be a Pre-Trial Review on (*date*   ) at (*time*   )] before the Judge at the [Royal Courts of Justice][Court (trial centre)] at which, except for urgent matters In the meantime, the Court will hear any further applications for Directions or Orders.

21. DEFINITION AND REDUCTION OF ISSUES

by (*date*   ) the parties list and discuss the issues in the claim [including the experts' reports and statements] and attempt to define and narrow the issues [including those issues the subject of discussion by the experts].

22. TRIAL BUNDLE

The parties agree and file a trial bundle and exchange and file skeleton arguments and chronologies not more than 7 and not less than 3 days before the start of the trial.

23. TRIAL TIMETABLE (*only for use at final CMC or PTR*)

(1) the parties agree a timetable for the trial, subject to the approval of the trial Judge, and file it with the trial bundle.

(2) subject to the approval of the trial Judge, the timetable for the trial will be:

(a) opening speeches to last no more than   minutes,

(b) the statements served stand as the evidence in chief of the Claimants' witnesses of fact who are to give, evidence on the [first] morning/afternoon/day of the trial,

(c) the statements served stand as the evidence in chief of the Defendants' witnesses of fact who are to give evidence on the [second] morning/afternoon/day of the trial,

(d) the reports of the experts served stand as their evidence in chief and the experts in the field(s) of (*specify*) give oral evidence on the [third] morning /afternoon/day of the trial,
(e) closing submissions be made on the [fourth] morning/afternoon/day of the trial.

24. SETTLEMENT
If the claim or part of the claim is settled the parties must immediately inform the Court, whether or not it is then possible to file a draft Consent Order to give effect to the settlement.

25. OTHER DIRECTIONS
(*The parties may here set out drafts of other Directions or Orders sought*).

26. COSTS
the costs of this application be;

(a) in the case, or
(b) summarily assessed at £   and paid by   , or
(c) the (*party/parties*) in any event to be the subject of a detailed assessment,
(d) the (*party*) pay the (*party*) the sum of £   on account of such costs on or before (*date*).

Dated

CONTENTIOUS PROBATE

A–018

Allocation questionnaire

To be completed by, or on behalf of,

[   ]

who is [1st][2nd][3rd][ ][Claimant][Defendant]
[Part 20 claimant] in this claim

In the

Claim No.

Last date for filing with court office

Please read the notes on page five before completing the questionnaire.

You should note the date by which it must be returned and the name of the court it should be returned to since this may be different from the court where the proceedings were issued.

If you have settled this claim (or if you settle it on a future date) and do not need to have it heard or tried, you must let the court know immediately.

Have you sent a copy of this completed form to the other party(ies)? ☐ Yes ☐ No

A Settlement

Do you wish there to be a one month stay to attempt to settle the claim, either by informal discussion or by alternative dispute resolution? ☐ Yes ☐ No

B Location of trial

Is there any reason why your claim needs to be heard at a particular court? ☐ Yes ☐ No

If Yes, say which court and why?

C Pre-action protocols

If an approved pre-action protocol applies to this claim, complete **Part 1** only. If not, complete **Part 2** only. If you answer 'No' to the question in either Part 1 or 2, please explain the reasons why on a separate sheet and attach it to this questionnaire.

Part 1	The* [ ] protocol applies to this claim.
*please say which protocol	Have you complied with it? ☐ Yes ☐ No

Part 2	No pre-action protocol applies to this claim.
	Have you exchanged information and/or documents (evidence) with the other party in order to assist in settling the claim? ☐ Yes ☐ No

N150 Allocation questionnaire (11.00)

D Case management information

What amount of the claim is in dispute? £ [ ]

Applications

Have you made any application(s) in this claim? ☐ Yes ☐ No

If Yes, what for? [ ] For hearing on [ ]
(e.g. summary judgment, add another party)

Witnesses

So far as you know at this stage, what witnesses of fact do you intend to call at the trial or final hearing including, if appropriate, yourself?

Witness name	Witness to which facts

Experts

Do you wish to use expert evidence at the trial or final hearing? ☐ Yes ☐ No

Have you already copied any experts' report(s) to the other party(ies)? ☐ None yet obtained ☐ Yes ☐ No

Do you consider the case suitable for a single joint expert in any field? ☐ Yes ☐ No

Please list any single joint experts you propose to use and any other experts you wish to rely on. Identify single joint experts with the initials 'SJ' after their name(s).

Expert's name	Field of expertise (e.g. orthopaedic surgeon, surveyor, engineer)

Do you want your expert(s) to give evidence orally at the trial or final hearing? ☐ Yes ☐ No

If Yes, give the reasons why you think oral evidence is necessary:

Track

Which track do you consider is most suitable for your claim? Tick one box ☐ small claims track ☐ fast track ☐ multi-track

If you have indicated a track which would not be the normal track for the claim, please give brief reasons for your choice

E Trial or final hearing

How long do you estimate the trial or final hearing will take? ____ days ____ hours ____ minutes

Are there any days when you, an expert or an essential witness will not be able to attend court for the trial or final hearing? ☐ Yes ☐ No

If Yes, please give details

Name	Dates not available

F Proposed directions *(Parties should agree directions wherever possible)*

Have you attached a list of the directions you think appropriate for the management of the claim? ☐ Yes ☐ No

If Yes, have they been agreed with the other party(ies)? ☐ Yes ☐ No

G Costs

*Do **not** complete this section if you have suggested your case is suitable for the small claims track **or** you have suggested one of the other tracks and you do not have a solicitor acting for you.*

What is your estimate of your costs incurred to date? £ _____

What do you estimate your overall costs are likely to be? £ _____

In substantial cases these questions should be answered in compliance with CPR Part 43

H Other information

Have you attached documents to this questionnaire?	☐ Yes ☐ No
Have you sent these documents to the other party(ies)?	☐ Yes ☐ No
If Yes, when did they receive them?	
Do you intend to make any applications in the immediate future?	☐ Yes ☐ No
If Yes, what for?	

In the space below, set out any other information you consider will help the judge to manage the claim.

Signed _____ Date _____

[Counsel][Solicitor][for the][1st][2nd][3rd][   ]
[Claimant][Defendant][Part 20 claimant]

Please enter your firm's name, reference number and full postal address including (if appropriate) details of DX, fax or e-mail

			if applicable
		fax no.	
		DX no.	
Tel. no.	Postcode	e-mail	
Your reference no.			

CONTENTIOUS PROBATE 279

Listing questionnaire (Pre-trial checklist)

A–019

In the	
Claim No.	
Last date for filing with court office	
Date(s) fixed for trial or trial period	

To be completed by, or on behalf of,

who is [1st][2nd][3rd][ ][Claimant][Defendant]
[Part 20 claimant][Part 20 defendant] in this claim

This form must be completed and returned to the court no later than the date given above. If not, your statement of case may be struck out or some other sanction imposed.

If the claim has settled, or settles before the trial date, you must let the court know immediately.

Legal representatives only: You must **attach** estimates of costs incurred to date, and of your likely overall costs. In substantial cases, these should be provided in compliance with CPR Part 43.

For multi-track claims only, you must also **attach** a proposed timetable for the trial itself.

A Confirmation of compliance with directions

1. I confirm that I have complied with those directions already given which require action by me. ☐Yes ☐No

   If you are unable to give confirmation, state which directions you have still to comply with and the date by which this will be done.

Directions	Date

2. I believe that additional directions are necessary before the trial takes place. ☐Yes ☐No

   If Yes, you should attach an application and a draft order.

   · Include in your application all directions needed to enable the claim *to be tried on the date, or within the trial period, already fixed. These should include any issues relating to experts and their evidence, and any order sought in respect of directions still requiring action by any other party.*

3. Have you agreed the additional directions you are seeking with the other party(ies)? ☐Yes ☐No

B Witnesses

1. How many witnesses (including yourself) will be giving evidence on your behalf at the trial? *(Do not include experts - see Section C)*

N170 Listing questionnaire (Pre-trial checklist) (IN FORCE DECEMBER 2, 2002)

APPENDIX I

Witnesses continued

2. If the trial date is not yet fixed, are there any days within the trial period you or your witnesses would wish to avoid if possible? *(Do not include experts - see Section C)*

Please give details

Name of witness	Dates to be avoided, if possible	Reason

Please specify any special facilities or arrangements needed at court for the party or any witness (e.g. witness with a disability).

3. Will you be providing an interpreter for any of your witnesses? ☐ Yes ☐ No

C Experts

You are reminded that you may not use an expert's report or have your expert give oral evidence unless the court has given permission. If you do not have permission, you must make an application (see section A2 above)

1. Please give the information requested for your expert(s)

Name	Field of expertise	Joint expert?	Is report agreed?	Has permission been given for oral evidence?
		☐Yes ☐No	☐Yes ☐No	☐Yes ☐No
		☐Yes ☐No	☐Yes ☐No	☐Yes ☐No
		☐Yes ☐No	☐Yes ☐No	☐Yes ☐No

2. Has there been discussion between experts? ☐ Yes ☐ No

3. Have the experts signed a joint statement? ☐ Yes ☐ No

4. If your expert is giving oral evidence and the trial date is not yet fixed, is there any day within the trial period which the expert would wish to avoid, if possible? ☐ Yes ☐ No

If Yes, please give details

Name	Dates to be avoided, if possible	Reason

D Legal representation

1. Who will be presenting your case at the trial? ☐ You ☐ Solicitor ☐ Counsel

2. If the trial date is not yet fixed, is there any day within the trial period that the person presenting your case would wish to avoid, if possible? ☐ Yes ☐ No

If Yes, please give details

Name	Dates to be avoided, if possible	Reason

E The trial

1. Has the estimate of the time needed for trial changed? ☐ Yes ☐ No

   If Yes, say how long you estimate the whole trial will take, including both parties' cross-examination and closing arguments   ☐ days ☐ hours ☐ minutes

2. If different from original estimate have you agreed with the other party(ies) that this is now the **total** time needed? ☐ Yes ☐ No

3. Is the timetable for trial you have attached agreed with the other party(ies)? ☐ Yes ☐ No

Fast track cases only

The court will normally give you 3 weeks notice in the fast track of the date fixed for a fast track trial unless, in exceptional circumstances, the court directs that shorter notice will be given.

Would you be prepared to accept shorter notice of the date fixed for trial? ☐ Yes ☐ No

F Document and fee checklist

Tick as appropriate

I attach to this questionnaire -

☐ An application and fee for additional directions   ☐ A proposed timetable for trial

☐ A draft order   ☐ An estimate of costs

☐ Listing fee

Signed

[Counsel][Solicitor][for the][1st][2nd][3rd][ ]
[Claimant][Defendant]
[Part 20 claimant][Part 20 defendant]

Date

Please enter your [firm's] name, reference number and full postal address including (if appropriate) details of DX, fax or e-mail

Postcode

Tel. no.	DX no.	E-mail
Fax no.	Ref. no.	

Statements of Case

Note:

A–020 There is never a "one size fits all" statement of case. Each one must be regarded as a made-to-measure item. However, what follows is a set of "template" forms which can be the starting point and will also serve as a reminder of what must be contained in any statement of case so as to conform with Part 57 and the Part 57 PD.

(I) Indorsements of Claim Form under "Brief details of Claim"

Note:

A–021 Part 57 r.7 contains the requirement that the nature of the interest of the claimant and each defendant in the estate must be stated and that if that interest is disputed such a dispute must be declared and reasons given.

(a) Propounding a will

The claimant claims as the executor/sole residuary legatee of the will dated [   ] of AB deceased who died on [   ].

The defendant is joined in this claim because he has entered a caveat on [date] and appeared to the warning on [date] and claims as [the only lawful child of the deceased] and entitled to the estate of the deceased in the event of an intestacy.

The claimant seeks an order that the Court shall pronounce for the said will in solemn form of law.

OR

The defendant is joined in this claim because he has entered a caveat on [date] and appeared to the warning on [date] and claims as the named executor in a pretended will dated [   ] *OR* is the sole residuary legatee in a pretended will dated [   ].

And continue as above

Note:

If there is more than one named executor, or residuary legatee, or person entitled on intestacy, join them as defendants.

There can be variations where an executor seeks to propound a will.

CONTENTIOUS PROBATE

For example:

— where he seeks the omission of an interlineation which is unexecuted and unattested

— where he seeks proof of a lost will and seeks to admit a draft, or a copy

— where he seeks to propound a will, but not a codicil to it; or vice versa.

— where he seeks proof of a privileged will.

— where the rules as to the validity of wills under the conflicts of laws rules (Wills Act 1963) require an order in favour of a particular will.

In all cases the particulars of claim will state the grounds; see below.

(b) Claiming an intestacy
The claimant claims as the sole person entitled to his estate on the intestacy of AB deceased who died on [date] survived by the claimant as his only child; (*i.e.* state the reason why the claimant is entitled to the estate under the intestacy rules)

The defendant is joined in this claim because he has entered a caveat (etc. as above) and claims to be the sole executor/residuary legatee under a pretended will dated [ ].

The claimant seeks an order that he be granted letters of administration of the estate of the deceased and that the Court shall pronounce against the validity of the said pretended will.

(c) Claiming revocation of an existing common form grant
The claimant claims as [state interest in estate whether under an intestacy or under a will which it is sought to propound] to have {the probate of a pretended will dated [ ] and granted on [ ] out of the [Registry] revoked} OR {the letters of administration granted on [ ] out of the [Registry] revoked}

The defendant is joined in this claim as {the executor named in the pretended will and the person to whom the said grant was issued} OR {the person who in the event of an intestacy would be entitled to [share in] the deceased's estate and the person to whom the said letters of administration were issued}

The claimant seeks an order that the said grant of {probate} {letters of administration} be revoked and that the Court {do pronounce for the validity of [will dated] in solemn form of law] OR {do pronounce against the validity of the said pretended will dated [ ]}.

APPENDIX I

(d) Claiming revocation of an existing solemn form grant

The claimant claims as {state interest as above} in the estate of AB deceased who died on [date].

By an order of Mr Justice [   ] dated [   ] in the High Court of Justice Chancery Division [District Registry] in a claim the short title is [   ] the Court pronounced in solemn form in favour of a will dated [   ] and on [   ] a grant thereto was issued out of the [Registry].

The defendant is joined to this claim as the person to whom the grant was made and as the sole residuary legatee under the will dated [   ] the subject of the said Order and he obtained that order by concealing the existence of a later will dated [   ] and by fraudulently alleging [etc. as the case may be]

The claimant seeks an order that the said Order be set aside and that the said grant dated [   ] be revoked and that the Court {do pronounce for the will dated [   ] in solemn form of law and against the will which was the subject of the said Order } OR that the claimant be granted letters of administration to the estate of AB deceased and that the Court do pronounce against the will which was the subject of the said Order.

(e) Where the claimant contests the interest of a person in the estate

The claimant claims as [define interest — *e.g.* only issue of the deceased, or a brother or sister of the whole blood] and is entitled to a grant of letters of administration to the estate of AB deceased.

The defendant is joined to this claim because he has entered a caveat {etc. as in form (a) above} and has claimed {*e.g.* when entering an appearance to the warning} that he is a person entitled to share in the estate as [a brother of the deceased of the whole blood].

The claimant denies the interest of the defendant for the reasons set out in the Particulars of Claim and seeks an Order that he be entitled to a grant of letters of administration of the estate of AB deceased.

CONTENTIOUS PROBATE

(II) Layout of Form N2 (See form N2 above)

General heading A–022

IN THE HIGH COURT OF JUSTICE
CHANCERY DIVISION
[[ ] District Registry]
[or [   ] County Court
Chancery Business]
Claim No. [   ]

In the estate of [A.B.] deceased (Probate)[3]
Claimant   C.D.
                   and
Defendant   E.F.

Brief details of claim

{ *see above*}

PARTICULARS OF CLAIM

{ see below}

Human Rights Act endorsement no issues raised

Signature of legal representative.
Dated [   ]

STATEMENT OF TRUTH

* {I believe} {The Claimant believes} that the facts stated in this claim form are true.
*I am duly authorised by the claimant to sign this statement.
signed [   ] date [   ]
**delete as appropriate*

Full name [   ]
Name of claimant's solicitor's firm [   ]
Position or office held [   ]
   if signing on behalf of a company

---

[3] Note requirement as to marking of all probate claims at the top in this way by virtue of Part 57 PD, para. 2.1.

Claimant's or claimant's solicitor's address to which documents should be sent if different from overleaf including (if appropriate) details of DX, fax or e-mail.

Note: see CPR Part 7 and Part 7 PD, Part 22 and Part 22 PD and Part 57 and Part 57 PD for the formal rules as to claim forms both generally and in probate claims and as to statements of truth.

(III) Particulars of claim

Specimen forms.

(a) Where the claimant seeks to propound a particular will

A–023 PARTICULARS OF CLAIM

1. The claimant is the sole executor named in the last will dated [ ] of AB deceased who died on [ ]
2. The defendant entered a caveat against a grant on [ ] and an appearance to the warning to that caveat was entered by him on [ ]. In the appearance the defendant contends that {the said will is invalid because [ ]}
3. The claimant disputes the allegations of the defendant for the reason that {the will was executed by the deceased and his signature was attested by two witnesses in compliance with s.9 of the Wills Act 1837}.

AND the claimant claims:

(1) That the Court shall pronounce for the force and validity of the said will dated [ ] in solemn form of law.
(2) That the claimant may be entitled to an order for his costs.

Note: Part 57, r.7 requires the interest of each party to be stated and if denied, that this interest is denied and why.

(b) Where the claimant seeks an intestacy

PARTICULARS OF CLAIM

1. The claimant is [describe relationship to deceased — *e.g.* the only issue of the deceased or a/the brother of the deceased — showing entitlement on an intestacy.

CONTENTIOUS PROBATE

2. The defendant has on [date] entered an appearance to a warning of a caveat dated [ ] and claims an interest in the estate of the deceased as [the sole executor] [residuary legatee] under a pretended will dated [ ].
3. The pretended will is invalid on the ground that:
    (i) It was lawfully revoked under section [18] [20] Wills Act 1837
    Particulars
    {*e.g.* of marriage after the will not made in contemplation of that marriage}
    {*e.g.* of destruction}

Note: The plea may also arise that the document is not a will either because it does not appear on its face to be a testamentary document, or because there was no immediate testamentary intention when it was made; see *Corbett v Newey* [1998] Ch. 57.

(ii) It was not executed in accordance with the Wills Act 1837
Particulars
{*e.g.* attesting witnesses not together when testator signed. Refer to statements of attesting witnesses}.

(iii) It was not executed by the deceased.
Particulars
{*e.g.* forgery, or impersonation}
Refer to report of handwriting expert or statement of private detective.

(iv) It was executed by the deceased while he was under the age of 18 years.
Particulars
[Date of birth. Not a privileged will.]

(v) The deceased was at the time when the pretended will was executed not of sound mind memory or understanding.
Particulars.
{Set out in detail the facts and matters which will be relied on so as to comply with Part 57, r.7(4). Refer to any medical notes, or report and the state why by virtue of those facts the deceased's capacity was not such as to satisfy the *Banks v Goodfellow* test; see Ch.5 para. 5–003 above for the essential ingredients of the test}.

(vi) The execution of the pretended will by the deceased was obtained by the {fraud} {undue influence} of the defendant.

Particulars
{State all facts and matters which will be relied on so as to comply with Part 57, r.7(4)}

(vii) The deceased did not know and approve of the terms of the pretended will.
Particulars
{State all facts and matters which will be relied on so as to comply with Part 57, r.7(3).

Note:
There will inevitably be variations so as to deal with codicils, or a series of wills which are claimed to be invalid for various reasons.

AND the claimant claims

(1) That the Court shall pronounce against the force and validity of the pretended will dated [   ] {and the will dated [   ]} {and the codicil dated [   ] to the will dated [   ]}

(2) A grant of letters of administration of the estate of the deceased.

(3) Costs.

(c) Where the claimant seeks to propound an earlier will

The particulars of claim will follow the same format as at (b) above and must comply with part 57, r.7(3) and (4). The claimant will have to give particulars of why the will put forward by the defendant is not valid.

Apart from the grounds set out above, the claimant may want to rely on the principle of conditional revocation (see Ch.9 para. 9–025 above) and set out the facts and matters Uwhich that claimant will rely upon in showing that the earlier will was revoked by the later will (or by destruction) conditionally on the validity of the later will or of gifts in it being valid. As that later will is not valid, the earlier one is revived. (See *Re Jones* [1976] Ch. 200 and *Re Finnemore* [1991] 1 W.L.R. 793).

In cases where an earlier will is being put forward, the prayer will run as follows:
AND the claimant claims;

(1) That the Court shall pronounce against the pretended will put forward by the defendant dated [   ].

(2) That the Court shall pronounce for the force and validity of the said will dated [   ] in solemn form of law

(3) Costs.

CONTENTIOUS PROBATE

(d) Where the claimant seeks revocation of an existing common form grant

Forms (a) (b) and (c) above can all be adapted here and the Particulars of Claim will be directed as to why the grant should be revoked. Compliance with Part 57, r.7(4) is essential.

The prayer will run as follows:
AND the claimant claims:

(1) Revocation of the said grant of [probate] [letters of administration] dated [ ].
{(2) That the Court shall pronounce against the pretended will put forward by the defendant dated [ ].} {*i.e.* the will which was the subject of the revoked probate; not needed if the grant was of letters of administration}.
{(3) That the Court shall pronounce for the force and validity of the said will dated [ ] in solemn form of law} {*i.e.* if there is to be a will proved in solemn form}.

(4) Costs.

Note: In the case of a claim seeking revocation of a solemn form grant, the Particulars of Claim will have to state all the facts and matters relevant to the plea of fraud, or any other ground on which it is alleged that the Order should be set aside.

(e) Other variations

Particulars of Claim will be required of:

— parentage and family pedigree in interest claims. This may also require proof of foreign law where the law of succession governing the estate of the deceased does not give that person an interest in the estate, or conversely, gives the claimant an interest which is greater than that which he might have under the English law; *e.g.* fixed shares for children of the deceased.

— particulars of loss or accidental destruction, or destructions while not of capacity, in claims to prove copies. In these cases it is necessary to set out, or annex the full text of the will which it is desired to admit to probate.

— particulars of foreign law in claims where it is desired to admit to proof a foreign will which may be valid under the Wills Act 1963. A translation of any material document should be provided with the particulars. Foreign law must be particularised.

(IV) Defence and Counterclaim

A–024 Generally; see Part 57, rr.7 and 8, and Part 20 and Part 20 PD, especially Part 20 PD, para. 6.1.

It is vital to remember that, when pleading on behalf of a defendant, he must serve a counterclaim setting out any contention he may have as regards any claim or any entitlement to a grant; Part 57, r.8. Likewise, if he is disputing any interest of the claimant he must say so and why he disputes it; Part 57, r.7(2).

Note that the general rules in Parts 15 and 16 and the Practice Direction to each Part (and in particular Part 16, r.5) require allegations in the Particulars of Claim which the defendant does not admit, or which he denies, to be dealt with in the Defence in the usual way. Failing to observe this rule can lead to embarrassing admissions. See the current White Book for the rules and the practice in the Notes. Under the CPR a comprehensive response is now required by a Defence. Part 57 reinforces this by requiring defendants to assert their contrary interest and to state what they dispute and give the reasons for that; Part 57, r.7(2).

(a) Defence alleging non-compliance with s.9 of the Wills Act 1837

(See Particulars of Claim form (a) under (III) above, to which this would be the Defence)

{Heading as on Claim Form}

DEFENCE AND COUNTERCLAIM

DEFENCE

1. The defendant denies that the will dated [ ] was executed in accordance with s.9 of the Wills Act 1837.
Particulars.
{*e.g.* attesting witnesses not together when testator signed. Refer to statements of attesting witnesses}.

COUNTERCLAIM

2. The true last will of the deceased is dated [ ].
OR

2. The deceased died intestate and the defendant is [one of the persons] [the sole person] entitled to his estate on that intestacy.
Particulars
{set out relationships; family tree}

AND the defendant counterclaims:

(1) That the Court shall pronounce against the force and validity of the will dated [ ] propounded by the claimant.

{(2) That the Court shall pronounce for the force and validity of the will dated [ ] in solemn form of law}

{(3) A grant of letters of administration of the estate of the deceased}.

Note:

(2) is not needed if there is no will which the defendant wishes to put forward and (3) is only needed in a case where the defendant is entitled to a grant of letters.

Note:
Any Defence (and Counterclaim) must include the Statement of Truth as in Parts 9, 15, 15PD and 22. (See above)

(b) Defence alleging inherent invalidity of the will being propounded by the Claimant

DEFENCE AND COUNTERCLAIM

DEFENCE

1. The defendant denies that the will alleged by the claimant to be the true last will of the deceased is the true last will.
Particulars

{Complete as in Form (b) in Part (III) above}.

COUNTERCLAIM

Assert the defendant's contrary interest as in form (a) above. The Prayer is also to follow the same form with variations as fit the claim.

See also the Note to form (a) above.

(c) Defence alleging destruction or revocation by marriage

{Heading as in Claim Form}

DEFENCE AND COUNTERCLAIM

DEFENCE

1. The defendant denies that the will alleged by the claimant to be the true last will of the deceased is the true last will.

Particulars
The will alleged by the claimant to be the last will was destroyed by the deceased in conformity with s.20 of the Wills Act 1837 in the following manner and in the following circumstances [as stated]

COUNTERCLAIM

{ Adapt forms above so that the defendant asserts either another will, or an intestacy and seek relief in the prayer as in those forms accordingly}

(d) Variations

Other variations to Defences and Counterclaims will be:

— allegation that will not valid under Wills Act 1963 where there is a conflict of laws problem
— allegation that a codicil should be admitted to probate as well as the document(s) propounded by the claimant

(e) Notice under Part 57, r.7(5); "notice to cross-examine"
{Heading as in Claim Form}

DEFENCE

1. The defendant does not admit that the will propounded by the claimant dated [   ] is the true last will of the deceased {as a will executed in accordance with s.9 of the Wills Act 1837} AND/OR {that the deceased knew and approved of the terms thereof}.

2. The defendant gives notice under Part 57, r.7(5) that he does not raise any positive case, but insists on the alleged will being proved in solemn form and for that purpose will cross-examine the witnesses who attested the alleged will.

3. {Deny/not admit any other matters in the Claim form as may be required.}

Note:
No Counterclaim will arise in such a case.

Such a notice MUST be given in the defence. This notice means that the attesting witnesses must attend Court to give evidence and be cross-examined. This is so even if the claimant wants to proceed on a summary application for judgment under Part 24; see Part 57 PD paras 5.1 and 5.2. Paragraph 5.2 means that the defendant can require the attesting witnesses to attend such an application.

(V) Reply and Defence to Counterclaim

See generally Parts 16.7 and 20 and Part 20 PD, para. 6.2. **A–025**
There is no specific form but in general terms it should look like this:

{Heading as in Claim Form}

REPLY AND DEFENCE TO COUNTERCLAIM

REPLY

1. {The claimant must deal with any matters which are not dealt with by the "implied joinder" on any issues raised in the defence. It may be necessary to amend the Particulars of Claim if, for example, a new will is put in by the defendant}.

A form of words which can open the Reply is:

"Save and in so far as the same consists of admissions and save as contained in this Reply, the Claimant joins issue with the Defendant on his Defence."

DEFENCE TO COUNTERCLAIM

{Here the claimant will need to meet all items in the Counterclaim which need to be met by way of Defence, bearing in mind the general rules under part 16 and the specific rules in part 57 about the need to state the interest put forward and why if it be the case that it is disputed, any contrary interest is so disputed}.

(VI) Compromise and Discontinuance

A–026 *CPR Forms*

Application Notice

You should provide this information for listing the application

1. How do you wish to have your application dealt with
   a) at a hearing? ☐
   b) at a telephone conference? ☐ } *complete all questions below*
   c) without a hearing? ☐ *complete Qs 5 and 6 below*

2. Give a time estimate for the hearing/conference ____(hours) ____(mins)

3. Is this agreed by all parties? ☐ Yes ☐ No

4. Give dates of any trial period or fixed trial date ____

5. Level of judge ____

6. Parties to be served ____

In the	
Claim no.	
Warrant no. (If applicable)	
Claimant (including ref.)	
Defendant(s) (including ref.)	
Date	

Note You must complete Parts A **and** B, **and** Part C if applicable. Send any relevant fee and the completed application to the court with any draft order, witness statement or other evidence; and sufficient copies for service on each respondent.

Part A

1. Enter your full name, or name of solicitor
   I (We)[1] ____ (on behalf of)(the claimant)(the defendant)

2. State clearly what order you are seeking and if possible attach a draft
   intend to apply for an order (a draft of which is attached) that[2]

3. Briefly set out why you are seeking the order. Include the material facts on which you rely, identifying any rule or statutory provision
   because[3]

Part B

I (We) wish to rely on: *tick one box*

the attached (witness statement)(affidavit) ☐   my statement of case ☐

4. If you are not already a party to the proceedings, you must provide an address for service of documents
   evidence in Part C in support of my application ☐

   Signed ____   Position or office held ____
   (Applicant)('s Solicitor)('s litigation friend)   (if signing on behalf of firm or company)

Address to which documents about this claim should be sent (including reference if appropriate)[3]

		if applicable
	fax no.	
	DX no.	
Tel. no. Postcode	e-mail	

The court office at

is open from 10am to 4pm Monday to Friday. When corresponding with the court please address forms or letters to the Court Manager and quote the claim number.

N244 Application Notice (April 2000)

Part C   Claim No.

I (We) wish to rely on the following evidence in support of this application:

Statement of Truth

*(I believe) *(The applicant believes) that the facts stated in Part C are true
*delete as appropriate

Signed   **Position or office held**

(Applicant)('s Solicitor)('s litigation friend)   (if signing on behalf of firm or company)

Date

Note:

This application notice will be needed when it is proposed that the Court be asked to approve a compromise of a probate claim on behalf of a person under a disability within Part 21.

It may also be used to ask the Court to hear the claim on written evidence so as to allow a solemn form grant to issue.

The application notice should be accompanied with a draft of the proposed terms of settlement in the form of a draft minute of order, statements from those of full capacity stating that they agree with the terms, and the instructions to counsel and his Opinion supporting the settlement of the claim on behalf of the patient or the minor.

The same application notice can be used to discontinue the claim under Part 57, r.11. The terms on which this is to happen can be served with the Notice. The same observation applies to an application under Part 57, r.10 where there has been a failure by a defendant to acknowledge service or file a defence, and in that case the claimant will want to set out what directions are needed for the claim to proceed; *e.g.* that there be a trial on written evidence.

See forms of Order below.

ORDERS OF THE COURT

(a) *Order following a compromise where there has been either an application under Part 57, r.11 by one party, or a discontinuance under an agreement to settle the claim, in each case the Court being asked to make a common form order.*

HEADING AS IN CLAIM FORM

Master/District Judge [   ]/ The Hon. Mr Justice [   ]
Dated [   ]
[Parties]
UPON THE APPLICATION of the [claimant/defendant] by Application Notice dated [   ]
AND UPON HEARiNG [the solicitors/counsel] for the claimant and the defendant
AND UPON READING the documents recorded in the Court file as having been read [AND the parties having agreed the terms set out in the Schedule to this Order]
IT IS [BY CONSENT] ORDERED as follows:

(1) That this claim be discontinued and [a grant of probate of the will of the deceased dated [   ]] [letters of administration of the estate of the deceased] be granted to the claimant if entitled thereto

(2) That on the application for the grant by the claimant Caveat No. [   ] entered on [date] do cease to have effect

(3) That the costs of all parties be subject to a detailed assessment on the standard basis if not agreed and be raised and paid out of the estate in the course of administration.

THE SCHEDULE
[TERMS OF COMPROMISE]

Note variations:

— costs may be agreed otherwise than as above and the personal representative may want his costs on the indemnity basis under Part 48, r.4.
— where there has been a renunciation by the person entitled under the will to the grant, a grant of letters of administration with will annexed is the appropriate order.
— where a party is in receipt of LSC funding and is liable for any costs, there must be an order for costs to be determined under s.11 of the Access to Justice Act 1999 and in accordance with paras 22 and 23 of the Costs Part 44 Practice Direction and under Regs 8–13 of the CLS (Costs) Regulations 2000.
— where any money is to be paid to a child or a patient, the costs of that party which are payable to his solicitor must be assessed under Part 48, r.5, unless there is no need to do so under para. 51 of the Part 48 Costs PD.

(b) *Order made on compromise of probate claim; s.49 of the Administration of Justice Act 1985 invoked*
Heading as in claim form.
Master/District Judge [   ]/ The Hon. Mr Justice [   ]
Dated [   ]
[Parties]
UPON HEARING [the solicitors/counsel] for the claimant and the defendant
AND UPON READING the documents recorded in the Court file as having been read
AND the parties having agreed the terms set out in the Schedule to this Order
AND the Court being satisfied

(i) that consents by or on behalf of every relevant beneficiary (as defined by s.49 of the Administration of Justice Act 1985) have been given to the making of this Order

[(ii) that the said Order is for the benefit of those relevant beneficiaries who are minors]

IT IS BY CONSENT ORDERED as follows:

(1) The Court hereby pronounces for the force and validity of the last will of the deceased dated [   ] being exhibit [   ] in the statement of testamentary documents of [   ] dated [   ] and marked "A" and pronounces against the force and validity of the will of the deceased dated [   ] being exhibit [   ] in the statement of testamentary documents of [   ] dated [   ] and marked "B"

(2) That a grant of probate of the will dated [   ] and marked "A" shall be made to [the claimant] [if entitled thereto][4]

(3) That on the application for the grant by the claimant Caveat No. [   ] entered on [date] do cease to have effect

(4) [Order as to costs]

The Schedule

[Terms of compromise]

Note:
If the agreement is that further proceedings in the claim be stayed on the terms set out in the Schedule, then the Order will be in "Tomlin" form as follows:—

[Formal parts as above]

It is by consent ordered [as above]

And it is by consent ordered that all further proceedings in this claim be stayed except for the purpose of carrying the terms set out in the Schedule hereto into effect and for that purpose the parties have permission to apply.[5]

The Schedule

The terms

---

[4] The words "if entitled thereto" are not required if it can be shown, either that the person in whose favour the grant is ordered is solely entitled without the exercise of any discretion under the NCPR 1987, or if it can be shown that all persons to whom, a grant could be made are before the Court. See Practice Direction (Compromise of Action) [1972] 1 W.L.R. 1215.

[5] See Chancery Guide Ch. 9, para. 9.15. Note that if the agreed terms as to the payment of costs are within the Schedule. If so, there is no need for the Court to direct any assessment of costs, and no need for detailed assessment will arise. See Part 47, r.6 note 1A in White Book.

Note:
In the case of a Tomlin form of order it may be necessary to revoke the grant pending suit under s.117 of the Supreme Court Act and discharge that administrator.

(c) *Orders made after a trial by the court where there is no compromise agreement*
Formal parts of order
The Hon. Mrs Justice [   ]
Dated [   ]
[Parties]
UPON the trial of this claim
AND UPON HEARING [counsel] [the solicitor] for the claimant and the defendant
AND UPON HEARING oral evidence
AND UPON READING the documents recorded on the Court file as having been read
IT IS ORDERED as follows:

(1) The Court hereby pronounces for the force and validity of the last will of the deceased dated [   ] being exhibit [   ] in the statement of testamentary documents of [   ] dated [   ] and marked "A" and pronounces against the force and validity of the will of the deceased dated [   ] being exhibit [   ] in the statement of testamentary documents of [   ] dated [   ] and marked "B"

(2) That a grant of probate of the will dated [   ] and marked "A" shall be made to [the claimant] [if entitled thereto][6]

OR in a case where a grant is revoked

(2) The grant of probate [letters of administration of the estate of the deceased] granted to [   ] out of the [Registry] on [date] be revoked

(3) That on the application for the grant by the claimant Caveat No. [   ] entered on [date] do cease to have effect

(4) The costs of this claim be assessed and paid as follows: the costs of the claimant be assessed on the indemnity

---

[6] The words "if entitled thereto" are not required if it can be shown either that the person in whose favour the grant is ordered is solely entitled without the exercise of any discretion under the NCPR 1987, or if it can be shown that all persons to whom a grant could be made are before the Court. See Practice Direction (Compromise of Action) [1972] 1 W.L.R. 1215.

basis if not agreed and be raised and paid out of the estate in due course of administration and that there be no order as to the costs of the defendant

OR

(4) The costs of the claimant be assessed on the standard [indemnity] basis if not agreed and it is ordered that the defendant do pay to the claimant his costs as assessed or agreed

(5) That leave to appeal to the defendant to the Court of Appeal be [granted] [refused] [and that the latest time for filing the notice of appeal be extended to [date]].[7]

VARIATIONS:

— *where the attempt to revoke a grant fails*

"It is ordered that the grant of probate of the will dated [ ] of the deceased/letters of administration of the estate of the deceased be handed out to [the claimant] or his solicitors"

— *where the order is in favour of a will which is found not to have been destroyed with the intention to revoke, or by accident*

"The Court pronounces in favour of the force and validity of the last will of AB deceased a true reconstruction of which is set out in the Schedule to this Order

And it is ordered that probate of the said reconstructed will be granted to [the claimant] [limited until the original will or more authentic copy thereof be proved]"

This form of order can be used in a modified form where there is a copy only of the will which is propounded by the Court.

(d) *Costs orders*:

Its is impossible to cover all variations. There may be an allowance of costs in favour of a losing party down to the service between all parties of statements of testamentary documents, for until that has been completed, a party may not know the case he

---

[7] (See Part 52, r.4 and Ch.19 para. 19–011 above on appeals.

has to make or meet. Thereafter he may take an active role at his peril.

(e) *Other orders and undertakings:*
In some cases there may have been matters reserved to the trial judge from the Master or District Judge at a pre-trial hearing. For example, a reserved order for the advocates for the parties are usually costs, or a costs order which will have to be picked up at the end of the trial and excluded from any order which might conflict with it. It is also possible that other orders have been made, such a freezing orders, or even a caution placed on the title to real property, which will have to be removed. In cases where the order is complex, ask to draft and agree a minute which can be shown to the judge for approval.

APPENDIX I

Rectification of Wills under Section 20 of the Administration of Justice Act 1982

Precedents

Form 1

Draft Claim form seeking rectification under s.20 of the Administration of Justice Act 1982

A–027 *Note the 6 months time period for issue from the date of the grant, failing which the leave of the Court will be required.*

Claim Form

In the

	for court use only
Claim No.	
Issue date	

Claimant(s)

Seal

Defendant(s)

Brief details of claim

Value

£

Defendant's name and address

Amount claimed	
Court fee	
Solicitor's costs	
Total amount	

The court office at

is open between 10am and 4pm Monday to Friday. When corresponding with the court, please address forms or letters to the Court Manager and quote the claim number.

N1 Claim form (CPR Part 7) (January 2002)

CONTENTIOUS PROBATE

| Claim No. | |

Does, or will, your claim include any issues under the Human Rights Act 1998?   ☐ Yes   ☐ No

Particulars of Claim (attached) (to follow)

Statement of Truth
*(I believe) (The Claimant believes) that the facts stated in these particulars of claim are true.
*I am duly authorised by the claimant to sign this statement

Full name _____

Name of claimant's solicitor's firm _____

signed _____ position or office held _____
*(Claimant) (Litigation friend) (Claimant's solicitor)
(if signing on behalf of firm or company)

*delete as appropriate

Claimant's or claimant's solicitor's address to which documents or payments should be sent if different from overleaf including (if appropriate) details of DX, fax or e-mail.

IN THE HIGH COURT OF JUSTICE
CHANCERY DIVISION
[[ ] District Registry]
Chancery Business
Claim No. [HC....]

In the Estate of AB deceased (Probate)
Between

Claimant	CD
	And
Defendants	(1) EF
	(2) GH (the personal representative of AB deceased)[8]

BRIEF DETAILS OF CLAIM

The claimant claims as the residuary legatee under the will date [ ] of the above named AB who died on [ ] and whose will was admitted to probate on [date]. The claimant seeks rectification of the Will under s.20 of the Administration of Justice Act 1982. The first defendant EF is the pecuniary legatee, the terms of whose legacy as set out in the Will is the subject of this claim and the second defendant GH is the proving executor.

PARTICULARS OF CLAIM

1. AB died on [date] ("the testator"). His last will is dated [date]; "the Will".

2. The terms of the Will which are relevant to this claim, which is for rectification of the Will under s.20 of the Administration of Justice Act 1982 ("the Act") are as follows.

   {Set out the material parts of the Will which are the subject of the rectification claim}

   OR where there has been an omission, state that the Will does not contain at a certain point the terms which were the subject of the instructions referred to below.

3. The testator instructed the firm of [ ] & Co, Mr/Ms X acting, to include within his will the following legacy {or devise, or terms, as the case may be}

4. The instructions were given orally on [date] or [in writing by letter dated [   ]] {refer to notes of attendance}.

---

[8] Note the requirement under Part 57, r.12(2) to join all personal representative as a party. The other defendant is a beneficiary concerned in the claim.

5. The draft will was sent to the testator on [date] for his approval and was returned as approved on [date].
6. An engrossment was prepared at X & Co. on [date] and on [date] the testator executed the Will in the presence of the two attesting witnesses whose names appear on it.
7. A grant of Probate in respect of the estate of the testator was issued out of the [   ] Probate Registry on [date] to GH.[9]
8. The claim is based on s.20(1)(a) OR (b)) (OR both paras.) of the Act.
9. "The Will contains the following clerical error:
{The reference in the legacy to the sum of £500,000 to Ms EF in Clause was a clerical error for the sum of £50,000. The letter of instructions refers to the sum of £50,000, and the draft and the engrossment failed to carry out the testator's intentions in regard to that legacy by referring to the sum of £500,000, which is a clerical error}
OR the engrossment contained the reference in error to the sum of £500,000 which failed to carry out the testator's intentions as contained in his letter of instructions and the draft approved by him on [   ]."
Alternative based on s.20(1)(b)
"The instructions in the letter dated [   ] were to provide that the legacy to Ms EF for £50,000 was contingent on her attaining the age of 25 years with a gift over to the RSPC should she die under that age without issue/ or/ that the legacy was to be settled on Ms EF for life. The solicitors at X & Co. failed to understand the instructions of the testator and made the said legacy one which was immediately vested on the death of the testator /or/ an absolute one. Accordingly the terms of Clause [   ] of the Will are so expressed that they fail to carry out the testator's intentions in consequence of a failure to understand his instructions".
AND the claimant claims
   (1) Rectification of the Will by [the omission of the figure 500,000 in clause [   ] and the insertion of

---

[9] Note: this must be no earlier than 6 months from the date on which the Claim Form is to be issued; s.20(2). The grant must be lodged with the Court on issue, if the claimant has it. If he does not, the defendant must do so within 14 days of service. Unlike 1975 Act claims, there is no requirement on the claimant in a claim to rectify under section 20 to file an official copy of the grant and the documents admitted to probate; see Part 57, r.16(3).

the figure 50,000 in it place]OR [the insertion of the words at the end of Clause [ ] "contingent on her attaining the age of 25 years and if she shall fail to attain that age leaving issue living at her death they shall take the said sum of £50,000 and if more than one in equal shares absolutely and in default thereof to the RSPCA of [addressl [RC No. [ ]] absolutely . . ."
(2) [That the Court do pronounce in favour of the Will as so rectified in solemn form of law.][10]
(3) Costs

Human Rights Act endorsement

Dated etc.

Statement of Truth etc.

As in Form NI

General Notes.

(i) In the text above there is reference made to the alternative way in which a will can be rectified under s.20 by means of the procedure under NCPR r.55, in cases where the relief is unopposed.

In such claims the adviser needs to:—

— draft a letter to those with an interest which may be prejudiced by an application to rectify; this will include not just those entitled under the will, but may include those with interests on intestacy.

— draft the application, which is an affidavit headed in the name of the deceased and under rule 55. It is worth calling the Registry to discover whether the Registrar will require a summons.

— serve the application and affidavit in support on those with an interest

— draft a further affidavit if necessary in support of the application if further comments in support emerge. The District Judge or Registrar may require a hearing to sort out who should be notified, the state of play as regards

---

[10] This is not strictly required in a claim under s.20, but in claims where it may be thought desirable to have a solemn form order where, for example, there are numerous interests to be bound by a solemn form order, such relief may be sought. It may will also be necessary to seek such relief where the claim is based on the inherent jurisdiction to omit words, and the claim is founded on want of knowledge and approval of the words to be omitted. The same would apply where there had been a fraudulent insertion of words.

opposition, and whether there should be notification by a Summons.

(ii) Note that if there is opposition from a person with an interest, the only course is to issue a Part 7 Claim Form in the Chancery Division.

Form 2

Order in Rectification Claim; s.20 claim

Heading as in Claim Form

The Hon. Mr Justice [　]
Dated [　]

UPON the trial of this claim
AND UPON HEARING [counsel for the claimant and for the defendants]
AND UPON READING the documents recorded in the Court file as having been read
IT IS ORDERED as follows:

1. That the Will dated [　] of [AB] deceased who died on [　] and whose will was admitted to probate issued out of the [　] Probate Registry on [date] be rectified pursuant to s.20 of the Administration of Justice Act 1982 in the following manner:

    By the deletion of the figures "500,000" in clause [　] thereof and the insertion of the words "50,000"

2. That the costs of this claim be {paid by the [　] defendant to the claimant such costs to be assessed (if not agreed) on the {standard} basis} OR {That (i) the costs of all parties raised and paid out the estate of the deceased in due course of administration and (ii) that before payment the costs of the claimant and the [　] defendant to be assessed on the standard basis unless agreed and the costs of the [　] defendant as the personal representative be assessed on the indemnity basis unless agreed}[11]

3. That in accordance with Part 57 PD, para. 11.1 a copy of this Order shall be sent to the Principal Registry of the Family Division and that it shall be endorsed on or

---

[11] See page 300 above where the various forms of costs orders are discussed.

permanently annexed to the grant of probate issued on [ ] out of the [ ] Registry.

General notes

1. A variation of this Order can be used in an application in the Probate Registry under NCPR r.55. The recitals to the Order can refer to the non-objection by the persons with an interest in the application. The application is in the form of an affidavit with the final paragraph containing the terms of the Order which the applicant wants to make. There is no fee for making the application, although there will be a swearing fee for the affidavit (£5) and £2 per exhibit. See Form 3 below.
2. Compromise orders can be made under s.20. Terms of settlement can go in a schedule and a Tomlin Form can be used. But the rectification must form part of the Order of the Court to be effective under s.20.

Form 3

Affidavit for application under NCPR Rule 55.

In the High Court of Justice
Family Division
[The Principal] [The [ ] District] Probate Registry
In the Estate of AB deceased

I [ ] of [ ] [rank, profession, or occupation] make oath and say as follows:—
1. I make this affidavit [on behalf of] [CD] who is the applicant. Save where the contrary appears I depose to the facts contained herein from my own knowledge [or from the knowledge acquired by me whilst acting for CD as his solicitor] [state means of deponent's knowledge as appropriate].
2. AB died on [date] ("the testator"). His last will is dated [date]; "the Will".
3. The terms of the Will which are relevant to this application which is made under NCPR r.55, for rectification of the Will under s.20 of the Administration of Justice Act 1982 ("the Act") are as follows.

{set out the material parts of the Will which are the subject of the rectification claim}

OR where there has been an omission, state that the Will does not contain at a certain point the terms which were the subject of the instructions referred to below.

4. The testator instructed the firm of [   ] & Co, Mr/Ms X acting, to include within his will the following legacy {or devise or terms as the case may be}

5. The instructions were given orally on [date] or [in writing by letter dated [   ]] {refer to notes of attendance}.

6. The draft will was sent to the testator on [date] for his approval and was returned as approved on [date].

7. An engrossment was prepared at X & Co. on [date] and on [date] the testator executed the Will in the presence of the two attesting witnesses whose names appear on it.

8. A grant of Probate in respect of the estate of the testator was issued out of the [   ] Probate Registry on [date] to GH.[12]

9. The claim is based on s.20(1)(a) OR (b)) (OR both paras.) of the Act.

10. "The Will contains the following clerical error:—

The reference in the legacy to the sum of £500,000 to Ms EF in Clause was a clerical error for the sum of £50,000. The letter of instructions refers to the sum of £50,000, and the draft and the engrossment failed to carry out the testator's intentions in regard to that legacy by referring to the sum of £500,000, which is a clerical error}

OR the engrossment contained the reference in error to the sum of £500,000 which failed to carry out the testator's intentions as contained in his letter of instructions and the draft approved by him on [   ]."

{Alternative based on s.20(i)(b)}

"The instructions in the letter dated [   ] were to provide that the legacy to Ms EF for £50,000 was contingent on her attaining the age of 25 years with a gift over to the RSPC should she die under that age without issue/ or/ that the legacy was to be settled on Ms EF for life. The solicitors at X & Co. failed to understand the instructions of the testator and made the said legacy one which was immediately vested on the death of the testator /or/ an absolute one. Accordingly the terms of Clause [   ] of the Will are so expressed that they fail to carry out the

---

[12] Note: this must be no earlier than 6 months from the date on which the Claim Form is to be issued; s.20(2). The grant must be lodged with the Court on issue, if the claimant has it. If he does not the defendant must do so within 14 days of service. Unlike 1975 Act claims there is no requirement on the claimant in a claim under section 20 to file an official copy of the grant and the documents admitted to probate; see Part 57, r.16(3).

testator's intentions in consequence of a failure to understand his instructions".

10. The notification of this application has been to the following persons who are all interested under either the Will [or in the event of a partial intestacy] as persons who might be prejudiced by the rectification applied for. [State persons notified and exhibit notification under exhibit [¹]

11. There is now produced and shown to me marked [²] a bundle of written comments contained in letters from those persons which shows that they will not oppose this application.

12. [I have not had any response from [Mr X] and [Ms Y] who were notified as will be seen from [ ]¹ and I ask the Registry to assume that they do not oppose this application.

13. [I await clear responses from [Mr WI and [Mr Z]] [I would ask the Registry to direct a hearing date at which Mr W and Mr Z attend to state whether or not they oppose this application] {and other such variations on the evidence to ensure that all interested parties may be notified and are not opposing the application}.

14. I seek an Order on behalf of the applicant CD that there be an order as follows:

Rectification of the Will by [the omission of the figure 500,000 in clause [ ] and the insertion of the figure 50,000 in its place] OR [the insertion of the words at the end of Clause [ ] "contingent on her attaining the age of 25 years and if she shall fail to attain that age leaving issue living at her death they shall take the said sum of £50,000 and if more than one in equal shares absolutely and in default thereof to the RSPCA of [address] [RC No.[ ]] absolutely . . ."

15. I also seek an order that CD recovers the costs of this application out of the estate of AB deceased.

Sworn etc.

Form 4

Draft Summons in a NCPR r.55 application to rectify. (NCPR r.61).

In the High Court of Justice
Family Division
[The Principal] [The [ ] District Probate Registry
In the Estate of AB deceased

Let all parties concerned attend one of the District Judges [the Registrar] of this Division in Chambers at the [Principal Registry of the Family Division at First Avenue House 42–49 High

Holborn London WC1V 6NP] OR [The [ ] District Probate Registry at [ ]] on [date] at [time] on the hearing of an application by [named party] that the Will of AB deceased dated [ ] and admitted to probate on [ ] in favour of [ ] be rectified pursuant to Rule 55 of the Non Contentious Probate Rules 1987 and that an order for the costs of this application be dealt with. The evidence in support of this Summons is in the affidavit of [ ] sworn on [ ] and served herewith.

This summons was taken out by [ ] of [ ] Solicitors for the [named party] To [solicitor] for [named party or parties]

Note:

A summons, as opposed to an affidavit which can be used as the application under rule 55, may be ordered by the Court if it feels that this is a proper method of giving notice to those with an interest.

There is no fee for the issue of the Summons. There may be a £10 fee if the Court is asked to settle the form of Summons.

Appendix II

Statutes and Rules of Court and other procedural material

WILLS ACT 1837

CHAPTER 26

s.1 Meaning of certain words in this Act:

The words and expressions herein-after mentioned, which in their ordinary signification have a more confined or a different meaning, shall in this Act, except where the nature of the provision or the context of the Act shall exclude such construction, be interpreted as follows; (that is to say,) the word "will" shall extend to a testament, and to a codicil, and to an appointment by will or by writing in the nature of a will in exercise of a power, and also to an appointment by will of a guardian of a child, and to any other testamentary disposition; and the words "real estate" shall extend to manors, advowsons, messuages, lands, tithes, rents, and hereditaments, whether corporeal, incorporeal, or personal, [. . .] and to any estate, right, or interest (other than a chattel interest) therein; and the words "personal estate" shall extend to leasehold estates and other chattels real, and also to monies, shares of government and other funds, securities for money (not being real estates), debts, choses in action, rights, credits, goods, and all other property whatsoever which by law devolves upon the executor or administrator, and to any share or interest therein; and every word importing the singular number only shall extend and be applied to several persons or things as well as one person or thing; and every word importing the masculine gender only shall extend and be applied to a female as well as a male.

B–001

s.3 All property may be disposed of by will; contingent interests; rights of entry; and property acquired after execution of the will.

B–002 It shall be lawful for every person to devise, bequeath, or dispose of, by his will executed in manner herein-after required, all real estate and all personal estate which he shall be entitled to, either at law or in equity, at the time of his death, and which, if not so devised, bequeathed, or disposed of, would devolve [. . .] upon his executor or administrator; and the power hereby given shall extend [. . .] to all contingent, executory or other future interests in any real or personal estate, whether the testator may or may not be ascertained as the person or one of the persons in whom the same respectively may become vested, and whether he may be entitled thereto under the instrument by which the same respectively were created, or under any disposition thereof by deed or will; and also to all rights of entry for conditions broken, and other rights of entry; and also to such of the same estates, interests, and rights respectively, and other real and personal estate, as the testator may be entitled to at the time of his death, notwithstanding that he may become entitled to the same subsequently to the execution of his will.

s.7 No will of a person under age valid.

B–003 No will made by any person under the age of [eighteen years] shall be valid.

s.9 Signing and attestation of wills.

B–004 No will shall be valid unless—

(a) it is in writing, and signed by the testator, or by some other person in his presence and by his direction; and

(b) it appears that the testator intended by his signature to give effect to the will; and

(c) the signature is made or acknowledged by the testator in the presence of two or more witnesses present at the same time; and

(d) each witness either —

(i) attests and signs the will; or
(ii) acknowledges his signature, in the presence of the testator (but not necessarily in the presence of any other witness),
but no form of attestation shall be necessary.

s.10 Appointments by will to be executed like other wills, and to be valid, although other required solemnities are not observed.

No appointment made by will, in exercise of any power, shall be valid, unless the same be executed in manner herein-before required; and every will executed in manner herein-before required shall, so far as respects the execution and attestation thereof, be a valid execution of a power of appointment by will, notwithstanding it shall have been expressly required that a will made in exercise of such power should be executed with some additional or other form of execution or solemnity. **B–005**

s.11 Soldiers and mariners wills excepted.

Provided always, that any soldier being in actual military service, or any mariner or seaman being at sea, may dispose of his personal estate as he might have done before the making of this Act. **B–006**

s.13 Publication of will not be requisite.

Every will executed in manner herein-before required shall be valid without any other publication thereof. **B–007**

s.14 Will not to be void on account of incompetency of attesting witness.

If any person who shall attest the execution of a will shall at the time of the execution thereof or at any time afterwards be incompetent to be admitted a witness to prove the execution thereof, such will shall not on that account be invalid. **B–008**

s.15 Gifts to an attesting witness to be void.

If any person shall attest the execution of any will to whom or to whose wife or husband any beneficial devise, legacy, estate, interest, gift, or appointment, of or affecting any real or personal estate (other than and except charges and directions for the payment of any debt or debts), shall be thereby given or made, such devise, legacy, estate, interest, gift, or appointment shall, so far only as concerns such person attesting the execution of such will, or the wife or husband of such person, or any person claiming under such person or wife or husband, be utterly null and void, and such person so attesting shall be admitted as a witness to prove the execution of such will, or to prove the validity or invalidity thereof, notwithstanding such devise, legacy, estate, interest, gift, or appointment mentioned in such will. **B–009** *s.16 Creditor attesting to be admitted a witness.*

B–010 In case by any will any real or personal estate shall be charged with any debt or debts, and any creditor, or the wife or husband of any creditor, whose debt is so charged, shall attest the execution of such will, such creditor notwithstanding such charge shall be admitted a witness to prove the execution of such will, or to prove the validity or invalidity thereof.

s.17 Executor shall be admitted a witness.

B–011 No person shall, on account of his being an executor of a will, be incompetent to be admitted a witness to prove the execution of such will, or a witness to prove the validity or invalidity thereof.

s.18 Wills to be revoked by marriage, except in certain cases.

B–012 (1) Subject to subsections (2) to (4) below, a will shall be revoked by the testator's marriage.

(2) A disposition in a will in exercise of a power of appointment shall take effect notwithstanding the testator's subsequent marriage unless the property so appointed would in default of appointment pass to his personal representatives.

(3) Where it appears from a will that at the time it was made the testator was expecting to be married to a particular person and that he intended that the will should not be revoked by the marriage, the will shall not be revoked by his marriage to that person.

(4) Where it appears from a will that at the time it was made the testator was expecting to be married to a particular person and that he intended that a disposition in the will should not be revoked by his marriage to that person,—

(a) that disposition shall take effect notwithstanding the marriage; and
(b) any other disposition in the will shall take effect also, unless it appears from the will that the testator intended the disposition to be revoked by the marriage.

s.18A Effect of dissolution or annulment of marriage on wills.

B–013 (1) Where, after a testator has made a will, an order or decree of a court of civil jurisdiction in England and Wales dissolves or annuls his marriage or his marriage is dissolved or annulled and the divorce or annulment is entitled to recognition in England and Wales by virtue of Part II of the Family Law Act 1986—

  (a) provisions of the will appointing executors or trustees or conferring a power of appointment, if they appoint or confer the power on the former spouse, shall take effect as if the former spouse had died on the date on which the marriage is dissolved or annulled, and
  (b) any property which, or an interest in which, is devised or bequeathed to the former spouse shall pass as if the former spouse had died on that date,

except in so far as a contrary intention appears by the will.

(2) Subsection (1)(b) above is without prejudice to any right of the former spouse to apply for financial provision under the Inheritance (Provision for Family and Dependants) Act 1975.

s.19 No will to be revoked by presumption.

No will shall be revoked by any presumption of an intention on the ground of an alteration in circumstances. **B–014**

s.20 No will to be revoked but by another will or codicil, or by a writing executed like a will, or by destruction.

No will or codicil, or any part thereof, shall be revoked otherwise than as aforesaid, or by another will or codicil executed in manner herein-before required, or by some writing declaring an intention to revoke the same, and executed in the manner in which a will is herein-before required to be executed, or by the burning, tearing, or otherwise destroying the same by the testator, or by some person in his presence and by his direction, with the intention of revoking the same. **B–015**

s.21 No alteration in a will shall have any effect unless executed as a will.

No obliteration, interlineation, or other alteration made in any will after the execution thereof shall be valid or have any effect, except so far as the words or effect of the will before such alteration shall not be apparent, unless such alteration shall be executed in like manner as herein-before is required for the **B–016** execution of the will; but the will, with such alteration as part thereof, shall be deemed to be duly executed if the signature of the testator and the subscription of the witnesses be made in the margin or on some other part of the will opposite or near to such alteration, or at the foot or end of or opposite to a memorandum referring to such alteration, and written at the end or some other part of the will.

s.22 No will revoked to be revived otherwise than by Re-execution or a Codicil to revive it.

B–017 No will or codicil, or any part thereof, which shall be in any manner revoked, shall be revived otherwise than by the re-execution thereof, or by a codicil executed in manner herein-before required and showing an intention to revive the same; and when any will or codicil which shall be partly revoked, and afterwards wholly revoked, shall be revived, such revival shall not extend to so much thereof as shall have been revoked before the revocation of the whole thereof, unless an intention to the contrary shall be shown.

s.23 A devise not to be rendered inoperative by any subsequent conveyance or act.

B–018 No conveyance or other Act made or done subsequently to the execution of a will of or relating to any real or personal estate therein comprised, except an act by which such will shall be revoked as aforesaid, shall prevent the operation of the will with respect to such estate or interest in such real or personal estate as the testator shall have power to dispose of by will at the time of his death.

s.24 A will shall be construed to speak from the death of the testator.

B–019 Every will shall be construed, with reference to the real estate and personal estate comprised in it, to speak and take effect as if it had been executed immediately before the death of the testator, unless a contrary intention shall appear by the will.

s.25 Residuary devise shall include estates comprised in lapsed and void devises.

B–020 Unless a contrary intention shall appear by the will, such real estate or interest therein as shall be comprised or intended to be comprised in any devise in such will contained, which shall fail or be void by reason of the death of the devisee in the lifetime of the testator, or by reason of such devise being contrary to law or otherwise incapable of taking effect shall be included in the residuary devise (if any) contained in such will.

s.26 A general devise of the testator's lands shall include copyhold and leasehold as well as freehold lands.

A devise of the land of the testator, or of the land of the testator in any place or in the occupation of any person mentioned in his will, or otherwise described in a general manner, and any other general devise which would describe a [. . .] leasehold estate if the testator had no freehold estate which could be described by it, shall be construed to include the [. . .] leasehold estates of the testator, or his [. . .] leasehold estates, or any of them, to which such description shall extend, as the case may be, as well as freehold estates, unless a contrary intention shall appear by the will. **B–021**

s.27 A general gift shall include estates over which the testator has a general power of appointment.

A general devise of the real estate of the testator, or of the real estate of the testator in any place or in the occupation of any person mentioned in his will, or otherwise described in a general manner, shall be construed to include any real estate, or any real estate to which such description shall extend (as the case may be), which he may have power to appoint in any manner he may think proper, and shall operate as an execution of such power, unless a contrary intention shall appear by the will; and in like manner a bequest of the personal estate of the testator, or any bequest of personal property described in a general manner, shall be construed to include any personal estate, or any personal estate to which such description shall extend (as the case may be), which he may have power to appoint in any manner he may think proper, and shall operate as an execution of such power, unless a contrary intention shall appear by the will. **B–022**

s.28 A devise without any words of limitation shall be construed to pass as free.

Where any real estate shall be devised to any person without any words of limitation, such devise shall be construed to pass the fee simple, or other the whole estate or interest which the testator had power to dispose of by will in such real estate, unless a contrary intention shall appear by the will. **B–023** *s.29 The words "die without issue," or "die without leaving issue," shall be construed to mean die without issue living at the death.*

B–024 In any devise or bequest of real or personal estate the words "die without issue," or "die without leaving issue," or "have no issue," or any other words which may import either a want or failure of issue of any person in his lifetime or at the time of his death, or an indefinite failure of his issue, shall be construed to mean a want or failure of issue in the lifetime or at the time of the death of such person, and not an indefinite failure of his issue, unless a contrary intention shall appear by the will, by reason of such person having a prior estate tail, or of a preceding gift, being, without any implication arising from such words, a limitation of an estate tail to such person or issue, or otherwise:

Provided, that this Act shall not extend to cases where such words as aforesaid import if no issue described in a preceding gift shall be born, or if there shall be no issue who shall live to attain the age or otherwise answer the description required for obtaining a vested estate by a preceding gift to such issue.

s.30 No devise to trustees or executors, except for a term or a presentation to a church, shall pass a chattel interest.

B–025 Where any real estate (other than or not being a presentation to a church) shall be devised to any trustee or executor, such devise shall be construed to pass the fee simple or other the whole estate or interest which the testator had power to dispose of by will in such real estate, unless a definite term of years, absolute or determinable, or an estate of freehold, shall thereby be given to him expressly or by implication.

s.31 Trustees under an unlimited devise, where the trust may endure beyond the life of a person beneficially entitled for life, shall take the fee.

B–026 Where any real estate shall be devised to a trustee, without any express limitation of the estate to be taken by such trustee, and the beneficial interest in such real estate, or in the surplus rents and profits thereof, shall not be given to any person for life, or such beneficial interest shall be given to any person for life, but the purposes of the trust may continue beyond the life of such person, such devise shall be construed to vest in such trustee the fee simple, or other the whole legal estate which the testator had power to dispose of by will in such real estate, and not an estate determinable when the purposes of the trust shall be satisfied.

s.33 Gifts to children or other issue who leave issue living as the testator's death shall not lapse.

(1) Where—   B–027
   (a) a will contains a devise or bequest to a child or remoter descendant of the testator; and
   (b) the intended beneficiary dies before the testator, leaving issue; and
   (c) issue of the intended beneficiary are living at the testator's death,

then, unless a contrary intention appears by the will, the devise or bequest shall take effect as a devise or bequest to the issue living at the testator's death.

(2) Where —
   (a) a will contains a devise or bequest to a class of persons consisting of children or remoter descendants of the testator; and
   (b) a member of the class dies before the testator, leaving issue; and
   (c) issue of that member are living at the testator's death,

then, unless a contrary intention appears by the will, the devise or bequest shall take effect as if the class included the issue of its deceased member living at the testator's death.

(3) Issue shall take under this section through all degrees, according to their stock, in equal shares if more than one, any gift or share which their parent would have taken and so that no issue shall take whose parent is living at the testator's death and so capable of taking.

(4) For the purposes of this section—
   (a) the illegitimacy of any person is to be disregarded; and
   (b) a person conceived before the testator's death and born living thereafter is to be taken to have been living at the testator's death.

s.34 Act not to extend to wills made before 1838, nor to estates pur autre vie of persons who die before 1838.

This Act shall not extend to any will made before the first day of   B–028
January one thousand eight hundred and thirty-eight, and every will re-executed or republished, or revived by any codicil, shall

for the purposes of this Act be deemed to have been made at the time at which the same shall be so re-executed, republished or revived, and this Act shall not extend to any estate pur autre vie of any person who shall die before the first day of January one thousand eight hundred and thirty-eight.

s.35 Act not to extend to Scotland.

B–029 This Act shall not extend to Scotland.

WILLS (SOLDIERS AND SAILORS ACT 1918

CHAPTER 58

s.1 Explanation of s.II of 7 Will. 4 & 1 Vict. c.26.

B–030 In order to remove doubts as to the construction of the Wills Act 1837, it is hereby declared and enacted that section eleven of that Act authorises and always has authorised any soldier being in actual military service, or any mariner or seaman being at sea, to dispose of his personal estate as he might have done before the passing of that Act, though under the age of eighteen years.

s.2

B–031 Section eleven of the Wills Act, 1837, shall extend to any member of His Majesty's naval or marine forces not only when he is at sea but also when he is so circumstanced that if he were a soldier he would be in actual military service within the meaning of that section.

s.3

B–032 (1) A testamentary disposition of any real estate in England or Ireland made by a person to whom section eleven of the Wills Act 1837, applies, and who dies after the passing of this Act, shall, notwithstanding that the person making the disposition was at the time of making it under [eighteen years] of age or that the disposition has not been made in such manner or form as was at the passing of this Act required by law, be valid in any

case where the person making the disposition was of such age and the disposition has been made in such manner and form that if the disposition had been a disposition of personal estate made by such a person domiciled in England or Ireland it would have been valid.
(2) [. . .]

s.4

Where any person dies after the passing of this Act having made a will which is, or which, if it had been a disposition of property, would have been rendered valid by section eleven of the Wills Act, 1837, any appointment contained in that will of any person as guardian of the infant children of the testator shall be of full force and effect. **B–033**

s.5

(1) This Act may be cited as the Wills (Soldiers and Sailors) Act, 1918. **B–034**
(2) For the purposes of section eleven of the Wills Act, 1837, and this Act the expression "soldier" includes a member of the Air Force, and references in this Act to the said section eleven include a reference to that section as explained and extended by this Act.

LAW OF PROPERTY ACT 1925

CHAPTER 20

s.204 Orders of court conclusive.

(1) An order of the court under any statutory or other jurisdiction shall not, as against a purchaser, be invalidated on the ground of want of jurisdiction, or of want of any concurrence, consent, notice, or service, whether the purchaser has notice of any such want or not. **B–035**
  (2) This section has effect with respect to any lease, sale, or other act under the authority of the court, and purporting to be in pursuance of any statutory power notwithstanding any exception in such statute.
  (3) This section applies to all orders made before or after the commencement of this Act.

ADMINISTRATION OF ESTATES ACT 1925

CHAPTER 23

s.27 Protection of persons acting on probate or administration.

B–036 (1) Every person making or permitting to be made any payment or disposition in good faith under a representation shall be indemnified and protected in so doing, notwithstanding any defect or circumstance whatsoever affecting the validity of the representation.

(2) Where a representation is revoked, all payments and dispositions made in good faith to a personal representative under the representation before the revocation thereof are a valid discharge to the person making the same; and the personal representative who acted under the revoked representation may retain and reimburse himself in respect of any payments or dispositions made by him which the person to whom representation is afterwards granted might have properly made.

s.37 Validity of conveyance not affected by revocation of representation.

B–037 (1) All conveyances of any interest in real or personal estate made to a purchaser either before or after the commencement of this Act by a person to whom probate or letters of administration have been granted are valid, notwithstanding any subsequent revocation or variation, either before or after the commencement of this Act, of the probate or administration.

(2) This section takes effect without prejudice to any order of the court made before the commencement of this Act, and applies whether the testator or intestate died before or after such commencement.

SUPREME COURT ACT 1981

CHAPTER 54

s.105 Applications.

B–038 Applications for grants of probate or administration and for the revocation of grants may be made to—

    (a) the Principal Registry of the Family Division (in this Part referred to as "the Principal Registry"); or

    (b) a district probate registry.

s.106 Grants by district probate registrars.

(1) Any grant made by a district probate registrar shall be made in the name of the High Court under the seal used in the registry. **B–039**
(2) [. . .]
(3) [. . .]
(4) [. . .]

s.107 No grant where conflicting applications.

Subject to probate rules, no grant in respect of the estate, or part of the estate, of a deceased person shall be made out of the Principal Registry or any district probate registry on any application if, at any time before the making of a grant, it appears to the registrar concerned that some other application has been made in respect of that estate or, as the case may be, that part of it and has not been either refused or withdrawn. **B–040**

s.108 Caveats.

(1) A caveat against a grant of probate or administration may be entered in the Principal Registry or in any district probate registry. **B–041**
(2) On a caveat being entered in a district probate registry, the district probate registrar shall immediately send a copy of it to the Principal Registry to be entered among the caveats in that Registry.

s.109 Refusal of grant where capital transfer tax unpaid.

(1) Subject to subsections (2) and (3), no grant shall be made, and no grant made outside the United Kingdom shall be resealed, except on the production of an account prepared in pursuance of ["the Inheritance Act 1984"] showing by means of such receipt or certification as may be prescribed by the Commissioners of Inland Revenue (in this and the following section referred to as "the Commissioners") either— **B–042**

   (a) that the capital transfer tax payable on the delivery of the account has been paid; or

   (b) that no such tax is so payable.

(2) Arrangements may be made between the President of the Family Division and the Commissioners providing for the purposes of this section in such cases as may be specified in the

arrangements that the receipt of certification of an account may be dispensed with or that some other document may be substituted for the account required by [the Inheritance Act 1984].

(3) Nothing in subsection (1) applies in relation to a case where the delivery of the account required by that Part of that Act has for the time being been dispensed with by any regulations under [section 256(1) of the Inheritance Act 1984].

s.110 Documents to be delivered to Commissioners of Inland Revenue.

B–043 Subject to any arrangements which may from time to time be made between the President of the Family Division and the Commissioners, the Principal Registry and every district probate registry shall, within such period after a grant as the President may direct, deliver to the Commissioners or their proper officer the following documents—

(a) in the case of a grant of probate or of administration with the will annexed, a copy of the will;

(b) in every case, such certificate or note of the grant as the Commissioners may require.

s.111 Records of grants.

B–044 (1) There shall continue to be kept records of all grants which are made in the Principal Registry or in any district probate registry.

(2) Those records shall be in such form, and shall contain such particulars, as the President of the Family Division may direct.

s.112 Summons to executor to prove or renounce.

B–045 The High Court may summon any person named as executor in a will to prove, or renounce probate of, the will, and to do such other things concerning the will as the court had power to order such a person to do immediately before the commencement of this Act.

s.113 Power of court to sever grant.

B–046 (1) Subject to subsection (2), the High Court may grant probate or administration in respect of any part of the estate of a deceased person, limited in any way the court thinks fit.

(2) Where the estate of a deceased person is known to be insolvent, the grant of representation to it shall not be severed under subsection (1) except as regards a trust estate in which he had no beneficial interest.

s.114 Number of personal representatives.

(1) Probate or administration shall not be granted by the High Court to more than four persons in respect of the same part of the estate of a deceased person.

(2) Where under a will or intestacy any beneficiary is a minor or a life interest arises, any grant of administration by the High Court shall be made either to a trust corporation (with or without an individual) or to not less than two individuals, unless it appears to the court to be expedient in all the circumstances to appoint an individual as sole administrator.

(3) For the purpose of determining whether a minority or life interest arises in any particular case, the court may act on such evidence as may be prescribed.

(4) If at any time during the minority of a beneficiary or the subsistence of a life interest under a will or intestacy there is only one personal representative (not being a trust corporation), the High Court may, on the application of any person interested or the guardian or receiver of any such person, and in accordance with probate rules, appoint one or more additional personal representatives to act while the minority or life interest subsists and until the estate is fully administered.

(5) An appointment of an additional personal representative under subsection (4) to act with an executor shall not have the effect of including him in any chain of representation.

B–047

s.115 Grants to trust corporations.

(1) The High Court may—

B–048

(a) where a trust corporation is named in a will as executor, grant probate to the corporation either solely or jointly with any other person named in the will as executor, as the case may require; or

(b) grant administration to a trust corporation, either solely or jointly with another person;
and the corporation may act accordingly as executor or administrator, as the case may be.

(2) Probate or administration shall not be granted to any person as nominee of a trust corporation.

(3) Any officer authorised for the purpose by a trust corporation or its directors or governing body may, on behalf of the corporation, swear affidavits, give security and do any other act which the court may require with a view to the grant to the corporation of probate or administration; and the acts of an officer so authorised shall be binding on the corporation.

s.116 Power of court to pass over prior claims to grant.

B–049 (1) If by reason of any special circumstances it appears to the High Court to be necessary or expedient to appoint as administrator some person other than the person who, but for this section, would in accordance with probate rules have been entitled to the grant, the court may in its discretion appoint as administrator such person as it thinks expedient.

(2) Any grant of administration under this section may be limited in any way the court thinks fit.

s.117 Administration pending suit.

B–050 (1) Where any legal proceedings concerning the validity of the will of a deceased person, or for obtaining, recalling or revoking any grant, are pending, the High Court may grant administration of the estate of the deceased person in question to an administrator pending suit, who shall, subject to subsection (2), have all the rights, duties and powers of a general administrator.

(2) An administrator pending suit shall be subject to the immediate control of the court and act under its direction; and, except in such circumstances as may be prescribed, no distribution of the estate, or any part of the estate, of the deceased person in question shall be made by such an administrator without the leave of the court.

(3) The court may, out of the estate of the deceased, assign an administrator pending suit such reasonable remuneration as it thinks fit.

s.118 Effect of appointment of minor as executor.

B–051 Where a testator by his will appoints a minor to be an executor, the appointment shall not operate to vest in the minor the estate, or any part of the estate, of the testator, or to constitute him a personal representative for any purpose, unless and until probate is granted to him in accordance with probate rules.

s.119 Administration with will annexed.

B–052 (1) Administration with the will annexed shall be granted, subject to and in accordance with probate rules, in every class of case in which the High Court had power to make such a grant immediately before the commencement of this Act.

(2) Where administration with the will annexed is granted, the will of the deceased shall be performed and observed in the same manner as if probate of it had been granted to an executor.

s.121 Revocation of grants and cancellation of resealing at instance of court.

(1) Where it appears to the High Court that a grant either ought not to have been made or contains an error, the court may call in the grant and, if satisfied that it would be revoked at the instance of a party interested, may revoke it. **B–053**

(2) A grant may be revoked under subsection (1) without being called in, if it cannot be called in.

(3) Where it appears to the High Court that a grant resealed under the Colonial Probates Acts 1892 and 1927 ought not to have been resealed, the court may call in the relevant document and, if satisfied that the resealing would be cancelled at the instance of a party interested, may cancel the resealing.

In this and the following subsection "the relevant document" means the original grant or, where some other document was sealed by the court under those Acts, that document.

(4) A resealing may be cancelled under subsection (3) without the relevant document being called in, if it cannot be called in.

s.122 Examination of person with knowledge of testamentary document.

(1) Where it appears that there are reasonable grounds for believing that any person has knowledge of any document which is or purports to be a testamentary document, the High Court may, whether or not any legal proceedings are pending, order him to attend for the purpose of being examined in open court. **B–054**

(2) The court may—

(a) require any person who is before it in compliance with an order under subsection (1) to answer any question relating to the document concerned; and

(b) if appropriate, order him to bring in the document in such manner as the court may direct.

(3) Any person who, having been required by the court to do so under this section, fails to attend for examination, answer any question or bring in any document shall be guilty of contempt of court.

s.123 Subpoena to bring in testamentary document.

B–055 Where it appears that any person has in his possession, custody or power any document which is or purports to be a testamentary document, the High Court may, whether or not any legal proceedings are pending, issue a subpoena requiring him to bring in the document in such manner as the court may in the subpoena direct.

s.128 Interpretation of Part V and other probate provisions.

B–056 In this part, and in the other provisions of this Act relating to probate causes and matters, unless the context otherwise requires—

"administration" includes all letters of administration of the effects of deceased persons, whether with or without a will annexed, and whether granted for general, special or limited purposes;

"estate" means real and personal estate, and

"real estate" includes—

(a) chattels real and land in possession, remainder or reversion and every interest in or over land to which the deceased person was entitled at the time of his death, and

(b) real estate held on trust or by way of mortgage or security, but not [. . .] money secured or charged on land;

"grant" means a grant of probate or administration;

"grant" means a grant of probate or administration;

"non-contentious or common form probate business" means the business of obtaining probate and administration where there is no contention as to the right thereto, including—

(a) the passing of probates and administrations through the High Court in contentious cases where the contest has been terminated,

(b) all business of a non-contentious nature in matters of testacy and intestacy not being proceedings in any action, and

(c) the business of lodging caveats against the grant of probate or administration;

"Principal Registry" means the Principal Registry of the Family Division;

"probate rules" means rules of court made under section 127;

"trust corporation" means the Public Trustee or a corporation either appointed by the court in any particular case to be a trustee or authorised by rules made under section 4(3) of the Public Trustee Act 1906 to act as a custodian trustee;

"will" includes a nuncupative will and any testamentary document of which probate may be granted.

ADMINISTRATION OF JUSTICE ACT 1982

CHAPTER 53

s.20 Rectification.

(1) If a court is satisfied that a will is so expressed that it fails to carry out the testator's intentions, in consequence — **B–057**

    (a) of a clerical error; or
    (b) of a failure to understand his instructions,

it may order that the will shall be rectified so as to carry out his intentions.

(2) An application for an order under this section shall not, except with the permission of the court, be made after the end of the period of six months from the date on which representation with respect to the estate of the deceased is first taken out.

(3) The provisions of this section shall not render the personal representatives of a deceased person liable for having distributed any part of the estate of the deceased, after the end of the period of six months from the date on which representation with respect to the estate of the deceased is first taken out, on the ground that they ought to have taken into account the possibility that the court might permit the making of an application for an order under this section after the end of that period; but this subsection shall not prejudice any power to recover, by reason of the making of an order under this section, any part of the estate so distributed.

(4) In considering for the purposes of this section when representation with respect to the estate of a deceased person was first taken out, a grant limited to settled land or to trust property shall be left out of account, and a grant limited to real estate or to personal estate shall be left out of account unless a grant limited to the remainder of the estate has previously been made or is made at the same time.

s.21 Interpretation of wills — general rules as to evidence.

(1) This section applies to a will— **B–058**

    (a) in so far as any part of it is meaningless;
    (b) in so far as the language used in any part of it is ambiguous on the face of it;

(c) in so far as evidence, other than evidence of the testator's intention, shows that the language used in any part of it is ambiguous in the light of surrounding circumstances.

(2) In so far as this section applies to a will extrinsic evidence, including evidence of the testator's intention, may be admitted to assist in its interpretation.

ADMINISTRATION OF JUSTICE ACT 1985

CHAPTER 61

s.47 Power of High Court to make judgments binding on persons who are not parties.

B–059 (1) This section applies to actions in the High Court relating to the estates of deceased persons or to trusts and falling within any description specified in rules of court.

(2) Rules of court may make provision for enabling any judgment given in an action to which this section applies to be made binding on persons who—

(a) are or may be affected by the judgment and would not otherwise be bound by it; but
(b) have in accordance with the rules been given notice of the action and of such matters connected with it as the rules may require.

(3) Different provision may be made under this section in relation to actions of different descriptions.

s.48 Power of High Court to authorise action to be taken in reliance on counsel's opinion.

B–060 (1) Where—

(a) any question of construction has arisen out of the terms of a will or a trust; and
(b) an opinion in writing given by a [person who has a 10 year High Court qualification, within the meaning of section 71 of the Courts and Legal Services Act 1990.] has been obtained on that question by the personal representatives or trustees under the will or trust,

the High Court may, on the application of the personal representatives or trustees and without hearing argument, make an order authorising those persons to take such steps in reliance on the said opinion as are specified in the order.

(2) The High Court shall not make an order under subsection (1) if it appears to the court that a dispute exists which would make it inappropriate for the court to make the order without hearing argument.

s.49 Powers of High Court on compromise of probate action.

(1) Where on a compromise of a probate action in the High Court— **B–061**

    (a) the court is invited to pronounce for the validity of one or more wills, or against the validity of one or more wills, or for the validity of one or more wills and against the validity of one or more other wills; and

    (b) the court is satisfied that consent to the making of the pronouncement or, as the case may be, each of the pronouncements in question has been given by or on behalf of every relevant beneficiary,

the court may without more pronounce accordingly.

(2) In this section—

"probate action" means an action for the grant of probate of the will, or letters of administration of the estate, of a deceased person or for the revocation of such a grant or for a decree pronouncing for or against the validity of an alleged will, not being an action which is non-contentious or common form probate business; and

"relevant beneficiary", in relation to a pronouncement relating to any will or wills of a deceased person, means—

    (a) a person who under any such will is beneficially interested in the deceased's estate; and

    (b) where the effect of the pronouncement would be to cause the estate to devolve as on an intestacy (or partial intestacy), or to prevent it from so devolving, a person who under the law relating to intestacy is beneficially interested in the estate.

s.50 Power of High Court to appoint substitute for, or to remove, personal representative.

(1) Where an application relating to the estate of a deceased person is made to the High Court under this subsection by or on behalf of a personal representative of the deceased or a beneficiary of the estate, the court may in its discretion — **B–062**

(a) appoint a person (in this section called a substituted personal representative) to act as personal representative of the deceased in place of the existing personal representative or representatives of the deceased or any of them; or
(b) if there are two or more existing personal representatives of the deceased, terminate the appointment of one or more, but not all, of those persons.

(2) Where the court appoints a person to act as a substituted personal representative of a deceased person, then—

(a) if that person is appointed to act with an executor or executors the appointment shall (except for the purpose of including him in any chain of representation) constitute him executor of the deceased as from the date of the appointment; and
(b) in any other case the appointment shall constitute that person administrator of the deceased's estate as from the date of the appointment.

(3) The court may authorise a person appointed as a substituted personal representative to charge remuneration for his services as such, on such terms (whether or not involving the submission of bills of charges for taxation by the court) as the court may think fit.

(4) Where an application relating to the estate of a deceased person is made to the court under subsection (1), the court may if it thinks fit, proceed as if the application were, or included an application for the appointment under the Judicial Trustees Act 1896 of a judicial trustee in relation to that estate.

(5) In this section "beneficiary" in relation to the estate of a deceased person, means a person who under the will of the deceased or under the law relating to intestacy is beneficially interested in the estate.

(6) In *section 1* of the Judicial Trustees Act 1896, after *subsection (6)* there shall be added—

"(7) Where an application relating to the estate of a deceased person is made to the court under this section, the court may, if it thinks fit, proceed as if the application were, or included, an application under section 50 of the Administration of Justice Act 1985 (power of High Court to appoint substitute for, or to remove, personal representative).".

ACCESS TO JUSTICE ACT 1999

CHAPTER 22

s.11 Costs in funded cases.

(1) Except in prescribed circumstances, costs ordered against an individual in relation to any proceedings or part of proceedings funded for him shall not exceed the amount (if any) which is a reasonable one for him to pay having regard to all the circumstances including— **B–063**

> (a) the financial resources of all the parties to the proceedings, and
>
> (b) their conduct in connection with the dispute to which the proceedings relate;

and for this purpose proceedings, or a part of proceedings, are funded for an individual if services relating to the proceedings or part are funded for him by the Commission as part of the Community Legal Service.

(2) In assessing for the purposes of subsection (1) the financial resources of an individual for whom services are funded by the Commission as part of the Community Legal Service, his clothes and household furniture and the tools and implements of his trade shall not be taken into account, except so far as may be prescribed.

(3) Subject to subsections (1) and (2), regulations may make provision about costs in relation to proceedings in which services are funded by the Commission for any of the parties as part of the Community Legal Service.

(4) The regulations may, in particular, make provision—

> (a) specifying the principles to be applied in determining the amount of any costs which may be awarded against a party for whom services are funded by the Commission as part of the Community Legal Service,
>
> (b) limiting the circumstances in which, or extent to which, an order for costs may be enforced against such a party,
>
> (c) as to the cases in which, and extent to which, such a party may be required to give security for costs and the manner in which it is to be given,
>
> (d) requiring the payment by the Commission of the whole or part of any costs incurred by a party for whom services are not funded by the Commission as part of the Community Legal Service,

(e) specifying the principles to be applied in determining the amount of any costs which may be awarded to a party for whom services are so funded,
(f) requiring the payment to the Commission, or the person or body by which the services were provided, of the whole or part of any sum awarded by way of costs to such a party, and
(g) as to the court, tribunal or other person or body by whom the amount of any costs is to be determined and the extent to which any determination of that amount is to be final.

WILLS ACT 1963

CHAPTER 44

s.1 General rule as to formal validity.

B–064 A will shall be treated as properly executed if its execution conformed to the internal law in force in the territory where it was executed, or in the territory where, at the time of its execution or of the testator's death, he was domiciled or had his habitual residence, or in a state of which, at either of those times, he was a national.

s.2 Additional rules.

B–065 (1) Without prejudice to the preceding section, the following shall be treated as properly executed—

(a) a will executed on board a vessel or aircraft of any description, if the execution of the will conformed to the internal law in force in the territory with which, having regard to its registration (if any) and other relevant circumstances, the vessel or aircraft may be taken to have been most closely connected;
(b) a will so far as it disposes of immovable property, if its execution conformed to the internal law in force in the territory where the property was situated;
(c) a will so far as it revokes a will which under this Act would be treated as properly executed or revokes a provision which under this Act would be treated as comprised in a properly executed will, if the execution of the later will conformed to any law by reference to which the revoked will or provision would be so treated;

(d) a will so far as it exercises a power of appointment, if the execution of the will conformed to the law governing the essential validity of the power.

(2) A will so far as it exercises a power of appointment shall not be treated as improperly executed by reason only that its execution was not in accordance with any formal requirements contained in the instrument creating the power.

s.3 Certain requirements to be treated as formal.

Where (whether in pursuance of this Act or not) a law in force outside the United Kingdom falls to be applied in relation to a will, any requirement of that law whereby special formalities are to be observed by testators answering a particular description, or witnesses to the execution of a will are to possess certain qualifications, shall be treated, notwithstanding any rule of that law to the contrary, as a formal requirement only.

B–066

s.4 Construction of wills.

The construction of a will shall not be altered by reason of any change in the testator's domicile after the execution of the will.

B–067

s.6 Interpretation.

(1) In this Act—

B–068

"internal law" in relation to any territory or state means the law which would apply in a case where no question of the law in force in any other territory or state arose;

"state" means a territory or group of territories having its own law of nationality;

"will" includes any testamentary instrument or act, and "testator" shall be construed accordingly.

(2) Where under this Act the internal law in force in any territory or state is to be applied in the case of a will, but there are in force in that territory or state two or more systems of internal law relating to the formal validity of wills, the system to be applied shall be ascertained as follows—

(a) if there is in force throughout the territory or state a rule indicating which of those systems can properly be applied in the case in question, that rule shall be followed; or

(b) if there is no such rule, the system shall be that with which the testator was most closely connected at the relevant time, and for this purpose the relevant time is the time of the testator's death where the matter is to be determined by reference to circumstances prevailing at his death, and the time of execution of the will in any other case.

(3) In determining for the purposes of this Act whether or not the execution of a will conformed to a particular law, regard shall be had to the formal requirements of that law at the time of execution, but this shall not prevent account being taken of an alteration of law affecting wills executed at that time if the alteration enables the will to be treated as properly executed.

s.7 Short title, commencement, repeal and extent.

B–069 (1) This Act may be cited as the Wills Act 1963.
(2) This Act shall come into operation on 1st January 1964.
(3) [. . .]
(4) This Act shall not apply to a will of a testator who died before the time of the commencement of this Act and shall apply to a will of a testator who dies after that time whether the will was executed before or after that time, but so that the repeal of the Wills Act 1861 shall not invalidate a will executed before that time.
(5) It is hereby declared that this Act extends to Northern Ireland, [. . .]

(i) Orders

NON-CONTENTIOUS PROBATE RULES 1987/2024 (EXTRACTS)

r.1 Citation and commencement

These Rules may be cited as the Non-Contentious Probate Rules 1987 and shall come into force on 1st January 1988.

B–070

r.2 Interpretation

(1) In these Rules, unless the context otherwise requires—
"the Act" means the Supreme Court Act 1981;
"authorised officer" means any officer of a registry who is for the time being authorised by the President to administer any oath or to take any affidavit required for any purpose connected with his duties;
"the Crown" includes the Crown in right of the Duchy of Lancaster and the Duke of Cornwall for the time being;
"district judge" means a district judge of the Principal Registry;
"grant" means a grant of probate or administration and includes, where the context so admits, the resealing of such a grant under the Colonial Probates Act 1892 and 1927;
"gross value"in relation to any estate means the value of the estate without deduction for debts, incumbrances, funeral expenses or inheritance tax (or other capital tax payable out of the estate);
"judge" means a judge of the High Court;
"oath" means the oath required by rule 8 to be sworn by every applicant for a grant;
"personal applicant" means a person other than a trust corporation who seeks to obtain a grant without employing a solicitor or probate practitioner, and "personal application" has a corresponding meaning;
"probate practitioner" means a person to whom section 23(1) of the Solicitors Act 1974 does not apply by virtue of section 23(2) of that Act.
"registrar" means the district probate registrar of the district probate registry—

B–071

(i) to which an application for a grant is made or is proposed to be made,

(ii) in rules 26, 40, 41 and 61(2), from which the grant issued, and

(iii) in rules 46, 47 and 48, from which the citation has issued or is proposed to be issued;

"registry" means the Principal Registry or a district probate registry;

"the senior district judge" means the Senior District Judge of the Family Division or, in his absence, the senior of the district judges in attendance at the Principal Registry;

"the Treasury Solicitor" means the solicitor for the affairs of Her Majesty's Treasury and includes the solicitor for the affairs of the Duchy of Lancaster and the solicitor of the Duchy of Cornwall;

"trust corporation" means a corporation within the meaning of section 128 of the Act as extended by section 3 of the Law of Property (Amendment) Act 1926.

(2) A form referred to by number means the form so numbered in the First Schedule; and such forms shall be used wherever applicable, with such variation as a district judge or registrar may in any particular case direct or approve.

r.3 Application of other rules

B–072 (1) Subject to the provisions of these rules and to any enactment, the Rules of the Supreme Court 1965 as they were in force immediately before 26th April 1999 shall apply, with any necessary modifications to non-contentious probate matters, and any reference in these rules to those rules shall be construed accordingly.

(2) Nothing in Order 3 of the Rules of the Supreme Court shall prevent time from running in the Long Vacation.

r.4 Application for grants through solicitors or probate practitioners

B–073 (1) A person applying for a grant through a solicitor or probate practitioner may apply at any registry or sub-registry.

(2) Every solicitor or probate practitioner through whom an application for a grant is made shall give the address of his place of business within England and Wales.

r.5 Personal applications

(1) A personal applicant may apply for a grant at any registry or sub-registry.   B–074

(2) Save as provided for by rule 39 a personal applicant may not apply through an agent, whether paid or unpaid, and may not be attended by any person acting or appearing to act as his adviser.

(3) No personal application shall be proceeded with if—

(a) it becomes necessary to bring the matter before the court by action or summons, unless a judge, district judge or registrar so permits;

(b) an application has already been made by a solicitor [or probate practitioner] on behalf of the applicant and has not been withdrawn; or

(c) the district judge or registrar so directs.

(4) After a will has been deposited in a registry by a personal applicant, it may not be delivered to the applicant or to any other person unless in special circumstances the district judge or registrar so directs.

(5) A personal applicant shall produce a certificate of the death of the deceased or such other evidence of the death as the district judge or registrar may approve.

(6) A personal applicant shall supply all information necessary to enable the papers leading to the grant to be prepared in the registry.

(7) Unless the district judge or registrar otherwise directs, every oath or affidavit required on a personal application shall be sworn or executed by all the deponents before an authorised officer.

(8) No legal advice shall be given to a personal applicant by an officer of a registry and every such officer shall be responsible only for embodying in proper form the applicant's instructions for the grant.

r.6 Duty of district judge or registrar on receiving application for grant

(1) A district judge or registrar shall not allow any grant to issue until all inquiries which he may see fit to make have been answered to his satisfaction.   B–075

(2) Except with the leave of a district judge or registrar, no grant of probate or of administration with the will annexed shall issue within seven days of the death of the deceased and no grant of administration shall issue within fourteen days thereof.

r.7 Grants by registrars

B–076 (1) No grant shall be made by a registrar—

(a) in any case in which there is contention, until the contention is disposed of; or

(b) in any case in which it appears to him that a grant ought not to be made without the directions of a judge or a district judge.

(2) In any case in which paragraph (1)(b) applies, the registrar shall send a statement of the matter in question to the Principal Registry for directions.

(3) A district judge may either confirm that the matter be referred to a judge and give directions accordingly or may direct the registrar to proceed with the matter in accordance with such instructions as are deemed necessary, which may include a direction to take no further action in relation to the matter.

r.8 Oath in support of grant

B–077 (1) Every application for a grant other than one to which rule 39 applies shall be supported by an oath by the applicant in the form applicable to the circumstances of the case, and by such other papers as the district judge or registrar may require.

(2) Unless otherwise directed by a district judge or registrar, the oath shall state where the deceased died domiciled.

(3) Where the deceased died on or after 1st January 1926, the oath shall state whether or not, to the best of the applicant's knowledge, information and belief, there was land vested in the deceased which was settled previously to his death and not by his will and which remained settled land notwithstanding his death.

(4) On an application for a grant of administration the oath shall state in what manner all persons having a prior right to a grant have been cleared off and whether any minority or life interest arises under the will or intestacy.

r.9 Grant in additional name

B–078 Where it is sought to describe the deceased in a grant by some name in addition to his true name, the applicant shall depose to the true name of the deceased and shall specify some part of the estate which was held in the other name, or give any other reason for the inclusion of the other name in the grant.

r.10 Marking of wills

(1) Subject to paragraph (2) below, every will in respect of which **B–079** an application for a grant is made—

(a) shall be marked by the signatures of the applicant and the person before whom the oath is sworn; and

(b) shall be exhibited to any affidavit which may be required under these Rules as to the validity, terms, condition or date of execution of the will.

(2) The district judge or registrar may allow a facsimile copy of a will to be marked or exhibited in lieu of the original document.

r.11 Engrossments for purposes of record

(1) Where the district judge or registrar considers that in any **B–080** particular case a facsimile copy of the original will would not be satisfactory for purposes of record, he may require an engrossment suitable for facsimile reproduction to be lodged.

(2) Where a will—

(a) contains alterations which are not to be admitted to proof; or

(b) has been ordered to be rectified by virtue of section 20(1) of the Administration of Justice Act 1982,

there shall be lodged an engrossment of the will in the form in which it is to be proved.

(3) Any engrossment lodged under this rule shall reproduce the punctuation, spacing and division into paragraphs of the will and shall follow continuously from page to page on both sides of the paper.

r.12 Evidence as to due execution of will

(1) Subject to paragraphs (2) and (3) below, where a will **B–081** contains no attestation clause or the attestation clause is insufficient, or where it appears to the district judge or registrar that there is doubt about the due execution of the will, he shall before admitting it to proof require an affidavit as to due execution from one or more of the attesting witnesses or, if no attesting witness is conveniently available, from any other person who was present when the will was executed; and if the district judge or registrar, after considering the evidence, is

satisfied that the will was not duly executed, he shall refuse probate and mark the will accordingly.

(2) If no affidavit can be obtained in accordance with paragraph (1) above, the district judge or registrar may accept evidence on affidavit from any person he may think fit to show that the signature on the will is in the handwriting of the deceased, or of any other matter which may raise a presumption in favour of due execution of the will, and may if he thinks fit require that notice of the application be given to any person who may be prejudiced by the will.

(3) A district judge or registrar may accept a will for proof without evidence as aforesaid if he is satisfied that the distribution of the estate is not thereby affected.

r.13 Execution of will of blind or illiterate testator

B–082 Before admitting to proof a will which appears to have been signed by a blind or illiterate testator or by another person by direction of the testator, or which for any other reason raises doubt as to the testator having had knowledge of the contents of the will at the time of its execution, the district judge or registrar shall satisfy himself that the testator had such knowledge.

r.14 Evidence as to terms, condition and date of execution of will

B–083 (1) Subject to paragraph (2) below, where there appears in a will any obliteration, interlineation, or other alteration which is not authenticated in the manner prescribed by section 21 of the Wills Act 1837, or by the re-execution of the will or by the execution of a codicil, the district judge or registrar shall require evidence to show whether the alteration was present at the time the will was executed and shall give directions as to the form in which the will is to be proved.

(2) The provisions of paragraph (1) above shall not apply to any alteration which appears to the district judge or registrar to be of no practical importance.

(3) If a will contains any reference to another document in such terms as to suggest that it ought to be incorporated in the will, the district judge or registrar shall require the document to be produced and may call for such evidence in regard to the incorporation of the document as he may think fit.

(4) Where there is a doubt as to the date on which a will was executed, the district judge or registrar may require such evidence as he thinks necessary to establish the date.

r.15 Attempted revocation of will

Any appearance of attempted revocation of a will by burning, tearing, or otherwise destroying and every other circumstance leading to a presumption of revocation by the testator, shall be accounted for to the district judge's or registrar's satisfaction. **B–084**

r.16 Affidavit as to due execution, terms, etc., of will

A district judge or registrar may require an affidavit from any person he may think fit for the purpose of satisfying himself as to any of the matters referred to in rules 13, 14 and 15, and in any such affidavit sworn by an attesting witness or other person present at the time of the execution of a will the deponent shall depose to the manner in which the will was executed. **B–085**

r.17 Wills proved otherwise than under section 9 of the Wills Act 1837

(1) Rules 12 to 15 shall apply only to a will that is to be established by reference to section 9 of the Wills Act 1837 (signing and attestation of wills). **B–086**

(2) A will that is to be established otherwise than as described in paragraph (1) of this rule may be so established upon the district judge or registrar being satisfied as to its terms and validity, and includes (without prejudice to the generality of the foregoing)—

(a) any will to which rule 18 applies; and

(b) any will which, by virtue of the Wills Act 1963, is to be treated as properly executed if executed according to the internal law of the territory or state referred to in section 1 of that Act.

r.18 Wills of persons on military service and seamen

Where the deceased died domiciled in England and Wales and it appears to the district judge or registrar that there is prima facie evidence that a will is one to which section 11 of the Wills Act 1837 applies, the will may be admitted to proof if the [district judge or] registrar is satisfied that it was signed by the testator or, if unsigned, that it is in the testator's handwriting. **B–087** *r.19 Evidence of foreign law*

B–088 Where evidence as to the law of any country or territory outside England and Wales is required on any application for a grant, the district judge or registrar may accept—

(a) an affidavit from any person whom, having regard to the particulars of his knowledge or experience given in the affidavit, he regards as suitably qualified to give expert evidence of the law in question; or

(b) a certificate by, or an act before, a notary practising in the country or territory concerned.

r.20 Order of priority for grant where deceased left a will

B–089 Where the deceased died on or after 1st January 1926 the person or persons entitled to a grant in respect of a will shall be determined in accordance with the following order of priority, namely—

(a) the executor (but subject to rule 36(4)(d) below);

(b) any residuary legatee or devisee holding in trust for any other person;

(c) any other residuary legatee or devisee (including one for life) or where the residue is not wholly disposed of by the will, any person entitled to share in the undisposed of residue (including the Treasury Solicitor when claiming bona vacantia on behalf of the Crown), provided that—

(i) unless a district judge or registrar otherwise directs, a residuary legatee or devisee whose legacy or devise is vested in interest shall be preferred to one entitled on the happening of a contingency, and

(ii) where the residue is not in terms wholly disposed of, the district judge or registrar may, if he is satisfied that the testator has nevertheless disposed of the whole or substantially the whole of the known estate, allow a grant to be made to any legatee or devisee entitled to, or to share in, the estate so disposed of, without regard to the persons entitled to share in any residue not disposed of by the will;

(d) the personal representative of any residuary legatee or devisee (but not one for life, or one holding in trust for any other person), or of any person entitled to share in any residue not disposed of by the will;

(e) any other legatee or devisee (including one for life or one holding in trust for any other person) or any creditor of the deceased, provided that, unless a district judge or registrar otherwise directs, a legatee or devisee whose legacy or devise is vested in interest shall be preferred to one entitled on the happening of a contingency;

(f) the personal representative of any other legatee or devisee (but not one for life or one holding in trust for any other person) or of any creditor of the deceased.

r.21 Grants to attesting witnesses, etc

Where a gift to any person fails by reason of section 15 of the Wills Act 1837, such person shall not have any right to a grant as a beneficiary named in the will, without prejudice to his right to a grant in any other capacity. **B–090**

r.22 Order of priority for grant in case of intestacy

(1) Where the deceased died on or after 1st January 1926, wholly intestate, the person or persons having a beneficial interest in the estate shall be entitled to a grant of administration in the following classes in order of priority, namely— **B–091**

(a) the surviving husband or wife;

(b) the children of the deceased and the issue of any deceased child who died before the deceased;

(c) the father and mother of the deceased;

(d) brothers and sisters of the whole blood and the issue of any deceased brother or sister of the whole blood who died before the deceased;

(e) brothers and sisters of the half blood and the issue of any deceased brother or sister of the half blood who died before the deceased;

(f) grandparents;

(g) uncles and aunts of the whole blood and the issue of any deceased uncle or aunt of the whole blood who died before the deceased;

(h) uncles and aunts of the half blood and the issue of any deceased uncle or aunt of the half blood who died before the deceased.

(2) In default of any person having a beneficial interest in the estate, the Treasury Solicitor shall be entitled to a grant if he claims bona vacantia on behalf of the Crown.

(3) If all persons entitled to a grant under the foregoing provisions of this rule have been cleared off, a grant may be made to a creditor of the deceased or to any person who, notwithstanding that he has no immediate beneficial interest in the estate, may have a beneficial interest in the event of an accretion thereto.

(4) Subject to paragraph (5) of rule 27, the personal representative of a person in any of the classes mentioned in paragraph (1) of this rule or the personal representative of a creditor of the deceased shall have the same right to a grant as the person whom he represents provided that the persons mentioned in sub-paragraphs (b) to (h) of paragraph (1) above shall be preferred to the personal representative of a spouse who has died without taking a beneficial interest in the whole estate of the deceased as ascertained at the time of the application for the grant.

r.23 Order of priority for grant in pre-1926 cases

B–092 Where the deceased died before 1st January 1926, the person or persons entitled to a grant shall, subject to the provisions of any enactment, be determined in accordance with the principles and rules under which the court would have acted at the date of death.

r.24 Right of assignee to a grant

B–093 (1) Where all the persons entitled to the estate of the deceased (whether under a will or on intestacy) have assigned their whole interest in the estate to one or more persons, the assignee or assignees shall replace, in the order of priority for a grant of administration, the assignor or, if there are two or more assignors, the assignor with the highest priority.

(2) Where there are two or more assignees, administration may be granted with the consent of the others to any one or more (not exceeding four) of them.

(3) In any case where administration is applied for by an assignee the original instrument of assignment shall be produced and a copy of the same lodged in the registry.

r.25 Joinder of administrator

(1) A person entitled in priority to a grant of administration **B–094** may, without leave, apply for a grant with a person entitled in a lower degree, provided that there is no other person entitled in a higher degree to the person to be joined, unless every other such person has renounced.

(2) Subject to paragraph (3) below, an application for leave to join with a person entitled in priority to a grant of administration a person having no right or no immediate right thereto shall be made to a district judge or registrar, and shall be supported by an affidavit by the person entitled in priority, the consent of the person proposed to be joined as administrator and such other evidence as the district judge or registrar may direct.

(3) Unless a district judge or registrar otherwise directs, there may without any such application be joined with a person entitled in priority to administration-

(a) any person who is nominated under paragraph (3) of rule 32 or paragraph (3) of rule 35;

(b) a trust corporation.

r.26 Additional personal representatives

(1) An application under section 114(4) of the Act to add a **B–095** personal representative shall be made to a district judge or registrar and shall be supported by an affidavit by the applicant, the consent of the person proposed to be added as personal representative and such other evidence as the district judge or registrar may require.

(2) On any such application the district judge or registrar may direct that a note shall be made on the original grant of the addition of a further personal representative, or he may impound or revoke the grant or make such other order as the circumstances of the case may require.

r.27 Grants where two or more persons entitled in same degree

(1) Subject to paragraphs (1A), (2) and (3) below, where, on an **B–096** application for probate, power to apply for a like grant is to be reserved to such other of the executors as have not renounced probate, notice of the application shall be given to the executor or executors to whom power is to be reserved; and, unless the district judge or registrar otherwise directs, the oath shall state that such notice has been given.

(1A) Where power is to be reserved to executors who are partners in a firm, notice need not be given to them under paragraph (1) above if probate is applied for by another partner in that firm.

(2) Where power is to be reserved to partners of a firm, notice for the purposes of paragraph (1) above may be given to the partners by sending it to the firm at its principal or last known place of business.

(3) A district judge or registrar may dispense with the giving of notice under paragraph (1) above if he is satisfied that the giving of such a notice is impracticable or would result in unreasonable delay or expense.

(4) A grant of administration may be made to any person entitled thereto without notice to other persons entitled in the same degree.

(5) Unless a district judge or registrar otherwise directs, administration shall be granted to a person of full age entitled thereto in preference to a guardian of a minor, and to a living person entitled thereto in preference to the personal representative of a deceased person.

(6) A dispute between persons entitled to a grant in the same degree shall be brought by summons before a district judge or registrar.

(7) The issue of a summons under this rule in a registry shall be noted forthwith in the index of pending grant applications.

(8) If the issue of a summons under this rule is known to the district judge or registrar, he shall not allow any grant to be sealed until such summons is finally disposed of.

r.28 Exceptions to rules as to priority

B–097 (1) Any person to whom a grant may or is required to be made under any enactment shall not be prevented from obtaining such a grant notwithstanding the operation of rules 20, 22, 25 or 27.

(2) Where the deceased died domiciled outside England and Wales rules 20, 22, 25 or 27 shall not apply except in a case to which paragraph (3) of rule 30 applies.

r.43 Standing searches

B–098 (1) Any person who wishes to be notified of the issue of a grant may enter a standing search for the grant by lodging at, or sending by post to any registry or subregistry, a notice in Form 2.

(2) A person who has entered a standing search will be sent an office copy of any grant which corresponds with the particulars given on the completed Form 2 and which—

CONTENTIOUS PROBATE 351

- (a) issued not more than twelve months before the entry of the standing search; or
- (b) issues within a period of six months after the entry of the standing search.

(3)(a) Where an applicant wishes to extend the said period of six months, he or his solicitor or probate practitioner may lodge at, or send by post to, the registry or sub-registry at which the standing search was entered written application for extension.

- (b) An application for extension as aforesaid must be lodged, or received by post, within the last months of the said period of six months, and the standing search shall thereupon be effective for an additional period of six months from the date on which it was due to expire.
- (c) A standing search which has been extended as above may be further extended by the filing of a further application for extension subject to the same conditions as set out in sub-paragraph (b) above.

r.44 Caveats

(1) Any person who wishes to show cause against the sealing of a grant may enter a caveat in any registry or sub-registry, and the district judge or registrar shall not allow any grant to be sealed (other than a grant *ad colligenda bona* or a grant under section 117 of the Act) if he has knowledge of an effective caveat; provided that no caveat shall prevent the sealing of a grant on the day on which the caveat is entered. **B–099**

(2) Any person wishing to enter a caveat (in these Rules called "the caveator"), or a solicitor or probate practitioner on his behalf, may effect entry of a caveat—

- (a) by completing Form 3 in the appropriate book at any registry or sub- registry; or
- (b) by sending by post at his own risk a notice in Form 3 to any registry or sub-registry and the proper officer shall provide an acknowledgment of the entry of the caveat.

(3)(a) Except as otherwise provided by this rule or by rules 45 or 46, a caveat shall be effective for a period of six months from the date of entry thereof, and where a caveator wishes to extend the said period of six months, he or his solicitor or probate practitioner may lodge at, or send by post to, the registry or sub-registry at which the caveat was entered a written application for extension.

(b) An application for extension as aforesaid must be lodged, or received by post, within the last month of the said period of six months, and the caveat shall thereupon (save as otherwise provided by this rule) be effective for an additional period of six months from the date on which it was due to expire.

(c) A caveat which has been extended as above may be further extended by the filing of a further application for extension subject to the same conditions as set out in sub-paragraph (b) above.

(4) An index of caveats entered in any registry or sub-registry shall be maintained and upon receipt of an application for a grant, the registry or sub-registry at which the application is made shall cause a search of the index to be made and the appropriate district judge or registrar shall be notified of the entry of a caveat against the sealing of a grant for which the application has been made.

(5) Any person claiming to have an interest in the estate may cause to be issued from the nominated registry a warning in Form 4 against the caveat, and the person warning shall state his interest in the estate of the deceased and shall require the caveator to give particulars of any contrary interest in the estate; and the warning or a copy thereof shall be served on the caveator forthwith.

(6) A caveator who has no interest contrary to that of the person warning, but who wishes to show cause against the sealing of a grant to that person, may within eight days of service of the warning upon him (inclusive of the day of such service), or at any time thereafter if no affidavit has been filed under paragraph (12) below, issue and serve a summons for directions.

(7) On the hearing of any summons for directions under paragraph (6) above the district judge or registrar may give a direction for the caveat to cease to have effect.

(8) Any caveat in force when a summons for directions is issued shall remain in force until the summons has been disposed of unless a direction has been given under paragraph (7) above or until it is withdrawn under paragraph (11) below.

(9) The issue of a summons under this rule shall be notified forthwith to the nominated registry.

(10) A caveator having an interest contrary to that of the person warning may within eight days of service of the warning upon him (inclusive of the day of such service) or at any time thereafter if no affidavit has been filed under paragraph (12) below, enter an appearance in the nominated registry by filing Form 5; and he shall serve forthwith on the person warning a copy of Form 5 sealed with the seal of the court.

(11) A caveator who has not entered an appearance to a warning may at any time withdraw his caveat by giving notice at the registry or sub-registry at which it was entered, and the caveat shall thereupon cease to have effect; and, where the caveat has been so withdrawn, the caveator shall forthwith give notice of withdrawal to the person warning.

(12) If no appearance has been entered by the caveator or no summons has been issued by him under paragraph (6) of this rule, the person warning may at any time after eight days of service of the warning upon the caveator (inclusive of the day of such service) file an affidavit in the nominated registry as to such service and the caveat shall thereupon cease to have effect provided that there is no pending summons under paragraph (6) of this rule.

(13) Unless a district judge or, where application to discontinue a caveat is made by consent, a registrar by order made on summons otherwise directs, any caveat in respect of which an appearance to a warning has been entered shall remain in force until the commencement of a probate action.

(14) Except with the leave of a district judge, no further caveat may be entered by or on behalf of any caveator whose caveat is either in force or has ceased to have effect under paragraphs (7) or (12) of this rule or under rule 45(4) or rule 46(3).

(15) In this rule, "nominated registry" means the registry nominated for the purpose of this rule by the senior district judge or in the absence of any such nomination the Leeds District Probate Registry.

r.45 Probate actions

(1) Upon being advised by the court concerned of the commencement of a probate action the senior district judge shall give notice of the action to every caveator other than the plaintiff in the action in respect of each caveat that is in force.

B–100

(2) In respect of any caveat entered subsequent to the commencement of a probate action the senior district judge shall give notice to that caveator of the existence of the action.

(3) Unless a district judge by order made on summons otherwise directs, the commencement of a probate action shall operate to prevent the sealing of a grant (other than a grant under section 117 of the Act) until application for a grant is made by the person shown to be entitled thereto by the decision of the court in such action.

(4) Upon such application for a grant, any caveat entered by the plaintiff in the action, and any caveat in respect of which notice of the action has been given, shall cease to have effect.

r.46 Citations

B–101 (1) Any citation may issue from the Principal Registry or a district probate registry and shall be settled by a district judge or registrar before being issued.

(2) Every averment in a citation, and such other information as the district judge or registrar may require, shall be verified by an affidavit sworn by the person issuing the citation (in these Rules called the "citor"), provided that the district judge or registrar may in special circumstances accept an affidavit sworn by the citor's solicitor [or probate practitioner].

(3) The citor shall enter a caveat before issuing a citation and, unless a district judge by order made on summons otherwise directs, any caveat in force at the commencement of the citation proceedings shall, unless withdrawn pursuant to paragraph (11) of rule 44, remain in force until application for a grant is made by the person shown to be entitled thereto by the decision of the court in such proceedings, and upon such application any caveat entered by a party who had notice of the proceedings shall cease to have effect.

(4) Every citation shall be served personally on the person cited unless the district judge or registrar, on cause shown by affidavit, directs some other mode of service, which may include notice by advertisement.

(5) Every will referred to in a citation shall be lodged in a registry before the citation is issued, except where the will is not in the citor's possession and the district judge or registrar is satisfied that it is impracticable to require it to be lodged.

(6) A person who has been cited to appear may, within eight days of service of the citation upon him (inclusive of the day of such service), or at any time thereafter if no application has been made by the citor under paragraph (5) of rule 47 or paragraph (2) of rule 48, enter an appearance in the registry from which the citation issued by filing Form 5 and shall forthwith thereafter serve on the citor a copy of Form 5 sealed with the seal of the registry.

r.47 Citation to accept or refuse or to take a grant

(1) A citation to accept or refuse a grant may be issued at the instance of any person who would himself be entitled to a grant in the event of the person cited renouncing his right thereto.

B–102

(2) Where power to make a grant to an executor has been reserved, a citation calling on him to accept or refuse a grant may be issued at the instance of the executors who have proved the will or the survivor of them or of the executors of the last survivor of deceased executors who have proved.

(3) A citation calling on an executor who has intermeddled in the estate of the deceased to show cause why he should not be ordered to take a grant may be issued at the instance of any person interested in the estate at any time after the expiration of six months from the death of the deceased, provided that no citation to take a grant shall issue while proceedings as to the validity of the will are pending.

(4) A person cited who is willing to accept or take a grant may, after entering an appearance, apply ex parte by affidavit to a district judge or registrar for an order for a grant to himself.

(5) If the time limited for appearance has expired and the person cited has not entered an appearance, the citor may-

(a) in the case of a citation under paragraph (1) of this rule, apply to a district judge or registrar for an order for a grant to himself;

(b) in the case of a citation under paragraph (2) of this rule, apply to a district judge or registrar for an order that a note be made on the grant that the executor in respect of whom power was reserved has been duly cited and has not appeared and that all his rights in respect of the executorship have wholly ceased; or

(c) in the case of a citation under paragraph (3) of this rule, apply to a district judge or registrar by summons (which shall be served on the person cited) for an order requiring such person to take a grant within a specified time or for a grant to himself or to some other person specified in the summons.

(6) An application under the last foregoing paragraph shall be supported by an affidavit showing that the citation was duly served.

(7) If the person cited has entered an appearance but has not applied for a grant under paragraph (4) of this rule, or has failed to prosecute his application with reasonable diligence, the citor may—

(a) in the case of a citation under paragraph (1) of this rule, apply by summons to a district judge or registrar for an order for a grant to himself;

(b) in the case of a citation under paragraph (2) of this rule, apply by summons to a district judge or registrar for an order striking out the appearance and for the endorsement on the grant of such a note as is mentioned in sub-paragraph (b) of paragraph (5) of this rule; or

(c) in the case of a citation under paragraph (3) of this rule, apply by summons to a district judge or registrar for an order requiring the person cited to take a grant within a specified time or for a grant to himself or to some other person specified in the summons;

and the summons shall be served on the person cited.

r.48 Citation to propound a will

B–103 (1) A citation to propound a will shall be directed to the executors named in the will and to all persons interested thereunder, and may be issued at the instance of any citor having an interest contrary to that of the executors or such other persons.

(2) If the time limited for appearance has expired, the citor may—

(a) in the case where no person has entered an appearance, apply to a district judge or registrar for an order for a grant as if the will were invalid and such application shall be supported by an affidavit showing that the citation was duly served; or

(b) in the case where no person who has entered an appearance proceeds with reasonable diligence to propound the will, apply to a district judge or registrar by summons, which shall be served on every person cited who has entered an appearance, for such an order as is mentioned in paragraph (a) above.

r.49 Address for service

B–104 All caveats, citations, warnings and appearance shall contain an address for service in England and Wales.

r.50 Application for order to attend for examination or for subpoena to bring in a will

(1) An application under section 122 of the Act for an order requiring a person to attend for examination may, unless a probate action has been commenced, be made to a district judge or registrar by summons which shall be served on every such person as aforesaid.

(2) An application under section 123 of the Act for the issue by a district judge or registrar of a subpoena to bring in a will shall be supported by an affidavit setting out the grounds of the application, and if any person served with the subpoena denies that the will is in his possession or control he may file an affidavit to that effect in the registry from which the subpoena issued.

B–105

r.51 Grants to part of an estate under section 113 of the Act

An application for an order for a grant under section 113 of the Act to part of an estate may made to a [district judge or] registrar, and shall be supported by an affidavit setting out the grounds of the application, and

(a) stating whether the estate of the deceased is known to be insolvent; and

(b) showing how any person entitled to a grant in respect of the whole estate in priority to the applicant has been cleared off.

B–106

r.52 Grants of administration under discretionary powers of court, and grants and colligenda bona

An application for an order for—

(a) a grant of administration under section 116 of the Act; or

(b) a grant of administration ad colligenda bona,

may be made to a district judge or registrar and shall be supported by an affidavit setting out the grounds of the application.

B–107

r.53 Applications for leave to swear to death

An application for leave to swear to the death of a person in whose estate a grant is sought may be made to a district judge or

B–108

registrar, and shall be supported by an affidavit setting out the grounds of the application and containing particulars of any policies of insurance effected on the life of the presumed deceased together with such further evidence as the district judge or registrar may require.

r.54 Grants in respect of nuncupative wills and copies of wills

B–109 (1) Subject to paragraph (2) below, an application for an order admitting to proof a nuncupative will, or a will contained in a copy or reconstruction thereof where the original is not available, shall be made to a district judge or registrar.

(2) In any case where a will is not available owing to its being retained in the custody of a foreign court or official, a duly authenticated copy of the will may be admitted to proof without the order referred to in paragraph (1) above.

(3) An application under paragraph (1) above shall be supported by an affidavit setting out the grounds of the application, and by such evidence on affidavit as the applicant can adduce as to—

- (a) the will's existence after the death of the testator or, where there is no such evidence, the facts on which the applicant relies to rebut the presumption that the will has been revoked by destruction;

- (b) in respect of a nuncupative will, the contents of that will; and

- (c) in respect of a reconstruction of a will, the accuracy of that reconstruction.

(4) The district judge or registrar may require additional evidence in the circumstances of a particular case as to due execution of the will or as to the accuracy of the copy will, and may direct that notice be given to persons who would be prejudiced by the application.

r.55 Application for rectification of a will

B–110 (1) An application for an order that a will be rectified by virtue of section 20(1) of the Administration of Justice Act 1982 may be made to a district judge or registrar, unless a probate action has been commenced.

(2) The application shall be supported by an affidavit, setting out the grounds of the application, together with such evidence

as can be adduced as to the testator's intentions and as to whichever of the following matters as are in issue:

(a) in what respects the testator's intentions were not understood; or

(b) the nature of any alleged clerical error.

(3) Unless otherwise directed, notice of the application shall be given to every person having an interest under the will whose interest might be prejudiced, or such other person who might be prejudiced by the rectification applied for and any comments in writing by any such person shall be exhibited to the affidavit in support of the application.

(4) If the district judge or registrar is satisfied that, subject to any direction to the contrary, notice has been given to every person mentioned in paragraph (3) above, and that the application is unopposed, he may order that the will be rectified accordingly.

r.57 Index of grant applications

(1) The senior district judge shall maintain an index of every pending application for a grant made in any registry or sub-registry.   **B–111**

(2) Every registry or sub-registry in which an application is made shall cause the index to be searched and shall record the result of the search.

r.58 Inspection of copies of original wills and other documents

An original will or other document referred to in section 124 of the Act shall not be open to inspection if, in the opinion of a district judge or registrar, such inspection would be undesirable or otherwise inappropriate.   **B–112**

r.59 Issue of copies of original wills and other documents

Where copies are required of original wills or other documents deposited under section 124 of the Act, such copies may be facsimile copies sealed with the seal of the court and issued either as office copies or certified under the hand of a district judge or registrar to be true copies.   **B–113** *r.60 Costs*

B–114 (1) Order 62 of the Rules of the Supreme Court 1965 shall not apply to costs in non-contentious probate matters, and Parts 43, 44 (except rules 44.9 to 44.12), 47 and 48 of the Civil Procedure Rules 1998 ("the 1998 Rules") shall apply to costs in those matters, with the modifications contained in paragraphs (3) to (7) of this rule.

(2) Where detailed assessment of a bill of costs is ordered, it shall be referred—

- (a) where the order was made by a district judge, to a district judge, a costs judge or an authorised court officer within rule 43.2(1)(d)(iii) or (iv) of the 1998 Rules;

- (b) where the order was made by a registrar, to that registrar or, where this is not possible, in accordance with sub-paragraph (a) above.

(3) Every reference in Parts 43, 44, 47 and 48 of the 1998 Rules to a district judge shall be construed as referring only to a district judge of the Principal Registry.

(4) The definition of "costs officer" in rule 43.2(1)(c) of the 1998 Rules shall have effect as if it included a paragraph reading—

"(iv) a district probate registrar."

(5) The definition of "authorised court officer" in rule 43.2(1)(d) of the 1998 Rules shall have effect as if paragraphs (i) and (ii) were omitted.

(6) Rule 44.3(2) of the 1998 Rules (costs follow the event) shall not apply.

(7) Rule 47.4(2) of the 1998 Rules shall apply as if after the words "Supreme Court Costs Office" there were inserted ", the Principal Registry of the Family Division or such district probate registry as the court may specify".

(8) Except in the case of an appeal against a decision of an authorised court officer (to which rules 47.20 to 47.23 of the 1998 Rules apply), an appeal against a decision in assessment proceedings relating to costs in non-contentious probate matters shall be dealt with in accordance with the following paragraphs of this rule.

(9) An appeal within paragraph (8) above against a decision made by a district judge, a costs judge (as defined by rule 43.2(1)(b) of the 1998 Rules) or a registrar, shall lie to a judge of the High Court.

CONTENTIOUS PROBATE

(10) CPR r.52 of the 1998 Rules applies to every appeal within paragraph (8) above, and any reference in CPR r.52 to a judge or a district judge shall be taken to include a district judge of the Principal Registry of the Family Division.

(11) The 1998 Rules shall apply to an appeal to which CPR r.52 or rules 47.20 to 47.23 of those Rules apply in accordance with paragraph (8) above in the same way as they apply to any other appeal within CPR r.52 or rules 47.20 to 47.23 of those Rules as the case may be; accordingly the Rules of the Supreme Court 1965 and the County Court Rules 1981 shall not apply to any such appeal.

r.61 Power to require applications to be made by summons

(1) Subject to rule 7(2), a district judge or registrar may require **B–115** any application to be made by summons to a district judge or registrar in chambers or a judge in chambers or open court.

(2) An application for an inventory and account shall be made by summons to a district judge or registrar.

(3) A summons for hearing by a district judge or registrar shall be issued out of the registry in which it is to be heard.

(4) A summons to be heard by a judge shall be issued out of the Principal Registry.

r.62 Transfer of applications

A district judge or registrar to whom any application is made **B–116** under these Rules may order the transfer of the application to another district judge or registrar having jurisdiction.

r.62A Exercise of a registrar's jurisdiction by another registrar

A registrar may hear and dispose of an application under these **B–117** Rules on behalf of any other registrar by whom the application would otherwise have been heard, if that other registrar so requests or an application in that behalf is made by a party making an application under these Rules; and where the circumstances require it, the registrar shall, without the need for any such request or application, hear and dispose of the application.

r.63 Power to make orders for costs

On any application dealt with by him on summons, the registrar **B–118** shall have full power to determine by whom and to what extent the costs are to be paid.

r.64 Exercise of powers of judge during Long Vacation

B–119 All powers exercisable under these Rules by a judge in chambers may be exercised during the Long Vacation by a district judge.

r.65 Appeals from district judges or registrars

B–120 (1) An appeal against a decision or requirement of a district judge or registrar shall be made by summons to a judge.

(2) If, in the case of an appeal under the last foregoing paragraph, any person besides the appellant appeared or was represented before the district judge or registrar from whose decision or requirement the appeal is brought, the summons shall be issued within seven days thereof for hearing on the first available day and shall be served on every such person as aforesaid.

(3) This rule does not apply to an appeal against a decision in proceedings for the assessment of costs.

r.66 Service of summons

B–121 (1) A judge or district judge or, where the application is to be made to a district probate registrar, that registrar, may direct that a summons for the service of which no other provision is made by these Rules shall be served on such person or persons as the judge, district judge or registrar may direct.

(2) Where by these Rules or by any direction given under the last foregoing paragraph a summons is required to be served on any person, it shall be served not less than two clear days before the day appointed for the hearing, unless a judge or district judge or registrar at or before the hearing dispenses with service on such terms, if any, as he may think fit.

r.67 Notices, etc.

B–122 Unless a district judge or registrar otherwise directs or these Rules otherwise provide, any notice or other document required to be given to or served on any person may be given or served in the manner prescribed by Order 65 Rule 5 of the Rules of the Supreme Court 1965

r.68 Application to pending proceedings

B–123 Subject in any particular case to any direction given by a judge or district judge or registrar, these Rules shall apply to any proceedings which are pending on the date on which they come into force as well as to any proceedings commenced on or after that date.

NON-CONTENTIOUS PROBATE RULES 1987/2024

SCHEDULE 1 FORMS

Form 6

Rule 56

Notice of Election to Redeem Life Interest

In the High Court of Justice   B–124
Family Division
The Principal [*or* .... District probate] Registry
            In the estate of .... deceased.
Whereas .... of .... died on the .... day of ....
20 ....
wholly/partially intestate leaving his/her/lawful wife/husband and .... lawful issue of the said deceased:
   And whereas Probate/Letters of Administration of the estate of the said ....
were granted to me, the said ....
[and to .... of ....] at the Probate Registry on the .... day of ....20 ....;
And whereas [the said .... has ceased to be a personal representative because ....] and I am [now] the sole personal representative:
   Now I, the said .... hereby give notice in accordance with section 47A of the Administration of Estates Act 1925 that I elect to redeem the life interest to which I am entitled in the estate of the late ....
by retaining £..... its capital value, and £..... the costs of the transaction.
Dated the .... day of .... 20.........
(Signed)
To the senior district judge of the Family Division.

NON-CONTENTIOUS PROBATE FEES ORDER 1999/688

Art 1 Citation and commencement

B–125 This Order may be cited as the Non-Contentious Probate Fees Order 1999 and shall come into force on April 26, 1999.

Art 2 Interpretation

B–126 In this Order, unless the context otherwise requires—

(a) a fee referred to by number means the fee so numbered in Schedule 1 to this Order,

(b) "assessed value" means the value of the net real and personal estate (excluding settled land if any) passing under the grant as shown—

   (i) in the Inland Revenue affidavit (for a death occurring before 13th March 1975), or
   (ii) in the Inland Revenue account (for a death occurring on or after 13th March 1975), or
   (iii) in a case in which, in accordance with arrangements made between the President of the Family Division and the Commissioners of Inland Revenue, or regulations made under section 256(1)(a)of the Inheritance Tax Act 1984 and from time to time in force, no such affidavit or account is required to be delivered, in the oath which is sworn to lead to the grant,

and in the case of an application to reseal a grant means the value, as so shown, passing under the grant upon its being resealed;

(c) "authorised place of deposit" means any place in which, by virtue of a direction given under section 124 of the Supreme Court Act 1981 original wills and other documents under the control of the High Court (either in the principal registry or in any district registry) are deposited and preserved;

(d) "grant" means a grant of probate or letters of administration;

(e) "district registry" includes the probate registry of Wales, any district probate registry and any subregistry attached to it;

(f) "the principal registry" means the Principal Registry of the Family Division and any sub-registry attached to it.

Art 3 Fees to be taken

The fees set out in column 2 of Schedule 1 to this Order shall be taken in the principal registry and in each district registry in respect of the items described in column 1 in accordance with and subject to any directions specified in column 1.

B–127

Art 5 Exemptions, reductions and remissions

(1) Where it appears to the Lord Chancellor that the payment of any fee prescribed by this Order would, owing to the exceptional circumstances of the particular case, involve undue hardship, he may reduce or remit the fee in that case.

B–128

(1A) Subject to paragraph (1B), where a fee has been paid at a time—

(a) where the Lord Chancellor, if he had been aware of all the circumstances, would have reduced the fee under article 5(1), the amount by which the fee would have been reduced shall be refunded; and

(b) where the Lord Chancellor, if he had been aware of all the circumstances, would have remitted the fee under article 5(1), the fee shall be refunded.

(1B) No refund shall be made under paragraph (1A) unless the party who paid the fee applies within 6 months of paying the fee.

(1C) The Lord Chancellor may extend the period of 6 months referred to in paragraph (1B) if he considers that there is good reason for an application being made after the end of the period of 6 months.

(2) Where by any convention entered into by Her Majesty with any foreign power it is provided that no fee shall be required to be paid in respect of any proceedings, the fees specified in this Order shall not be taken in respect of those proceedings.

(3) Where any application for a grant is withdrawn before the issue of a grant, a registrar may reduce or remit a fee.

(4) Fee 7 shall not be taken where a search is made for research or similar purposes by permission of the President of the Family Division for a document over 100 years old filed in the principal registry or a district registry or another authorised place of deposit.

B–129 Para. 1

Column 1 Number and description of fee	Column 2 Amount of fee
1. Application for a grant On an application for a grant (or for resealing a grant) other than on an application to which fee 3 applies, where the assessed value of the estate exceeds £5,000	£50
2. Personal application fee Where the application under fee 1 is made by a personal applicant (not being an application to which fee 3 applies) fee 2 is payable in addition to fee 1, where the assessed value of the estate exceeds £5,000	£80
3. Special applications (1) For a duplicate or second or subsequent grant (including one following a revoked grant) in respect of the same deceased person, other than a grant preceded only by a grant limited to settled land, to trust property, or to part of the estate	£15
(2) On an application for a grant in respect of an estate exempt from inheritance tax by virtue of section 154 if the Inheritance Tax Act 1984 (exemption for members of the armed forces etc.)	£8
4. Caveats For the entry or the extension of a caveat	£15
5. Search On an application for a standing search to be carried out in an estate, for each period of six months including the issue of a copy grant and will, if any (irrespective of the number of pages)	£5
6. Deposit of wills On depositing a will for safe custody in the principal registry or a district registry	£15
7. Inspection On inspection of any will or other document retained by the registry (in the presence of an officer of the registry)	£15
8. Copy documents On a request for a copy of any document whether or not provided as a certified copy:	
(a) for the first copy	£5
(b) for every subsequent copy of the same document if supplied at the same time	£1
(c) where copies of any document are made available on a computer disk or in other electronic form, for each such copy	£3
(d) where a search of the index is required, in addition to fee 8(a), (b) (c) as apropriate, for each period of 4 years searched after the first 4 years	£3

9. Oaths Except on a personal application for a grant for administering an oath,	
9.1 for each deponent to each affidvit	£5
9.2 for marking each exhibit	£2
10. Determination of costs For determining cost	The same fees as are payable from time to time for determining costs under the Supreme Court Fees Order 1999 (the relevant fees are set out in fee 3 in Schedule 1 to that Order)
11. Settling documents For perusing and settling citations, advertisements, oaths, affidavits, or other documents, for each document settled	£10

(ii) Civil Procedure Rules (extracts)

Part 36

Scope of this Part

B–130 36.1 (1) This Part contains rules about—

(a) offers to settle and payments into court; and
(b) the consequences where an offer to settle or payment into court is made in accordance with this Part.

(2) Nothing in this Part prevents a party making an offer to settle in whatever way he chooses, but if that offer is not made in accordance with this Part, it will only have the consequences specified in this Part if the court so orders.

(Part 36 applies to Part 20 claims by virtue of rule 20.3)

Part 36 offers and Part 36 payments — general provisions

36.2 (1) An offer made in accordance with the requirements of this Part is called—

(a) if made by way of a payment into court, 'a Part 36 payment';
(b) otherwise 'a Part 36 offer'.—

(Rule 36.3 sets out when an offer has to be made by way of a payment into court)

(2) The party who makes an offer is the 'offeror'.

(3) The party to whom an offer is made is the 'offeree'.

(4) A Part 36 offer or a Part 36 payment—

(a) may be made at any time after proceedings have started; and
(b) may be made on appeal proceedings.

(5) A Part 36 offer or a Part 36 payment shall not have the consequences set out in this Part while the claim is being dealt with on the small claims track unless the court orders otherwise.

(Part 26 deals with allocation to the small claims track)
(Rule 27.2 provides that Part 36 does not apply to small claims)

A defendant's offer to settle a money claim requires a Part 36 payment

36.3 (1) Subject to rules 36.5(5) and 36.23, an offer by a defendant to settle a money claim will not have the consequences set out in this Part unless it is made by way of a Part 36 payment.

(2) A Part 36 payment may only be made after proceedings have started.

(Rule 36.5(5) permits a Part 36 offer to be made by reference to an interim payment)
(Rule 36.10 makes provision for an offer to settle a money claim before the commencement of proceedings)
(Rule 36.23 makes provision for where benefit is recoverable under the Social Security (Recovery of Benefit) Act 1997

Defendant's offer to settle the whole of a claim which includes both a money claim and a non-money claim

36.4 (1) This rule applies where a defendant to a claim which includes both a money claim and a non-money claim wishes—

(a) to make an offer to settle the whole claim which will have the consequences set out in this Part; and
(b) to make a money offer in respect of the money claim and a non – money offer in respect of the non-money claim.

(2) The defendant must—

(a) make a Part 36 payment in relation to the money claim; and
(b) make a Part 36 offer in relation to the non-money claim.

(3) The Part 36 payment notice must—

(a) identify the document which sets out the terms of the Part 36 offer; and
(b) state that if the claimant gives notice of acceptance of the Part 36 payment he will be treated as also accepting the Part 36 offer.

(Rule 36.6 makes provision for a Part 36 payment notice)

(4) If the claimant gives notice of acceptance of the Part 36 payment, he shall also be taken as giving notice of acceptance of the Part 36 offer in relation to the non-money claim.

Form and content of a Part 36 offer

36.5 (1) A Part 36 offer must be in writing.

(2) A Part 36 offer may relate to the whole claim or to part of it or to any issue that arises in it.

(3) A Part 36 offer must—
(a) state whether it relates to the whole of the claim or to part of it or to an issue that arises in it and if so to which part or issue;
(b) state whether it takes into account any counterclaim; and
(c) if it is expressed not to be inclusive of interest, give the details relating to interest set out in rule 36.22(2).

(4) A defendant may make a Part 36 offer limited to accepting liability up to a specified proportion.

(5) A Part 36 offer may be made by reference to an interim payment. (Part 25 contains provisions relating to interim payments)

(6) A Part 36 offer made not less than 21 days before the start of the trial must—
(a) be expressed to remain open for acceptance for 21 days from the date it is made; and
(b) provide that after 21 days the offeree may only accept it if—
(i) the parties agree the liability for costs; or
(ii) the court gives permission.

(7) A Part 36 offer made less than 21 days before the start of the trial must state that the offeree may only accept it if—

(a) the parties agree the liability for costs; or
(b) the court gives permission.

(Rule 36.8 makes provision for when a Part 36 offer is treated as being made)

(8) If a Part 36 offer is withdrawn it will not have the consequences set out in this Part.

Notice of a Part 36 payment

36.6 (1) A Part 36 payment may relate to the whole claim or part of it or to an issue that arises in it.

(2) A defendant who makes a Part 36 payment must file with the court a notice ('Part 36 payment notice') which—

(a) states the amount of the payment;
(b) states whether the payment relates to the whole claim or to part of it or to any issue that arises in it and if so to which part or issue;
(c) states whether it takes into account any counterclaim;
(d) if an interim payment has been made, states that the defendant has taken into account the interim payment; and
(e) if it is expressed not to be inclusive of interest, gives the details relating to interest set out in rule 36.22(2).

(Rule 25.6 makes provision for an interim payment)
(Rule 36.4 provides for further information to be included where a defendant wishes to settle the whole of a claim which includes a money claim and a non-money claim)
(Rule 36.23 makes provision for extra information to be included in the payment notice in a case where benefit is recoverable under the Social Security (Recovery of Benefit) Act 1997)

(3) The offeror must—

(a) serve the Part 36 payment notice on the offeree; and
(b) file a certificate of service of the notice.

(5) A Part 36 payment may be withdrawn or reduced only with the permission of the court.

. . . . . .

Time when a Part 36 offer or a Part 36 payment is made and accepted

36.8 (1) A Part 36 offer is made when received by the offeree.

(2) A Part 36 payment is made when written notice of the payment into court is served on the offeree.

(3) An improvement to a Part 36 offer will be effective when its details are received by the offeree.

(4) An increase in a Part 36 payment will be effective when notice of the increase is served on the offeree.

(5) A Part 36 offer or Part 36 payment is accepted when notice of its acceptance is received by the offeror.

Clarification of a Part 36 offer or a Part 36 payment notice

36.9 (1) The offeree may, within 7 days of a Part 36 offer or payment being made, request the offeror to clarify the offer or payment notice.

(2) If the offeror does not give the clarification requested under paragraph (1) within 7 days of receiving the request, the offeree may, unless the trial has started, apply for an order that he does so.

(3) If the court makes an order under paragraph (2), it must specify the date when the Part 36 offer or Part 36 payment is to be treated as having been made.

Court to take into account offer to settle made before commencement of proceedings

36.10 (1) If a person makes an offer to settle before proceedings are begun which complies with the provisions of this rule, the court will take that offer into account when making any order as to costs.

(2) The offer must—

(a) be expressed to be open for at least 21 days after the date it was made;
(b) if made by a person who would be a defendant were proceedings commenced, include an offer to pay the costs of the offeree incurred up to the date 21 days after the date it was made; and
(c) otherwise comply with this Part.

(3) If the offeror is a defendant to a money claim—

　(a) he must make a Part 36 payment within 14 days of service of the claim form; and

　(b) the amount of the payment must be not less than the sum offered before proceedings began.

(4) An offeree may not, after proceedings have begun, accept—

　(a) an offer made under paragraph (2); or

　(b) a Part 36 payment made under paragraph (3),

without the permission of the court.

(5) An offer under this rule is made when it is received by the offeree.

Time for acceptance of a defendant's Part 36 offer or Part 36 payment

36.11 (1) A claimant may accept a Part 36 offer or a Part 36 payment made not less than 21 days before the start of the trial without needing the court's permission if he gives the defendant written notice of acceptance not later than 21 days after the offer or payment was made.

(Rule 36.13 sets out the costs consequences of accepting a defendant's offer or payment without needing the permission of the court)

　(2) If—

　　(a) a defendant's Part 36 offer or Part 36 payment is made less than 21 days before the start of the trial; or

　　(b) the claimant does not accept it within the period specified in paragraph (1)—

　　　(i) if the parties agree the liability for costs, the claimant may accept the offer or payment without needing the permission of the court;

　　　(ii) if the parties do not agree the liability for costs the claimant may only accept the offer or payment with the permission of the court.

　(3) Where the permission of the court is needed under paragraph (2) the court will, if it gives permission, make an order as to costs.

Time for acceptance of a claimant's Part 36 offer

36.12 (1) A defendant may accept a Part 36 offer made not less than 21 days before the start of the trial without needing the court's permission if he gives the claimant written notice of acceptance not later than 21 days after the offer was made.

(Rule 36.14 sets out the costs consequences of accepting a claimant's offer without needing the permission of the court)

    (2) If—

        (a) a claimant's Part 36 offer is made less than 21 days before the start of the trial; or

        (b) the defendant does not accept it within the period specified in paragraph (1)—

            (i) if the parties agree the liability for costs, the defendant may accept the offer without needing the permission of the court;

            (ii) if the parties do not agree the liability for costs the defendant may only accept the offer with the permission of the court.

    (3) Where the permission of the court is needed under paragraph (2) the court will, if it gives permission, make an order as to costs.

Costs consequences of acceptance of a defendant's Part 36 offer or Part 36 payment

36.13 (1) Where a Part 36 offer or a Part 36 payment is accepted without needing the permission of the court the claimant will be entitled to his costs of the proceedings up to the date of serving notice of acceptance.

    (2) Where—

        (a) a Part 36 offer or a Part 36 payment relates to part only of the claim; and

        (b) at the time of serving notice of acceptance the claimant abandons the balance of the claim,

the claimant will be entitled to his costs of the proceedings up to the date of serving notice of acceptance, unless the court orders otherwise.

(3) The claimant's costs include any costs attributable to the defendant's counterclaim if the Part 36 offer or the Part 36 payment notice states that it takes into account the counterclaim.

(4) Costs under this rule will be payable on the standard basis if not agreed.

Costs consequences of acceptance of a claimant's Part 36 offer

36.14 Where a claimant's Part 36 offer is accepted without needing the permission of the court the claimant will be entitled to his costs of the proceedings up to the date upon which the defendant serves notice of acceptance.

The effect of acceptance of a Part 36 offer or a Part 36 payment

36.15 (1) If a Part 36 offer or Part 36 payment relates to the whole claim and is accepted, the claim will be stayed.

(2) In the case of acceptance of a Part 36 offer which relates to the whole claim—

(a) the stay will be upon the terms of the offer; and
(b) either party may apply to enforce those terms without the need for a new claim.

(3) If a Part 36 offer nr a Part 36 payment which relates to part only of the claim is accepted—

(a) the claim will be stayed to that part; and
(b) unless the parties have agreed costs, the liability for costs shall be decided by the court.

(4) If the approval of the court is required before a settlement can be binding, any stay! which would otherwise arise on the acceptance of a Part 36 offer or a Part 36 payment will take effect only when that approval has been given.

(5) Any stay arising under this rule will not affect the power of the court—

(a) to enforce the terms of a Part 36 offer;
(b) to deal with any question of costs (including interest on costs) relating to the proceedings;
(c) to order payment out of court of any sum paid into court.

(6) Where—
    (a) a Part 36 offer has been accepted; and
    (b) a party alleges that—
        (i) the other party has not honoured the terms of the offer; and
        (ii) he is therefore entitled to a remedy for breach of contract,

the party may claim the remedy by applying to the court without the need to start a new claim unless the court orders otherwise.

Payment out of a sum in court on the acceptance of a Part 36 payment

36.16 Where a Part 36 payment is accepted the claimant obtains payment out of the sum in court by making a request for payment in the practice form.

Acceptance of a Part 36 offer or a Part 36 payment made by one or more, but not all, defendants

36.17 (1) This rule applies where the claimant wishes to accept a Part 36 offer or a Part 36 payment made by one or more, but not all, of a number of defendants.

(2) If the defendants are sued jointly or in the alternative, the claimant may accept the offer or payment without needing the permission of the court in accordance with rule 36.11(1) if—
    (a) he discontinues his claim against those defendants who have not made the offer or payment; and
    (b) those defendants give written consent to the acceptance of the offer or payment.

(3) If the claimant alleges that the defendants have a several liability to him the claimant may—
    (a) accept the offer or payment in accordance with rule 36.11(1); and
    (b) continue with his claims against the other defendants if he is entitled to do so.

(4) In all other cases the claimant must apply to the court for—

(a) an order permitting a payment out to him of any sum in court; and
(b) such order as to costs as the court considers appropriate.

Other cases where a court order is required to enable acceptance of a Part 36 offer or a Part 36 payment

36.18 (1) Where a Part 36 offer or a Part 36 payment is made in proceedings to which rule 21.10 applies—

(a) the offer or payment may be accepted only with the permission of the court; and
(b) no payment out of any sum in court shall be made without a court order.

(Rule 21.10 deals with compromise etc. by or on behalf of a child or patient)

(2) Where the court gives a claimant permission to accept a Part 36 offer or payment after the trial has started—

(a) any money in court may be paid out only with a court order; and
(b) the court must, in the order, deal with the whole costs of the proceedings.

(3) Where a claimant accepts a Part 36 payment after a defence of tender before claim has been put forward by the defendant, the money in court may be paid out only after an order of the court.

(Rule 37.3 requires a defendant who wishes to rely on a defence of tender before claim to make a payment into court)

Restriction on disclosure of a Part 36 offer or a Part 36 payment

36.19 (1) A Part 36 offer will be treated as 'without prejudice except as to costs'.

(2) The fact that a Part 36 payment has been made shall not be communicated to the trial judge until all questions of liability and the amount of money to be awarded have been decided.

(3) Paragraph (2) does not apply—

(a) where the defence of tender before claim has been raised;
(b) where the proceedings have been stayed under rule 36.15 following acceptance of a Part 36 offer or Part 36 payment; or
(c) where—
  (i) the issue of liability has been determined before any assessment of the money claimed; and
  (ii) the fact that there has or has not been a Part 36 payment may be relevant to the question of the costs of the issue of liability.

Costs consequences where claimant fails to do better than a Part 36 offer or a Part 36 payment

36.20 (1) This rule applies where at trial a claimant—

(a) fails to better a Part 36 payment; or
(b) fails to obtain a judgment which is more advantageous than a defendant's Part 36 offer.

(2) Unless it considers it unjust to do so, the court will order the claimant to pay any costs incurred by the defendant after the latest date on which the payment or offer could have been accepted without needing the permission of the court.

(Rule 36.11 sets out the time for acceptance of a defendant's Part 36 offer or Part 36 payment)

Costs and other consequences where claimant does better than he proposed in his Part 36 offer

36.21 (1) This rule applies where at trial—

(a) a defendant is held liable for more; or
(b) the judgment against a defendant is more advantageous to the claimant,

than the proposals contained in a claimant's Part 36 offer.

(2) The court may order interest on the whole or part of any sum of money (excluding interest) awarded to

CONTENTIOUS PROBATE 379

the claimant at a rate not exceeding 10% above base rate for some or all of the period starting with the latest date on which the defendant could have accepted the offer without needing the permission of the court.

(3) The court may also order that the claimant is entitled to—

   (a) his costs on the indemnity basis from the latest date when the defendant could have accepted the offer without needing the permission of the court; and
   (b) interest on those costs at a rate not exceeding 10% above base rate.

(4) Where this rule applies, the court will make the orders referred to in paragraphs (2) and (3) unless it considers it unjust to do so.

(Rule 36.12 sets out the latest date when the defendant could have accepted the offer)

(5) In considering whether it would be unjust to make the orders referred to in paragraphs (2) and (3) above, the court will take into account all the circumstances of the case including—

   (a) the terms of any Part 36 offer;
   (b) the stage in the proceedings when any Part 36 offer or Part 36 payment was made;
   (c) the information available to the parties at the time when the Part 36 offer or Part 36 payment was made; and
   (d) the conduct of the parties with regard to the giving or refusing to give information for the purposes of enabling the offer or payment into court to be made or evaluated.

(6) Where the court awards interest under this rule and also awards interest on the same sum and for the same period under any other poyier, the total rate of interest may not exceed 10% above base rate.

Interest

36.22 (1) Unless—

   (a) a claimant's Part 36 offer which offers to accept a sum of money; or

(b) a Part 36 payment notice,

indicates to the contrary, any such offer or payment will be treated as inclusive of all interest until the last date on which it could be accepted without needing the permission of the court.

(2) Where a claimant's Part 36 offer or Part 36 payment notice is expressed not to be inclusive of interest, the offer or notice must state—

(a) whether interest is offered; and
(b) if so, the amount offered, the rate or rates offered and the period or periods for which it is offered.

Deduction of benefits

36.23 (1) This rule applies where a payment to a claimant following acceptance of a Part 36 offer or Part 36 payment into court would be a compensation payment as defined in s.1 of the Social Security (Recovery of Benefits) Act 1997.

(2) A defendant to a money claim may make an offer to settle the claim which will have the consequences set out in this Part, without making a Part 36 payment if—

(a) at the time he makes the offer he has applied for, but not received, a certificate of recoverable benefit; and
(b) he makes a Part 36 payment not more than 7 days after he receives the certificate.

(Section 1 of the 1997 Act defines 'recoverable benefit')

(3) A Part 36 payment notice must state—

(a) the amount of gross compensation;
(b) the name and amount of any benefit by which that gross amount is reduced in accordance with section 8 and Schedule 2 to the 1997 Act; and
(c) that the sum paid in is the net amount after deduction of the amount of benefit.

(4) For the purposes of rule 36.20, a claimant fails to better a Part 36 payment if he fails to obtain

judgment for more than the gross sum specified in the Part 36 payment notice.

(5) Where—

   (a) a Part 36 payment has been made; and
   (b) application is made for the money remaining in court to be paid out,

the court may treat the money in court as being reduced by a sum equivalent to any further recoverable benefits paid to the claimant since the date of payment into court and may direct payment out accordingly.

Part 43

Scope of this Part

43.1 This Part contains definitions and interpretation of certain matters set out in the rules about costs contained in Parts 44 to 48. **B–131**

(Part 44 contains general rules about costs; Part 45 deals with fixed costs; Part 46 deals with fast track trial costs; Part 47 deals with the detailed assessment of costs and related appeals and Part 48 deals with costs payable in special cases)

Definitions and application

43.2 (1) In Parts 44 to 48, unless the context otherwise requires—

   (a) 'costs' includes fees, charges, disbursements, expenses, remuneration, reimbursement allowed to a litigant in person under rule 48.6, any additional liability incurred under a funding arrangement and any fee or reward charged by a lay representative for acting on behalf of a party in proceedings allocated to the small claims track;
   (b) 'costs judge' means a taxing master of the Supreme Court;
   (c) 'costs officer' means —

　　　　(i) a costs judge;
　　　　(ii) a district judge; and
　　　　(iii) an authorised court officer;
　　(d) 'authorised court officer' means any officer of—
　　　　(i) a county court;
　　　　(ii) a district registry;
　　　　(iii) the Principal Registry of the Family Division; or
　　　　(iv) the Supreme Court Costs Office, whom the Lord Chancellor has authorised to assess costs.
　　(e) 'fund' includes any estate or property held for the benefit of any person or class of person and any fund to which a trustee or personal representative is entitled in his capacity as such;
　　(f) 'receiving party' means a party entitled to be paid costs;
　　(g) 'paying party' means a party liable to pay costs;
　　(h) 'assisted person' means an assisted person within the statutory provisions relating to legal aid;
　　(i) 'LSC funded client' means an individual who receives services funded by the Legal Services Commission as part of the Community Legal Service within the meaning of Part I of the Access to Justice Act 1999;
　　(j) 'fixed costs' means the amounts which are to be allowed in respect of solicitors' charges in the circumstances set out in Section I of Part 45.
　　(k) 'funding arrangement' means an arrangement where a person has —
　　　　(i) entered into a conditional fee agreement or a collective conditional fee agreement which provides for a success fee within the meaning of section 58(2) of the Courts and Legal Services Act 1990;
　　　　(ii) taken out an insurance policy to which section 29 of the Access to Justice Act 1999 (recovery of insurance premiums by way of costs) applies; or
　　　　(iii) made an agreement with a membership organisation to meet his legal costs;
　　(l) 'percentage increase' means the percentage by which the amount of a legal representative's fee

can be increased in accordance with a conditional fee agreement which provides for a success fee;

(m) 'insurance premium' means a sum of money paid or payable for insurance against the risk of incurring a costs liability in the proceedings, taken out after the event that is the subject matter of the claim;

(n) 'membership organisation' means a body prescribed for the purposes of section 30 of the Access to Justice Act 1999 (recovery where body undertakes to meet costs liabilities); and

(o) 'additional liability' means the percentage increase, the insurance premium, or the additional amount in respect of provision made by a membership organisation, as the case may be.

(2) The costs to which Parts 44 to 48 apply include —

(a) the following costs where those costs may be assessed by the court —

(i) costs of proceedings before an arbitrator or umpire;
(ii) costs of proceedings before a tribunal or other statutory body; and
(iii) costs payable by a client to his solicitor; and

(b) costs which are payable by one party to another party under the terms of a contract, where the court makes an order for an assessment of those costs.

(3) Where advocacy or litigation services are provided to a client under a conditional fee agreement, costs are recoverable under Parts 44 to 48 notwithstanding that the client is liable to pay his legal representative's fees and expenses only to the extent that sums are recovered in respect of the proceedings, whether by way of costs or otherwise.

(4) In paragraph (3), the reference to a conditional fee agreement is to an agreement which satisfies all the conditions applicable to it by virtue of section 58 of the Courts and Legal Services Act 1990.

Meaning of summary assessment

43.3 'Summary assessment' means the procedure by which the court, when making an order about costs, orders payment of a sum of money instead of fixed costs or 'detailed assessment'.

Meaning of detailed assessment

43.4 'Detailed assessment' means the procedure by which the amount of costs is decided by a costs officer in accordance with Part 47.

Part 44

Scope of this Part

B–132 44.1 This Part contains general rules about costs and entitlement to costs.

(The definitions contained in Part 43 are relevant to this Part)

Solicitor's duty to notify client

44.2 Where—

(a) the court makes a costs order against a legally represented party; and
(b) the party is not present when the order is made,

the party's solicitor must notify his client in writing of the costs order no later than 7 days after the solicitor receives notice of the order.

Court's discretion and circumstances to be taken into account when exercising its discretion as to costs

44.3 (1) The court has discretion as to—

(a) whether costs are payable by one party to another;
(b) the amount of those costs; and

(c) when they are to be paid.

(2) If the court decides to make an order about costs—
 (a) the general rule is that the unsuccessful party will be ordered to pay the costs of the successful party; but
 (b) the court may make a different order.

(3) The general rule does not apply to the following proceedings—
 (a) proceedings in the Court of Appeal on an application or appeal made in connection with proceedings in the Family Division; or
 (b) proceedings in the Court of Appeal from a judgment, direction, decision or order given or made in probate proceedings or family proceedings.

(4) In deciding what order (if any) to make about costs, the court must have regard to all the circumstances, including—
 (a) the conduct of all the parties;
 (b) whether a party has succeeded on part of his case, even if he has not been wholly successful; and
 (c) any payment into court or admissible offer to settle made by a party which is drawn to the court's attention (whether or not made in accordance with Part 36).

(Part 36 contains further provisions about how the court's discretion is to be exercised where a payment into court or an offer to settle is made under that Part)

(5) The conduct of the parties includes—
 (a) conduct before, as well as during, the proceedings and in particular the extent to which the parties followed any relevant pre-action protocol;
 (b) whether it was reasonable for a party to raise, pursue or contest a particular allegation or issue;
 (c) the manner in which a party has pursued or defended his case or a particular allegation or issue; and
 (d) whether a claimant who has succeeded in his claim, in whole or in part, exaggerated his claim.

(6) The orders which the court may make under this rule include an order that a party must pay—

   (a) a proportion of another party's costs;
   (b) a stated amount in respect of another party's costs;
   (c) costs from or until a certain date only;
   (d) costs incurred before proceedings have begun;
   (e) costs relating to particular steps taken in the proceedings;
   (f) costs relating only to a distinct part of the proceedings; and
   (g) interest on costs from or until a certain date, including a date before judgment.

(7) Where the court would otherwise consider making an order under paragraph (6)(f), it must instead, if practicable, make an order under paragraph (6)(a) or (c).

(8) Where the court has ordered a party to pay costs, it may order an amount to be paid on account before the costs are assessed.

(9) Where a party entitled to costs is also liable to pay costs the court may assess the costs which that party is liable to pay and either—

   (a) set off the amount assessed against the amount the party is entitled to be paid and direct him to pay any balance; or
   (b) delay the issue of a certificate for the costs to which the party is entitled until he has paid the amount which he is liable to pay.

Costs orders relating to funding arrangements

44.3A (1) The court will not assess any additional liability until the conclusion of the proceedings, or the part of the proceedings, to which the funding arrangement relates.

('Funding arrangement' and 'additional liability' are defined in rule 43.2)

(2) At the conclusion of the proceedings, or the part of the proceedings, to which the funding arrangement relates the court may—

(a) make a summary assessment of all the costs, including any additional liability;
(b) make an order for detailed assessment of the additional liability but make a summary assessment of the other costs; or
(c) make an order for detailed assessment of all the costs.

(Part 47 sets out the procedure for the detailed assessment of costs)

Limits on recovery under funding arrangements

44.3B (1) A party may not recover as an additional liability—

(a) any proportion of the percentage increase relating to the cost to the legal representative of the postponement of the payment of his fees and expenses;
(b) any provision made by a membership organisation which exceeds — the likely cost to that party of the premium of an insurance policy against the risk of incurring a liability to pay the costs of other parties to the proceedings;
(c) any additional liability for any period in the proceedings during which he failed to provide information about a funding arrangement in accordance with a rule, practice direction or court order;
(d) any percentage increase where a party has failed to comply with

(i) a requirement in the costs practice direction; or
(ii) a court order,

to disclose in any assessment proceedings the reasons for setting the percentage increase at the level stated in the conditional fee agreement.

(2) This rule does not apply in an assessment under rule 48.9 (assessment of a solicitor's bill to his client).

(Rule 3.9 sets out the circumstances the court will consider on an application for relief from a sanction for failure to comply with any rule, practice direction or court order)

Basis of assessment

44.4 (1) Where the court is to assess the amount of costs (whether by summary or detailed assessment) it will assess those costs—

(a) on the standard basis; or
(b) on the indemnity basis,

but the court will not in either case allow costs which have been unreasonably incurred or are unreasonable in amount.

(Rule 48.3 sets out how the court decides the amount of costs payable under a contract)

(2) Where the amount of costs is to be assessed on the standard basis, the court will—

(a) only allow costs which are proportionate to the matters in issue; and
(b) resolve any doubt which it may have as to whether costs were reasonably incurred or reasonable and proportionate in amount in favour of the paying party.

(Factors which the court may take into account are set out in rule 44.5)

(3) Where the amount of costs is to be assessed on the indemnity basis, the court will resolve any doubt which it may have as to whether costs were reasonably incurred or were reasonable in amount in favour of the receiving party.

(4) Where—

(a) the court makes an order about costs without indicating the basis on which the costs are to be assessed; or
(b) the court makes an order for costs to be assessed on a basis other than the standard basis or the indemnity basis, the costs will be assessed on the standard basis.

(6) Where the amount of a solicitor's remuneration in respect of non-contentious business is regulated by any general orders made under the Solicitors Act 1974 the amount of the costs to be allowed in respect of any such business which falls to be

assessed by the court will be decided in accordance with those general orders rather than this rule and rule 44.5.

Factors to be taken into account in deciding the amount of costs

44.5 (1) The court is to have regard to all the circumstances in deciding whether costs were—

(a) if it is assessing costs on the standard basis—

(i) proportionately and reasonably incurred; or
(ii) were proportionate and reasonable in amount, or

(b) if it is assessing costs on the indemnity basis—

(i) unreasonably incurred; or—
(ii) unreasonable in amount.

(2) In particular the court must give effect to any orders which have already been made.

(3) The court must also have regard to—

(a) the conduct of all the parties, including in particular—

(i) conduct before, as well as during, the proceedings; and
(ii) the efforts made, if any, before and during the proceedings in order to try to resolve the dispute;

(b) the amount or value of any money or property involved;
(c) the importance of the matter to all the parties;
(d) the particular complexity of the matter or the difficulty or novelty of the questions raised;
(e) the skill, effort, specialised knowledge and responsibility involved;
(f) the time spent on the case; and
(g) the place where and the circumstances in which work or any part of it was done.

(Rule 35.4(4) gives the court power to limit the amount that a party may recover with regard to the fees and expenses of an expert)

Fixed costs

44.6   A party may recover the fixed costs specified in Part 45 in accordance with that Part.

Procedure for assessing costs

44.7   Where the court orders a party to pay costs to another party (other than fixed costs) it may either—

(a) make a summary assessment of the costs; or
(b) order detailed assessment of the costs by a costs officer,

unless any rule, practice direction or other enactment provides otherwise.

(The costs practice direction sets out the factors which will affect the court's decision under this rule)

Time for complying with an order for costs

44.8   A party must comply with an order for the payment of costs within 14 days of—

(a) the date of the judgment or order if it states the amount of those costs;
(b) if the amount of those costs (or part of them) is decided later in accordance with Part 47, the date of the certificate which states the amount; or
(c) in either case, such later date as the court may specify.

(Part 47 sets out the procedure for detailed assessment of costs)

. . . . . .

Costs following allocation and re-allocation

44.11 (1)   Any costs orders made before a claim is allocated will not be affected by allocation.

(2)   Where —

(a) a claim is allocated to a track; and

CONTENTIOUS PROBATE 391

(b) the court subsequently re-allocates that claim to a different track,

then unless the court orders otherwise, any special rules about costs applying—

(i) to the first track, will apply to the claim up to the date of re-allocation; and
(ii) to the second track, will apply from the date of re-allocation.

(Part 26 deals with the allocation and re-allocation of claims between tracks

Cases where costs orders deemed to have been made

44.12 (1) Where a right to costs arises under—

(a) rule 3.7 (defendant's right to costs where claim struck out for non-payment of fees);
(b) rule 36.13(1) (claimant's right to costs where he accepts defendant's Part 36 offer or Part 36 payment);
(c) rule 36.14 (claimant's right to costs where defendant accepts the claimant's Part 36 offer); or
(d) rule 38.6 (defendant's right to costs where claimant discontinues),

a costs order will be deemed to have been made on the standard basis.

(2) Interest payable pursuant to s.17 of the Judgments Act 1838 or section 74 of the County Courts Act 1984 on the costs deemed we have been ordered under paragraph (1) shall begin to run from the date on which the event which gave rise to the entitlement to costs occurred.

Costs-only proceedings

44.12A(1) This rule sets out a procedure which may be followed where—

(a) the parties to a dispute have reached an agreement on all issues (including which party is to pay the costs) which is made or confirmed in writing; but

(b) they have failed to agree the amount of those costs; and
(c) no proceedings have been started.

(2) Either party to the agreement may start proceedings under this rule by issuing a claim form in accordance with Part 8.

(3) The claim form must contain or be accompanied by the agreement or confirmation.

(4) In proceedings to which this rule applies the court—

(a) may

(i) make an order for costs to be determined by detailed assessment; or
(ii) dismiss the claim; and

(b) must dismiss the claim if it is opposed.

(5) Rule 48.3 (amount of costs where costs are payable pursuant to a contract) does not apply to claims started under the procedure in this rule. (Rule 7.2 provides that proceedings are started when the court issues a claim form at the request of the claimant)

(Rule 8.1(6) provides that a practice direction may modify the Part 8 procedure)

Special situations

44.13(1) Where the court makes an order which does not mention costs—

(a) the general rule is that no party is entitled to costs in relation to that order; but
(b) this does not affect any entitlement of a party to recover costs out of a fund held by him as trustee or personal representative, or pursuant to any lease, mortgage or other security.

(2) The court hearing an appeal may, unless it dismisses the appeal, make orders about the costs of the proceedings giving rise to the appeal as well as the costs of the appeal.

(3) Where proceedings are transferred from one court to another, the court to which they are transferred may deal with all the costs, including the costs before the transfer.

(4) Paragraph (3) is subject to any order of the court which ordered the transfer.

Court's powers in relation to misconduct

44.14 (1) The court may make an order under this rule where—

    (a) a party or his legal representative, in connection with a summary or detailed assessment, fails to comply with a rule, practice direction or court order; or

    (b) it appears to the court that the conduct of a party or his legal representative, before or during the proceedings which gave rise to the assessment proceedings, was unreasonable or improper.

(2) Where paragraph (1) applies, the court may—

    (a) disallow all or part of the costs which are being assessed; or

    (b) order the party at fault or his legal representative to pay costs which he has caused any other party to incur.

(3) Where—

    (a) the court makes an order under paragraph (2) against a legally represented party; and

    (b) the party is not present when the order is made,

the party's solicitor must notify his client in writing of the order no later than 7 days after the solicitor receives notice of the order.

Providing information about funding arrangements

44.15 (1) A party who seeks to recover an additional liability must provide information about the funding arrangement to the court and to other parties as required by a rule, practice direction or court order.

(2) Where the funding arrangement has changed, and the information a party has previously provided in accordance with paragraph (1) is no longer accurate, that party must file notice of the change and serve it on all other parties within 7 days.

(3) Where paragraph (2) applies, and a party has already filed—

    (a) an allocation questionnaire; or
    (b) a pre-trial check list (listing questionnaire)

he must file and serve a new estimate of costs with the notice.

(The costs practice direction sets out—

- the information to be provided when a party issues or responds to a claim form, files an allocation questionnaire, a pre-trial check list, and a claim for costs;
- the meaning of estimate of costs and the information required in it)

(Rule 44.3B sets out situations where a party will not recover a sum representing any additional liability)

Adjournment where legal representative seeks to challenge disallowance of any amount of percentage increase

44.16 Where—

    (a) the court disallows any amount of a legal representative's percentage increase in summary or detailed assessment proceedings; and
    (b) the legal representative applies for an order that the disallowed amount should continue to be payable by his client,

the court may adjourn the hearing to allow the client to be—

    (i) notified of the order sought; and
    (ii) separately represented.

(Regulation 3(2)(b) of the Conditional Fee Agreements Regulations 2000 provides that a conditional fee agreement which provides for a success fee must state that any amount of a percentage increase disallowed on assessment ceases to be payable unless the court is satisfied that it should continue to be so payable. Regulation 5(2)(b) of the Collective Conditional Fee Agreements Regulations 2000 makes similar provision in relation to collective conditional fee agreements).

Application of costs rules

44.17 This Part and Part 45 (fixed costs), Part 46 (fast track trial costs), Part 47 (procedure for detailed assessment of costs and default provisions) and Part 48 (special cases), do not apply to the assessment of costs in proceedings to the extent that—

(a) section 11 of the Access to Justice Act 1999, and provisions made under that Act, or
(b) regulations made under the Legal Aid Act 1988

make different provision. (The costs practice direction sets out the procedure to be followed where a party was wholly or partially funded by the Legal Services Commission).

Part 48

Pre-commencement disclosure and orders for disclosure against a person who is not a party

48.1 (1) This paragraph applies where a person applies—   **B–133**

(a) for an order under—

(i) section 33 of the Supreme Court Act 1981; or
(ii) section 52 of the County Courts Act 1984,

(which give the court powers exercisable before commencement of proceedings); or

(b) for an order under—

(i) section 34 of the Supreme Court Act 1981; or
(ii) section 53 of the County Courts Act 1984,

(which give the court power to make an order against a non-party for disclosure of documents, inspection of property etc.).

(2) The general rule is that the court will award the person against whom the order is sought his costs—

(a) of the application; and
(b) of complying with any order made on the application.

(3) The court may however make a different order, having regard to all the circumstances, including—

    (a) the extent to which it was reasonable for the person against whom the order was sought to oppose the application; and

    (b) whether the parties to the application have complied with any relevant pre-action protocol.

Costs orders in favour of or against non-parties

48.2 (1) Where the court is considering whether to exercise its power under section 51 of the Supreme Court Act 1981((costs are in the discretion of the court) to make a costs order in favour of or against a person who is not a party to proceedings—

    (a) that person must be added as a party to the proceedings for the purposes of costs only; and

    (b) he must be given a reasonable opportunity to attend a hearing at which the court will consider the matter further.

(2) This rule does not apply—

    (a) where the court is considering whether to—

        (i) make an order against the Legal Services Commission;

        (ii) make a wasted costs order (as defined in 48.7), and

    (b) in proceedings to which rule 48.1 applies (pre-commencement disclosure and orders for disclosure against a person who is not a party).

Amount of costs where costs are payable pursuant to a contract

48.3 (1) Where the court assesses (whether by the summary or detailed procedure) costs which are payable by the paying party to the receiving party under the terms of a contract, the costs payable under those terms are, unless the contract expressly provides otherwise, to be presumed to be costs which—

    (a) have been reasonably incurred; and

    (b) are reasonable in amount, and the court will assess them accordingly.

(The costs practice direction sets out circumstances where the court may order otherwise)

(2) This rule does not apply where the contract is between a solicitor and his client.

Limitations on court's power to award costs in favour of trustee or personal representative

48.4 (1) This rule applies where—

(a) a person is or has been a party to any proceedings in the capacity of trustee or personal representative; and

(b) rule 48.3 does not apply.

(2) The general rule is that he is entitled to be paid the costs of those proceedings, insofar as they are not recovered from or paid by any other person, out of the relevant trust fund or estate.

(3) Where he is entitled to be paid any of those costs out of the fund or estate, those costs will be assessed on the indemnity basis.

Costs where money is payable by or to a child or patient

48.5 (1) This rule applies to any proceedings where a party is a child or patient and

(a) money is ordered or agreed to be paid to, or for the benefit of, that party; or

(b) money is ordered to be paid by him or on his behalf.

('Child' and 'patient' are defined in rule 2.3)

(2) The general rule is that—

(a) the court must order a detailed assessment of the costs payable by any party who is a child or patient to his solicitor; and

(b) on an assessment under paragraph (a), the court must also assess any costs payable to that party in the proceedings, unless the court has issued a default costs certificate in relation to those costs under rule 47.11.

(3) The court need not order detailed assessment of costs in the circumstances set out in the costs practice direction.

(4) Where—
- (a) a claimant is a child or patient; and
- (b) a detailed assessment has taken place under paragraph (2)(a), the only amount payable by the child or patient to his solicitor is the amount which the court certifies as payable.

(This rule applies to a counterclaim by or on behalf of a child or patient by virtue of rule 20.3)

Litigants in person

48.6 (1) This rule applies where the court orders (whether by summary assessment or detailed assessment) that the costs of a litigant in person are to be paid by any other person.

(2) The costs allowed under this rule must not exceed, except in the case of a disbursement, two-thirds of the amount which would have been allowed if the litigant in person had been represented by a legal representative.

(3) The litigant in person shall be allowed—
- (a) costs for the same categories of—
    - (i) work; and
    - (ii) disbursements,

    which would have been allowed if the work had been done or the disbursements had been made by a legal representative on the litigant in person's behalf;
- (b) the payments reasonably made by him for legal services relating to the conduct of the proceedings; and
- (c) the costs of obtaining expert assistance in assessing the costs claim.

(4) The amount of costs to be allowed to the litigant in person for any item of work claimed shall be—
- (a) where the litigant can prove financial loss, the amount that he can prove he has lost for time reasonably spent on doing the work; or
- (b) where the litigant cannot prove financial loss, an amount for the time reasonably spent on

doing the work at the rate set out in the practice direction.

(5) A litigant who is allowed costs for attending at court to conduct his case is not entitled to a witness allowance in respect of such attendance in addition to those costs.

(6) For the purposes of this rule, a litigant in person includes—

(a) a company or other corporation which is acting without a legal representative; and
(b) a barrister, solicitor, solicitor's employee or other authorised litigator (as defined in the Courts and Legal Services Act 1990(i) who is acting for himself.

Part 52

Scope and interpretation

52.1 (1) The rules in this Part apply to appeals to—

(a) the civil division of the Court of Appeal;
(b) the High Court; and
(c) a county court.

(2) This Part does not apply to an appeal in detailed assessment proceedings against a decision of an authorised court officer.

(Rules 47.21 to 47.26 deal with appeals against a decision of an authorised court officer in detailed assessment proceedings)

(3) In this Part—

(a) 'appeal' includes an appeal by way of case stated;
(b) 'appeal court' means the court to which an appeal is made;
(c) 'lower court' means the court, tribunal or other person or body from whose decision an appeal is brought;
(d) 'appellant' means a person who brings or seeks to bring an appeal;
(e) 'respondent' means—

(i) a person other than the appellant who was a party to the proceedings in the lower court and who is affected by the appeal; and

(ii) a person who is permitted by the appeal court to be a party to the appeal; and

(f) 'appeal notice' means an appellant's or respondent's notice.

(4) This Part is subject to any rule, enactment or practice direction which sets out special provisions with regard to any particular category of appeal.

Parties to comply with the practice direction

52.2 All parties to an appeal must comply with the relevant practice direction.

Permission

52.3 (1) An appellant or respondent requires permission to appeal—

(a) where the appeal is from a decision of a judge in a county court or the High Court, except where the appeal is against—

(i) a committal order;
(ii) a refusal to grant habeas corpus; or
(iii) a secure accommodation order made under section 25 of the Children Act 1989; or

(b) as provided by the relevant practice direction.

(Other enactments may provide that permission is required for particular appeals)

(2) An application for permission to appeal may be made—

(a) to the lower court at the hearing at which the decision to be appealed was made; or
(b) to the appeal court in an appeal notice.

(Rule 52.4 sets out the time limits for filing an appellant's notice at the appeal court. Rule 52.5 sets out the time limits for filing a respondent's notice at the appeal court. Any application for permission to appeal to the appeal court must be made in the appeal notice (see rules 52.4(1) and 52.5(3))

(Rule 52.13(1) provides that permission is required from the Court of Appeal for all appeals to that court from a decision of a county court or the High Court which was itself made on appeal)

    (3) Where the lower court refuses an application for permission to appeal, a further application for permission to appeal may be made to the appeal court.

    (4) Where the appeal court, without a hearing, refuses permission to appeal, the person seeking permission may request the decision to be reconsidered at a hearing.

    (5) A request under paragraph (4) must be filed within 7 days after service of the notice that permission has been refused.

    (6) Permission to appeal will only be given where—

        (a) the court considers that the appeal would have a real prospect of success; or
        (b) there is some other compelling reason why the appeal should be heard.

    (7) An order giving permission may—

        (a) limit the issues to be heard; and
        (b) be made subject to conditions.

(Rule 3.1(3) also provides that the court may make an order subject to conditions)
(Rule 25.15 provides for the court to order security for costs of an appeal)

Appellant's notice

52.4 (1) Where the appellant seeks permission from the appeal court it must be requested in the appellant's notice.

    (2) The appellant must file the appellant's notice at the appeal court within—

        (a) such period as may be directed by the lower court; or
        (b) where the court makes no such direction, 14 days after the date of the decision of the lower court that the appellant wishes to appeal.

(3) Unless the appeal court orders otherwise, an appeal notice must be served on each respondent—

    (a) as soon as practicable; and
    (b) in any event not later than 7 days,

after it is filed.

Respondent's notice

52.5 (1) A respondent may file and serve a respondent's notice.

(2) A respondent who—

    (a) is seeking permission to appeal from the appeal court; or
    (b) wishes to ask the appeal court to uphold the order of the lower court for reasons different from or additional to those given by the lower court,

must file a respondent's notice.

(3) Where the respondent seeks permission from the appeal court it must be requested in the respondent's notice.

(4) A respondent's notice must be filed within—

    (a) such period as may be directed by the lower court; or
    (b) where the court makes no such direction, 14 days after the date in paragraph (5).

(5) The date referred to in paragraph (4) is—

    (a) the date the respondent is served with the appellant's notice where—

        (i) permission to appeal was given by the lower court; or
        (ii) permission to appeal is not required;

    (b) the date the respondent is served with notification that the appeal court has given the appellant permission to appeal; or
    (c) the date the respondent is served with notification that the application for permission to appeal and the appeal itself are to be heard together.

(6) Unless the appeal court orders otherwise a respondent's notice must be served on the appellant and any other respondent—

(a) as soon as practicable; and
(b) in any event not later than 7 days,

after it is filed.

Variation of time

52.6 (1) An application to vary the time limit for filing an appeal notice must be made to the appeal court.

(2) The parties may not agree to extend any date or time limit set by—

(a) these Rules;
(b) the relevant practice direction; or
(c) an order of the appeal court or the lower court.

(Rule 3.1(2)(a) provides that the court may extend or shorten the time for compliance with any rule, practice direction or court order (even if an application for extension is made after the time for compliance has expired))
(Rule 3.1(2)(b) provides that the court may adjourn or bring forward a hearing)

Stay

52.7 Unless—

(a) the appeal court or the lower court orders otherwise; or
(b) the appeal is from the Immigration Appeal Tribunal,

an appeal shall not operate as a stay of any order or decision of the lower court.

Amendment of appeal notice

52.8 An appeal notice may not be amended without the permission of the appeal court.

Striking out appeal notices and setting aside or imposing conditions on permission to appeal

52.9 (1) The appeal court may—

(a) strike out the whole or part of an appeal notice;
(b) set aside permission to appeal in whole or in part;
(c) impose or vary conditions upon which an appeal may be brought.

(2) The court will only exercise its powers under paragraph (1) where there is a compelling reason for doing so.

(3) Where a party was present at the hearing at which permission was given he may not subsequently apply for an order that the court exercise its powers under sub-paragraphs (1)(b) or (1)(c).

Appeal court's powers

52.10 (1) In relation to an appeal the appeal court has all the powers of the lower court.

(Rule 52.1(4) provides that this Part is subject to any enactment that sets out special provisions with regard to any particular category of appeal — where such an enactment gives a statutory power to a tribunal, person or other body it may be the case that the appeal court may not exercise that power on an appeal)

(2) The appeal court has power to—

(a) affirm, set aside or vary any order or judgment made or given by the lower court;—
(b) refer any claim or issue for determination by the lower court;
(c) order a new trial or hearing;
(d) make orders for the payment of interest;
(e) make a costs order.

(3) In an appeal from a claim tried with a jury the Court of Appeal may, instead of ordering a new trial—

(a) make an order for damages; or
(b) vary an award of damages made by the jury.

(4) The appeal court may exercise its powers in relation to the whole or part of an order of the lower court.

(Part 3 contains general rules about the court's case management powers)

Hearing of appeals

52.11 (1) Every appeal will be limited to a review of the decision of the lower court unless—

(a) a practice direction makes different provision for a particular category of appeal; or
(b) the court considers that in the circumstances of an individual appeal it would be in the interests of justice to hold a re-hearing.

(2) Unless it orders otherwise, the appeal court will not receive—

(a) oral evidence; or
(b) evidence which was not before the lower court.

(3) The appeal court will allow an appeal where the decision of the lower court was—

(a) wrong; or
(b) unjust because of a serious procedural or other irregularity in the proceedings in the lower court.

(4) The appeal court may draw any inference of fact which it considers justified on the evidence.

(5) At the hearing of the appeal a party may not rely on a matter not contained in his appeal notice unless the appeal court gives permission.

Non-disclosure of Part 36 offers and payments

52.12 (1) The fact that a Part 36 offer or Part 36 payment has been made must not be disclosed to any judge of the appeal court who is to hear and finally determine an appeal until all questions (other than costs) have been determined.

(2) Paragraph (1) does not apply if the Part 36 offer or Part 36 payment is relevant to the substance of the appeal.

(3) Paragraph (1) does not prevent disclosure in any application in the appeal proceedings if disclosure of

the fact that a Part 36 offer or Part 36 payment has been made is properly relevant to the matter to be decided.

Part 57

I Probate claims

General

B–135 57.2 (1) This Section contains rules about probate claims.

(2) Probate claims in the High Court are assigned to the Chancery Division.

(3) Probate claims in the county court must only be brought in—

  (a) a county court where there is also a Chancery district registry;
  (b) the Central London County Court.

(4) All probate claims are allocated to the multi-track.

How to start a probate claim

57.3 A probate claim must be commenced—

  (a) in the relevant office; and
  (b) using the procedure in Part 7.

Acknowledgment of Service and Defence

57.4 (1) A defendant who is served with a claim form must file an acknowledgment of service.

(2) Subject to paragraph (3), the period for filing an acknowledgment of service is—

  (a) if the defendant is served with a claim form which states that particulars of claim are to follow, 28 days after service of the particulars of claim; and
  (b) in any other case, 28 days after service of the claim form.

(3) If the claim form is served out of the jurisdiction under rule 6.19, the period for filing an acknowledgment of service is 14 days longer than the relevant

period specified in rule 6.22 or the practice direction supplementing Section 3 of Part 6.

(4) Rule 15(4) (which provides the period for filing a defence) applies as if the words 'under Part 10' were omitted from rule 15.4(1)(b).

Lodging of testamentary documents and filing of evidence about testamentary documents

57.5 (1) Any testamentary document of the deceased person in the possession or control of any party must be lodged with the court.

(2) Unless the court directs otherwise, the testamentary documents must be lodged in the relevant office—

(a) by the claimant when the claim form is issued; and

(b) by a defendant when he acknowledges service.

(3) The claimant and every defendant who acknowledges service of the claim form must in written evidence—

(a) describe any testamentary document of the deceased of which he has any knowledge or, if he does not know of any such testamentary document, state that fact, and

(b) if any testamentary document of which he has knowledge is not in his possession or under his control, give the name and address of the person in whose possession or under whose control it is or, if he does not know the name or address of that person, state that fact.

(A specimen form for the written evidence about testamentary documents is annexed to the practice direction.)

(4) Unless the court directs otherwise, the written evidence required by paragraph (3) must be filed in the relevant office—

(a) by the claimant, when the claim form is issued; and

(b) by a defendant when he acknowledges service.

(5) Except with the permission of the court, a party shall not be allowed to inspect the testamentary documents or written evidence lodged or filed by any

other party until he himself has lodged his testamentary documents and filed his evidence.

(6) The provisions of paragraphs (2) and (4) may be modified by a practice direction under this Part.

Revocation of existing grant

57.6 (1) In a probate claim which seeks the revocation of a grant of probate or letters of administration every person who is entitled, or claims to be entitled, to administer the estate under that grant must be made a party to the claim.

(2) If the claimant is the person to whom the grant was made, he must lodge the probate or letters of administration in the relevant office when the claim form is issued.

(3) If a defendant has the probate or letters of administration under his control, he must lodge it in the relevant office when he acknowledges service.

(4) Paragraphs (2) and (3) do not apply where the grant has already been lodged at the court, which in this paragraph includes the Principal Registry of the Family Division or a district probate registry.

Contents of statements of case

57.7 (1) The claim form must contain a statement of the nature of the interest of the claimant and of each defendant in the estate.

(2) If a party disputes another party's interest in the estate he must state this in his statement of case and set out his reasons.

(3) Any party who contends that at the time when a will was executed the testator did not know of and approve its contents must give particulars of the facts and matters relied on.

(4) Any party who wishes to contend that—

(a) a will was not duly executed;
(b) at the time of the execution of a will the testator was not of sound mind, memory and understanding; or

(c) the execution of a will was obtained by undue influence or fraud,

must set out the contention specifically and give particulars of the facts and matters relied on.

(5) (a) A defendant may give notice in his defence that he does not raise any positive case, but insists on the will being proved in solemn form and, for that purpose, will cross-examine the witnesses who attested the will.
 (b) If a defendant gives such a notice, the court will not make an order for costs against him unless it considers that there was no reasonable ground for opposing the will.

Counterclaim

57.8 (1) A defendant who contends that he has any claim or is entitled to any remedy relating to the grant of probate of the will, or letters of administration of the estate, of the deceased person must serve a counterclaim making that contention.

(2) If the claimant fails to serve particulars of claim within the time allowed, the defendant may, with the permission of the court, serve a counterclaim and the probate claim shall then proceed as if the counterclaim were the particulars of claim.

Probate counterclaim in other proceedings

57.9 (1) In this rule 'probate counterclaim' means a counterclaim in any claim other than a probate claim by which the defendant claims any such remedy as is mentioned in rule 57.1(2)(a).

(2) Subject to the following paragraphs of this rule, this Part shall apply with the necessary modifications to a probate counterclaim as it applies to a probate claim.

(3) A probate counterclaim must contain a statement of the nature of the interest of each of the parties in the estate of the deceased to which the probate counterclaim relates.

(4) Unless an application notice is issued within 7 days after the service of a probate counterclaim for an order under rule 3.1(2)(e) or 3.4 for the probate counterclaim to be dealt with in separate proceedings or to be struck out, and the application is granted, the court shall order the transfer of the proceedings to either—

    (a) the Chancery Division (if it is not already assigned to that Division) and to either the Royal Courts of Justice or a Chancery district registry (if it is not already proceeding in one of those places); or

    (b) if the county court has jurisdiction, to a county court where there is also a Chancery district registry.

(5) If an order is made that a probate counterclaim be dealt with in separate proceedings, the order shall order the transfer of the probate counterclaim as required under paragraph (4).

Failure to acknowledge service or to file a defence

57.10 (1) A default judgment cannot be obtained in a probate claim and rule 10.2 and Part 12 do not apply.

(2) If any of several defendants fails to acknowledge service the claimant may—

    (a) after the time for acknowledging service has expired; and

    (b) upon filing written evidence of service of the claim form and (if no particulars of claim were contained in or served with the claim form) the particulars of claim on that defendant;

proceed with the probate claim as if that defendant had acknowledged service.

(3) If no defendant acknowledges service or files a defence then, unless on the application of the claimant the court orders the claim to be discontinued, the claimant may, after the time for acknowledging service or for filing a defence (as the case may be) has expired, apply to the court for an order that the claim is to proceed to trial.

(4) When making an application under paragraph (3) the claimant must file written evidence of service of the claim form and (if no particulars of claim were contained in or served with the claim form) the particulars of claim on each of the defendants.

(5) Where the court makes an order under paragraph (3), it may direct that the claim be tried on written evidence.

Discontinuance and dismissal

57.11 (1) Part 38 does not apply to probate claims.

(2) At any stage of a probate claim the court, on the application of the claimant or of any defendant who has acknowledged service, may order that—

(a) the claim be discontinued or dismissed on such terms as to costs or otherwise as it thinks just; and
(b) a grant of probate of the will, or letters of administration of the estate, of the deceased person be made to the person entitled to the grant.

II Rectification of wills

Rectification of Wills

57.12 (1) This Section contains rules about claims for the rectification of a will. **B–136**

(Section 20 of the Administration of Justice Act 1982 – provides for rectification of a will. Additional provisions are contained in rule 55 of the Non-Contentious Probate Rules 1987.)

(2) Every personal representative of the estate shall be joined as a party.

(3) The practice direction makes provision for lodging the grant of probate or letters of administration with the will annexed in a claim under this Section.

Part 57 Practice Direction

I Probate claims

General

B–137 1.1 This Section of this practice direction applies to contentious probate claims.
1.2 The rules and procedure relating to non-contentious probate proceedings (also known as 'common form') are the Non-Contentious Probate Rules 1987 as amended.

How to start a probate claim

2.1 A claim form and all subsequent court documents relating to a probate claim must be marked at the top 'In the estate of [*name*] deceased (Probate)'.
2.2 The claim form must be issued out of

- (1) Chancery Chambers at the Royal Courts of Justice; or
- (2) one of the Chancery district registries; or
- (3) if the claim is suitable to be heard in the county court—
  - (a) a county court in a place where there is also a Chancery district registry; or
  - (b) the Central London County Court.

There are Chancery district registries at Birmingham, Bristol, Cardiff, Leeds, Liverpool, Manchester, Newcastle upon Tyne and Preston.

(Section 32 of the County Courts Act 1984 identifies which probate claims may be heard in a county court.)

2.3 When the claim form is issued, the relevant office will send a notice to Leeds District Probate Registry, Coronet House, Queen Street, Leeds, LS1 2BA, DX 26451 Leeds (Park Square), telephone 0113 243 1505, requesting that all testamentary documents, grants of representation and other relevant documents currently held at any probate registry are sent to the relevant office.

2.4 The commencement of a probate claim will, unless a court otherwise directs, prevent any grant of probate or letters of administration being made until the probate claim has been disposed of.

(Rule 45 of the Non-Contentious Probate Rules 1987 makes provision for notice of the probate claim to be given, and section 117 of the Supreme Court Act 1981 for the grant of letters of administration pending the determination of a probate claim. Paragraph 8 of this practice direction makes provision about an application for such a grant.)

Testamentary documents and evidence about testamentary documents

3.1 Unless the court orders otherwise, if a testamentary document is held by the court (whether it was lodged by a party or it was previously held at a probate registry) when the claim has been disposed of the court will send it to the Leeds District Probate Registry.

3.2 The written evidence about testamentary documents required by this Part—

(1) should be in the form annexed to this practice direction; and

(2) must be signed by the party personally and not by his solicitor or other representative (except that if the party is a child or patient the written evidence must be signed by his litigation friend).

3.3 In a case in which there is urgent need to commence a probate claim (for example, in order to be able to apply immediately for the appointment of an administrator pending the determination of the claim) and it is not possible for the claimant to lodge the testamentary documents or to file the evidence about testamentary documents in the relevant office at the same time as the claim form is to be issued, the court may direct that the claimant shall be allowed to issue the claim form upon his giving an undertaking to the court to lodge the documents and file the evidence within such time as the court shall specify.

Case management

4 In giving case management directions in a probate claim the court will give consideration to the questions—

(1) whether any person who may be affected by the claim and who is not joined as a party should be joined as a party or given notice of the claim, whether under rule 19.8A or otherwise; and

(2) whether to make a representation order under rule 19.6 or rule 19.7.

Summary judgment

5.1 If an order pronouncing for a will in solemn form is sought on an application for summary judgment, the evidence in support of the application must include written evidence proving due execution of the will.

5.2 If a defendant has given notice in his defence under rule 57.7(5) that he raises no positive case but—

(1) he insists that the will be proved in solemn form; and

(2) for that purpose he will cross-examine the witnesses who attested the will;

any application by the claimant for summary judgment is subject to the right of that defendant to require those witnesses to attend court for cross-examination.

Settlement of a probate claim

6.1 If at any time the parties agree to settle a probate claim, the court may—

(1) order the trial of the claim on written evidence, which will lead to a grant in solemn form;

(2) order that the claim be discontinued or dismissed under rule 57.11, which will lead to a grant in common form; or

(3) pronounce for or against the validity of one or more wills under section 49 of the Administration of Justice Act 1985.

(For a form of order which is also applicable to discontinuance and which may be adapted as appropriate, see Practice Form No. CH38)

(Section 49 of the Administration of Justice Act 1985 permits a probate claim to be compromised without a trial if every 'relevant beneficiary', as defined in that section, has consented to the proposed order. It is only available in the High Court.)

6.2 Applications under section 49 of the Administration of Justice Act 1985 may be heard by a master or district judge and must be supported by written evidence identifying the relevant beneficiaries and exhibiting the written consent of each of them. The written evidence of testamentary documents required by rule 57.5 will still be necessary.

Application for an order to bring in a will, etc.

7.1 Any party applying for an order under section 122 of the Supreme Court Act 1981 ('the 1981 Act') must serve the application notice on the person against whom the order is sought.

(Section 122 of the 1981 Act empowers the court to order a person to attend court for examination, and to answer questions and bring in documents, if there are reasonable grounds for believing that such person has knowledge of a testamentary document. Rule 50(1) of the Non-Contentious Probate Rules 1987 makes similar provision where a probate claim has not been commenced.)

7.2 An application for the issue of a witness summons under section 123 of the 1981 Act—

(1) may be made without notice; and

(2) must be supported by written evidence setting out the grounds of the application.

(Section 123 of the 1981 Act empowers the court, where it appears that any person has in his possession, custody or power a testamentary document, to issue a witness summons ordering such person to bring in that document. Rule 50(2) of the Non-Contentious Probate Rules makes similar provision where a probate claim has not been commenced.)

7.3 An application under section 122 or 123 of the 1981 Act should be made to a master or district judge.

7.4 A person against whom a witness summons is issued under section 123 of the 1981 Act who denies that the testamentary document referred to in the witness summons is in his possession or under his control may file written evidence to that effect.

Administration pending the determination of a probate claim

8.1 An application under section 117 of the Supreme Court Act 1981 for an order for the grant of administration pending the determination of a probate claim should be made by application notice in the probate claim.

8.2 If an order for a grant of administration is made under section 117 of the 1981 Act—

(1) Rules 69.4 to 69.7 shall apply as if the administrator were a receiver appointed by the court;

(2) if the court allows the administrator remuneration under rule 69.7, it may make an order under section

117(3) of the 1981 Act assigning the remuneration out of the estate of the deceased; and

(3) every application relating to the conduct of the administration shall be made by application notice in the probate claim.

8.3 An order under section 117 may be made by a master or district judge.

8.4 If an order is made under section 117 an application for the grant of letters of administration should be made to the Principal Registry of the Family Division, First Avenue House, 42–49 High Holborn, London WC1V 6NP.

8.5 The appointment of an administrator to whom letters of administration are granted following an order under section 117 will cease automatically when a final order in the probate claim is made but will continue pending any appeal.

II Rectification of wills

Scope of this Section

B–138 9. This Section of this practice direction applies to claims for the rectification of a will.

Lodging the grant

10.1 If the claimant is the person to whom the grant was made in respect of the will of which rectification is sought, he must, unless the court orders otherwise, lodge the probate or letters of administration with the will annexed with the court when the claim form is issued.

10.2 If a defendant has the probate or letters of administration in his possession or under his control, he must, unless the court orders otherwise, lodge it in the relevant office within 14 days after the service of the claim form on him.

Orders

11.1 A copy of every order made for the rectification of a will shall be sent to the Principal Registry of the Family Division for filing, and a memorandum of the order shall be endorsed on, or permanently annexed to, the grant under which the estate is administered.

Pre-Action Behaviour in Other Cases

4.1 In cases not covered by any approved protocol, the court will expect the parties, in accordance with the overriding objective and the matters referred to in CPR 1.1(2)(a), (b) and (c), to act reasonably in exchanging information and documents relevant to the claim and generally in trying to avoid the necessity for the start of proceedings.

4.2 Parties to a potential dispute should follow a reasonable procedure, suitable to their particular circumstances, which is intended to avoid litigation. The procedure should not be regarded as a prelude to inevitable litigation. It should normally include—

(a) the claimant writing to give details of the claim;

(b) the defendant acknowledging the claim letter promptly;

(c) the defendant giving within a reasonable time a detailed written response; and

(d) the parties conducting genuine and reasonable negotiations with a view to settling the claim economically and without court proceedings.

4.3 The claimant's letter should—

(a) give sufficient concise details to enable the recipient to understand and investigate the claim without extensive further information;

(b) enclose copies of the essential documents which the claimant relies on;

(c) ask for a prompt acknowledgement of the letter, followed by a full written response within a reasonable stated period;
(For many claims, a normal reasonable period for a full response may be one month.)

(d) state whether court proceedings will be issued if the full response is not received within the stated period;

(e) identify and ask for copies of any essential documents, not in his possession, which the claimant wishes to see;

(f) state (if this is so) that the claimant wishes to enter into mediation or another alternative method of dispute resolution; and

(g) draw attention to the court's powers to impose sanctions for failure to comply with this practice direction and, if the recipient is likely to be unrepresented, enclose a copy of this practice direction.

4.4 The defendant should acknowledge the claimant's letter in writing within 21 days of receiving it. The acknowledgement should state when the defendant will give a full written response. If the time for this is longer than the period stated by the claimant, the defendant should give reasons why a longer period is needed.

4.5 The defendant's full written response should as appropriate—

(a) accept the claim in whole or in part and make proposals for settlement; or

(b) state that the claim is not accepted.

If the claim is accepted in part only, the response should make clear which part is accepted and which part is not accepted.

4.6 If the defendant does not accept the claim or part of it, the response should—

(a) give detailed reasons why the claim is not accepted, identifying which of the claimant's contentions are accepted and which are in dispute;

(b) enclose copies of the essential documents which the defendant relies on;

(c) enclose copies of documents asked for by the claimant, or explain why they are not enclosed;

(d) identify and ask for copies of any further essential documents, not in his possession, which the defendant wishes to see; and
(The claimant should provide these within a reasonably short time or explain in writing why he is not doing so.)

(e) state whether the defendant is prepared to enter into mediation or another alternative method of dispute resolution.

4.7 If the claim remains in dispute, the parties should promptly engage in appropriate negotiations with a view to settling the dispute and avoiding litigation.

4.8 Documents disclosed by either party in accordance with this practice direction may not be used for any purpose other than resolving the dispute, unless the other party agrees.

4.9 The resolution of some claims, but by no means all, may need help from an expert. If an expert is needed, the parties should wherever possible and to save expense engage an agreed expert.

4.10 Parties should be aware that, if the matter proceeds to litigation, the court may not allow the use of an expert's report, and that the cost of it is not always recoverable.

(iii) Chancery Guide (Extract)

Chapter 24 — Probate and Inheritance Claims

Key Rules and PD: CPR Part 57 and PD 57

Probate

24.1 In general, contentious probate proceedings follow the **B–139** same pattern as an ordinary claim but there are important differences and Part 57 and PD 57 should be carefully studied. Particular regard should be had to the following:

(1) A defendant must file an acknowledgment of service. An additional 14 days is provided for doing so.

(2) Save where the court orders otherwise, the parties must at the outset of proceedings lodge all testamentary documents in their possession and control with the court. At the same time parties must file written evidence describing any testamentary document of the deceased of which they have knowledge, stating, if any such document is not in the party's possession or control, the name and address, if known, of the person in whose possession or under whose control the document is. In the case of a claimant, these materials must be lodged at the time when the Claim Form is issued. In the case of a defendant, these materials must be lodged when service is acknowledged. If these requirements are not complied with it is likely that the claim will not be issued and, correspondingly, that the acknowledgment of service will not be permitted to be lodged.

(3) The court will generally ensure that all persons with any potential interest in the proceedings are joined as parties or served with notice under Part 19.8A.

(4) A default judgment cannot be obtained in a probate claim. Where, however, no defendant acknowledges service or files a defence, the claimant may apply for an order that the claim proceed to trial and seek a direction that the claim be tried on written evidence.

(5) If an order pronouncing for a will in solemn form is sought under Part 24, the evidence in support must include written evidence proving due execution of the will. In such a case, if a defendant has given notice under rule 57.11 that he raises no positive case but requires that the will be proved in solemn form and that, to that end, he wishes to cross examine the attesting witnesses, then the Claimant's application for summary judgment is subject to the right of such a defendant to require the attesting witnesses to attend for cross examination.

(6) A defendant who wishes to do more than test the validity of the will by cross examining the attesting witnesses must set up by Counterclaim his positive case in order to enable the court to make an appropriate finding or declaration as to which is the valid will, or whether a person died intestate or as the case may be.

(7) The proceedings may not be discontinued without permission. Even if they are compromised, it will usually be necessary to have an order stating to whom the grant is to be made, either under rule 57.11 (leading to a grant in common form), or after a trial on written evidence under paragraph 6.1(1) of PD 57 (leading to a grant in solemn form) or under section 49 of the Administration of Justice Act 1985 and paragraph 6.1(3) of PD 57 (again leading to a grant in solemn form).

24.2 When the court orders trial of a contentious probate claim on written evidence, or where the court is asked to pronounce in solemn form under Part 24, it is normally necessary for an attesting witness to sign a witness statement or swear an affidavit of due execution of any will or codicil sought to be admitted to probate. The will or codicil is at that stage in the court's possession and cannot be handed out of court for use as an exhibit to the witness statement or affidavit, so that the attesting witness has to attend at the Royal Courts of Justice.

24.3 Where an attesting witness is unable to attend the Royal Courts of Justice in order to sign his or her witness statement or swear his or her affidavit in the presence of an officer of the court, the solicitor concerned may request from Room TM7.09, Thomas More Building, a photographic copy of the will or codicil in question. This will be certified as authentic by the court and may be exhibited to the witness statement or affidavit of due execution in lieu of the original. The witness statement or affidavit must in that case state that the exhibited document is an authenticated copy of the document signed in the witness' presence.

24.4 When a probate claim is listed for trial outside London, the solicitor for the party responsible for preparing the court bundle must write to Room TM7.09 and request that the testamentary documents be forwarded to the appropriate District Registry.

Inheritance (Provision for Family and Dependants) Act 1975

24.5 Claims under the Inheritance (Provision for Family and Dependants) Act 1975 in the Chancery Division are issued by way of a Part 8 claim. Ordinarily they will be heard by the Master. At present they are governed by RSC Order 99, but this is to be replaced by additbns to Part 57 and PD 57 before the end of 2002. The following paragraphs describe the procedure as it will be under the new rules.

24.6 The written evidence filed with such a claim must exhibit an official copy of the grant of probate or letters of administration together with every testamentary document in respect of which probate or letters of administration was granted.

24.7 A defendant must file and serve acknowledgment of service not later than 21 days after service of the Part 8 claim form. Any written evidence (subject to any extension agreed or directed) must likewise be served and filed no later than 21 days after service.

24.8 The personal representatives of the deceased are necessary defendants to a claim under the 1975 Act and the written evidence filed by a defendant who is a personal representative must comply with paragraph 15 of PD 57.

24.9 On the hearing of a claim under the 1975 Act, the personal representatives must produce the original grant of representation to the deceased's estate. It the court makes an order under the Act, the original grant together with a sealed copy of the order must be sent to the Principal Registry of the Family Division for a memorandum of the order to be endorsed on or permanently annexed to the grant.

24.10 Where claims under the 1975 Act are compromised the consent order lodged must comply with paragraph 9.14 of this Guide.

Appendices (Extracts)

Appendix 1 — Guidelines on Statements of Case

B–140 1. The document must be as brief and concise as possible.
2. The document must be set out in separate consecutively numbered paragraphs and sub-paragraphs.
3. So far as possible each paragraph or sub-paragraph should contain no more than one allegation.
4. The document should deal with the case on a point by point basis, to allow a point by point response.
5. Where the CPR require a party to give particulars of an allegation or reasons for a denial (see rule 16.5 (2)), the allegation or denial should be stated first and then the particulars or reasons listed one by one in separate numbered sub-paragraphs.
6. A party wishing to advance a positive case must identify that case in the document; a simple denial is not sufficient.
7. Any matter which if not stated might take another party by surprise should be stated.
8. Where they will assist, headings, abbreviations and definitions should be used and a glossary annexed.
9. Contentious headings, abbreviations, paraphrasing and definitions should not be used; every effort should be made to ensure that headings, abbreviations and definitions are in a form that will enable them to be adopted without issue by the other parties.
10. Particulars of primary allegations should be stated as particulars and not as primary allegations.
11. Schedules or appendices should be used if this would be helpful, for example where lengthy particulars are necessary.
12. The names of any witness to be called may be given, and necessary documents (including an expert's report) can be attached or served contemporaneously if not bulky (PD 16; Guide paragraph 2.11). Otherwise evidence should not be included.
13. A response to particulars stated in a schedule should be stated in a corresponding schedule.
14. A party should not set out lengthy extracts from a document in his or her statement of case. If an extract has to be included, it should be placed in a schedule.
15. The document must be signed by the individual person or persons who drafted it not, in the case of a solicitor, in the name of the firm only.

Appendix 2 — Guidelines on Bundles

Bundles of documents must comply with paragraph 3 of PD 39 Miscellaneous Provisions relating to Hearings. These guidelines are additional to those requirements, and they should be followed wherever possible.

1. The preparation of bundles requires co-operation between the legal representatives for all parties, and in many cases a high level of co-operation. It is the duty of all legal representatives to co-operate to the necessary level. Where a party is acting in person it is also that party's duty to co-operate as necessary with the other parties' legal representatives.
2. Bundles should be prepared in accordance with the following guidance.

Avoidance of duplication

3. No more than one copy of any one document should be included, unless there is good reason for doing otherwise. One such reason may be the use of a separate core bundle.
4. If the same document is included in the chronological bundles and is also an exhibit to an affidavit or witness statement, it should be included in the chronological bundle and where it would otherwise appear as an exhibit a sheet should instead be inserted. This sheet should state the page and bundle number in the chronological bundles where the document can be found.
5. Where the court considers that costs have been wasted by copying unnecessary documents, a special costs order may be made against the relevant person.

Chronological order and organisation

6. In general documents should be arranged in date order starting with the earliest document.
7. If a contract or other transactional document is central to the case it may be included in a separate place provided that a page is inserted in the chronological run of documents to indicate where it would have appeared chronologically and where it is to be found instead. Alternatively transactional documents may be placed in a separate bundle as a category.

Pagination

8. This is covered by paragraph 3 of the PD, but it is permissible, instead of numbering the whole bundle, to number documents separately within tabs. An exception to consecutive page numbering arises in the case of the core bundle. For this it may be preferable to retain the original numbering with each bundle represented by a separate divider.

9. Page numbers should be inserted in bold figures, at the bottom of the page and in a form that can clearly be distinguished from any other pagination on the document.

Format and presentation

10. Where possible, the documents should be in A4 format. Where a document has to be read across rather than down the page, it should so be placed in the bundle as to ensure that the top of the text starts nearest the spine.

11. Where any marking or writing in colour on a document is important, for example on a conveyancing plan, the document must be copied in colour or marked up correctly in colour.

12. Documents in manuscript, or not easily legible, should be transcribed; the transcription should be marked and placed adjacent to the document transcribed.

13. Documents in a foreign language should be translated; the translation should be marked and placed adjacent to the document translated; the translation should be agreed or, if it cannot be agreed, each party's proposed translation should be included.

14. The size of any bundle should be tailored to its contents. There is no point having a large lever-arch file with just a few pages inside. On the other hand bundles should not be overloaded as they tend to break. **No bundle should contain more than 300 pages.**

15. Binders and files must be strong enough to withstand heavy use.

16. Large documents, such as plans, should be placed in an easily accessible file. If they will need to be opened up often, it may be sensible for the file to be larger than A4 size.

Indices and labels

17. Indices should, if possible, be on a single sheet. It is not necessary to waste space with the full heading of the action. Documents should be identified briefly but properly, *e.g.* "AGS3 – Defendants Accounts".

18. Outer labels should use large lettering, *e.g.* "A. Pleadings." The full title of the action and solicitors' names and addresses should be omitted. A label should be used on the front as well as on the spine.

19. A label should also be stuck on to the front inside cover of a file at the top left, in such a way that it can be seen even when the file is open.

Staples etc.

20. All staples, heavy metal clips etc. should be removed.

Statements of case

21. Statements of case should be assembled in 'chapter' form, *i.e.* claim form followed by particulars of claim, followed by further information, irrespective of date.

22. Redundant documents, *e.g.* particulars of claim overtaken by amendments, requests for further information recited in the answers given, should generally be excluded. Backsheets to statements of case should also be omitted.

Witness statements, affidavits and expert reports

23. Where there are witness statements, affidavits and/or expert reports from two or more parties, each party's witness statements etc. should, in large cases, be contained in separate bundles.

24. The copies of the witness statements, affidavits and expert reports in the bundles should have written on them, next to the reference to any document, the reference to that document in the bundles. This can be done in manuscript.

25. Documents referred to in, or exhibited to, witness statements, affidavits and expert reports should be put in a separate bundle and not placed behind the statement concerned, so that the reader can see both the text of the statement and the document referred to at the same time.

26. Backsheets to affidavits and witness statements should be omitted.

New Documents

27. Before a new document is introduced into bundles which have already been delivered to the court -indeed before it is copied — steps should be taken to ensure that it carries an appropriate bundle/page number, so that it can be added to the court documents. It should not be stapled, and it should be prepared with punch holes for immediate inclusion in the binders in use.

28. If it is expected that a large number of miscellaneous new documents will from time to time be introduced, there should be a special tabbed empty loose-leaf file for that purpose. An index should be produced for this file, updated as necessary.

Inter-Solicitor Correspondence

29. It is seldom that all inter-solicitor correspondence is required. Only those letters which are likely to be referred to should be copied. They should normally be placed in a separate bundle.

Core bundle

30. Where the volume of documents needed to be included in the bundles, and the nature of the case, makes it sensible, a separate core bundle should be prepared for the trial, containing those documents likely to be referred to most frequently.

Basis of agreement of bundles

31. See Chapter 7, paragraph 13.

Photocopy authorities

32. If authorities, extracts from text-books etc. are photocopied for convenience for use in court, the photocopies should be placed in a separate bundle with an index and dividers. Reduced size copies (*i.e.* 2 pages of original to each A4 sheet) should not be used. Where only a short passage from a long case is needed, the headnote and key pages only should be copied and the usher should be asked to have the full volume in court. Whenever possible the parties' advocates should liaise about these bundles in order to avoid duplication of copies.

Appendix 3 — Guidelines on Skeleton Arguments, Chronologies, Indices and Reading Lists

Skeleton arguments

1. A skeleton argument is intended to identify both for the parties and the court those points which are, and those that are not, in issue, and the nature of the argument in relation to those points which are in issue. It is not a substitute for oral argument.
2. Every skeleton argument should therefore:

   (1) identify concisely:

   (a) the nature of the case generally, and the background facts insofar as they are relevant to the matter before the court;
   (b) the propositions of law relied on with references to the relevant authorities;
   (c) the submissions of fact to be made with reference to the evidence;

   (2) be as brief as the nature of the issues allows — it should not normally exceed 20 pages of double-spaced A4 paper and in many cases it should be much shorter than this;

   (3) be in numbered paragraphs and state the name (and contact details) of the advocate(s) who prepared it;

   (4) avoid arguing the case at length;

   (5) avoid formality and make use of abbreviations, *e.g.* C for Claimant, A/345 for bundle A page 345, 1.1.95 for 1st January 1995 etc.

3. Paragraph 1 also applies to written summaries of opening speeches and final speeches. Even though in a large case these may necessarily be longer, they should still be as brief as the case allows.

Reading lists

4. The documents which the Judge should if possible read before the hearing may be identified in a skeleton argument, but must in any event be listed in a separate reading list, if possible agreed between the advocates, which must be lodged with the agreed bundles, together with an estimate, if possible agreed, of the time required for the reading.

Chronologies and indices

5. Chronologies and indices should be non-contentious and agreed with the other parties if possible. If there is a material dispute about any event stated in the chronology, that should be stated in neutral terms and the competing versions shortly stated.
6. If time and circumstances allow its preparation, a chronology or index to which all parties have contributed and agreed can be invaluable.
7. Chronologies and indices once prepared can be easily updated and may be of continuing usefulness throughout the case.

Appendix 4 — Guidelines on Witness Statements

1. The function of a witness statement is to set out in writing the evidence in chief of the maker of the statement. Accordingly witness statements should, so far as possible, be expressed in the witness's own words. This guideline applies unless the perception or recollection of the witness of the events in question is not in issue.
2. Witness statements should be as concise as the circumstances of the case allow. They should be written in consecutively numbered paragraphs. They should present the evidence in an orderly and readily comprehensible manner. They must be signed by the witness, and contain a statement that he or she believes that the facts stated in his or her witness statement are true. They must indicate which of the statements made are made from the witness' own knowledge and which are made on information and belief, giving the source of the information or basis for the belief.
3. Inadmissible material should not be included. Irrelevant material should likewise not be included.
4. Any party on whom a witness statement is served who objects to the relevance or admissibility of material contained in a witness statement should notify the other party of his or her objection within 28 days after service of the witness statement in question and the parties concerned should attempt to resolve the matter as soon as possible. If it is not possible to resolve the matter, the party who objects should make an appropriate application, normally at the PTR, if there is one, or otherwise at trial.
5. It is incumbent on solicitors and counsel not to allow the costs of preparation of witness statements to be unnecessarily increased by over-elaboration of the statements. Any unnecessary elaboration may be the subject of a special order as to costs.

6. Witness statements must contain the truth, the whole truth and nothing but the truth on the issues covered. Great care must be taken in the preparation of witness statements. No pressure of any kind should be placed on a witness to give other than a true and complete account of his or her evidence, It is improper to serve a witness statement which is known to be false or which the maker does not in all respects actually believe to be true. In addition, a professional adviser may be under an obligation to check where practicable the truth of facts stated in a witness statement if he or she is put on enquiry as to their truth. If a party discovers that a witness statement which he or she has served is incorrect he or she must inform the other parties immediately.

7. A witness statement should simply cover those issues, but only those issues, on which the party serving the statement wishes that witness to give evidence in chief. Thus it is not, for example, the function of a witness statement to provide a commentary on the documents in the trial bundle, nor to set out quotations from such documents, nor to engage in matters of argument. Witness statements should not deal with other matters merely because they may arise in the course of the trial.

8. Witness statements very often refer to documents, If there could be any doubt as to what document is being referred to, or if the document has not previously been made available on disclosure, it may be helpful for the document to be exhibited to the witness statement. If, to assist reference to the documents, the documents referred to are exhibited to the witness statement, they should nevertheless not be included in trial bundles in that form: see Appendix 2 paragraph 4. If (as is normally preferable) the documents referred to in the witness statement are not exhibited, care should be taken in identifying them, for example by reference to the lists of documents exchanged on disclosure. In preparation for trial, it will be necessary to insert cross-references to the trial bundles so as to identify the documents: see Appendix 2 paragraph 24.

9. If a witness is not sufficiently fluent in English to give his evidence in English, the witness statement should be in the witness' own language and a translation provided, If a witness is not fluent in English but can make himself understood in broken English and can understand written English, the statement need not be in his own words provided that these matters are indicated in the statement itself. It must however be written so as to express as accurately as possible the substance of his evidence.

Appendix 5

Part 1: Judge's Application Information Form

Title as in claim form

Application Information

1. [— DATE APPLICATION TO BE HEARD —]

2. DETAILS OF SOLICITOR/PARTY LODGING THE APPLICATION

    a. [Name]

    b. [Address]

    c. [Telephone No.]

    d. [Reference]

    e. [Acting for Claimant(s)/Defendant(s)]

3. DETAILS OF COUNSEL/OR OTHER ADVOCATE

    a. [Name]

    b. [Address of Chambers/Firm]

    c. [Telephone No.]

4. DETAILS OF OTHER PART(Y'S)(IES) SOLICITORS

    a. [Name]

    b. [Address]

    c. [Telephone No.]

    d. [Reference]

    [Acting for Claimant(s)/Defendant(s)]

CONTENTIOUS PROBATE

Part 2: WRITTEN EVIDENCE LODGMENT FORM

CHANCERY CHAMBERS

TO FILING SECTION — ROOM TM 3.07

CLAIM NO:

SHORT TITLE:

Herewith Affidavit or witness statement of ....

/of if other document specify ....

filed in respect of:—

1. Application before Judge on...
2. Application before Master on ....
3. Charging Order
4. Garnishee Order
5. Permission to issue [claim for] possession
6. Service by alternative method
7. Service out of Jurisdiction
8. Evidence
9. Oral examination of debtor
10. To enable a Master's order to be drawn
11. Other (Specify) ....

Signed:

Solicitor for Claimant/Defendant

other (please specify)

Telephone No:

Ref:

Appendix III

Mental and Medical Conditions Relevant to Testamentary Capacity

Mental and medical conditions which may affect testamentary capacity

Practitioners will be aware that many different mental disorders may affect testamentary capacity, and it must be emphasised that a mental health diagnosis alone does not imply lack of testamentary capacity, rather it must always be specifically determined by the tests laid down in Chapter 5. In this brief appendix, the sorts of mental conditions which may give rise to problems with testamentary capacity will be outlined, with the pertinent characteristics being described. Moreover, it is not the precise diagnosis which matters but the manifestations of the illness which the individual shows and their effects on the abilities necessary for testamentary capacity. Clearly, testamentary capacity requires adequate memory function, a capacity for analysis and understanding of consequences and an absence of delusions which could be expected to affect choice of beneficiaries. **C–001**

Failure for full intelligence to develop and traumatic injuries to the brain

Children who sustain brain injuries in the womb or at the time of birth or have other conditions such as Down's syndrome, a genetic disease, which is perhaps the most frequent and familiar example of such conditions, may in consequence never develop full intellectual capacity. In the past a variety of terms have been used to describe such cases, such as mental deficiency, mental **C–002** handicap or mental subnormality. However in more recent years the less stigmatising term of learning difficulty has been preferred. Severity may range from mild impairment, where there may be testamentary capacity, to very severe cases where the making of a will would be totally and obviously impossible.

By the time such individuals reach adulthood, they are likely to have had extensive neurological, psychological and educational assessments on record and will be in a steady state of impairment so that assessment of testamentary capacity is not likely to be problematical.

Very similar situations may arise where there have been severe head injuries after acquisition of full intelligence. Again, there is likely to have been detailed assessment of the injury and its consequences, particularly if there has been personal injury litigation.

Affective disorders

C–003 These can be described as disorders of mood and include depression, a very common condition, and the far less common mania. Individuals may at different times manifest both mania and depression, so-called manic depressive psychosis or bipolar affective disorder. Both mania and depression are characteristically temporary conditions which are amenable to treatment. However, depression in particular may be very long-term and refractory to treatment in some individuals. Both mania and depression have a tendency to recur. Both may have a sudden onset. This is particularly so in depression when there is a clear external triggering life event such as bereavement, a sudden stroke or other catastrophic loss or serious illness.

Depression may affect capacity when the severely depressed patient becomes apathetic and withdrawn to the extent that their state may even be mistaken for dementia, a state sometimes called pseudo-dementia. Alternatively, both mania and depression may give rise to delusions (false beliefs which cannot be dispelled by appeals to logic) and, if so, these too may be relevant to capacity if, and only if, their content is such as to affect disposition of property.

Schizophrenia

C–004 This is a major psychosis which may affect the individual for prolonged periods, though remissions of severity may occur. It does not affect intelligence or memory but is often accompanied by thought disorder, behavioural abnormalities and by delusions, often of a paranoid nature. Auditory hallucinations, typically voices which may tell them to do certain things, are also an important feature. A diagnosis of schizophrenia does not, however, preclude testamentary capacity but clearly will if the individual has hallucinations or delusions which are relevant to disposition of assets.

Alcohol and other substance abuse

This is a complex area which will only briefly be mentioned here. Suffice it to say that some drugs, for example amphetamines, may result in states resembling schizophrenia. Alcohol may affect capacity in a number of situations. Particularly devastating is the complication of chronic heavy drinking and poor nutrition, Korsakoff's syndrome, where there is a very severe defect of short-term memory and a striking degree of confabulation (the creation of false memories to fill the memory gaps). This would very likely preclude testamentary capacity. Some individuals, particularly older alcoholics, may go on to a dementing disorder, alcoholic dementia. Withdrawal of drugs may also result in psychotic episodes, the delirium tremens of alcohol withdrawal being a good example, a form of delirium (see below) characterised by florid visual hallucinations, 'seeing pink elephants' according to popular lore. It goes without saying that when in a drunk or a drugged state, testamentary capacity may be temporarily compromised. C–005

Delirium (confusional state)

Delirium refers to mental states, which are typically but not universally of acute onset and of limited duration, and which are secondary to physical causes outside the brain. Delirium can be defined as a syndrome characterised by global cognitive impairment, disturbances of attention, reduced level of consciousness, (ranging from drowsiness, to stupor to coma, and often referred to as clouding of consciousness), increased or reduced psychomotor activity, (*i.e.* restlessness or reduced activity) and disturbed sleep-wake cycle. Visual hallucinations and delusions may also occur. Delirious states are also commonly referred to as confusional states or acute confusional states and a variety of other terms have also been used in the past but are best avoided. C–006

There are many physical causes. Any severe illness may give rise to delirium, particularly in childhood or old age or where there is pre-existing brain damage such as in Parkinson's disease or where there is a pre-existing dementia (see below). Infections are a particularly common cause, especially chest infections, but there is a very long list of other possible precipitating diseases which may be responsible. Delirium may also result from drugs, especially those that have intended effects on the central nervous system such as sedatives, tranquillisers and narcotics, anti-Parkinsonian drugs, anti-epileptics, anti-depressants and anti-psychotics. Withdrawal of sedative and narcotic drugs may also give rise to delirium as mentioned above in the example of delirium tremens from alcohol withdrawal.

Many of the precipitants of delirium are themselves acute in nature and account for delirium's typically acute onset. If the precipitants are short-term conditions, as is frequently the case, then delirium will be of relatively short duration also, broadly recovering in step with the resolution of the precipitating cause. However, there are other causes which are chronic rather than acute, for example delirium may well result from advanced malignant disease (carcinomatosis) and in such instances delirium may have an insidious onset with persistence from then on until the patient's death. For this reason, the term *acute confusional state* is best abandoned as an alternative term for delirium.

Clouding of consciousness (reduced level of consciousness) is an important feature of delirium which is helpful in distinguishing it from dementia. However, it must be borne in mind that there may not be clouding all the time during a delirious episode, particularly when it is of milder degree. Another feature which is prominent in delirium, in contrast to dementia where it is uncommon, is variability. Over short time periods the individual may vary from being extremely confused and restless to having less severe or near normal mental functioning, often described as a 'lucid interval' (see further discussion below). There is a tendency for delirium to be worse in the evening and night, perhaps because of the diminution in visual information helping the delirious person to re-orientate himself.

Delirious states are more likely in old age and in childhood than in middle life, perhaps because the child's brain has not reached full capacity and that the elderly may have subtle losses of brain capacity. Physical illness is far more common in older age groups so that they have both increased vulnerability and increased likelihood of precipitating conditions. They also tend to receive far more prescribed drugs. Thus delirium is an integral part of medicine of the elderly and is frequently seen in any illness episode, but most particularly in final illness leading to the old person's death, especially if such drugs as morphine are used to control pain. This is not uncommonly the very time that an old person may choose to make or revise a will and, coupled with the rising prevalence of dementia with age, accounts for the observation that contested probate cases so often involve the elderly.

Dementia

Dementia is a clinical syndrome due to disease of the brain, **C-007** which is usually chronic and progressive, comprising a global impairment of intellectual functions including memory, thinking, orientation, comprehension and judgement but without clouding of consciousness. There may be associated disturbances of emotional control, behaviour, mood and motivation. Visual hallucinations and delusions may also occur. The similarities of dementia to delirium are obvious, clouding of consciousness being a key point of distinction. However, where clouding is not present at the time of an examination, the distinction cannot be made by the character of the confusion itself or by simple mental tests. Distinguishing between delirium and dementia relies rather on the time pattern, between that of the often sudden onset and typically short duration of delirium and the long-term and progressive nature of the confusion in dementia. A careful past history from a carer or relative (for the patient himself cannot usually give a reliable history) is thus of the greatest importance.

It is clear therefore that both dementia and delirium are well capable of affecting testamentary capacity and in very similar ways, *i.e.* memory deficits, impairment of reasoning and judgement and, possibly, because of delusions. So, although from the medical point of view it is very important to make the distinction between them, as prognosis and treatment of the two are quite different, from the testamentary capacity point of view the distinction is less important and the precise cause totally irrelevant. It should also be borne in mind that dementia predisposes to delirium when triggering physical illness or drug administration occurs. So when a slow steady deterioration of a dementia changes to a period of marked deterioration the reason will usually be the occurrence of a super-added episode of delirium.

Dementia is particularly a disease of age, for although there are dementias which occur at earlier ages, these are far less common. The prevalence of dementia rises with age and is somewhat more common in women, perhaps mainly because of their greater survival rates so that they remain in a demented state longer than men on average.

There are many causes of dementia but two predominate, Alzheimer's disease and vascular dementia; and this account will concentrate on these two causes, of which the former is the more common. Sometimes the two may coexist.

Alzheimer's disease

C–008 Alzheimer's disease has a characteristic brain pathology; large numbers of what are called plaques and neurofibrillary tangles occurring in silver stained microscopical sections of the cerebral cortex. (Plaques are relatively large structures 10–200 microns in diameter where degenerative cell constituents surround a central core of amyloid protein fibrils; the smaller tangles are at first intracellular but progress to replacement of a dead nerve cell when a skein of helically twisted neurofibrils, abnormal forms of a normal structure found inside neurones.) Obviously it is not possible to biopsy the brain to prove the diagnosis so that it can only become certain after post mortem study of the brain so that in life it can only be diagnosed by a consideration of the mental state, its evolution with time, and the exclusion of other causes.

It is now clear that Alzheimer's disease has important genetic causes, and there are a number of different genetic abnormalites which have already been identified in different individuals. A broad distinction can be made clinically between early onset and late onset cases. The early onset cases, formerly called pre-senile dementia, and typically developing in the 40–60 age group, are strongly familial (*i.e.* have a far stronger genetic background) and are much more severe and more rapidly progressive. It is this group of cases that was described by Alois Alzheimer in his classical paper. Clinical descriptions of this group have also emphasised other neurological manifestations in this pre-senile type with particular emphasis on dysphasia; (see discussion below).

In contrast, cases with later onset in old age, formerly called senile dementia, tend to be less severe, more slowly progressive and show a far weaker familial pattern. They tend to have smaller numbers of plaques and tangles than the pre-senile group. They are often given the alternative name of senile dementia of Alzheimer type ('SDAT').

The characteristic time pattern of development of SDAT is that it is a very slow and insidiously developing disease. By the time relatives have become concerned by loss of intellectual function and have sought medical help, the doctor taking a careful history will usually find that there has been a long history, often as long as ten years, of deteriorating mental function already. This deterioration has often not been appreciated by relatives, who have made undue allowances and have put the insidious deterioration down simply to age. In the absence of such a long past history, doctors should be very hesitant to diagnose SDAT. It is not a condition where onset is sudden or rapid.

Progression in SDAT typically continues in a slow but inexorable manner in a very steady way with little short-term variability. SDAT has little effect on physical health until the final stage is reached, except that some weight loss often occurs, so there is often a period of many years from diagnosis to death unless other physical illness intervenes or unless the propensity for demented people to have accidents causes fractures or other major injuries. Fracture of the femur is a common consequence of such accidents and may lead to a period of rapid physical decline leading to death. Later in the dementing process, continence is often affected, first urinary incontinence and later faecal incontinence also. In its final and most severe stages the victim of SDAT may become bedridden, doubly incontinent, and need virtually total care including spoon feeding.

Vascular dementia

This comprises a group of pathologies giving rise to progressive dementia. They account for a smaller proportion of the dementias of old age than SDAT. The best known sub-type of vascular dementia is multi-infarct dementia ('MID'). MID results from progressive loss of brain tissue as a result of a series of strokes, many of which may be totally unrecognised at the time they occur because they are too minor or have been regarded as 'blackouts' or transient ischaemic attacks. However, other episodes may involve a clinically obvious stroke with evidence of limb weakness and other neurological signs. The progress of MID is generally more rapid than SDAT and may sometimes be seen to be 'step-wise' with each downwards step in intellectual capacity being due to a further stroke. There is an association of MID with high blood pressure as this is a powerful risk factor for stroke. Careful examination of the patient with MID may show evidence of strokes by the presence of exaggerated limb reflexes, an abnormal plantar reflex or other neurological signs and this helps to distinguish MID from SDAT where such signs do not occur. C–009

In more recent years an important second sub-type due to small vessel disease has been given greater prominence than before. Here diffuse cerebral damage from inadequate blood supply occurs rather than the multiple focal areas of damage occurring in MID.

Other dementias

These are many in number but uncommon. They include such genetic diseases as Huntington's disease and Creutzfelt Jacob disease, the variant form of which is due to the spread to humans of the prion protein of BSE (mad cow disease or, more C–010 properly, bovine spongiform encephalopathy). Far more numerically important than these rare diseases are dementias associated with Parkinson's disease and Lewy body disease but even their contribution is dwarfed by the prevalence of SDAT and vascular dementia. Readers requiring fuller details of these less frequent dementias may read fuller accounts in textbooks such as 'The New Oxford Textbook of Psychiatry' (Oxford University Press, 2000) or 'Psychiatry of the Elderly' (Jacoby and Oppenheimer, 13th edition, Oxford University Press, 2002).

Lucid intervals

C–011 This concept has been referred to briefly above. It should be emphasised that they tend to be periods of *relative* lucidity and not a complete return to mental normality, but such relative improvement may be sufficient to support testamentary capacity nonetheless. Lucid intervals are unlikely to be seen in SDAT, given its pattern of slow but steady deterioration and general lack of hour to hour or day to day variation. MID tends to be more variable and may give lucid intervals. However delirium, whether due to illness or drugs, very often shows such variability so that there may well be lucid intervals. Generally speaking, those with delirium are more likely to be lucid during the day and to deteriorate in the evening and night when sensory stimulation declines. However, an exception to this general pattern is when delirium occurs as a consequence of night sedation. Then the worst confusion is likely to be in the mornings when the hangover effect is maximal.

Social facade

C–012 Individuals with well developed social skills who develop dementia may, on casual conversation, appear to be alert and mentally able, at least whilst sticking to conversational generalities. Yet when conversation requires factual recall it may readily be appreciated that memory and orientation are grossly impaired. This is what is referred to as a 'well preserved social facade' and it may easily mislead lay observers, and indeed may similarly mislead professional observers such as nurses or doctors. The use of simple and brief mental test scores which involve asking a set series of questions which comprise orientation questions and short-term and long-term memory tasks, can be particularly useful in this context as well as providing a semi-quantitative estimation of the degree of memory impairment and disorientation. Commonly used tests are the mini-mental state examination (scored out of 30) and the abbreviated mental test score (scored out of 10). Such tests are, of course, non-specific and do not distinguish between dementia and delirium and may also be impaired where there is depression and attendant lack of concentration or when there is dysphasia, so that speech and language difficulties hinder performance.

It should be re-emphasised that such tests are merely general and semi-quantitative indications of the degree of impairment of orientation and memory. They are not themselves tests of testamentary capacity, though it is obvious that severe impairments make capacity far less likely to be present. Testamentary capacity must be assessed by specific questions, echoing the dicta of *Banks v Goodfellow*, that investigate whether the individual understands the nature of a will, knows the extent of what he has to dispose of, knows what individuals have moral claims on his bounty and is able to assess their relative claims, and that this judgement is not affected by any delusions that he may have.

Dysphasia

Dysphasia is not a mental illness but a disorder of speech and language caused by damage in the cortical speech area of the parietal lobe of the dominant hemisphere of the brain. This is most often seen as an accompaniment of stroke accompanied by dominant side hemiplegia (paralysis of limbs on the dominant side). Dysphasia can be a mild problem, consisting mainly of word-finding difficulty, with all gradations of severity up to the person having virtually no speech or understanding of speech, with the person perhaps only being able to utter a handful of words, often just yes and no and even these not necessarily being used appropriately.

C–013

Dysphasia is often subdivided into motor or executive dysphasia, where the main deficit is in the production of speech, and receptive dysphasia, where the main problem is in the understanding of language. In truth, pure forms of motor or receptive dysphasia probably never occur, the two co-existing. However most cases show more marked motor problems than receptive ones.

The result of this is that a severely dysphasic patient cannot reliably communicate and therefore cannot give instructions for a will. Intellectual capacity becomes impossible to assess because of the communication difficulties.

Though typically seen in stroke or other focal injury to the brain, for example after trauma, dysphasia has also been stressed as an important concomitant of dementia in the pre-senile type of Alzheimer's disease. There is a view, particularly among psychiatrists as opposed to geriatricians, that dysphasia is also an important feature of SDAT. However my own view based on my own research and experience is that this belief is mistaken and that all that can be found in SDAT is a poverty of vocabulary and some minor word finding difficulty and not dysphasia proper. Indeed language function may be well preserved even in very advanced dementia. Of course, because MID is caused by multiple strokes, it is perfectly possible to find genuine dysphasia in that form of dementia, though only in the occasional case.

Undue influence

C–014 Undue influence may also be an issue when the validity of a will is under question. In general terms, physically or mentally frail individuals who come to depend on carers may be particularly vulnerable to their undue influence, especially where they have become the main source of information about others who ought to be considered as objects of a testator's bounty. The carer can all too easily keep visitors at bay and then poison the patient's opinion of them on the basis of their not having visited. Underlying personality is perhaps more important than the degree of mental frailty and overall dependence; stubborn personalities are less likely to be influenced than those of a more compliant cast of mind.

Which expert?

C–015 Lawyers may have difficulty in deciding which type of expert should be instructed to produce a report in contested probate cases involving mental and physical impairment. They have the choice of using an adult psychiatrist, or if the individual is elderly, a psychogeriatrician or geriatrician.

An adult psychiatrist would be appropriate where the mental problem was in a younger person. As regards the choice in an elderly person between psychogeriatician and geriatrician it is generally appropriate to use the former where the mental disability is not accompanied by physical problems of any magnitude and to prefer a geriatrician if there is a combination of mental and physical problems.

Index

Abroad—
  foreign wills, 4–023
Accept or refuse grant, citation to, 11–020, B–102
Acknowledgment—
  attestation of will, 4–009, 4–010
  caveats, 11–004
  service of claim form, 11–090—11–093, A–013
ACTAPS draft protocol, 11–129, D–001—D–008
Actual undue influence—
  equity, in, 7–002, 7–004, 7–005, 7–007
  probate, in, 7–009—7–014
Administration—
  definition, B–056
  pending suit, 12–028, 14–006, B–050
  will annexed, with, B–052
ADR, 12–045, 12–046
Advertisement—
  citations, 11–021
Affidavit—
  citations, 11–021
  due execution, B–085
  Inland Revenue, certificate of delivery of, A–001
  subpoenas, 11–031
  terms of will, B–085
Agent—
  signature on will by, 4–005
Aircraft—
  execution or attestation of will aboard, 4–023
Airman—
  privileged wills, 4–019
Alcohol—
  testamentary capacity, effect on, 5–018
Allocation of track, 12–002
  allocation questionnaire, 11–105, 12–002, A–018
Alternative dispute resolution, 12–045, 12–046
Alzheimer's disease 5–001, 5–002. *See also* Testamentary capacity

Appeals—
  applicable rules, 19–005
  Civil Procedure Rules, B–134
  costs, 11–045, 16–010, 19–027, 19–028
  application for permission, 19–018
  Court of Appeal, to, 19–001
  criteria, 19–012
  dealing with application for permission, 19–016, 19–017
  decision whether to appeal, 19–006, 19–007
  destination, 19–001
  final decision, 19–001, 19–002, 19–004
  Form N161, 9–1011
  fresh evidence, 19–021
  Non-Contentious Probate Rules, B–120
  notice of appeal, 19–008—19–010, A–015
  Part 36 offers, 19–028
  permission to appeal, 13–019, 19–003
    costs, 19–018
    dealing with application, 19–016, 19–017
    refusal, 19–017
  principles upon which appellate court will act, 19–019—19–025
  procedure, 19–005
  re-trials, 19–019, 19–026
  real prospect of success, 19–012, 19–013
  rectification of will, 20–033
  refusal of permission, 19–017
  route, 19–001—19–004
  service of appeal notice to respondent, 19–014, 19–015
  skeleton argument, 19–011
  time limits, 19–003, 19–008—19–010
  written submission to appeal notice, 19–014, 19–015
  wrong decision of lower court, 19–020, 19–022—19–024

INDEX

Application—
  case management conference directions, B–016
  caveat, removal of, 11–015
  conflicting, B–040
  discontinuance, A–026
    claimant, 14–002
    defendant, 14–002
  grant *ad colligenda bona*, 11–042
  grant of probate, B–038
  permission to appeal, 19–016, 19–017, 19–018
  private hearing, 13–002
  rectification of will, 10–041
  revocation of grant, B–038
  subpoenas, 11–030
  summons, by, 11–025
Approval of contents of will. *See* Knowledge and approval
Attestation of will, 4–001, 4–006, 4–007—4–010
  acknowledgment by testator, 4–009, 4–010
  aircraft, aboard, 4–023
  blind persons, 4–008, B–082
  failure, 4–007
  gifts to attesting witness, B–009
  incompetence of attesting witness, B–008
  informal clause, 4–016
  manner, 4–007
  number of witnesses, 4–007
  omnia praesumuntur rite esse acta, 4–016
  paralysed, 4–005, 6–004
  presence of both witnesses, 4–008, 4–011, 4–015
  presumption of due execution, 4–016
  rationale of requirement, 4–007
  regular clause, 4–016
  signature in presence of both witnesses, 4–001, 4–007—4–010
  simultaneous presence of both witnesses, 4–008
  unconscious testator, 4–008
  vessel, aboard, 4–023

Banks v Goodfellow test, 5–002—5–009, 5–021
  authorities, approval of earlier, 5–006
  claims to which effect ought to be given, understanding, 5–003, 5–004, 5–008, 5–009

Banks v Goodfellow test—*cont.*
  Dan v Vancleve, 5–006
  disorder of the mind or insane delusions, relevance of, 5–003, 5–004, 5–006
  extent of property being disposed, understanding, 5–003, 5–004, 5–008, 5–009
  Harwood v Baker, 5–008
  issue in case, 5–005
  judges deciding case, 5–005
  memory, 5–007
  partial unsoundness of mind, 5–004, 5–005, 5–006
  standard of capacity, 5–009
  understanding of testator, 5–003, 5–004, 5–008
Barry v Butlin, rule in, 6–007—6–011
Beneficiary—
  assessment of costs, seeking, 16–011
  charity, 14–012
  compromise of claim, consent to, 14–010, 14–011
  joining those with beneficial interests, 11–055
  secret trusts and certainty of, 10–031
  third-party, 10–007
Blind persons—
  attestation of will, 4–008
  execution of will, 4–005, B–082
  knowledge and approval, 6–004, 6–013—6–023
  signature, 4–005
Blood tests—
  legitimacy, 2–009
  parentage, 2–009
Bona vacantia, 16–017
Bundles, 12–037—12–039, 12–044
Burden of proof—
  conditional revocation, 9–032
  hearing, 13–005
  mutual wills, 10–006
  rectification of will, 10–045, 20–020
  revocation, 9–022
  secret trusts, 10–040
  shifting, 13–005
  testamentary capacity, 5–014—5–020
    alcohol, effect of, 5–018
    basic principle, 5–014
    diabetes, 5–015—5–017
    drugs, effect of, 5–018
    drunkenness, 5–018
    execution of will, 5–015
    factual context of the making of the will, 5–015

INDEX

Burden of proof—*cont.*
  testamentary capacity—*cont.*
    intermittent attacks of confusion, 5–017
    lucid intervals, 5–014
    previous mental illness, 5–014
    probate in common form, seeking, 5–014
    rebuttable presumptions, 5–014
    recovering and then losing capacity, 5–017
    temporary incapacity, 5–018
    validity of will questioned, 5–014
    whole history of mental decline, consideration of, 5–019
  testamentary intention, 3–008
  undue influence, 7–012
Burning of will, 9–017, 9–019

Calderbank letters, 14–020, 14–021
Capacity. *See* Testamentary capacity
Capital gains tax, 14–024, 20–022
Capital transfer tax—
  unpaid, B–042
Case management conference—
  attendance by representative, 12–007
  case summary, 12–007
  Chancery Order, 12–024
  directions, 12–004, 12–008
    Form PF 50, A–016
    non-compliance, 12–025, 12–039, 12–044
    variation, 12–009
  disclosure, 12–004
  expert evidence, 12–004
  fixing date for, 12–002
  Form PF 52, 12–024, A–017
  inadequate representation at, 12–007
  Inheritance (Provision for Family and Dependants) Act 1975, claims under, 12–033
  inspection, 12–004
  likely topics, 12–066
  listing questionnaire, 12–002, 12–038, A–019
  non-compliance with directions, 12–025, 12–039, 12–044
  not required, where, 12–002
  orders on—
    compliance, 12–025, 12–039, 12–044
    making, 12–024
  parties, 12–004
  pleadings, conformity of, 12–004
  pre-trial checklist, 12–002, A–019

Case management conference—*cont.*
  preparation for hearing, 12–004—12–009
  single joint expert, 12–004
  specimen order, 12–006
  statements of documents, 12–004, A–006
  telephone conference, 12–009
  testamentary documents, 11–080, 12–004
  venue, 12–009
  video conferences, 12–009
  wasted costs order, 12–007
  witness statements, 12–004
Case summary, 12–007
Caution, registration of, 12–029, 12–030
Caveats, A–003, B–041
  See also Starting claims
  acknowledgment by registry of form, 11–004
  address for service, B–104
  agreement to discontinue, 11–015
  appearance, to warning, 11–009, 11–011
  caveator, 11–004
  ceasing to have effect, 11–010, 11–015, 11–018, 11–042
  citations, 11–021
  claim form, issue of, 11–016, 11–017
  contrary interest, 11–012, 11–013
  costs, 11–043—11–045
  date from which time runs, 11–004
  discontinuance, 11–015
  discovery, 11–005
  entering an appearance, 11–009, 11–011, 11–012, 11–014
    action after, 11–015—11–016
  fees, 11–004, 11–017, 11–021
  Form 3, 11–004, A–003
  Form 4, 11–006, 11–007, 11–008, A–004
  Form 5, 11–014, A–005
  grant *ad colligenda bona*, 11–004, 11–042
  grant *ad litem*, 11–016
  improper uses, 11–003
  issue, 11–004
  issuing and serving summons for directions, 11–010, 11–011, 11–013
  letters of administration, 11–004
  meaning, 11–002
  no appearance entered to warning, 11–018

INDEX

Caveats—*cont.*
  Non-Contentious Probate Rules,
    11–003, B–099
    address for service, B–104
    fee, 11–004
    Form 3, 11–004, A–003
    notice, 11–016
    procedure, 11–004
    withdrawal of caveat, 11–018
  problem areas, 11–041, 11–042
  procedure for issue, 11–004
  reasons for use, 11–003
  removal application, 11–015
  renewal, 11–017
  rules governing use, 11–002
  service, 11–005
  unless order, imposition of, 11–015
  use, 11–003
  warning—
    entering an appearance to,
      11–009, 11–011
    Form 4, 11–006, 11–007, 11–008,
      A–004
    interest of person in estate,
      stating, 11–008
    issue, 11–008
    issuing and serving summons for
      directions, 11–010, 11–011
    no appearance entered to
      warning, 11–018
    procedure, 11–006—11–008
    reasons, 11–007
    responses to Form 4,
      11–009—11–011
    service, 11–008
    withdrawal, 11–018
Challenging the will—
  contentious probate claims,
    1–001—1–007
Chancery Guide, 12–037, B–139
Charity beneficiaries—
  compromise of claim, 14–012
  costs, 16–017
Chattel interest, B–025
Children—
  See also Minors
  gifts to, B–027
  legitimacy. *See* Legitimacy;
    Parentage
Citation to see the proceedings,
  15–002
Citations—
  accept or refuse grant, to, 11–020,
    B–102
  advertisement, 11–021
  affidavit, 11–021
  caveat, issue of, 11–021
  citor, 11–021

Citations—*cont.*
  draft, 11–021
  entering an appearance, 11–021,
    11–022, 11–024
  Form 5, 11–021, A–005
  intermeddling, 11–020, 11–021
  no appearance entered, 11–021,
    11–023
  Non-Contentious Probate Rules,
    11–019, B–101
    accept or refuse grant, to, B–102
    address for service, B–104
    fees, 11–021
    procedure, 11–021
    summons, application by, 11–025
  personal service, 11–021
  procedure, 11–019, 11–021
  propound a will, to, 11–020,
    11–022—11–027, A–021,
    B–103
  purpose, 11–019
  service, 11–021, 11–024
  specimen form, 11–021
  take a grant, to, 11–020
  types, 11–020
  use, 11–019, 11–027
  will referred to in, 11–021
Civil Procedure Rules—
  appeals, B–134
  claim form *See* Claim form
  contentious and non-contentious
    probate, distinction between,
    1–001
  costs, 16–001, B–131, B–132
  cross-examine, notice to,
    11–049—11–051
  early disclosure, 11–132—11–138
  fraud, 8–007
  non-parties, notice to, 11–056
  Part 36 offers. *See* Part 36 offers
  policy, 11–064
  pre-action protocols,
    11–128—11–131
    cases not covered by, B–138
  probate claims, B–134, B–136
  rectification of wills, B–135, B–137
Claim form, 1–001, A–010
  See also Starting claims
  acknowledgment of service, 11–089,
    11–090—11–093, A–013
  assignment of case to multi-track,
    11–062
  caveats, issue and, 11–016, 11–017
  claimant—
    caveator, 11–047, 11–048
    conflict of interest, 11–048
    contents of claim form,
      11–062—11–068

Claim form—*cont.*
claimant—*cont.*
costs, 11–049
deciding in which court to bring claim, 11–058—11–060
executor, 11–048
factors against being, 11–049—11–052
fees, 11–049, 11–061
identification, 11–047—11–052
lodging testamentary documents 11–064, 11–077—11–082. *And see* Testamentary documents
notice to cross-examine, 11–049—11–051, 11–076, 13–006
payment of issue fee, 11–061
person warning the caveat, 11–048
persons joined as defendants, 11–065
statement of case, 11–070—11–076
testamentary documents 11–064, 11–077—11–082. *And see* Testamentary documents
unique features of claim, 11–064
contents, 11–062—11–068
county court, issue in, 11–058—11–060
defendant—
codicils, 11–055
contrary interest to the claimant, 11–053, 11–054
identification, 11–053—11–056
identification of correct, 11–053, 11–054
intestacy, 11–054
joining those with beneficial interests, 11–055
revocation claims, 11–054
fee, 11–061, 11–085
Form 205D, 11–089
Form N2, 11–062
Form N2A, 11–062
Form N2B, 11–062
Form N3, 11–062, 11–090
Form N205D, 11–062
Form N1A, 11–046
formal requirements, 11–046
High Court, issue in, 11–058—11–060
Human Rights Act 1998, 11–066
indorsements, A–021
issue—
choice of court, 11–058—11–060

Claim form—*cont.*
issue—*cont.*
fee paid by claimant, 11–061, 11–085
notice of, 11–089
relevant court offices, 11–085
joining defendants, 11–055, 11–065
lodging testamentary documents, 11–064, 11–077—11–082
Non-Contentious Probate Rules, 11–016, 11–040
notes for completion, A–011, A–012
notice of issue, 11–089, A–014
particulars of claim, 11–067, 11–068, A–022, A–023
See also Statement of case
failure to serve, 11–097
parties 11.065. *See also* Claimant; Defendant
revocation claim, 11–083, 11–084
service, 11–068, 11–086—11–088
acknowledgment, 11–090—11–093, A–013
extension of time for, 11–088
outside jurisdiction, 11–087
time for, 11–088
within jurisdiction, 11–086
statement of case, 11–067—11–076
capacity in which claimant is claiming, 11–070
clarity, need for, 11–073
drafting, 11–070—11–076
facts in support, 11–072
grounds on which will is invalid, 11–069, 11–071—11–075
notice to cross-examine, 11–076
particulars of claim, 11–067, 11–068
Practice Direction, 11–067
setting out, 11–074
setting out grounds on which will is invalid, 11–069, 11–071—11–075
statement of interest of each party, 11–069, 11–070
striking out, 11–119
subpoenas as alternative to, 11–034
testamentary documents 11–064, 11–077—11–082. *And see* Testamentary documents
venue for claim, 11–058—11–060
which claim form to use, 11–062—11–068
Claimant—
See also Claim form
amendment of claim, 11–104
caveator, 11–047, 11–048

Claimant—*cont.*
  conflict of interest, 11–048
  costs, 11–049
  deciding in which court to bring claim, 11–058—11–060
  defence to counterclaim, 11–106—11–110
  executor, 11–048
  factors against being, 11–049—11–052
  fees, 11–049
  further pleadings, 11–111
  identification, 11–047—11–052
  lodging testamentary documents, 11–064
  notice to cross-examine, 11–049—11–051, 11–076
  person warning the caveat, 11–048
  reply to counterclaim, 11–103—11–105, 11–111, A–025
Claims—
  default judgment, 11–115
  form. *See* Claim form
  further information, requests for, 11–120
  inexcusable delay, 11–121
  limitation. *See* Limitation of claims
  starting. *See* Caveats; Citations; Claim form; Limitation of claims; Starting claims; Subpoenas
  striking out, 11–119
  summary judgment, 11–118
Clerical error—
  rectification of will, 10–041, 10–043, 10–044, 20–001
Client care, 12–042, 12–043
Closing speeches, 13–017, 13–018
CMC. *See* Case management conference
Codicil—
  revocation of earlier will, 9–012
Commencement of claims. *See* Caveats; Citations; Claims; Starting claims; Subpoenas
Committal—
  breach of order, 17–003
Common form grant, 15–005—15–009
  discontinuance, 15–005
  false statement, grant obtained by, 15–007
  lodging, 15–006
  non-contentious probate, 15–005
  consent, 15–005
  reliance on, 15–006

Common form grant—*cont.*
  revocation, 15–005
    effect, 15–007
    false statement, grant obtained by, 15–007
    orders, 15–008, 15–009
    third party dealings, 15–007
    uses, 15–005
  validity, 15–006
  voidable, 15–007
Competing wills—
  interest claims, 2–002
Compromise of claim—
  See also Discontinuance; Part 36 offers
  Administration of Justice Act 1985, order under, 14–010
  application notice, A–026
  Calderbank letters, 14–020, 14–021
  charity beneficiaries, 14–012
  choice, 14–009—14–011
  consent of beneficiaries, 14–010, 14–011
  CPR forms, A–026
  disability, persons under, 14–012
  Form NCH38, 14–011
  High Court powers, 14–010, 14–011, B–061
  inappropriate uses, 14–012
  litigation friend, 14–012
  mediate, offers to, 14–023
  open offers, 14–022
  order, A–009
    no agreement, where, A–027
  rectification of will, 20–023
  revocation of existing common form grant, 14–012
  taxation, 14–024—14–027
  uses, 14–012
  without prejudice offers, 14–019
    costs, save as to, 14–020, 14–021
  written evidence only, trial on, 14–009
Conditional revocation—
  absolute or qualified revocation, 9–025, 9–026
  assumed facts, truth of, 9–029
  burden of proof, 9–032
  dependent relative revocation, 9–025
  destruction of existing will in anticipation of new will, 9–027
  facts of case, 9–028
  general revocation clause in later will, 9–030, 9–031
  inferences, 9–032

INDEX

Conditional revocation—*cont.*
  intention of testator, 9–025
  meaning, 9–025
  mistaken beliefs, 9–029
  nature of qualification, 9–026
  new will, intention to make, 9–028
  performance or satisfaction of qualification, 9–026
Conditional wills, 3–003, 3–015—3–017
  execution of will, 3–016
  extrinsic evidence, 3–016
  intrinsic terms of will, 3–016
  not dating will, 3–016
Confidentiality, 12–010
Conflict of interest—
  executor, 11–048
Conflict of laws, 4–024
Consent—
  common form grant, 15–005
  compromise of claim, 14–010, 14–011
  orders, 15–005, 17–002
  rectification of will, 20–023
Construction of will, 20–002, B–067
Constructive trusts, 1–006
  agreement to share, 10–024
  arrangement to share, 10–024
  cohabitees, 10–023
  common intention to share ownership, 10–027
  conduct of parties, 10–025
  contributions to purchase price, 10–025, 10–026
  direct contribution to purchase price, 10–025, 10–026
  family assets, concept of, 10–023
  former matrimonial home, 10–023
  inference, 10–025
  spouses, 10–023
  typical case, 10–023
  understanding, reaching an, 10–024
Contempt of court, 12–010
Contentious probate claim—
  categories, 1–004
  claim form in. *See also* Claim Form
  context, 1–006
  decree pronouncing for or against will. *See* Decree pronouncing for or against will
  definition under CPR, 1–002
  grounds for claim, 1–005
  interest claims. *See* Interest claims; Parentage; Personation
  meaning, 1–002
  non-contentious probate distinguished, 1–001
  revocation of grant. *See* Revocation of grant

Contingent interests, B–002
Copies
  costs, B–016
  testamentary documents, 11–077
Copyhold, B–021
Costs, B–063
  advice to client, 16–002
  agreement, 16–023
  appeals, 11–045, 16–010, 19–027, 19–028
    application for permission, 19–018
  apportionment, 16–004
  assessment, 13–019
    beneficiary seeking, 16–011
    generally, 16–016
    indemnity basis, 11–044, 16–017
    standard basis, 16–017
  caveats, 11–043—11–045
  charities, 16–017
  Civil Procedure Rules, 16–001, B–131, B–132
  claimant, 11–049
  conduct-effect of—
    detailed assessment, 13–019
    determination, 11–044
    discontinuance, 14–003
    discretion, 11–044, 16–001, 16–009
    exceptions to general rule—
      conduct of party, 16–009
      fault of beneficiary, claim being the, 16–006
      fault of the deceased, claim being the, 16–005
      notice to cross-examine, 16–008
      reasonable grounds for opposing grant of probate, 16–007
  executor, 11–048
    proving will in solemn form, 16–011
  expert evidence, 12–004
  fault—
    beneficiary, of, 16–006
    deceased, of, 16–005
  following the event, 11–044, 16–001, 16–002
  fraud, 16–012
  general rule, 11–044, 16–001, 16–002
  grant pending suit, 16–013
  hearing, 13–019
  House of Lords, appeals to, 19–029, 19–030
  indemnities, 16–015, 16–021
  indemnity basis, 11–044, 16–017
  Larke v Nugus request, 16–009
  legal representatives, 16–022
  litigants in person, 16–022

Costs—*cont.*
  maintainers, 16–022
  more than one party bearing, 16–004
  muddled papers left, where, 16–005
  neutral personal representative, 16–018—16–021
  non-contentious probate, 11–043—11–045
  Non-Contentious Probate Rules, B–136
    power to make order for, B–118
  notice to cross-examine, 16–008
  Official Solicitor, 16–017
  Part 36 offers, 14–018, 16–017
  power to order, 16–004
  pre-emptive applications, 16–020
  Protocols, observance of 11–128—11–131
  public funding, 16–014, 16–023
  pure funders, 16–022
  rectification of will, 20–028—20–032
  scale fees, 11–045
  separate treatment, 16–004
  special rules, 16–010—16–014
  special status, parties with, 16–017
  standard basis of assessment, 16–017
  submissions, 13–019
  success on one issue but failure on another, 16–004
  summary assessment, 13–019
  testamentary capacity, lack of, 16–012
  Treasury Solicitor, 16–017
  undue influence, 16–012
  wasted costs order, 12–007, 16–022, 16–023
Counsel's opinion, B–060
Counterclaim—
  claims in nature of a probate claim, 11–098—11–102
  contents, 11–096
  defence, served with, 11–096
  defence to, 11–106—11–110
  permission to serve, 11–096
  reply to, 11–103—11–105, 11–111, A–025
  requirement to serve, 11–097
  separate to defence, service, 11–096
  service, 11–096
County court—
  Chancery District Registry, 11–058
  claim form issued in, 11–058, 11–059

County court—*cont.*
  jurisdiction, 11–060
  limit, 11–059, 11–060
Court of Appeal—
  appeals to 19–001. *And see* Appeals
Creditors, B–010
Cross-examination, 13–010, 13–011
  notice to cross-examine, 11–049—11–051, 11–076, 11–097, 13–006, 16–008
Crown, 16–017, B–077

Data protection, 12–016
Date—
  not dating will, 3–016
Deafness—
  knowledge and approval, 6–004, 6–013—6–023
Death—
  claims arising on, 1–001, 1–006
  pre-1838, B–028
Declarations—
  validity of an alleged will, against, 15–010
Decree pronouncing for or against will, 1–004
Deed of variation, 14–025, 20–022
Default judgment—
  non-availability, 11–115
Defence—
  See also Defendant
  contents, 11–096—11–102
  counterclaim, to, 11–106—11–110
  filing, 11–094
  notice to cross-examine, 11–097
  obedience to any order of court, stating, 11–117
  pleadings, A–024
  reply, 11–104, 11–111, A–025
  time for, 11–095
Defendant—
  acknowledgment of service, 11–090—11–093, A–013
  claims against another defendant, 11–112—11–114
  claims in nature of a probate claim, 11–098, 11–099
  codicils, 11–055
  contrary interest to the claimant, 11–053, 11–054
  counterclaim—
    contents, 11–096
    defence, served with, 11–096
    permission to serve, 11–096
    requirement to serve, 11–097
    served separate to defence, 11–096

INDEX

Defendant—*cont.*
  defence—
    contents, 11–096—11–102
    counterclaim served with, 11–096
    filing, 11–094
    notice to cross-examine, 11–097
    time for, 11–095
  Form N3, 11–090
  identification, 11–053—11–056
  intestacy, 11–054
  joining those with beneficial interests, 11–055, 11–065
  neutral, 11–117
  notice to cross-examine, 11–049, 11–076
  other proceedings, probate claim in, 11–098—11–102
  Part 20 claims, 11–112—11–114
  rejoinder, 11–111
  representation, 11–056
  revocation claims, 11–054
  statement of testamentary documents, 11–090, 11–091, A–006
Delay—
  inexcusable, 11–121
  striking out claim, 14–008
Delusions—
  testamentary capacity, 5–010—5–013
Dementia, 5–001
Dependent relative revocation. *See* Conditional revocation
Destruction of will, 9–017, 9–018—9–020, B–015
  attempted destruction, 9–019
  burning, 9–019
  duplicate wills, 9–020
  existing will destroyed in anticipation of new will, 9–027
  fraud, 9–022
  intention, 9–018, 9–021, 9–022
  presumption, 9–022
  subpoenas, 11–038
  sufficient act, 9–018—9–020
  tearing, 9–019
  uncompleted destruction, 9–019
Diabetes—
  testamentary capacity, 5–015—5–017
Directions—
  case management conference, 12–004, 12–008
    application, A–016
    Form PF 50, A–016
    non-compliance, 12–025, 12–039, 12–044

Directions—*cont.*
  case management conference—*cont.*
    variation, 12–009
  enforcement of order, 17–003
Disability, persons under, 11–065
  compromise of claim, 14–012
  Part 36 offers, 14–018
Disclosure—
  case management conference, 12–004
  confidentiality, 12–010
  contempt of court, 12–010
  copying costs, 12–016
  data protection, 12–016
  early, 11–132—11–138, 12–036
  electronic records, 12–016
  false statement, 12–010
  fishing expeditions, 12–016
  general principles, 12–010
  health records, 12–017—12–019
    medical ethics, 12–020
  Larke v Nugus, principle in, 12–016, 16–009
  legal professional privilege, 12–010, 12–013
  lifetime gifts, documents relating to, 12–010
  medical ethics, 12–020
  medical records, 12–017—12–019
  order for, 12–010
  pre-claim, 12–010, 12–012
  privilege, 12–010, 12–013—12–016
  procedure, 12–011
  reasonable search for documents, duty to make, 12–010
  relevant documents, 12–010
  specific, 12–010
  standard, 12–010
  statement, 12–011
  third-party, 12–012
  without prejudice communications, 12–010
Discontinuance—
  administration pending suit, 14–006
  agreement, 14–002—14–008
  application, A–026
    claimant, 14–002
    defendant, 14–002
  approval of court required, 14–007
  costs, 14–003
  jurisdiction, 14–006
  party seeking order, 14–002—14–008
  terms of compromise, 14–002
  terms of order, 14–005
  Tomlin order, 14–006

Discontinuance—*cont.*
  want of prosecution, striking out for, 14–008
Dishonesty
  acting, 8–002
  behaviour of honest people, 8–003
  carelessness and, 8–002
  fraud, 8–001, 8–002
  honesty, 8–002, 8–005
  meaning, 8–002
  misrepresentation, 8–004
  objective standard, 8–002
District probate registrars, B–039
Divorce—
  Inheritance (Provision for Family and Dependants) Act 1975, 9–010
  parentage, 2–006
  revocation of will, 9–010
DNA testing—
  legitimacy, 2–009
  parentage, 2–009
Doctor—
  testamentary capacity, opinion on, 5–021, 5–022, 5–024
  consequences, 5–024
  dealing with request, 5–023
Documents. *See* Testamentary documents
Drugs—
  testamentary capacity, effect on, 5–018
Drunkenness—
  testamentary capacity, 5–018

Electronic records, 12–016
Entry, rights of, B–002
Equitable estoppel—
  revocation, 9–001
Equity—
  limitation of claims, 11–121
  mutual wills. *See* Mutual wills
  rectification of will, 10–041
  secret trusts, 10–028
  undue influence—
    actual, 7–007
    actual undue influence, 7–002, 7–004, 7–005
    cheating, 7–005
    Class 1, 7–002
    Class 2, 7–002
    Class 2A, 7–003, 7–009
    Class 2B, 7–003, 7–007, 7–009
    classification, 7–002
    coercion, 7–005

Equity—*cont.*
  undue influence—*cont.*
    domination by wrongdoer of mind and will of complainant, 7–006
    establishing relationship, 7–003
    express undue influence, 7–002
    family loyalty, 7–008
    importunity, 7–007
    legitimate commercial pressure, 7–008
    overreaching, 7–005
    personal advantage, 7–005
    pressure, 7–007
    presumed undue influence, 7–002, 7–004
    rebutting presumption, 7–002, 7–003
    scope of doctrine, 7–005
    trust and confidence, relationship of, 7–002, 7–003
    unconscionable acts, 7–005
    unfair advantage, 7–004
    unfair and improper conduct, 7–005
    vulnerable, protection of, 7–005
Errors—
  See also rectification of will—
  clerical, 10–041, 10–043, 10–044, 20–001
  grants, 11–027
Estate—
  definition, B–056
Estoppel—
  proprietary. *See* Proprietary estoppel
Execution of will—
  agent, signature by, 4–005
  aircraft, aboard, 4–023
  attestation of will, 4–001, 4–006, 4–007—4–010
  acknowledgment by testator, 4–009, 4–010
  blind persons, 4–008, B–088
  failure, 4–007
  informal clause, 4–016
  manner, 4–007
  number of witnesses, 4–007
  omnia praesumuntur rite esse acta, 4–015, 4–016
  presence of both witnesses, 4–008, 4–015
  presumption of due execution, 4–016
  rationale of requirement, 4–007
  regular clause, 4–016
  simultaneous presence of both witnesses, 4–008

Execution of will—*cont.*
  attestation of will—*cont.*
    unconscious testator, 4–008
  blind testator, 4–005, B–088
  codicils, 3–013
  foreign wills, 4–023
  form of writing, 4–002
  formal validity, B–064, B–065, B–066
  holograph wills, 4–016
  indecipherable scrawl, 4–004
  invalid wills, 3–013
  knowledge and approval of contents. *See* Knowledge and approval
  lack of due execution, 4–001—4–024
  omnia praesumuntur rite esse acta, 4–015, 4–016
  operation of will on, 3–016
  paralysed testator, 4–005
  personal stamp of testator, 4–004
  position of signature, 4–001, 4–006
  presumption of due execution, 4–015, 4–016
  privileged wills. *See* Privileged wills
  requirements, 4–001—4–016
  signature, 4–002—4–005
    position, 4–001, 4–006
    presence of both witnesses, in, 4–001, 4–007—4–010
    standard form wills, 4–006
    substance capable of bearing signature, 4–002
  testamentary capacity, 5–020
    factual context of, 5–015
    slight degree of capacity required at time of execution, 5–020
  thumb prints, 4–004
  vesssel, aboard, 4–023
  Wills Act 1837, B–004
  writing requirement, 4–001, 4–002—4–005

Executor—
  admitting as witness, B–011
  claimant, 11–048
  conflict of interest, 11–048
  costs, 11–048
    proving will in solemn form, 16–011
  directions of court, seeking, 11–048
  minors, B–051
  refusing to prove will, 11–048

Expert evidence—
  capacity, 12–004
  case management conference, 12–004
  costs, 12–004
  single joint expert, 12–004

Express undue influence, 7–002
Extrinsic evidence—
  conditional wills, 3–016
  incorporation of documents, 3–011
  interpretation of will, 3–011
  testamentary intention, 3–005

Fee—
  caveats, 11–004, 11–017
  claim form, 11–061, 11–085
  conditional fee agreements, 18–006—18–008
  Non-Contentious Probate Rules, 11–004, 11–021, B–149—B–158
  starting claims, 11–061
  subpoenas, 11–032
Fishing expeditions, 12–016
Foreign law—
  Non-Contentious Probate Rules, B–094
Foreign wills, 4–023
Forgery, 8–008
Fraud—
  Civil Procedure Rules, 8–007
  destruction of will, 9–022
  dishonesty. *See* Dishonesty
  effect on will, 8–001
  example, 8–005
  forgery, 8–008
  grant in solemn form, 15–004
  knowledge and approval, 6–008, 6–026, 8–005
  misrepresentation, dishonest, 8–004
  mutual wills, 10–007
  personation, 2–004
  preparation of will, 8–005
  probate, in, 8–004
  proprietary estoppel, 10–011
  righteousness of transaction, 8–005
  seriousness, 8–007
  setting aside order for pronouncing will in solemn form, 8–006
  strangers benefiting from will, 8–005
  suspicion of, 8–005
  undue influence distinguished, 8–002
Freehold, B–021
Freezing orders, 12–027
Funding probate claims—
  conditional fee agreements, 18–006—18–008
  insurance policies, 18–005
  Legal Services Commission funding, 18–003, 18–004
  private funding, 18–001, 18–002

Further information, requests for, 11–120
Further pleadings, 11–111

Gender, B–001
Golden but tactless rule, 5–021, 5–022, 11–048
Grant *ad colligenda bona*, B–127
  application, 11–042
  caveats, 11–004
  Non-Contentious Probate Rules, 11–042
Grant *ad litem*—
  caveats, 11–016
Grant in common form—
  consent, 15–005
  discontinuance, 15–005
  distribution, 15–007
  false statement, grant obtained by, 15–007
  lodging, 15–006
  non-contentious probate, 15–005
  reliance on, 15–006
  revocation, 15–005
    effect, 15–007
    false statement, grant obtained by, 15–007
    orders, 15–008, 15–009
    third party dealings, 15–007
  uses, 15–005
  validity, 15–006
  voidable, 15–007
Grant pending suit, 11–042
  costs, 16–013
Grant in solemn form, 15–002—15–004
  fraud, 15–004
  revocation, 15–004
  summary judgment, 11–118
Guardians, appointment of, B–033

Health records—
  disclosure, 12–017—12–019
Hearing—
  admission to probate, 13–001
  adversarial trial, principles of, 13–001
  burden of proof, 13–005
  closing speeches, 13–017, 13–018
  costs, 13–019
  cross-examination, 13–010, 13–011
  estimated length, 12–038
  evidence
    cross-examination, 13–010, 13–011
    evidence in chief, 13–007—13–009
    re-examination, 13–012

Hearing—*cont.*
  final hearing, 13–002
  fixing trial date, 12–038
  general observations, 13–001
  inquisitorial role of court, 13–001
  interposing witnesses, 13–014
  justice at, 13–011
  no case to answer, submission of, 13–020
  obligations of court, 13–001
  opening speeches, 13–015
  order of speeches, 13–002—13–006
  permission to appeal, 13–019
  preparation. *See* Pre-trial procedure; Preparation for hearing
  private, 13–002
  public, 13–002
  re-examination, 13–012
  releasing witnesses, 13–013
  speeches, order of, 13–003—13–006
  standard of proof, 13–005
  submission of no case to answer, 13–020
  subpoena, after service of, 11–035, 11–036
  vigilance of court, 13–001
  window for trial, 12–038
High Court—
  Chancery Division, 11–058, 11–060
  claim form issued in, 11–058, 11–059
  compromise of claim, 14–010, 14–011, B–061
  contentious probate jurisdiction, 11–060
  Family Division (Probate), 11–060
  non-contentious probate jurisdiction, 11–060
  non-parties, power to bind, B–059
  orders—
    And See Orders
    carrying out, 15–011—15–016
    common form grant 15–005—15–009. *And See* Common form grant
    declarations against the validity of an alleged will, 15–010
    pending applications, 15–015
    Probateman computer records, 15–014, 15–015
    procedure for carrying out, 15–012—15–014
    revocation of solemn form grant, 15–004
    solemn form grant, 15–002—15–004
  personal representatives, B–062

Holograph wills, 4–016
Home Guard—
  privileged wills, 4–019
Honesty, 8–002
House of Lords, appeals to, 19–029, 19–030
Human assisted reproduction, 2–010
Human Rights Act 1998
  claim form, 11–066
Husband and wife. *See* Marriage

Immovable property—
  territory, 4–023
Impersonation. *See* Personation
Incorporation of documents, 3–003, 3–009—3–014
  document already in existence, 3–010
  duly executed codicil, 3–013
  extrinsic evidence, 3–011
  factual circumstances required, 3–010—3–012
  future documents, statement in will referring to, 3–012
  general words, 3–012
  intended documents, 3–012
  limits of rule, 3–012
  non-dispositive documents, 3–012
  revival, doctrine of, 3–014
  rule, 3–009—3–012
  terms of will ambiguous in light of surrounding circumstances, 3–011
  "that is certain which can be rendered certain", 3–012
Indemnities—
  costs, 16–015, 16–021
Inexcusable delay, 11–121
Inheritance (Provision for Family and Dependants) Act 1975
  case management conference, 12–033
  claim form, 12–032
  claims under, 1–007, 12–033—12–035, 17–002
  discretion, exercise of, 10–045
  divorce, 9–010
  Part 8 claims, 12–032
  spouse, claims by, 9–010
Inheritance Tax, 14–024, 14–025, 14–026
  rectification of will, 20–021, 20–022
Inland Revenue—
  affidavit, certificate of delivery of, A–001
  documents to be delivered to Commissioners, B–043

Innocent mistake—
  knowledge and approval, 6–026
Inspection—
  See also Disclosure
  right, 12–010
  testamentary documents, 11–079
Instructions for will—
  knowledge and approval, 6–005
Insurance policies—
  funding probate claims, 18–005
Intention—
  conditional revocation, 9–025, 9–026
  mutual wills, 10–006
  revocation of will
    conditional revocation, 9–025, 9–026
    instrument in writing, revocation by, 9–015, 9–016
    physical act of the testator, 9–017, 9–021, 9–022
    some writing declaring an intention to revoke, by, 9–016
  secret trusts, 10–030, 10–031—10–038
    communication, 10–030
    equivocal expression of wishes, 10–036
    example, 10–031, 10–032
    language in imperative form, certainty of, 10–031
    subject matter, certainty of, 10–031
    three certainties, 10–031
    whole course of dealing, 10–033—10–036
  testamentary. *See* Testamentary intention
Interest claims, 1–004
  challenging will, 2–002
  competing wills, 2–002
  entitlement, question of, 2–001
  essential issue, 2–001, 2–002
  factual issues raised, 2–003
  fraud, 2–004
  intestacy, 2–002
  parentage. *See* Parentage
  personation, 2–003, 2–004
  proof of identity, 2–004
Interim remedies, 15–006
  administration pending suit, 12–028, A–008
  caution, registration of, 12–029, 12–030
  freezing orders, 12–027

Interim remedies—*cont.*
  preservation of estate, 12–026, 12–031
  purpose, 12–026
  revocation claims, 12–026, 12–031
Interlineation—
  revocation, 9–023, 9–024
Intermeddling, 11–020, 11–021
Internal law—
  meaning, B–068
Intestacy—
  defendant, 11–054
  interest claims, 2–002
  Non-Contentious Probate Rules, B–091
  order of priority for grant, B–091
  parentage, 2–005
Invalid wills, 3–013
Issue
  death without, B–024

Judicial separation—
  legitimacy, 2–007
  parentage, 2–007

Knowledge and approval—
  Barry v Butlin, rule in, 6–007—6–011
  basic principle, 6–001
  blind testator, 6–004, 6–013—6–023
  circumstances giving rise to lack of, 6–026
  communicating contents of will, 6–004
  deafness, 6–004, 6–013—6–023
  discharging onus of proof, 6–009
  factual circumstances affecting, 6–003, 6–004
  fraud, 6–008, 6–026, 8–005
  inferences from the evidence, 6–003
  innocent mistake, 6–026
  instructions for will, 6–005
  insufficient evidence, where, 6–024
  issue, putting in, 6–002
  lack of, 6–001—6–027
  mistake, 6–026
  mute testator, 6–004, 6–013—6–023
  paralysed testator, 6–004
  part of contents, of, 6–006
  preparation of will by person other than testator, 6–003, 6–008, 6–009
  presumption, 6–002
  previous instructions, 6–005
  reading of will to testator, 6–004

Knowledge and approval—*cont.*
  requirement, 6–001
  righteousness of the transaction, proving, 6–002, 6–007
  standard of proof, 6–012
  stroke victims, 6–024
  suspicious circumstances, 6–003
    Barry v Butlin, rule in, 6–007—6–011
    complex wills, 6–010
    deaf testator, 6–013—6–023
    degree of suspicion, 6–011
    discharging onus of proof, 6–009
    independent advice, lack of, 6–010
    instructions for will, 6–009
    nature of suspicion, 6–007
    onus of proof, 6–009
    preparation of will by person benefiting, 6–008, 6–009
    seriousness of allegations, 6–012
    solicitor benefiting from will, 6–010, 6–011
    standard of proof, 6–012
    trivial allegations, 6–012
    true will, expression of, 6–008, 6–009
    vigilant and jealous, requirement that court be, 6–008, 6–009, 6–011
  testamentary capacity, lack of, 6–013—6–023

Lapsed devises, B–020
Larke v Nugus, principle in, 12–016, 16–009
Leasehold, B–021
Legal professional privilege, 12–010, 12–013
Legal representatives, 16–022
Legal Services Commission funding, 18–003, 18–004
Legitimacy—
  See also Parentage
  blood tests, 2–009
  common law presumption, 2–006—2–010
    act of marriage as recognition of child, 2–007
    before marriage, children conceived before, 2–006
    death of husband, 2–006
    divorce, 2–006
    DNA testing, 2–009
    evidence for rebuttal, 2–008, 2–009

Legitimacy—*cont.*
  common law presumption—*cont.*
    judicial separation, 2–007
    living apart by agreement, 2–007
    non-cohabitation, 2–007
    other person having intercourse with woman, 2–007
    rebutting presumption, 2–008—2–010
    standard of proof for rebuttal, 2–008
  DNA testing, 2–009
  blood tests, 2–009
  human assisted reproduction, 2–010
  judicial separation, 2–007
  mother, definition of, 2–010
  scientific evidence, 2–009, 2–010
  sperm donors, 2–010
  surrogacy, 2–010
Letters of administration—
  caveats, 11–004
Limitation of claims, 11–121—11–127
  equity, 11–121
  executors, action by, 11–122
  generally, 11–121, 11–122
  inexcusable delay, 11–121
  revocation claims, 11–123—11–127
    dealing with the estate during the claim, 11–124
    Inheritance (Family Provision) Act 1975, claims brought after orders made under, 11–125—11–127
  striking out, 11–121
  very late claims, 11–121
Listing questionnaire, 12–002, 12–038, A–019
Litigants in person, 12–039
  costs, 16–022
Litigation friend, 11–065, 14–012
Lost wills, 9–022, 11–038

Maintainers, 16–022
Mariners—
  privileged wills, 4–017—4–022, B–006, B–031
Marriage—
  annulment, 9–010, B–013
  dissolution, 9–010, B–013
  divorce, 9–010
  revocation of will, 9–005—9–009, B–012
    annulment of marriage, 9–010, B–013
    in contemplation of a marriage, 9–007—9–009

Marriage—*cont.*
  revocation of will—*cont.*
    dissolution of marriage, 9–010, B–013
    divorce, 9–010
    expectation of marriage, 9–005, 9–006
    extrinsic evidence, 9–009
    fiancée cases, 9–009
    general contemplation cases, 9–008
    "marriage" and "a marriage" distinguished, 9–008
    power of appointment, 9–005, 9–007
    pre-1983 law, 9–006, 9–007—9–009
    wife cases, 9–009
Mediation, 12–045, 12–046
  effect on costs, 14–023
  offers to mediate, 14–023
Medical ethics, 12–020
Medical evidence—
  testamentary capacity, 5–002, 5–021, 5–022
Medical records—
  disclosure, 12–017—12–019
  medical ethics, 12–020
  testamentary capacity, 5–021, 5–022
Mental illness—
  testamentary capacity, 5–002, 5–021, 5–022, C–001—C–015
Military service—
  privileged wills, 4–017—022, B–030, B–031
Minors, B–003
  See also Children
  executor, B–051
  privileged wills, 4–021, B–032, B–033
Mirror wills, 10–006
Mistake—
  knowledge and approval, 6–026
  rectification of will, 6–026
Mute testator—
  knowledge and approval, 6–004, 6–013—6–023
Mutual wills, 1–006
  agreement to make, 10–005
  application of doctrine, 10–005
  basic doctrine, 10–004
  burden of proof, 10–006
  consideration, 10–005
  contract, requirement for, 10–005
  enforceability of agreement, 10–008
  floating nature of obligation, 10–008, 10–009
  fraud, 10–007

Mutual wills—*cont.*
  intention, 10–006
  inter vivos gifts and dispositions, 10–008
  mirror wills, 10–006
  mutual benefits, 10–007
  operation of doctrine, 10–003, 10–004
  proof of, 10–006
  rectification of will, 20–001
  remarriage of survivor, 10–009
  terms of agreement, 10–005
  third-party beneficiary, 10–007
  trust, 10–004, 10–008
  withdrawal from agreement, 10–009

Negligence—
  professional, 1–007, 10–044
Neutral personal representative, 11–117, 16–018—16–021
No case to answer, submission of, 13–020
Non-contentious probate—
  contentious probate distinguished, 1–001
  costs, 11–043—11–045
  definition, 1–003, B–056
  fees, B–124—B–126
  Rules. *See* Non-Contentious Probate Rules
Non-Contentious Probate Rules, 1–003
  additional name, grant in, B–078
  address for service, B–104
  appeals, B–120
  application for grants through solicitors or probate practitioners, B–073
  assignee to a grant, right of, B–093
  attempted revocation of will, B–084
  attesting witnesses, grants to, B–090
  authorised officer, B–071
  blind testator, B–082
  caveats, 11–003, B–099
    address for service, B–104
    ceasing to have effect, 11–042
    fee, 11–004
    Form 3, 11–004, A–003
    notice, 11–016
    procedure, 11–004
    withdrawal of caveat, 11–018
  certificate of delivery of Inland Revenue affidavit, B–118
  citation, B–070

Non-Contentious Probate Rules—*cont.*
  citations, 11–019, B–101
    accept or refuse grant, to, B–102
    address for service, B–104
    fees, 11–021
    procedure, 11–021
    propound a will, to, B–103
  claim form, issue of, 11–016, 11–040
  commencement, B–070
  computerised records, 11–004
  condition of will, B–083
  copies, B–109
  costs, B–114
    power to make order for, B–118
  Crown, B–071
  date of execution of will, B–083
  district judge
    duty, B–075
    meaning, B–071
  due execution of will, evidence as to, B–081
  duty of district judge or registrar, B–075
  engrossment for purposes of record, B–080
  evidence as to due execution, B–081
  examination, application to attend for, B–105
  foreign law, B–088
  Form 2, A–003
  Form 3, 11–004, A–003
  Form 4, 11–006, 11–007, 11–008, A–004
  Form 5, 11–014, 11–021, A–005
  forms, B–124
  grant *ad colligenda bona*, 11–042, B–128
  grants of administration, B–107
  gross value, B–071
  illiterate testator, B–088
  index of grant applications, B–111
  interpretation, B–071
  intestacy, B–091
  joinder of administrator, B–094
  judge, B–071
  life interest, notice of election to redeem, B–124
  long vacation, exercise of powers of judge during, B–119
  marking of wills, B–079
  military service, B–087
  minors
  notices, B–122
  nuncupative wills, B–109
  oath, B–071, B–077
  order of priority of grant, B–089

INDEX

Non-Contentious Probate
Rules—*cont.*
original copies of wills—
inspection of, B–112
issue, B–113
other rules, application of, B–072
pending proceedings, application
to, B–123
personal applicant, B–071, B–074
pre-1926 cases, B–092
priority—
exceptions to rules, B–097
joinder of administration, B–094
pre-1926 cases, B–092
two or more persons entitled in
same degree, grants where,
B–096
probate actions, B–100
probate practitioner, B–071
proved otherwise than under s.9
Wills Act 1837, B–086
rectification of will,
20–034—20–041, B–110
registrar
duty, B–075
exercise of jurisdiction by
another, B–117
grants by, B–076
meaning, B–071
registry, B–071
seamen, B–087
senior district judge, B–071
service, 11–004
standing search procedure, 11–003,
A–002, B–110
subpoenas, 11–030, 11–031, B–105
summons—
power to require application by,
B–115
service, B–121
swear to death, application for
leave to, B–108
terms of will, evidence as to, B–083
transfer of applications, B–116
Treasury Solicitor, B–071
trust corporation, B–011, B–071
two or more persons entitled in
same degree, grants where,
B–096

Non-parties—
notice to, 11–056
power of High Court to bind,
B–059

Non-probate claims—
constructive trusts. *See*
Constructive trusts; Mutual
wills; Proprietary estoppel;
Rectification of will; Secret
trusts

Notice—
cross-examine, to, 11–049—11–051,
11–067, 11–097, 13–007,
16–008
issue of claim form, 11–089

Obliteration—
revocation, 9–023, 9–024
Official Solicitor, 16–017
omnia praesumuntur rite esse acta,
4–015, 4–016
Opening speeches, 13–015, 13–016
Orders—
agreed terms, 17–002
carrying out, 15–011—15–016
clarity, 17–002
committal for breach, 17–003
common form grant
15–005—15–009. *And See*
Common form grant
conclusive, B–035
consent, 15–005, 17–002
declarations against the validity of
an alleged will, 15–010
enforcement, 17–001—17–005
clarity of terms, 17–002
committal for breach, 17–003
consent orders, 17–002
correspondence, 17–003
directions of court, 17–003
disclosure, 17–003
out of jurisdiction, 17–002
post-grant remedies, 17–002,
17–005
procedure, 17–003
Supreme Court Act 1981, s.116,
application under, 17–003
Tomlin order, 17–003,
17–004
undertakings, 17–003
grant in solemn form,
15–002—15–004
pending applications, 15–015
post-grant remedies, 17–002,
17–005
Probateman computer records,
15–014, 15–015
procedure for carrying out,
15–012—15–014
revocation of solemn form grant,
15–004
solemn form grant,
15–002—15–004
Tomlin order, 14–006, 14–025,
17–003, 17–004

Paralysed testator—
  execution of will, 4–005
  knowledge and approval, 6–004
  signature, 4–005
Parentage—
  See also Legitimacy
  blood tests, 2–009
  common law presumption of legitimacy, 2–006—2–010
    act of marriage as recognition of child, 2–007
    before marriage, children conceived before, 2–006
    blood tests, 2–009
    death of husband, 2–006
    divorce, 2–006
    DNA testing, 2–009
    evidence for rebuttal, 2–008, 2–009
    judicial separation, 2–007
    living apart by agreement, 2–007
    non-cohabitation, 2–007
    other person having intercourse with woman, 2–007
    probability of illegitimacy, 2–008
    rebutting presumption, 2–008—2–010
    scientific evidence, 2–009, 2–010
    standard of proof for rebuttal, 2–008
  developments in law, 2–010
  divorce, 2–006
  DNA testing, 2–009
  human assisted reproduction, 2–010
  intestacy, 2–005
  issue, 2–005
  judicial separation, 2–007
  mother, definition of, 2–010
  scientific evidence, 2–009, 2–010
  sperm donors, 2–010
  surrogacy, 2–010
Parker v Felgate, rule in, 5–020
Part 20 claims, 11–112—11–114
Part 36 offers, 12–039, B–159
  acceptance of offer, 14–018
  appeals, 19–028
  costs, 14–018, 16–017
  disability, persons under, 14–018
  disclosure, 14–016
  effectiveness, 14–013, 14–018
  mistaken disclosure, 14–016
  money claims, 14–013
  nature of probate claims, 14–018
  pre-claim, 14–017
  purpose, 14–015, 14–018
  reasons for using, 14–015
  use in probate claims, 14–013

Particulars of claim, 11–067, 11–068, A–022, A–023
  See also Claim form; Statement of case
  failure to serve, 11–097
  statement of case, 11–067, 11–068
Pension schemes—
  secret trusts, 10–037
Personal estate—
  meaning, B–001
Personal representatives—
  additional, B–095
  High Court, B–062
  liability
    rectification of will, 10–041
  neutral, 11–117, 16–018—16–021
  number, B–001, B–047
  protection, B–036
  rectification of will—
    joining claim, 20–016
    liability, 10–041, 20–024
  removal, 17–002, B–062
  substitution, B–062
Personation—
  falsely assuming description, 2–004
  fraud, 2–004
  interest claims, 2–003, 2–004
  misdescription of legatee, 2–004
  precautions against, 12–022
  proof of identity, 2–004
  testator, 12–022
Power of appointment, 4–023, 9–005, 9–007, B–022
Pre-claim protocols, 11–128—11–131
Pre-trial procedure—
  administration pending suit, 12–028, A–008
  allocation of track, 12–002
  case management conference. *See* Case management conference
  checklist, 12–002, 12–038, A–019
  disclosure. *See* Disclosure
  Form N150, 12–005
  Form N170, 12–002, 12–038
  freezing orders, 12–027
  interim remedies. *See* Interim remedies
  listing questionnaire 12–002, 12–038, A–019
  management of claims by court, 12–002, 12–003
  preparation for hearing. *See* Preparation for hearing
  progress of claim, monitoring, 12–002
  timetable imposed by court, 12–002

INDEX

Pre-trial procedure—*cont.*
witness statements. *See* Witness statements
Preparation for hearing—
alternative dispute resolution, 12–045, 12–046
bundles, 12–037—12–039, 12–044
Chancery Guide, 12–037, B–139
client care, 12–042, 12–043
compliance with orders, 12–039, 12–044
counsel, 12–039
exchange of witness statements, 12–038
litigants in person, 12–039
matters to consider, 12–038, 12–039
mediation, 12–045, 12–046
Part 36 offers, 12–039
presentation—
documents, 12–037—12–039
witness evidence, 12–040
skeleton arguments, 12–039, 12–041, 12–044
time limits, 12–037—12–039
timetable, 12–038
witness summonses, 12–039
witnesses, 12–039
Preparation of will—
benefiting, by person, 6–003, 6–008, 6–009
fraud, 8–005
professional negligence, 1–007
suspicious circumstances, 6–008, 6–009
Presumed undue influence, 7–002, 7–004
Principal Registry, B–056
Prior claims to grant—
power of court to pass over, B–049
Private hearing—
application, 13–002
Privilege—
disclosure, 12–010, 12–013—12–016
Privileged wills, 4–001, 4–017—4–022
airman, 4–019
alterations, 4–022
armed forces, member of, 4–018, 4–019
doubtful cases, 4–020
effect of privilege, 4–017
exemption, 4–018—4–022
form, 4–022
guardians, appointment of, B–033
Home Guard, 4–019
inter-delineations, 4–022
letters, in, 4–022

Privileged wills—*cont.*
mariners, 4–018, 4–020, B–006, B–031
military service, 4–017—4–022, B–030, B–031
minors, 4–021, B–032, B–033
officers on half pay, 4–019
peace time, service in, 4–019
reserves, 4–019
scope of exemption, 4–019
seaman, 4–018, 4–019, 4–021
signature, 4–022
soldiers, 4–018, 4–019, 4–020, B–006, B–034
territorials, 4–019
testamentary intention, 4–022
verbal will, 4–022
witnesses, 4–022
writing, in, 4–022
Probate claim—
Civil Procedure Rules, B–135
definition, 11–045
funding. *See* Funding probate claims
Probate court—
function, 3–001
Probateman computer records, 15–014, 15–015
Procedure—
starting claims. *See* Caveats; Citations; Starting claims; Subpoenas
Professional negligence, 1–007
rectification of will, 10–044
Propound a will, citation to, 11–020, 11–022—11–027, A–021, B–124
Proprietary estoppel, 1–006
basis, 10–011
claims, 10–010
detriment, 10–013, 10–014, 10–017, 10–021
discretion of court, 10–016, 10–017
effect of successful claim, 10–010
example, 10–013
existing right, reliance on belief relating to, 10–013
expectation of claimant, 10–017, 10–021
fixed sum, award of, 10–022
fraud, 10–011
future rights, reliance on belief in, 10–013
modern form, 10–012—10–014
nature of claim, 10–010
origins, 10–011
proportionality, 10–017
Ramsden v Dyson principle, 10–011

Proprietary estoppel—*cont.*
  satisfying the equity,
    10–015—10–022
  unconscionability, 10–011, 10–014
  valuation of equity,
    10–015—10–022
Protocols—
  ACTAPS draft, 11–129
  pre-action, 11–128—11–131
  starting claims, 11–128—11–132
Publication—
  wills, B–007

Ramsden v Dyson principle, 10–011
Re-examination, 13–012
Real estate—
  meaning, B–001, B–056
Records of grants, B–044
  Probateman computer records,
    15–014, 15–015
Rectification of will, 1–006, B–057
  ACTAPS draft protocol, 20–018,
    D–001—D–008
  appeals, 20–033
  application, 10–041
  application form, 20–003
  assignment of claims, 20–012,
    20–015
  burden of proof, 10–045, 20–020
  capital gains tax, 20–022
  case management, 20–018
  Civil Procedure Rules, B–136,
    B–138
  claim form, 20–013, 20–014
  clerical error, 10–041, 10–043,
    10–044, 20–001
  compromise of claims, 20–023
  conflict of evidence, 20–018
  consent order, 20–023
  convincing evidence, 20–019
  costs, 20–028—20–032
  deed of variation distinguished,
    20–022
  discretion of court, 10–045
  distribution of estate, 10–045
  draft claim form, A–027, A–028
  effect of order, 20–021
  equity, 10–041, 10–042, 20–001
  evidence, 20–018, 20–019, B–058
  extrinsic evidence, 20–019
  failure to carry out testator's
    intentions, 10–041, 10–042,
    20–001
  failure to understand instructions,
    10–041, 10–043, 20–001
  funding, 20–003
  grounds, 20–001

Rectification of will—*cont.*
  inherent jurisdiction of court,
    20–001, 20–019, 20–021
  Inheritance Act 1975 claims,
    20–018
  inheritance tax, 20–021, 20–022
  intention, 20–001
  letter before claim, 20–018
  mistake, 6–026
  mutual wills, 20–001
  negotiations, 10–045
  Non-Contentious Probate Rules,
    20–034—20–041
  personal representatives—
    joining, 20–016
    liability, 10–041, 20–024
  post-January 1 cases, 10–041
  power of court, 10–041
  probate claim, not, 20–003
  procedure, 20–003,
    20–012—20–020
  professional negligence, 10–044
  recording the order of the court,
    20–025—20–027
  releasing file, 20–018
  secret trusts, 20–001
  speculation concerning testator's
    intention, 20–019
  standard of proof, 20–019
  statutory power, 10–041—10–045
  strong evidence, 20–019
  time limits, 10–041, 10–045,
    20–004—20–011, 20–018
  unopposed applications,
    20–034—20–041
Republication, 11–055
Revival, doctrine of, 3–014, 11–055,
  B–017
Revocation, 1–004, B–053
  action for breach of contract not to
    revoke will, 9–001
  alteration of will, 9–023, 9–024,
    B–016
  annulment of marriage, 9–010,
    B–013
  attempted, B–084
  burden of proof, 9–022
  burning of will, 9–017, 9–019
  claim form, 11–083, 11–084
  codicil, 9–012
  conditional. *See* Conditional
    revocation
  defendant, 11–054
  dependent relative revocation. *See*
    Conditional revocation
  destruction of will, 9–017,
    9–018—9–020, B–015

INDEX

Revocation—*cont.*
  determination whether, 9–002
  dissolution of marriage, 9–010, B–013
  divorce, 9–010
  duplicate wills, 9–020
  equitable estoppel, 9–001
  express revocation clause, 9–014
  instrument in writing, by, 9–003, 9–011—9–016, B–015
    express revocation clause, 9–014
    intention, 9–015, 9–016
    last and only will, description as, 9–014
    later will or codicil, 9–012, 9–013—9–016, B–015
    no revocation clause, where, 9–015
    some writing declaring an intention to revoke, by, 9–016
  intention, 9–011, 9–015, 9–021, 9–022
  interlineation, 9–023, 9–024
  irrevocable, expressed to be, 9–001
  later will or codicil, 9–012, 9–013—9–016, B–015
    express revocation clause, 9–014
  limitation of claims, 11–123—11–127
    dealing with the estate during the claim, 11–124
    Inheritance (Family Provision) Act 1975, claims brought after orders made under, 11–125—11–127
  lost wills, 9–022
  marriage, 9–005—9–009, B–012
    annulment, 9–010, B–013
    in contemplation of a marriage, 9–007—9–009
    dissolution, 9–010, B–013
    divorce, 9–010
    expectation of marriage, 9–005, 9–007
    extrinsic evidence, 9–009
    fiancée cases, 9–009
    general contemplation cases, 9–008
    "marriage" and "a marriage" distinguished, 9–008
    power of appointment, 9–005, 9–007
    pre-1983 law, 9–006, 9–007—9–009
    wife cases, 9–009
  modes, 9–003

Revocation—*cont.*
  mutual wills, 9–001
  Non-Contentious Probate Rules, B–117
  obliteration, 9–023, 9–024
  operation of law, 9–003, 9–004—9–010
    annulment of marriage, 9–010
    divorce, 9–010
    operation of marriage 9–005—9–009. *And see* Marriage
  partial, 9–023, 9–024
  physical act of the testator, 9–003, 9–017—9–024
    alteration, 9–023, 9–024
    attempted destruction, 9–019
    burning, 9–017, 9–019
    destruction of will, 9–017, 9–018—9–020
    duplicate wills, 9–020
    fraudulent destruction of will, 9–022
    intention, 9–017, 9–021, 9–022
    interlineation, 9–023, 9–024
    lost wills, 9–022
    obliteration, 9–023, 9–024
    partial revocation, 9–023, 9–024
    presumption of destruction, 9–022
    sufficient act of destruction, 9–017, 9–018—9–020
    tearing will, 9–017, 9–019
    uncompleted destruction, 9–019
  presumptions, 9–022, B–014
  tearing will, 9–017, 9–019
  validity of conveyance not affected by revocation of representation, B–037
  voluntary act of writing, 9–011, 9–012

Scientific evidence—
  legitimacy, 2–009, 2–010
  parentage, 2–009, 2–010
Scotland, B–029
Seaman—
  privileged wills, 4–017—4–022
Secret trusts, 1–006
  acceptance of the trust, 10–039
  basic rule, 10–028
  burden of proof, 10–040
  communication of intention, 10–030, 10–038
  equity, intervention of, 10–028
  family obligations, 10–031
  fully secret, 10–029, 10–039

INDEX

Secret trusts—*cont.*
  half secret, 10–029, 10–039
  honourable engagements, 10–031
  inconsistent dealings, 10–028
  intention, 10–030, 10–031—10–038
    beneficiaries, certainty of, 10–031
    communication, 10–030, 10–038
    equivocal expression of wishes, 10–036
    example, 10–031, 10–032
    language in imperative form, certainty of, 10–031
    subject matter, certainty of, 10–031
    three certainties, 10–031
    whole course of dealing, 10–033—10–036
  meaning, 10–028
  moral obligations, 10–031, 10–036
  ownership of property, 10–037
  pension schemes, 10–037
  rectification of will, 20–001
  requirements, 10–030
  semi-secret, 10–029
  three certainties, 10–031
  whole course of dealing, 10–033—10–036
Settlement. *See* Compromise of claim; Discontinuance; Part 36 offers
Severance—
  power of court, B–046
Signature—
  agent, by, 4–005
  attestation, 4–006
  blind testator, 4–005
  execution of will, 4–002—4–005
  indecipherable, 4–004
  initialled seal, 4–004
  paralysed testator, 4–005
  personal stamp of testator, 4–004
  position, 4–001, 4–006
  privileged wills, 4–022
  purpose, 4–003
  standard form wills, 4–006
  statement about testamentary documents, 11–082
  testamentary intention, 4–001, 4–006
  thumb print, 4–004
  Wills Act 1837, B–005
  witnesses, 4–011, 4–012
Silence—
  testamentary intention, 3–005
Single joint expert, 12–004
Skeleton arguments, 12–039, 12–041, 12–044

Soldiers—
  privileged wills, 4–017—4–022, B–006, B–034
Solemn form grant, 15–002—15–004
  revocation, 15–004
  summary judgment, 11–118
Solicitor—
  benefiting from will prepared for client, 6–010, 6–011
  professional conduct, 18–001
  professional negligence, 11–048
Specific performance, 9–001
Sperm donors, 2–010
Spouses. *See* Marriage
Standard form wills—
  execution of will, 4–006
  signature, 4–006
Standard of proof—
  forgery, 8–008
  hearing, 13–005
  knowledge and approval, 6–012
  suspicious circumstances, 6–012
  testamentary capacity, 5–014
Standing search procedure, 11–003, A–002, B–098
Starting claims—
  caveats. *See* Caveats
  citations. *See* Citations
  claim form. *See* Claim form
  claimant. *See* Claimant
  default judgment, non-availability of, 11–115, 11–116
  defendant. *See* Defendant
  early disclosure, principles of, 11–132—11–138
  pre-claim protocols, 11–125—11–132
  preliminary steps, 11–001
  probate claim
    definition, 11–045
    stages, 11–057
    statement of case 11–070—11–076. *And see* Statement of case
  steps to be taken by claimant—
    claim form, 11–062—11–066
    contents of claim form, 11–062—11–066
    deciding in which court to bring claim, 11–058—11–060
    issue and service of claim form, 11–083—11–089
    payment of fee, 11–061
    testamentary documents, statement of, 11–077—11–082
  subpoenas. *See* Subpoenas
State—
  definition, B–068

INDEX

Statements of case, 11–067—11–076, 12–004, A–020—A–026
  affirmative allegations not pleaded, avoiding, 11–073
  capacity in claimant is claiming, 11–069, 11–070
  clarity, need for, 11–073
  drafting, 11–069—11–076
  facts in support, 11–072
  grounds on which will is invalid, 11–071—11–075
  notice to cross-examine, 11–076
  particulars of claim, 11–067, 11–068
  Practice Direction, 11–067
  setting out, 11–074
  setting out grounds on which will is invalid, 11–071—11–075
  statement of interest of each party, 11–069, 11–070
Striking out claim, 11–119, 11–121
  delay, 14–008
  non-compliance with orders, 14–008
  want of prosecution, for, 14–008
Stroke victims—
  knowledge and approval, 6–024
Submission of no case to answer, 13–020
Subpoenas—
  affidavit, 11–031
  application by summons, 11–030
  claim form, as alternative to, 11–034
  compliance, 11–028
  contentious probate claim started, use after, 11–040
  destruction of will, 11–038
  difficult cases, 11–037
  evidence, 11–037, 11–038
  fee, absence of, 11–032
  formalities of execution, non-compliance with, 11–037
  hearing after service, 11–035, 11–036
  inappropriate uses, 11–039
  lost wills, 11–038
  meaning, 11–028
  Non-Contentious Probate Rules, 11–030, 11–031, B–105
  obtaining, 11–030, 11–031
  person having knowledge of testamentary document, attendance at court of, 11–029, B–054
  precedent, A–007
  produce a testamentary document, to, 11–029, B–055

Subpoenas—*cont.*
  recommended uses, 11–033
  refusal to hand over will, 11–033
  summons, 11–030, 11–031
  types, 11–029
  use, 11–028, 11–033, 11–034
  when to use, 11–033, 11–034
Summary judgment—
  solemn form proof, 11–118
Summons—
  application by, 11–025
  caveats, 11–010, 11–011
  executor to prove or renounce, to, B–045
  power to require application by, B–115
  service, B–121
  witness, 12–039
Surrogacy, 2–010
Suspicious circumstances, 6–003
  Barry v Butlin, rule in, 6–007—6–011
  complex wills, 6–010
  degree of suspicion, 6–011
  discharging onus of proof, 6–009
  independent advice, lack of, 6–010
  instructions for will, 6–009
  nature of suspicion, 6–007
  preparation of will by person benefiting, 6–008, 6–009
  seriousness of allegations, 6–012
  solicitor benefiting from will, 6–010, 6–011
  standard of proof, 6–012
  trivial allegations, 6–012
  true will, expression of, 6–008, 6–009
  vigilant and jealous, requirement that court be, 6–008, 6–009, 6–011

Taxation, 14–024—14–027
  See also Inland Revenue
  capital gains tax, 14–024
  inheritance tax, 14–024, 14–025, 14–026, 14–027
  websites, 14–024
Tearing will—
  destruction of will, 9–019
  revocation, 9–017, 9–019
Telephone conference, 12–009
Territorials—
  privileged wills, 4–019
Testamentary capacity—
  alcohol, effect of, 5–018
  Alzheimer's disease, 5–001, 5–002
  analysis of tests, 5–021

Testamentary capacity—*cont.*
  assessment, 5–002
  Banks v Goodfellow test,
    5–002—5–009, 5–021
    authorities, approval of earlier,
      5–006
    claims to which effect ought to
      be given, understanding,
      5–003, 5–004, 5–008, 5–009
    Dan v Vancleve, 5–006
    disorder of the mind or insane
      delusions, relevance of,
      5–003, 5–004, 5–006
    extent of property being
      disposed, understanding,
      5–003, 5–004, 5–008, 5–009
    Harwood v Baker, 5–008
    issue in case, 5–005
    judges deciding case, 5–005
    memory, 5–007
    nature of act, understanding,
      5–003, 5–004, 5–008
    partial unsoundness of mind,
      5–004, 5–005, 5–006
    probate in common form,
      seeking, 5–014
    sound and disposing mind and
      memory, 5–006—5–008
    standard of capacity, 5–009
    understanding of testator, 5–003,
      5–004, 5–008
  burden of proof, 5–014—5–020
    alcohol, effect of, 5–018
    basic principle, 5–014
    diabetes, 5–015—5–017
    drugs, effect of, 5–018
    drunkenness, 5–018
    execution of will, 5–015
    factual context of the making of
      the will, 5–015
    intermittent attacks of confusion,
      5–017
    lucid intervals, 5–014, 5–017
    previous mental illness, 5–014
    probate in common form,
      seeking, 5–014
    rebuttable presumptions, 5–014
    recovering and then losing
      capacity, 5–017
    temporary incapacity, 5–018
    validity of will questioned, 5–014
    whole history of mental decline,
      consideration of, 5–019
  case law, 5–002
  claims to which effect ought to be
    given, understanding, 5–003,
    5–004, 5–009
  confusion, 5–016, 5–017

Testamentary capacity—*cont.*
  costs, 16–012
  degree of soundness of mind,
    5–006
  delusions, 5–010—5–013
  dementia, 5–001
  demographic trends, influence of,
    5–001
  diabetes, 5–015—5–017
  disorder of the mind or insane
    delusions, relevance of, 5–003,
    5–004, 5–006
  doctor, opinion of, 5–021—5–024
    consequences of request, 5–024
    dealing with request, 5–023
  drugs, effect of, 5–018
  drunkenness, 5–018
  execution of will—
    factual context of, 5–015
    slight degree of capacity required
      at, 5–020
  extent of property being disposed,
    understanding, 5–003, 5–004,
    5–008, 5–009
  factual context of the making of
    the will, 5–015
  golden but tactless routine, 5–021,
    5–022, 11–048
  GP, presence of, 5–021, 5–022
  imperfect memory, 5–007
  importance of issue, 5–001
  insane delusions, 5–003, 5–004,
    5–010—5–013
  intermittent attacks of confusion,
    5–017
  issue of court, 5–002
  knowledge and approval, use of
    evidence of lack of capacity in
    cases involving, 6–013—6–023
  Larke v Nugus, 12–016, 16–009
  lay evidence, 5–021
  lucid intervals, 5–014, 5–017
  meaning of *see Banks v Goodfellow*
    test—
  medical evidence, 5–002, 5–021,
    5–022
  medical records, 5–021, 5–022
  memory, 5–007
  mental illness, 5–002, 5–021, 5–022,
    C–001—C–015
  nature of act, understanding,
    5–003, 5–004, 5–008
  nineteenth century case law, 5–002
  Parker v Felgate, rule in, 5–020
  partial unsoundness of mind,
    5–004, 5–005, 5–006

INDEX

Testamentary capacity—*cont.*
  previous mental illness, 5–014
  rebuttable presumptions, 5–014
  sound and disposing mind and memory, 5–006—5–008
  standard of proof, 5–014
  temporary incapacity, 5–018
  whole history of mental decline, consideration of, 5–019

Testamentary documents—
  apparent, 3–008
  attendance at court by person having knowledge of, 11–029, B–054
  case management conference, 11–080
  compliance with rules, 11–078
  copies, 11–077
  definition, 11–077
  further time to lodge, seeking, 11–078
  inspection, 11–079
  lodging, 11–064
  meaning of, 11–077
  obligation to lodge, 11–077—11–082
  original form, 11–077
  permission not to lodge, 11–078
  possession or control, 11–077
  release, 11–079
  removal from court, 11–079
  request for transfer to court, 11–080
  signature on statement, 11–082
  statement of, 11–077—11–082, 11–090, 11–091, A–006

Testamentary intention—
  abandonment of fixed and final intention, 3–007
  aggregate net result of documents, 3–001
  ambiguous expressions, 3–006
  apparently testamentary documents, 3–008
  ascertaining, 3–002
  burden of proof, 3–008
  clear expression of intention, 3–004
  conditional wills, 3–003, 3–015—3–017
    extrinsic evidence, 3–016
    interpretation of terms of will, 3–017
    intrinsic terms of will, 3–016
    not dating will, 3–016
    operation of will upon execution, 3–016
  evidence of, 3–004—3–007

Testamentary intention—*cont.*
  expression of wishes, documents containing, 3–006
  extrinsic evidence, 3–005
  fixed and final expression of wishes, 3–006, 3–007
  form of document, 3–002, 3–004
  imperfect documents, 3–007
  incorporation of documents, 3–003, 3–009—3–014
    document already in existence, 3–010
    duly executed codicil, 3–013
    extrinsic evidence, 3–0.11
    factual circumstances required, 3–010, 3–011
    future document, statement in will referring to, 3–012
    general words, 3–012
    inclusion of documents not duly executed, 3–011
    intended documents, 3–012
    invalid wills, 3–013
    limits of rule, 3–012
    non-dispositive documents, 3–012
    revival, doctrine of, 3–014
    rule, 3–009—3–012
    terms of will ambiguous in light of surrounding circumstances, 3–011
    "that is certain which can be rendered certain", 3–012
  lacking, 3–001—3–017
  language used, 3–002
  not to be a will, document expressed, 3–004
  number of wills, 3–001
  operate as a will, intention that document, 3–003, 3–006
  parol evidence, 3–006
  position of signature, 4–006
  positive assertion that document not intended to be a will, 3–004
  privileged wills, 4–022
  silence, 3–005
  temporary documents, 3–006
  two wills, leaving, 3–001
  underlying principle, 3–003
  unfinished documents, 3–007

Testator—
  acknowledgment by, 4–009, 4–010
  blind, 4–005, 6–004, B–082
  capacity. *See* Testamentary capacity
  illiterate, B–088

INDEX

Testator—*cont.*
  intention. *See* Testamentary intention
  mute, 6–004
  personal stamp of, 4–004
  signature, 4–004, 4–005
  unconscious, 4–008
  understanding of, 5–003, 5–004, 5–008
Third-party disclosure, 12–012
Thumb prints, 4–004
Tomlin order, 14–006, 14–025, 17–003, 17–004
Tracing papers, 15–015
Treasury Solicitor, B–071
Trust corporations, B–001, B–048, B–056, B–071
Trusts, B–026
  constructive. *See* Constructive trusts
  secret. *See* Secret trusts

Undertakings—
  enforcement, 17–003
Undue influence—
  actual
    equity, in, actual undue influence, 7–002, 7–004, 7–005
    probate, in, 7–009—7–014
  burden of proof, 7–012
  costs, 16–012
  equity, 7–001, 7–002—7–008
    abuse of position of trust and confidence, 7–004
    actual undue influence, 7–002, 7–004, 7–005, 7–007
    cheating, 7–005
    Class 1, 7–002
    Class 2, 7–002
    Class 2A, 7–003, 7–009
    Class 2B, 7–003, 7–007, 7–009
    classification, 7–002
    coercion, 7–005
    domination by wrongdoer of mind and will of complainant, 7–006
    establishing relationship, 7–003
    express undue influence, 7–002
    family loyalty, 7–008
    importunity, 7–007
    legitimate commercial pressure, 7–008
    personal advantage, 7–005
    pressure, 7–007
    presumed undue influence, 7–002, 7–004

Undue influence—*cont.*
  equity—*cont.*
    rebutting presumption, 7–002, 7–003
    scope of doctrine, 7–005
    trust and confidence, relationship of, 7–002, 7–003
    unconscionable acts, 7–005
    unfair advantage, 7–004
    unfair and improper conduct, 7–005
    vulnerable, protection of, 7–005
  fraud distinguished, 8–002
  general rule, 7–001
  nature of concept in probate, 7–001
  probate, in, 7–001, 7–009—7–014, 12–023
    actual undue influence, 7–009
    burden of proof, 7–012
    Class 2A undue influence, 7–009
    Class 2B undue influence, 7–009
    coercion, 7–011
    confinement, 7–011
    example, 7–012—7–014
    importunity, 7–010
    legitimate pressure, 7–010
    overpowering volition, 7–010
    scope of concept, 7–009
    threats, 7–010
    violence, 7–011

Vessel—
  execution or attestation of will aboard, 4–023

Want of prosecution, striking out for, 14–008
Warning—
  caveats
    entering an appearance, 11–009, 11–011
    Form 4, 11–006, 11–007, 11–008, A–004
    interest of person in estate, stating, 11–008
    issue, 11–008
    issuing and serving summons for directions, 11–010, 11–011
    no appearance entered to warning, 11–018
    procedure, 11–006—11–008
    reasons, 11–007
    responses to Form 4, 11–009—11–011
    service, 11–008

INDEX

Wasted costs order, 12–007, 16–022, 16–023
Wills—
  after execution, property acquired, B–002
  alteration, 9–023, 9–024, B–016
  ambulatory until death, 9–001
  appointments by, B–005
  attestation. *See* Attestation of will
  capacity. *See* Testamentary capacity
  conditional, 3–003, 3–015—3–017
    extrinsic evidence, 3–016
    interpretation of terms, 3–017
    intrinsic terms of will, 3–016
    operation of will, 3–016
  construction of words in, 20–002
  date—
    not dating will, 3–016
  destruction. *See* Destruction of will
  execution. *See* Execution of will
  foreign, 4–023
  forgery, 8–008
  form, 3–002
  holograph, 4–016
  instructions, 6–005
  interest claims. *See* Interest claims
  interlineation, 9–023, 9–024
  interpretation
    extrinsic evidence, 3–012
    invalid, 3–013
  knowledge and approval of contents. *See* Knowledge and approval
  language, 3–002
  lost, 9–022, 11–038
  meaning, B–001, B–056, B–068
  mirror, 10–006
  mutual. *See* Mutual wills
  number of, 3–001
  obliteration, 9–023, 9–024
  original copies
    inspection of, B–133
    issue, B–134
  privileged. *See* Privileged wills
  professional negligence in preparation, 1–007
  property disposed of by, B–002
  publication, B–007
  signature. *See* Signature
  speaking from the death of the testator, B–019
  subsequent conveyance or act, B–018

Wills—*cont.*
  testamentary capacity to make. *See* Testamentary capacity
  testamentary intention. *See* Testamentary intention
  validity 4–001—4–016. *See also* Execution of will
  words of limitation, B–023
  writing, requirement that will be in, 4–001, 4–002—4–005
Wills Act 1837, B–001—B–029
Without prejudice communications, 12–010
Without prejudice offers, 14–019
  costs, save as to, 14–020, 14–021
Witness statements, 12–004
  See also Witnesses
  contents, 12–022
  detail needed, 12–022, 12–023
  exchange, 12–023, 12–038
  form, 12–022
  impersonation, 12–021
  investigation agencies, use of, 12–023
  practical tips, 12–023
  preparation, 12–023
  schedule, 12–023
  types of witness, 12–021
Witness summary, 12–023
Witness summonses, 12–039
Witnesses—
  attestation by. *See* Attestation of will
  interposing, 13–014
  preparation for hearing, 12–039
  presentation of evidence, 12–040
  privilege, 12–016
  privileged wills, 4–022
  releasing, 13–013
  role, 12–016
  statements. *See* Witness statements
Writing—
  execution of will, 4–001, 4–002—4–005
  privileged wills, 4–022
  requirement that will be in, 4–001, 4–002—4–005
  revocation by instrument in, 9–003, 9–011—9–016, B–015
  wills required to be in, 4–001, 4–002—0051